COST DETERMINATION:

A Conceptual Approach

COST DETERMINATION:

A Conceptual Approach

JOEL S. DEMSKI

GERALD A. FELTHAM

The Iowa State University Press / *Ames, Iowa*

1 9 7 6

JOEL S. DEMSKI, professor of information and accounting systems in the Graduate School of Business, Stanford University, holds B.S.E. and M.B.A. degrees from the University of Michigan and the Ph.D. degree from the University of Chicago. He has served on the faculty of Columbia University and has been a visiting faculty member at the University of Chicago. Besides this book, he has authored *Information Analysis,* has coauthored *Cost Accounting: Accounting Data for Management's Decisions* (2nd edition), and has published articles in various journals, including the *Accounting Review, Journal of Accounting Research,* and *Management Science.*

GERALD A. FELTHAM, associate professor of accounting and management information systems at the University of British Columbia, holds the B. Comm. degree from the University of Saskatchewan and the Ph.D. degree from the University of California, Berkeley. He has served on the faculty of the University of Alberta and Stanford University. Besides this book, he has authored *Information Evaluation* and has published articles in the *Accounting Review.*

© 1976 The Iowa State University Press
Ames, Iowa 50010. All rights reserved

Composed by Science Press
Printed by the Iowa State University Press

First edition, 1976

Library of Congress Cataloging in Publication Data

Demski, Joel S.
  Cost determination.

  Bibliography: p.
  Includes index.
  1. Cost accounting. 2. Uncertainty. I. Feltham, Gerald A., 1938–   joint author.   II. Title.
HF5686.C8D295   657'.42   76–14421
ISBN 0–8138–0360–8

TO

Millie	*June*
Jay	*Tracy*
Rachel	*Shari*
Sybil	*Sandra*

CONTENTS

PREFACE

The genesis for this study arose when the AICPA approached us and our colleagues (Chuck Horngren, Bob Jaedicke, Bob Sprouse, and Bob Swieringa) in 1968 and asked for a study of cost measurement issues, including those that arise in defense procurement. We initially set out to explore these issues by analyzing the cost measurements "required" by a variety of decision contexts (see Jaedicke et al. 1969). This soon proved to be unsatisfactory, however, as we were unable to precisely identify what constituted cost in a given context and we found the concept of a "required" measurement to be inappropriate.

This, in turn, led us to the study reported here: an exploration of the single unifying theme of conscious choice among measurement alternatives. That is, by modeling these choices in terms of consistent choice among alternatives in the tradition of economic theory, we are able to offer a central theme that seems to capture the essence of cost measurement controversies, be they related to recognition, allocation, incidence, or whatever. For example, Thomas's (1974) view of the irresolvability of the allocation dilemma and Ijiri's (1975) multiperson focus based on an accountability notion are treated as part of a general resource allocation, or choice, paradigm.

As such, our study owes a deep legacy to J. M. Clark (1923). Indeed, without advances in economic theory in the last half-century, it is doubtful that refinement of Clark's theme would be feasible.

We are also indebted to numerous colleagues and institutions. The AICPA funded the early part of this study, and our respective schools continued to support us during our deliberations. Bob Sprouse and Bob Swieringa took part in and contributed toward countless discussions, and Bill Beaver and John Butterworth were particularly helpful in reading early drafts. Jack Kennelly introduced us to Iowa State University Press. Ursula Kaiser and Barbara Kent typed numerous versions of the manuscript.

Most important, however, is our debt to Chuck Horngren and Bob Jaedicke. They were active participants in numerous deliberations, read the various drafts, and wrote some of the earlier ones. The monograph remains a joint product, though as the primary authors we must accept final responsibility for its contents.

Finally, our families have been tolerant and supportive of as well as appropriately humored by our albatrosslike efforts. To say they supplied critical factors of production is to significantly understate their role in this venture. What the cost of these efforts was (as the reader will soon discover) remains problematic.

Joel S. Demski
Gerald A. Feltham

Watsonville, California

COST DETERMINATION:

A Conceptual Approach

1

"GOOD" ACCOUNTING

The accounting literature is replete with discourses on the pros and cons of particular cost measurement methods. Examples include the literature on direct costing, on how to measure assets for return on investment computations, on transfer pricing, and on alternative methods of allocating overhead to products or cost centers. A common concern in this literature is the question of which cost measures to report to users. Most discussions, however, are not founded on an explicit, common basis for resolving this question. This study develops an explicit common basis, or conceptual framework, for choosing among cost measurement alternatives.

Our approach to resolution of these cost issues is to focus on a central, unifying theme of normative economics. In other words, we examine cost measurement controversies within a resource allocation paradigm. The question of which cost measure to produce is modeled as a decision (or choice among alternatives). Then, as in consumer demand theory, we impose assumptions sufficient to allow us to state, in a particular setting, what the "best" cost measure would be, given exogenous specification of opportunities, tastes, and beliefs.

The purpose of this initial chapter is to introduce this resource allocation perspective and to contrast it with alternative approaches to the cost measurement question.

1.0 THE BASIC APPROACH

What is cost? What cost should be assigned to various products, processes, divisions, or actions? These, and other cost measurement questions, are essentially questions of information choice. In this study we suggest that these questions be

3

resolved by evaluating the expected impact of alternative cost measurements on the outcomes resulting from the actions selected by users of those measurements. Although this view is not revolutionary, it has two features that distinguish it from much of the current literature: (i) task specialization and (ii) formal recognition of the accountant's information choice problem.

More specifically, our analysis is based on developments in decision theory. The decision theory literature, however, has not recognized that the accountant must often make *information* decisions concerning what data to provide a *separate* decision maker who will select the *action.* In our analysis we recognize that these two decisions may be made by separate individuals. Furthermore, this task specialization model is readily extended to the evaluation of alternative procedures for motivating the decisions of subordinates.[1]

Given this task specialization, we focus on the accountant's information choice problem and formally consider the consequences of alternative cost measurements. This is in contrast to much of the accounting literature, which has tended either to ignore the consequences of alternative measurements or at best only to give them general consideration. Before amplifying our approach, which we term *information evaluation,* we consider two other general approaches that have had a major impact on the development of accounting thought.

1.1 HISTORICAL COMMUNICATION APPROACH

One approach, which we label the *historical communication* approach, dominated the accounting literature until about 1960. Its dominance has faded, but it is still widely used and advocated. This approach focuses on the establishment of principles or rules for the collection and processing of data. These rules might codify current practice, might stem from high authority, or might be derived from some theory or conceptual framework. In any event, there is an underlying belief that a unique set of rules can be established such that the resulting data are understood by any possible user. According to this approach, there are too many diverse uses to justify elaborate information systems tailored to every conceivable use. Potential uses are a consideration, but the best way to serve the user is to formulate clear rules for measuring costs. In this way, there will be minimal ambiguity about the meaning of cost, and the user can make his own adjustments for any shortcomings of the data provided.

The accounting literature contains much discussion as to which framework should be used in establishing these rules. The frameworks often differ as to the type of measurement unit used (for example, historical cost, replacement cost, net realizable value, etc.), but all are similar in that their ultimate output is a set of rules. The most widely used measurement unit is, of course, historical cost.

---

1. This could include motivation of the accountant to make information decisions that are consistent with, say, the firm's owners' goals.

The heavy reliance on historical cost and the conviction that rules are desirable are present in the following quotations:

> Accounting is thus not essentially a process of valuation, but the allocation of historical costs and revenues to the current and succeeding fiscal periods.... A history of cost and cost amortization is a consistent record of actual occurrences...and constitutes an essential starting point in financial interpretation. [American Accounting Association 1936, p. 188–89]

> It is no doubt an acceptable generalization to say that cost allocation is the fundamental process of accounting. And it is clearly recognized that original outlay-costs may be deferred (as assets), amortized (as expense) or abandoned (as losses). It is the duty of accounting theory in this connection to lay down the rules and reasons for making these distinctions. [Littleton 1937, p. 21]

The proponents of this historical communication approach maintain that the job of the accountant is to provide one type of clearly described data on a *caveat emptor* basis. The user should understand what the data represent and should proceed from that point. The major need is for an adequate set of standards, principles, definitions, or other guides to data collection. Two recent studies regarding cost accounting standards for government procurement illustrate this point:

> An important point should be noted about the relationship between costs and prices: if the contracting parties believe that cost accounting (under standards designed to enhance these conceptual objectives) will not furnish an agreeable result, they may make appropriate pricing adjustments; they need not change the cost measurement practices. [NAA Committee on Management Accounting Practices 1972, p. 55]

> Of the two main categories—a focus on total costs that have been incurred versus a focus on estimates of differential costs to be incurred—the former is clearly more desirable.... A and B, the negotiators in the episode at the beginning of this article *must* have standards. Without them, A and B have no practical way of reaching a meeting of the minds as to what the contract means by the word "cost," once the parties have agreed that reimbursement is to be based in part on cost. [Anthony 1970, p. 124]

Implicitly, this approach is based on the concept of absolute truth; there is a unique cost of producing an automobile, a barrel of oil, a space mission, an MBA, or a research project. By implication, the major problem facing the accountant is one of selecting a measurement procedure that identifies (or at least approximates) the true cost.

It is important to observe that the search for rules has not been based on an explicit comparison of the relative costs and benefits of alternative sets of rules. Instead, a global cost-benefit test is implied; a rather vague, general test that has concluded in favor of confining the alternatives to those based on a particular measurement unit, such as historical cost.

1.2 User Decision Model Approach

The historical communication approach of emphasizing measurement and classification of *the* cost provides a tractable basis for resolving cost measurement controversies *if* we can agree on *the* definition of cost. However, dissatisfaction with this approach has gradually arisen, in part because accountants do not agree. Furthermore, it fails to provide explicit consideration of heterogeneous users:

> Very few people in business have had the opportunity to reflect on the way in which the accounting model developed, particularly on how an instrument well adapted to detect fraud and measure tax liability has gradually been used as a general-purpose information source. Having been accustomed to information presented in this form, business people have adapted their concepts and patterns of thought and communication to it rather than adapting the information to the job or person. When one suggests the reverse process, as now seems not only logical but well within economic limits, he must expect a real reluctance to abandon a pattern of behavior that has a long history of working apparently quite well. [Fair 1960, pp. 229–30].

In response to such criticisms, the *user decision model approach* began to gain favor. This approach arose in the 1920s but did not receive much serious attention by accountants until the late 1950s.

The user decision model approach focuses on the decision method or model that, given some assumption, should be (or is) used for various classes of decisions. Models are postulated, and deductive reasoning is used to derive what data are relevant and how the data should be measured. Classes of decisions are identified; examples are capital investment decisions, pricing decisions, and output decisions. Most often, the models are drawn heavily from the classical economic theory of the firm, operations research, and more recently, from the behavioral theory of the firm. In contrast to the absolute truth theme of the historical communication approach, the user decision model approach has a theme of conditional truth. That is, it recognizes the possibility that different decision models may induce the generation of different data. These features led Clark to coin the often-heard phrase, "different costs for different purposes."[2]

Examples of the decision model approach are not difficult to cite; indeed, the development of "management accounting" in the last 25 years is based on this approach:

> More recently, accountants have turned a larger portion of their attention to this type of analysis, which we will call "managerial accounting." ... Management must determine what products to produce, what combinations of factors of production to use, what volume to produce, and what prices to place on output. The economist, concerned with the allocation of scarce resources, has built a supposedly rational structure explaining the activities of the firms which allocate these economic resources. The accountant has turned to this literature to determine what may be its relevancy to his task of serving management. ... Growing out of World War II, the mathematical technique of linear programming, and the entire field of operations research, has provided important tools for business in the solution of these problems. To some ac-

---

2. See Clark (1923), especially pp. 175–203.

countants, this is something to ignore; to others it involves the determination of the appropriate cost data to fit into models developed by others; to still others this offers a genuine opportunity to increase the service offered to management. [Moonitz and Nelson 1960, pp. 208–9]

Also, the extensive literature that has developed on direct costing is heavily based on the user decision model approach.[3] Sometimes, the exact model used for deriving a cost is not specified in all its details, but it is nevertheless the basis for the analysis. Consider, for example, the following passages taken from an early statement on direct costing:

> In such decisions [decisions on whether to sell special orders in situations where over-capacity exists], marginal income figures [that is, sales less variable costs] eliminate any confusion as to what the questioned sales add to overall profit. However, judgment and understanding are required in using marginal income figures for this purpose. It is necessary to consider the long range aspects of such business in order to avoid commitments which cannot be dropped when more profitable orders are available. [NACA 1953, p. 1106]

And, in commenting on the disadvantages of direct costing:

> Complete manufacturing cost is not determined in the process of costing production and supplementary allocation of fixed overhead on normal or some other volume base must be made to provide product costs for long-range planning and other long-range policy decisions. [NACA 1953, p. 1128]

Although the study is not explicit on the decision models related to the two classes of problems, different models are clearly felt to underly "short-run" pricing problems and "long-run" pricing problems.

The decision model approach is not, however, limited to direct costing and management accounting. An AAA Committee on External Reporting was charged to survey present external accounting practices and assess their merits. They chose the decision model approach:

> By choice and by necessity our general method is based on normative concepts. We start with normative investor's and creditor's valuation models and a normative dividend prediction model.... Note that we are not interested so much in how investors and creditors use accounting information in their decision processes as we are in what information they should be using to meet their goals. [AAA Committee on External Reporting 1969, pp. 79–80]

The user decision model approach has enriched the field of cost accounting because of its attempt to respond to differences among users. However, both the user decision model approach and the historical communication approach possess three fundamental defects.

First, truth—even if desirable—cannot be obtained without incurring a cost. Measurement consumes resources. Hence, consideration of measurement cost

---

3. Moreover, our original proposal for this research project was based on the user decision model approach. See Jaedicke et al. (1969).

must be an integral component of any theory of cost measurement. Of course, the two approaches do imply cost-benefit tests. The historical communications approach is based on the belief that differentiating among users is not worthwhile, whereas the user decision model approach is based on the belief that such differentiation is worthwhile. The difficulty, however, is that cost-benefit analysis is not an integral, explicit part of either approach.

Second, users operate in an uncertain world and explicit recognition of uncertainty casts doubt on the concept of a true cost, which implicitly presumes a certain world. As developed in Chapter 2, under uncertainty, a cost measure's value does not derive from how closely it represents an abstract concept but rather the state partition it induces. Hence, whether one measure or another is closer to, say, marginal cost is largely immaterial; the relevant question is what each reveals about an uncertain future.

Third, the concept of a true cost (whether conditional or absolute) is likely to be both illusory and irrelevant in a multiperson world. Two people in an organization are likely to possess different beliefs and tastes and therefore may react differently to particular measurements. Furthermore, communication between them may involve distortion or bluffing, such as when a manager communicates "tight" cost standards to a subordinate.

These three defects lead us to use the following approach.

1.3 INFORMATION EVALUATION APPROACH

In contrast with the foregoing two approaches, we adopt an explicit resource allocation perspective. Particular forms of measurement are viewed as desirable to the extent that they produce outcomes more desirable than the resources they consume. Replacement cost measures may, for example, be desirable, depending on the context and the relative cost of producing such measures. Similarly, a measurement system that systematically distorts a firm's cash balance may, in this view, be desirable, depending on the use to which the data will be put and the cost of producing more accurate measures.

Desirability, in turn, is determined in a conventional economic manner. That is, we explicitly consider available opportunities and prevailing tastes and beliefs. By implication, then, the focus is on analysis and not on prescription. In consumer demand theory, for example, we analyze the question of how much butter an individual should consume, but we do not categorically state a preferred amount of butter. Rather, this is a function of the individual's opportunities, tastes, and beliefs. Treating accounting measures as an economic commodity quite naturally produces the same outcome. We analyze the question of which cost measurements should be produced in a particular setting, but we do not categorically state preferred types of measurements. Rather, these are a function of the individual's opportunities, tastes, and beliefs.

The remainder of this chapter illustrates the information evaluation approach in two situations: *decision facilitating* and *decision influencing*. In the decision-facilitating case, the ultimate cost description is provided to the decision maker *before* he makes his decision. The purpose is to help resolve some form of uncertainty in the decision problem at hand. For example, the historical cost of supplies may serve as a basis for predicting the expected future costs of supplies.

In the decision-influencing case, however, the ultimate cost description is provided *after* the decision maker selects and implements his decision.[4] Only the measurement *method* can be conveyed to him prior to his selection. In this case, the cost measures are used to evaluate the decision maker's performance, with the purpose of motivating his action selections. Consequently, he is informed as to how his performance will be measured and how that measure will affect the outcomes that are relevant to his tastes.

2.0 A DECISION-FACILITATING ILLUSTRATION

Consider a decision of whether to accept or reject a special order for 1,000 units of a product that is a unique variation of a firm's regular output. Acceptance of this order would not interfere with regular sales, now or in the future. The incremental revenue will be $20,000, and production will require raw materials costing $5,000 plus 800 direct labor hours from department A and 200 hours from department B. The special order will be accepted if it has a positive expected contribution margin. Thus, if the expected incremental cost of labor and overhead is less than $15,000 ($20,000 − $5,000), the decision maker will accept the offer.

The accounting system currently uses a *plant-wide rate* to assign labor and variable overhead costs to production. The rate for the preceding period was $16 per hour and, without additional information, the decision maker will use this rate to predict the incremental labor and overhead cost for the special order. Hence, in the absence of additional information, he will reject the offer: $20,000 − $5,000 − $16(800 + 200) = −$1,000 < 0.

Now consider the question of whether this choice can be improved. We assume that the accountant is concerned about the quality of the data to be used in the decision. In particular, the $16 rate is based on the regular use of an equal number of hours from the two departments, and the accountant suspects that the rates for the two departments are not identical. A special analysis could be conducted to determine the departmental rates. The question, then, is whether the accountant should conduct this analysis and report the resulting data to the decision maker. The outcome of the analysis is not presently known, but the accountant feels that one of three findings will materialize: the rates for departments A and B will be, respectively, $12 and $20, $14 and $18, or $16 and $16. The re-

---

4. Quite clearly, a single measurement system could simultaneously provide measures for each situation in a multiperiod setting. An intermediate period's cost measures, that is, might help resolve future uncertainties as well as provide a measure for evaluating a manager's recent performance.

spective contribution margins will then be:

	Analysis Outcome		
Departmental rates (A & B)	$12 & $20	$14 & $18	$16 & $16
Expected incremental revenue	$20,000	$20,000	$20,000
Expected incremental costs			
Raw materials	$ 5,000	$ 5,000	$ 5,000
Labor & variable overhead			
Dept. A (800 hr)	9,600	11,200	12,800
Dept. B (200 hr)	4,000	3,600	3,200
Total	$18,600	$19,800	$21,000
Expected contribution margin	$ 1,400	$ 200	$−1,000

Moreover, the accountant perceives that if he learns and reports the actual rates, the decision maker will employ those rates in his decision. Hence, the offer will be accepted by the decision maker only if the rates of $12 and $20 or $14 and $18 are reported.

The accountant, then, has two alternatives: (i) do not perform the analysis, which guarantees an incremental gain to the firm of $0; (ii) perform the analysis, which guarantees an incremental gain to the firm of $1,400, $200, or $0, less the cost of the analysis. Choice between them will depend on his risk attitudes, his beliefs concerning how likely the three cost figures will be, and how costly the analysis is. Suppose that he is risk neutral and assigns respective probabilities of 0.2, 0.2, and 0.6 to the three events. The expected contribution margin from performing the analysis is, therefore,

$$0.2(\$1,400) + 0.2(\$200) + 0.6(0) - C = \$320 - C$$

where C denotes the cost of the analysis. The accountant should perform the analysis if its cost is not in excess of $320.

Alternatively, suppose that the accountant predicts that the decision maker will not accept the special order unless its expected contribution margin is at least $500. The order would then be accepted only if the departmental rates are $12 and $20. The expected contribution margin from performing the cost analysis would be

$$0.2(\$1,400) + 0.2(0) + 0.6(0) - C = \$280 - C.$$

Thus the decision by the accountant to supply particular information depends on his perception of the decision situation, the method of analysis employed by the decision maker, and the cost of supplying that information.

3.0   A DECISION-INFLUENCING ILLUSTRATION

The above example can be modified slightly to illustrate resolution of measurement controversies in circumstances where the decision maker's performance is to be (retrospectively) evaluated. Here, recall, the question is one of designing an evaluation scheme that will motivate the decision maker in a manner consistent with the firm's goals.

Suppose, then, that the decision maker must again decide whether to accept or reject the special order. The order, however, merely specifies the price of $20 per unit and the quantity is to depend on the customer's needs. Table 1.1 gives the

TABLE 1.1   ANALYSIS OF SPECIAL ORDER EXCLUSIVE OF IMPACT OF BONUS

Possible Demand Levels	500	1,000	1,500
Probability of Occurrence	0.3	0.4	0.3
Contribution Margin ($1.40 per unit)	$ 700	$1,400	$2,100
Incremental Fixed Overhead	1,200	1,200	1,200
Incremental Cash Flow	$ – 500	$ 200	$ 900
Direct Cost Measure of Income (as above)	$ – 500	$ 200	$ 900
Absorption Cost Measure of Income Contribution Margin	$ 700	$1,400	$2,100
Fixed Overhead Charge ($1.20 per unit)	600	1,200	1,800
Net	$ 100	$ 200	$ 300

possible demand levels and their probability of occurrence. For simplicity, we now assume that all incremental costs can be predicted with certainty; these include both the variable costs of $18.60 per unit and an increase in fixed overhead of $1,200.

We assume that the decision maker receives a bonus of 10% of the "income before bonus" (where income is subject to definition). The owner (the evaluator in this case) must choose between two possible methods for measuring the income associated with this special order. One method is to measure income by using the incremental contribution margin less the incremental fixed overhead; we term this the *direct cost measure*. The other method is to measure income by deducting an average fixed cost of $1.20 per unit from the contribution margin (any volume variance is ignored); we term this the *absorption cost measure*. The alternative measures are shown in Table 1.1.

The keys to choice between the two measures are the owner's preferences and the predicted behavior of the decision maker. If the owner is risk neutral he will prefer acceptance of the order in that the expected cash inflow is

$$0.3(-\$500) + 0.4(\$200) + 0.3(\$900) = \$200$$

and the expected bonus under either measure is $20. The decision maker will also prefer acceptance under both income measures if he is risk neutral. In that case, the owner would be indifferent between the two measures, unless there was a difference in computation costs.

On the other hand, if the decision maker is sufficiently risk averse, use of the direct cost measure may induce him to reject the order, while the absorption cost measure would induce him to accept it.[5] In that case, the owner should select the absorption cost measure.

Quite clearly, then, the best measure depends on the decision maker's behavior, as well as the cost of the alternative measures and the owner's perception of the decision situation. This implies that the performance measure must be tailored to the individual if the owner wishes to induce optimal decisions. In practice we generally find it uneconomical to do this. Instead, we often use one type of measure for a set of managers and account for individual differences by tailoring the bonus scheme, broadly interpreted.[6]

4.0 SUMMARY

Our approach to cost measurement controversies is to treat a cost measurement system as we would any other type of economic activity. This allows us to adopt an explicit resource allocation perspective; and we therefore regard the question of whether one measurement method is superior to another as an inherently contextual question. Good accounting, that is, will be defined in terms of the opportunities, tastes, and beliefs at hand. This provides a more inclusive, and we hope more insightful, paradigm than is offered by either the historical communication or user decision model approaches that dominate the present literature.

In subsequent chapters we use the term *cost assessment* instead of cost mea-

---

5. This would result, for example, if the decision maker's preferences were represented by the negative exponential utility function $1 - e^{-b/50}$, where b is the amount of his bonus. In that case, the expected utility of accepting the order is

Direct Cost Measure:

$$(0.3)(1 - e^{50/50}) + (0.4)(1 - e^{-20/50}) + (0.3)(1 - e^{-90/50}) = -0.13 < 0$$

Absorption Cost Measure:

$$(0.3)(1 - e^{-10/50}) + (0.4)(1 - e^{-20/50}) + (0.3)(1 - e^{-30/50}) = +0.32 > 0$$

Consequently, the decision maker would reject the order if the direct cost measure was used but accept it if the absorption cost measure was used.

6. The bonus scheme may include salary bonuses, stock options, club memberships, helmet stickers, and various subtle forms of praise and censure. In our example, a bonus equal to $-50ln$ $(1 - x/2,000)$, where x is the direct income measure, would induce the risk averse decision maker in the prior footnote to act as if he was risk neutral with respect to the income measure. This follows from the fact that

$$1 - e^{-(-50ln(1 - x/2,000))/50} = x/2,000 \text{ for } x < 2,000.$$

In that case the bonuses would be $-\$11.16$, $\$5.27$, and $\$29.89$, with an expected utility of 0.10.

surement. This is to stress the fact that much of our discussion, including the information evaluation approach, applies to both cost information and cost prediction. Moreover, we use the term cost assessment to refer to both the costing procedures and the resulting cost descriptions.

The study's basic assumptions and resource allocation perspective are developed in Chapters 2 and 3. The nature of cost assessment and its role in facilitating and influencing decisions within the firm are explored in Chapters 4 and 5. These two developments are then brought together in a number of illustrations that focus on short-run (Chapter 6) and long-run (Chapter 7) decisions. The analysis is extended to external reporting settings in Chapter 8 and, finally, a concluding summary (Chapter 9) is provided.

CONSISTENT CHOICE IN AN UNCERTAIN WORLD

Our study of cost assessment begins with two primitive notions. First, cost assessments are utilitarian in nature, serving a fundamental purpose of promoting economic activity. Second, alternative assessment procedures typically exist. As a result, a choice problem arises: Which assessment procedure do we prefer?

Our approach to this choice problem is normative. We address the question of what this choice should be, given a specific set of assumptions. In particular, we offer a formal, choice theoretic approach to the problem of selecting cost assessment procedures. Chapters 2 and 3 summarize those aspects of choice theory upon which we rely. The remaining chapters discuss the application of this theory to the evaluation of cost assessment alternatives in a variety of contexts.

The basic assumptions upon which we rely are discussed in the first section, where emphasis is placed on the concept of consistent individual choice under uncertainty. Since cost assessment problems are a subset of the more general problem of information system design, we then summarize, in the second section, the concept of consistent individual choice among informative alternatives. Finally, in the third section, we summarize the implications of our individual behavior assumptions for choice at the firm level, introducing some additional assumptions that allow us to reflect the owners' preferences and beliefs in terms of a single individual's preferences and beliefs.

1.0 TERMINOLOGY AND ASSUMPTIONS

We are fundamentally concerned with choice among cost assessment alternatives in a situation where (i) nontrivial cost assessment alternatives exist and

(ii) their fundamental purpose is promoting choice among action alternatives. The individual who selects the action alternative is termed the *decision maker,* and the individual who selects the cost assessment alternative is termed the *evaluator.* The decision maker and the evaluator may, of course, be the same individual; but we often find specialization of choice activity, both at the firm and social levels. Typically, for example, a firm's controller (evaluator) and production manager (decision maker) are different individuals.

Within this context of the evaluator's choice among cost assessment alternatives, we make three assumptions that heavily influence our description of the evaluator's choice problem, the statement of its optimal resolution, and its subsequent illustration. These assumptions are consistency, uncertainty, and free analysis.

1.1 THE STATE-ACT-OUTCOME PARADIGM

Before exploring these assumptions, however, we must explicate the basic nature of a choice problem. We begin with a motivating example and then formalize the implied structure.

Consider an individual who must decide whether to investigate the quality of a particular product. If he does *not* investigate and *if* the quality is acceptable, a \$400 net gain will materialize. (For simplicity, we assume here and throughout the illustration that only monetary consequences are of interest to the individual.) On the other hand, if he docs *not* investigate and *if* the quality is unacceptable, the customer will ultimately demand that the product be repaired and a \$250 net loss will result (for example, the \$400 original gain less a repair cost of \$650). Conversely, if he does investigate prior to delivery, any quality deficiency will be discovered and corrected. Unfortunately, investigation is expensive, and neither gain nor loss will result if the investigation alternative is selected. That is, investigation guarantees a gain of precisely \$0. (Investigation might, for example, cost \$400 regardless of product quality, so the net gain is \$400 − \$400 = \$0.)

To summarize, the individual must select between two alternatives: investigate or not investigate. We denote these alternatives, respectively, a^1 and a^2. The first, investigate, will result in neither gain nor loss, while the second will result in either a gain of \$400 or a loss of \$250.

Introduction of a "state" variable now provides a rich and convenient descriptive mechanism. Alternative a^2, not investigate, will result in either of two consequences. We therefore associate one consequence, say a \$400 gain, with one state, and the other consequence, a \$250 loss, with a second state. Denote the two states s^1 and s^2. Essentially, the state variable is "a description of the world, leaving no relevant aspect undescribed" (Savage 1954, p. 9). In our simple illustration, we might regard state s^1 as denoting an "in-control" production process and s^2 an "out-of-control" production process.

Observe, now, that by regarding s^1 and s^2 as mutually exclusive events we have completely described the choice problem originally posed. That is, a^1 will produce a \$0 consequence regardless of which state obtains, but a^2 will produce

TABLE 2.1   OUTCOME TABLE FOR INVESTIGATION EXAMPLE
$$p(s,a)$$

		Possible States	
		s^1	s^2
Choice Alternatives	a^1	\$0	\$0
	a^2	\$400	−\$250

a \$400 gain *if* state s^1 obtains and a \$250 loss *if* state s^2 obtains. Thus the question of which consequence will materialize upon selection of a^2 is characterized in terms of which state, s^1 or s^2, will obtain. A conventional outcome table is presented in Table 2.1.

A choice problem exists, then, when at least two alternative choices or actions are available and one must be selected. We denote the set of available actions A and its generic element a. Next we recognize a set of possible consequences, denoted X with generic element x. A consequence represents the primitive objects of choice, or whatever the individual deems desirable. "They might in general involve money, life, state of health, approval of friends, well-being of others, the will of God, or anything at all about which the person could possibly be concerned" (Savage 1954, p. 14).

Finally, to represent a specific action in terms of its consequences, we specify a set of states, denoted S with generic element s. One and only one member of S will obtain. And the possible consequences are specified by an *outcome function* p: $S \times A \rightarrow X$ such that $p(s,a) = x \in X$ for all states $s \in S$ and actions $a \in A$.[1] For convenience, we generally regard S, A, and X as finite sets.

We now endow this setting with behavior assumptions that will allow us to formally represent the criterion upon which choice should be made.[2]

1.2   EXPECTED UTILITY REPRESENTATION

Our first major assumption in this study concerns choice behavior. We assume that the evaluator consistently selects among cost assessment alternatives in a manner that can be represented by the expected utility hypothesis. Put another way, we assume that his choice behavior can be represented as though

---

1. The function p associates one and only one element of X with each possible (s,a) pair. An action is thus a mapping from S into X.

2. See Lea (1973) and particularly Savage (1954) for further discussion of this paradigm.

he selects the action with the maximum expected value of utility. We term such an individual *rational*.

To develop a description of rational choice, we assume that the individual in question is able to preferentially *rank* the various actions. For any pair of actions he is assumed able to tell which of the two he prefers or whether he is indifferent between them. We also assume that this ranking is *transitive*. For example, if a^1 is preferred to a^2 and a^2 is preferred to a^3, we then require that a^1 also be preferred to a^3.[3]

A convenient description of this preference assumption is provided by a binary preference relation, denoted $\succsim$. If a^1 is regarded to be at least as desirable as a^2, we denote this $a^1 \succsim a^2$. We then require that such a relation exist, be complete, and be transitive.[4]

These assumptions are sufficient to say a number of things about choice behavior (for example, see Arrow 1963; Nikaido 1968), but we are particularly interested in a class of behavior with a richer set of implications. In particular, we assume existence of probability and utility functions such that the expected utility of the possible outcomes from each action represents the primitive preference ordering encoded in $\succsim$. The probability function, denoted $\phi(s)$, represents the individual's state occurrence beliefs. The utility function, denoted $U(x)$, represents the individual's preferences with respect to the possible outcomes. The expected utility of action $a \in A$ is denoted

[2.1a]
$$E(U \mid a) = \sum_{s \in S} U(p(s,a))\,\phi(s).$$

Concisely stated, then, our rationality assumption is that functions $\phi(s)$ and $U(x)$ exist such that $a^1 \succsim a^2$ if and only if $E(U \mid a^1) \geq E(U \mid a^2)$ for all a^1, $a^2 \in A$. Put another way, we assume existence of an $E(U \mid a)$ measure that *represents* the individual's preference.[5] The individual can then be modeled as if he selects his most preferred action, $a^* \in A$, so as to maximize his expected utility measure:

[2.1b]
$$E(U \mid a^*) = \max_{a \in A} E(U \mid a).$$

---

3. Note that without the basic ranking ability we simply cannot talk about rational choice, because we admit to choice settings where our individual is unable to make a choice. Also, without transitivity, choice may whirl about in circles and needlessly consume resources. Suppose, to illustrate, a^1 is preferred to a^2, a^2 is preferred to a^3, but a^3 is preferred to a^1. The individual might, under these circumstances, currently possess a^3, pay \$100 to switch to a^2 (because a^2 is preferred to a^3), pay another \$100 to switch to a^1, and finally pay yet another \$100 to switch to a^3, arriving at his original position minus \$300.

4. A binary relation such as $\succsim$ is merely a subset of $A \times A$. For $a^1, a^2 \in A$, (a^1, a^2) is in the relation $\succsim$ if a^1 is ranked at least as good as a^2. We denote this $a^1 \succsim a^2$. $\succsim$ is complete if not $a^1 \succsim a^2$ implies $a^2 \succsim a^1$, for all $a^1, a^2 \in A$. Similarly, $\succsim$ is *transitive* if $a^1 \succsim a^2$ and $a^2 \succsim a^3$ implies $a^1 \succsim a^3$, for all $a^1, a^2, a^3 \in A$.

5. Conditions under which such a representation does exist have been explored in considerable depth. For the sake of completeness, the von Neumann-Morgenstern axiomatization is summarized in Appendix 2.1; deeper treatments are available in Savage (1954) and Krantz et al. (1971).

Observe that, given our assumptions, a complex choice problem can be decomposed into specification of an outcome function over the set of possible states and actions, a utility function over the set of possible outcomes and a probability function over the set of possible states. We shall rely on this characterization of rational choice in ensuing chapters and denote it $\{p, S, A, U, \phi\}$.[6]

To illustrate the expected utility representation, return to the investigation example in Table 2.1, which specifies the outcome function for the set of states $S = \{s^1, s^2\}$ and the set of actions $A = \{a^1, a^2\}$. We must further specify the individual's beliefs and cash flow preferences. Suppose that he regards the states as equally likely; then $\phi(s^1) = \phi(s^2) = 1/2$. Further suppose that his cash outcome preference is reflected by a negative exponential utility function of $U(x) = 1 - e^{-x/250}$. Then, using Equation [2.1a], we have

$$E(U \mid a^1) = (1 - e^0)(0.5) + (1 - e^0)(0.5)$$
$$= 0$$

and

$$E(U \mid a^2) = (1 - e^{-400/250})(0.5) + (1 - e^{250/250})(0.5)$$
$$= (0.798)(0.5) + (-1.718)(0.5)$$
$$= -0.46.$$

Since $E(U \mid a^1) > E(U \mid a^2)$, we know that investigation is the preferred action.[7]

1.3   UNCERTAINTY

Our second major assumption in this study is that in the general case choices are made under uncertainty. That is, the outcome that will be produced by a particular action will generally be regarded as uncertain at the time of choice. In our analysis, then, subjective certainty is merely a special case in which the individual assesses a probability of 1 that some specific state, say $\hat{s} \in S$, will occur. Then the expected utility measure reduces to

[2.1c] $$E(U \mid a^*) = \max_{a \in A} U(p(\hat{s}, a)).$$

To illustrate the special case of subjective certainty, again consider our investigation example. Suppose that the individual perceives that state s^2 will, in fact, obtain, that is, $\phi(s^1) = 0$ and $\phi(s^2) = 1$ (the process is not-in-control).

---

6. Also note that the utility measure is defined over alternative outcomes. On occasion, we suppress this dependency by working directly with the composition of the outcome and utility functions: $U(p(s, a)) = U(s, a)$.

7. Observe that our representation of the choice problem only specifies a utility function that is unique up to a positive linear transformation. That is, replacement of $U(x)$ with $\hat{U}(x) = \alpha + \beta\, U(x)$ will result in precisely the same choice for any real numbers $\beta > 0$ and α. Moreover, since $\beta > 0$ and α are arbitrary, we cannot use $U(x)$ or $\hat{U}(x)$ for making interpersonal utility comparisons.

Then the expected utilities associated with his two actions are

$$E(U \mid a^1) = (1 - e^0) = 0$$

and

$$E(U \mid a^2) = (1 - e^{250/250}) = -1.718.$$

The optimal action is again to investigate, $a^* = a^1$.[8]

For expositional reasons, some of our cost assessment illustrations will assume subjective certainty, but we regard this as a special case. In fact, we generally assume that both the evaluator and the decision maker perceive their respective choice problems as uncertain. This agrees with most views of the world; and it also provides entry to a number of cost assessment issues. Under subjective certainty, many—if not most—cost assessment problems disappear. For example, information has zero value in a subjectively certain world, and thus under subjective certainty we must relegate all historical cost reporting systems to zero value.

1.4   COSTLESS ANALYSIS

Our third major assumption is a world of costless analysis for the evaluator. The extensive assessments and computations implied by the model of rational choice in Equation [2.1], and its derivatives introduced in later sections, will be assumed to be a free good for the evaluator.

Regarding analysis as a free good has an important effect because we may then regard the specification of the choice alternatives, states, and outcome, probability, and utility functions as *complete*. Nothing of conceivable merit is omitted from the analysis. Before the fact, no specification error is conceivable. Totally unanticipated errors may, however, appear after the fact. For example, in our simple illustration, the product is assumed to be either acceptable or not acceptable; it may, however, turn out that the product is "slightly" inferior with a monetary return of $100. Had such an outcome been perceived before the choice was made, it would, with our free analysis assumption, have been included in the state and outcome specifications. Completeness, then, is an *ex ante* concept.

Introduction of a nontrivial analysis cost has a profound effect on our description of choice behavior; and it gives rise, as we shall see, to numerous cost assessment issues that do not exist under conditions of costless analysis.

---

8. Note that this same selection is made if we merely consider the cash flows instead of their utilities, that is, $p(s^2, a^1) = 0 > p(s^2, a^2) = -250$. This use of cash maximization occurs because, under subjective certainty, we may substitute any strictly increasing transformation of $U(\cdot)$ in Equation [2.1a] and continue to arrive at selection of the optimal action. Hence, if the outcome is assessed in cash and if the individual always prefers more to less cash, selection of the cash maximizing choice alternative will, in the certain case, ensure selection of a^*. But we are not afforded such liberty in the more general uncertain case. For example, using expected cash flows in the previous uncertain case would lead to incorrect selection of a^2.

Transformation of utility functions is further discussed in Chapter 3 (section 1.2).

Thus, in part of the study, we regard the decision maker as experiencing "costly" analysis in the sense that he finds it more beneficial to stop short of the extensive assessments and computations implied by Equation [2.1]. This introduces numerous additional cost assessment issues, but their *evaluation* must assume costless analysis if it is to be definitive. Hence, throughout the study, we assume costless analysis for the evaluator.

This completes the discussion of our major assumptions. The next question concerns how these assumptions combine to provide a structure for choice among cost assessment alternatives. At an abstract level, choice among cost assessment alternatives is identical to choice among information alternatives. We pursue this theme in the following section, where we introduce information and consistent choice among information alternatives.

2.0   USE AND CHOICE AMONG INFORMATIVE COMMODITIES

We begin our discussion of information by focusing on the anticipated receipt of information prior to selection of an action. This provides an opportunity to define the term information as well as to specify the nature of its rational use.

2.1   ANTICIPATED INFORMATION RECEIPT

Return to the basic description of rational choice embodied in Equation [2.1] and recall that we assume complete specification. Now consider the *anticipated* impact of receipt of some informative "message" or "signal." This might be historical cost data, a news media statement, conversation with another individual, receipt and perusal of a Sears Roebuck catalogue, and so on. What is important is the anticipated impact of this receipt on the specification of $\{p, S, A, U, \phi\}$. It is inconceivable that p, S, A, or U could be altered; these elements are, by definition, completely specified. The only question is which state $s \in S$ will in fact obtain. Hence, the only conceivable impact of information would be a revision of the individual's beliefs as to state occurrence. That is, the choice problem has been completely specified and uncertainty is entirely and completely embedded in state occurrence.

To formalize this theme, we denote the informative "message" or "signal" by y and its source by η. For later reference we denote the (generally finite) set of possible messages or signals by Y and the set of available sources by H. It will be convenient to regard H and Y as always including the null (or no information) source, denoted η^0, and its corresponding "signal," denoted y^0.

Before receipt of y from η, the individual's beliefs are encoded in the probability function $\phi(s)$; after receipt of y from η, they will be encoded in $\phi(s \mid y, \eta)$, the conditional probability of state s, given receipt of signal y from source η. Movement from $\phi(s)$ to $\phi(s \mid y, \eta)$ is accomplished in a Bayesian manner. Recall that our rationality assumption includes beliefs that are represented by a probability function. This implies that the probability calculus specifies the appropriate manner for manipulation and revision of these assessments. Hence, our choice behavior assumptions specify the optimal use of information in probability revision via Bayes's theorem.[9]

Specific details will depend on the basic distributions employed. For expositional convenience, we regard each source as a function or mapping from S into Y; that is, $\eta: S \to Y$ or $y = \eta(s)$. This convention merely requires that we define the state variable with sufficient richness to accommodate any past events, system "noise," or other factors that may affect the signal received. More important, however, it allows us to regard each source as forming a *partition* of the state space, S. To see this, define $S_{y\eta}$ to be the set of all states that are mapped by source η into specific signal $y \in Y$:

$$S_{y\eta} = \{s \in S \mid \eta(s) = y\}.$$

Quite clearly, now, $\{S_{y\eta}\}$ partitions S:[10] $\bigcup_{y \in Y} S_{y\eta} = S$ and for any distinct y^1, $y^2 \in Y$, $S_{y^1\eta} \cap S_{y^2\eta} = \phi$.

Bayesian revision of the probability measure, upon receipt of y from η, is now readily depicted. The probability of source η producing signal y, or partition $S_{y\eta}$, is simply $\phi(y \mid \eta) = \sum_{s \in S_{y\eta}} \phi(s)$; and the conditional probability measure is[11]

$$\phi(s \mid y, \eta) = \frac{\phi(y \mid s, \eta)\,\phi(s)}{\phi(y \mid \eta)}$$

$$= \begin{cases} \dfrac{\phi(s)}{\phi(y \mid \eta)} & \text{for all } s \in S_{y\eta} \\ 0 & \text{otherwise.} \end{cases}$$

In general, acquisition and use of information is costly; that is, the information source and the signal will influence the outcome associated with each pair of actions and states. Consequently, we expand the arguments of the outcome function to include the source:[12] $x = p(s, a, \eta)$. We may now interpret x as the net outcome, reflecting both the outcome from the decision maker's actions and

---

9. Consider the probability function defined over S. For any two subsets of S, which we term *events* and denote E_1 and E_2, we have $\phi(E_1 \cap E_2) = \phi(E_1 \mid E_2)\phi(E_2) = \phi(E_2 \mid E_1)\phi(E_1)$. Hence, assuming $\phi(E_2) > 0$, we have

$$\phi(E_1 \mid E_2) = \frac{\phi(E_2 \mid E_1)\phi(E_1)}{\phi(E_2)}$$

which is Bayes's theorem.

10. A collection of subsets G partitions S when $\bigcup_{g \in G} g = S$ and $g^1 \cap g^2 = \phi$ for all g^1, $g^2 \in G$, $g^1 \neq g^2$.

11. Observe that we engage in a slight notational liberty here by using y to refer to the message itself as well as the event $S_{y\eta}$.

12. Since the signal is a function of the state and the source, it need not be explicitly included as an argument of $p(\cdot)$; it is implicitly included.

the "cost" of providing him with information. If the source and signals are costless, then $p(s, a, \eta) = p(s, a)$.

In the general case of costly information acquisition, the choice problem upon receipt of signal y from source η is represented by

[2.2a] $$E(U \mid a, y, \eta) = \sum_{s \in S} U(p(s, a, \eta)) \phi(s \mid y, \eta)$$

and

[2.2b] $$E(U \mid \alpha^*(y, \eta), y, \eta) = \max_{a \in A} E(U \mid a, y, \eta).$$

where we employ $\alpha^*(y, \eta)$ to denote a most preferred action given receipt of signal y from source η.

Recall, now, that the null source and corresponding signal are contained, respectively, in H and Y. (This would be a constant function from S into $\{y^0\}$.) Hence, without loss of generality, we regard the statement in [2.2] as the basic representation of the individual's choice problem. For example, under subjective certainty we regard all η to be effectively null sources in that $\phi(\hat{s}) = 1$ for some $\hat{s} \in S$, and only signal $y = \eta(\hat{s})$ has a nonzero probability of occurrence.

Finally, observe that $E(U \mid a)$ and $E(U \mid a, y, \eta)$ may be identical for all $a \in A$. We impose no requirement that receipt of message y from system η alter the probability function with respect to those events that influence action outcomes. However, alteration of the probability function is the distinguishing feature of information. That is, signal y (from source η) is termed information with respect to the set of events G (a partition of S) if and only if $\phi(g) \neq \phi(g \mid y, \eta)$ for some $g \in G$.

Put somewhat differently, the concept of information is dependent on both the source and the problem addressed. The physical message y may be information if received from source η^1 but not if received from source η^2. Receipt of an income statement indicating an income of \$237 may not, for example, alter your beliefs unless the income statement has been audited. Additionally, receipt of a weather forecast indicating a 97% chance of rain may alter the probability function with respect to the events considered when choosing between attending a movie or a picnic but will not likely alter the probability assessments of the events considered in a marriage decision. The event specification relevant for one analysis need not be relevant for another. Consequently, receipt of y from η may alter the probability function in one situation but not the other. Hence, the definition of information is critically dependent on the choice context being addressed.[13]

---

13. It is not entirely clear how far we should push this issue before introduction of information system acquisition. We might, given our costless analysis assumption, envision the event specification as reflecting all conceivable differentiations. Then what is termed information in one choice context would also be termed information in any other contemporaneous context faced by the individual in question. It seems more useful, however, to view the event specification as payoff relevant in the sense of Marschak (1963) and define the term information with respect to that partition. This results in an individual-context specific definition.

To sum up, information is characterized by probability revision. Our specific rationality assumption, in turn, requires Bayesian probability revision for the use of information to be optimal.

2.2 INFORMATION SYSTEM CHOICE

Movement from the point of anticipated information use to selection of a most preferred information system is fairly straightforward. Recognize, however, that the element of choice is not the signal itself; rather, it is the source. In deciding to obtain information, the evaluator does not know the content of the information before it is acquired. For example, he selects a divisional profit-reporting method, not the profit figure itself. Similarly, in obtaining a weather report, we decide which reporting source's opinion to solicit, not the opinion itself. That is, η, not y, is the element of choice.

In a sense, then, we view selection of source η as a compound, two-stage "gamble." The first element of uncertainty is which signal will occur, and the second, following signal contingent action choice, is which consequence will be experienced. The utility measure associated with selection of source η, followed by selection of the most preferred action for whatever signal obtains, is given by

[2.3a] $$E(U \mid \alpha^*(\eta), \eta) = \sum_{y \in Y} \phi(y \mid \eta) E(U \mid \alpha^*(y, \eta), y, \eta)$$

where we employ $\alpha^*(\eta)$ to denote $\{\alpha^*(y, \eta)\}$.

Quite clearly, then, η^1 is as desirable as η^2 if and only if $E(U \mid \alpha^*(\eta^1), \eta^1) \geq E(U \mid \alpha^*(\eta^2), \eta^2)$; and the most preferred source is located by

[2.3b] $$E(U \mid \alpha^*(\eta^*), \eta^*) = \max_{\eta \in H} E(U \mid \alpha^*(\eta), \eta).$$

To illustrate these considerations, return to our earlier investigation example and suppose that our individual has an additional option of gathering some product cost data on a similar type of process before deciding whether to investigate the specific product in question. For simplicity, we assume that the cost data will indicate either y^1 ("low" cost) or y^2 ("high" cost). Four states are now explicitly recognized: s^{11} (in control, low cost), s^{12} (in control, high cost), s^{21} (not in control, low cost), and s^{22} (not in control, high cost), with respective probabilities of 0.40, 0.10, 0.25, and 0.25.[14]

Denoting the cost reporting source η, we therefore have $S_{y^1\eta} = \{s^{11}, s^{21}\}$ and $S_{y^2\eta} = \{s^{12}, s^{22}\}$. Also

$$\phi(y^1 \mid \eta) = \phi(s^{11}) + \phi(s^{21}) = 0.40 + 0.25 = 0.65$$

---

14. These data are consistent with a source that will report (i) a low cost on a similar process with probability 0.80 if the process in question is in control and (ii) a low cost on a similar process with probability 0.50 if the process in question is not in control. Further note that in terms of the original choice problem in Table 2.1 $s^1 = \{s^{11}, s^{12}\}$ and $s^2 = \{s^{21}, s^{22}\}$ are the states, but in the revised choice problem they constitute the set of *payoff relevant events*. This illustrates the basic point that we do not "ignore" states; rather, we elect not to distinguish among them.

and

$$\phi(y^2 \mid \eta) = \phi(s^{12}) + \phi(s^{22}) = 0.10 + 0.25 = 0.35.$$

The various conditional probabilities are given by

$$\phi(s^{11} \mid y^1, \eta) = \frac{\phi(s^{11})}{\phi(y^1 \mid \eta)} = \frac{0.40}{0.65}$$

$$\phi(s^{21} \mid y^1, \eta) = \frac{0.25}{0.65}$$

$$\phi(s^{12} \mid y^1, \eta) = \phi(s^{22} \mid y^1, \eta) = 0$$

$$\phi(s^{11} \mid y^2, \eta) = \phi(s^{21} \mid y^2, \eta) = 0$$

$$\phi(s^{12} \mid y^2, \eta) = \frac{\phi(s^{12})}{\phi(y^2 \mid \eta)} = \frac{0.10}{0.35}$$

and

$$\phi(s^{22} \mid y^2, \eta) = \frac{0.25}{0.35}.$$

Finally, suppose that acquisition and use of this information will cost $5. The expanded outcome function is given in Table 2.2. If signal y^1 is observed, we have, using [2.2],

$$E(U \mid \alpha^*(y^1, \eta), y^1, \eta) = \max \begin{cases} (1 - e^{-395/250})(40/65) + \\ \quad (1 - e^{255/250})(25/65) = -0.19 \\ (1 - e^{5/250})(40/65) + \\ \quad (1 - e^{5/250})(25/65) = -0.02 \end{cases}$$

$$= -0.02$$

with $\alpha^*(y^1, \eta) = a^1$. Similarly, if y^2 is observed

$$E(U \mid \alpha^*(y^2, \eta), y^2, \eta) = \max \begin{cases} (1 - e^{-395/250})(10/35) + \\ \quad (1 - e^{255/250})(25/35) = -1.04 \\ (1 - e^{5/250})(10/35) + \\ \quad (1 - e^{5/250})(25/35) = -0.02 \end{cases}$$

$$= -0.02$$

with $\alpha^*(y^2, \eta) = a^1$. And, using Equation [2.3a],

$$E(U \mid \alpha^*(\eta), \eta) = -0.02(0.65) - 0.02(0.35) = -0.02.$$

From the original example, however, we know that

$$E(U \mid \eta^0) = E(U \mid a^*) = 0 > E(U \mid \alpha^*(\eta), \eta).$$

Hence, no information is preferred to information source η.

This demonstrates that if a source is informative, in the sense that it alters

TABLE 2.2 OUTCOME FUNCTION FOR INVESTIGATION EXAMPLE
WITH INFORMATIVE ALTERNATIVE

$$p(s, a, \eta)$$

		Possible States			
		s^{11}	s^{12}	s^{21}	s^{22}
Choice Alternatives	a^1	$-\$5$	$-\$5$	$-\$5$	$-\$5$
	a^2	$\$395$	$\$395$	$-\$255$	$-\$255$

the probability function with respect to the payoff relevant events ($\{s^1, s^2\}$), this is not sufficient to select that source. It is, however, necessary because if a costly source does not alter that probability function it would never be preferred to the null system.[15]

Furthermore, no informative system will ever be preferred to the null system if its "cost" exceeds the "value of perfect information." The "value of perfect information" is the maximum amount, in dollars or other outcome units, that the individual would be willing to pay a clairvoyant to reveal which state will actually occur. More formally, in the scalar outcome case (and assuming suitable regularity), it is the value of p^* that equates

$$\sum_{s \in S} \left\{ \max_{a \in A} U(p(s, a) - p^*) \right\} \phi(s) = E(U \mid a^*).$$

p^* places an upper bound, in outcome units, on the amount by which information acquisition can improve the action selection. No information can be worth more than perfect information.

To illustrate, the maximum the individual would pay for state revelation in the investigation example is the value of p^* that equates $(1 - e^{-(400-p^*)/250})(0.5) + (1 - e^{+p^*/250})(0.5) = 0$. Therefore, $p^* = \$127$ and no system, regardless of how informative it is, would be selected in this situation if it cost more than $\$127$.[16]

Information, then, is characterized by an ability to alter the probability function. Whether a particular datum is information depends on both its source

---

15. In fact, the preferred action must not be a constant function of the information; otherwise, the individual's behavior is not affected by the information and the source in question is therefore without value. Such information is termed useless information. Alternatively, if the preferred action is not a constant function of the information, the information is termed *useful*.

16. See LaValle (1968) and Raiffa (1968) for more extensive discussion of the value of perfect information. Also see Avriel and Williams (1970) and Butterworth (1973) for discussions of various related bounds on the value of acquiring additional information.

and the choice context at hand; and how much we would be willing to pay for a particular source depends on the context at hand. Information use and choice among informative commodities are inherently contextual issues.

Indeed, an interesting question is whether the desirability of one source over another can ever be established without addressing the context in which the information is to be used. The answer is affirmative for a limited class of sources. In particular, if one *costless* source is as fine as or forms a subpartition of another *costless* source, then the latter will never be preferred to the former.[17]

To explore this, consider two costless sources η^1 and η^2 and further suppose η^1 is as fine as η^2. That is, for every $y^1 \in Y$ there exists a $y^2 \in Y$ such that $S_{y^1_{\eta^1}} \subset S_{y^2_{\eta^2}}$. Then the signal that source η^2 will produce can be expressed as a function of the signal from source η^1. The following proposition, due to Blackwell, summarizes the argument.[18]

Proposition 2.1:

Consider two costless sources η^1 and η^2. $E(U \mid \alpha^*(\eta^1), \eta^1) \geq E(U \mid \alpha^*(\eta^2), \eta^2)$ for all choice problems with finite S and Y if and only if η^1 is as fine as η^2.

Observe that even for the limited case of *costless* sources, this result cannot rank all sources. Fineness is a necessary and sufficient condition in this case, but it is also an incomplete relation.[19] We generally cannot rank all available sources by

---

17. Another conjecture here concerns sources of differing cost that produce exactly the same partition: the more costly one is never strictly preferred.

18. See Blackwell and Girshick (1954), Marschak and Radner (1972), and McGuire (1972) for discussion of this result, and Feltham (1972), Marshall (1972), and Butterworth (1973) for its application to resolution of accounting issues. The proof of this proposition is as follows:

Proof:

First assume that η^1 is as fine as η^2. Let $Y^1_{y^2} = \{y^1 \in Y \mid S_{y^1_{\eta^1}} \subset S_{y^2_{\eta^2}}\}$. Then, for any choice problem

$$
\begin{aligned}
E(U \mid \alpha^*(\eta^2), \eta^2) &= \sum_{y^2 \in Y} \phi(y^2 \mid \eta^2) \, E(U \mid \alpha^*(y^2, \eta^2), y^2, \eta^2) \\
&= \sum_{y^2 \in Y} \left[\sum_{y^1 \in Y^1_{y^2}} \phi(y^1 \mid \eta^1) \right] E(U \mid \alpha^*(y^2, \eta^2), y^2, \eta^2) \\
&\leq \sum_{y^1 \in Y} \phi(y^1 \mid \eta^1) \, E(U \mid \alpha^*(y^1, \eta^1), y^1, \eta^1) \\
&= E(U \mid \alpha^*(\eta^1), \eta^1).
\end{aligned}
$$

Now assume that η^1 is neither finer nor coarser than η^2. We demonstrate in a special case that neither system can be preferred in all choice problems. Suppose that $S = \{s^1, s^2, s^3\}$ and η^1 induces the partition $\{\{s^1, s^2\}, \{s^3\}\}$ while η^2 induces $\{\{s^1\}, \{s^2, s^3\}\}$. If $A = \{a^1, a^2\}$, then η^1 will be preferred in a choice problem where $U(p(s^1, a^1)) = U(p(s^2, a^1)) > U(p(s^1, a^2)) = U(p(s^2, a^2))$ and $U(p(s^3, a^1)) < U(p(s^3, a^2))$. However, η^2 will be preferred if $U(p(s^1, a^1)) > U(p(s^1, a^2))$ and $U(p(s^2, a^1)) = U(p(s^3, a^1)) < U(p(s^2, a^2)) = U(p(s^3, a^2))$. And, with finite S the required counterexample is readily guaranteed for any choice problem. Hence, to have $E(U \mid \alpha^*(\eta^1), \eta^1) \geq E(U \mid \alpha^*(\eta^2), \eta^2)$ for all choice problems, we must have η^1 as fine as η^2.

19. The two sources with $S = \{s^1, s^2, s^3\}$ illustrated in the proof provide an example of two sources noncomparable with respect to fineness.

fineness. We therefore cannot, in general, address the question of source selection —or choice among cost assessment alternatives—without reflecting on the individual's beliefs and preferences in a specific decision context. It is for this reason that we examine the question of cost assessment in terms of individual preferences and beliefs and not in terms of some set of belief or preference-free "standards." The latter are bound, in some cases, to incorrectly or incompletely rank the alternatives.[20]

2.3 CHOICE SPECIALIZATION

To this point we have focused on an individual's consistent choice among actions and the extension of this concept to consistent choice among informative sources. Our concern now turns to task specialization or selection of an information source and subsequent selection of a particular action by separate individuals. The source, recall, is generally selected by an *evaluator* and the action by a *decision maker*. The accountant, for example, often selects a divisional reporting method but does not become engaged in the division's detailed operations.

One might argue that such task specialization, while prevalent, is irrelevant because the evaluator's task is to identify the preferences and beliefs of the user of his information and to select the system deemed optimal by that user. The structure we present below treats this situation of identical preferences and opinions as a special case. But this case is far from universal. A divisional reporting system is designed to reflect the preferences and opinions of top management, not those of the division managers. To admit the latter would allow for manipulation of the reporting system.[21] Similarly, existing audit standards reflect an element of protection for the auditor. Moreover, we generally recognize the need to motivate decision makers in a multiperson organization. Incentive payment plans, stock options, and praise-censure practices are all common. The implication is that preferences and beliefs differ among the individuals in the organization. Hence, in the general case, we provide for divergent preferences and beliefs and view the evaluator as selecting the information system most desirable in terms of "his" preferences and beliefs. Precisely which preferences and beliefs the evaluator employs is a question with ethical overtones. But whatever their form, they are assumed to be consistent in the sense of admitting to an expected utility representation.[22]

With task specialization, the evaluator must predict the decision maker's choice

---

20. Marschak and Radner (1972) and McGuire (1972) discuss this in terms of measuring the "amount" of information any source could provide (irrespective of its cost). Application to choice among costly accounting systems and the role of standards to guide that choice is presented in Feltham (1972) and Demski (1973).

21. See Demski (1972b) for further discussion of this point.

22. On the other hand, it is not clear how far this distinction should be pressed because incentive schemes may be available that will produce unanimity among the evaluator and the decision makers. This is discussed in the following section. Also see Ijiri (1975) for further discussion of this preference issue.

behavior. We represent that prediction, without loss of generality, with the decision rule or function $\alpha: Y \times H \to A$. If source η is selected and produces signal y, the decision maker is predicted to select action $a = \alpha(y, \eta)$.[23] Hence, the evaluator's choice problem is restated in terms of:

[2.4a] $\quad E(U \mid \alpha(y, \eta), y, \eta) = \sum_{s \in S} U(p(s, \alpha(y, \eta), \eta)) \phi(s \mid y, \eta),$

[2.4b] $\quad E(U \mid \alpha(\eta), \eta) = \sum_{y \in Y} \phi(y \mid \eta) E(U \mid \alpha(y, \eta), y, \eta),$

and

[2.4c] $\quad E(U \mid \alpha(\eta^*), \eta^*) = \max_{\eta \in H} E(U \mid \alpha(\eta), \eta).$

With task specialization then, the evaluator's choice problem remains precisely as depicted in Equation [2.3], except that he now does not control selection of $a \in A$. He selects system η, which subsequently produces signal y. This signal is transmitted to the decision maker, who, in turn, selects the action $a \in A$ that he prefers. The outcome relevant to the evaluator depends on the state $s \in S$ that occurs, the decision maker's action, and his system selection, $x = p(s, a, \eta)$.[24] This process is depicted in Figure 2.1.

To illustrate the task specialization setting, return to our earlier investigation example and now assume a separate decision maker decides whether to investigate. We continue to regard the evaluator as described before, with a negative exponential utility function of $U(x) = 1 - e^{-x/250}$ and the beliefs tabulated earlier. In addition, the evaluator knows the decision maker will not investigate (select a^2) in the absence of additional information; but, if the cost data are provided, he will investigate only if a "high" cost is indicated (y^2 obtains).[25] Hence, using Equation [2.4b] we have

$$E(U \mid \alpha(\eta^0), \eta^0) = (1 - e^{-400/250})(0.5) + (1 - e^{250/250})(0.5)$$
$$= -0.46,$$

and

$$E(U \mid \alpha(\eta), \eta) = [(1 - e^{-395/250})(40/65) + (1 - e^{255/250})(25/65)](0.65)$$
$$+ [(1 - e^{5/250})][(10/35) + (25/35)](0.35)$$
$$= -0.13.$$

---

23. Observe that in general the evaluator will be uncertain as to the decision maker's choice behavior upon receipt of y from η. We could focus on this by explicitly introducing the evaluator's beliefs, $\phi(a \mid y, \eta)$. The decision rule formulation is identical, but more compact, provided we define s with sufficient richness to accommodate this form of uncertainty. The decision maker's act will thus depend on s, y, and η. But η partitions S, by convention, and the $a = \alpha(y, \eta)$ representation is therefore sufficient.

24. An interesting and perhaps significant phenomenon that we do not explicitly concern ourselves with here is the case where the evaluator's preferences are dependent on the consumption enjoyed by others (such as the decision maker). This is a familiar problem in welfare economics. See Graaff (1967).

25. These choices are consistent with various combinations of beliefs and preferences, such as $U(x) = -e^{-x/1,000}$, $\phi(s^{11}) = 0.48$, $\phi(s^{21}) = 0.20$, $\phi(s^{12}) = 0.12$, and $\phi(s^{22}) = 0.20$.

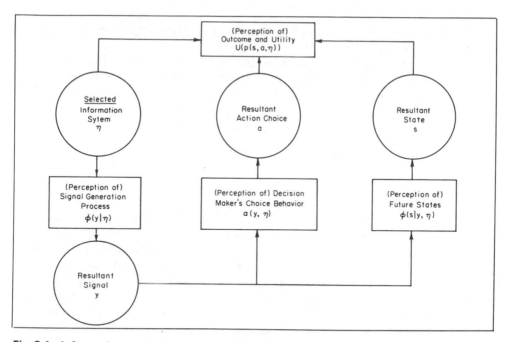

Fig. 2.1. Information evaluation process. This exhibit is taken from Feltham and Demski (1970) and Demski (1972).

Consequently, the cost information source is now preferred to the null information source, given the decision maker's anticipated action choice behavior.

Now compare our original choice characterization in Equation [2.1] with that in Equation [2.4]. The latter characterization abstractly depicts a choice problem in a situation where the choice produces an uncertain signal, which in turn induces an uncertain action choice, which ultimately results in an uncertain consequence. Equation [2.4] is a specialization of the basic theory in Equation [2.1] designed to highlight the characteristic structure of the evaluator's problem. And, just as we introduced information to assist in selection of $a^* \in A$, we might now introduce information to assist in selection of $\eta^* \in H$. Of course, any such information could not improve upon the case of perfect information supplied to the evaluator, coupled with action choice by the evaluator. Thus, in the scalar outcome case (again assuming suitable regularity), a necessary condition for employment by the evaluator of any informative source designed to improve his selection of $\eta^* \in H$ is that its "cost" not exceed p_α^*, where p_α^* equates[26]

$$\sum_{s \in S} \left\{ \max_{a \in A} U(p(s,a) - p_\alpha^*) \right\} \phi(s) = E(U \mid \alpha(\eta^*), \eta^*).$$

---

26. The issue of information seeking by the evaluator and formal statement and proof of this bound (along with several related bounds) are contained in Demski (1972a). Further observe here that p_α^*, properly interpreted, also bounds the improvement attainable by the evaluator through introduction of any information system that produces signals for the decision maker.

Indeed, many of the analyses contained in subsequent chapters can be interpreted as providing information for the evaluator.

In sum, the major impact of task specialization is lack of control, by the evaluator, over the action choice process.[27] By properly interpreting $\alpha(\eta)$, however, we may view [2.4] as the basic statement of the evaluator's choice problem. If the evaluator also selects the action, $\alpha(\eta)$ is interpreted as $\alpha^*(\eta)$ in Equation [2.3]; otherwise it is interpreted as the evaluator's representation of his beliefs about the decision maker's choice behavior.

3.0 EXTENSION TO FIRM CHOICE

The preceding expected utility characterization of consistent choice provides the basis for our exploration of choice among cost assessment alternatives. That characterization was developed from the perspective of a single, rational individual, but we may also interpret it in terms of consistent choice at the firm level. This may be done by somewhat casually assuming that Equation [2.4] characterizes the preferences of a "properly motivated" individual or team (as in Marschak and Radner (1972)). However, a much closer link between firm and individual choice behavior is available provided we are willing to make the requisite assumptions.

To sketch this setting, we proceed by considering an economy of rational individuals. Resource allocations by these individuals fall naturally into two broad categories: exchanges with other individuals and exchanges with "nature" (i.e., production). If a group of individuals agrees to engage in production, we have a firm. It might take the form of, say, a partnership or a corporation; the important characteristic is production specialization at the group level.

So viewed, the firm takes on an "entity" of its own (a fact long recognized in accounting convention). And it is the essence of this "entity" that presently concerns us. The individuals have consciously formed the firm and the firm specializes in production. Two facts become clear. First, the firm cannot consume; it merely acts as a productive agent for those who formed it. Second, these individuals, hereafter termed owners, are sovereign in directing its affairs. The firm is organized by the owners; it is concerned with productive activities but remains an agent of its owners. The open question is how we move from diverse owners' interests to direction of the firm's activities.

The appropriate normative framework for evaluating cost assessment alternatives from the point of view of the owners is, in general, unclear. In any specific

---

27. With the evaluator's outcome generally dependent upon his as well as the decision maker's choice, we have a game situation. Although we do not explore determination of η^* and $\alpha(\eta)$ in a game context (but, for simplicity treat $\alpha(\eta)$ as exogenously given), it should be clear that such an approach would provide a more thorough analysis of the class of problems we are addressing. See Baiman (1974) for one such example.

Further observe that Proposition 2.1 relies on the use of $\alpha^*(\eta)$. Hence, with task specialization (and $\alpha(\eta) \neq \alpha^*(\eta)$) the proposition does not necessarily hold.

context the owners may well disagree as to the ranking of any set of choice alternatives that affect the productive activities of the firm. Movement from their individual preferences to a group preference has long presented a challenge in the finance and economics literature. In a classic work in the area, Arrow (1963) demonstrates that, given some fairly simple requirements, it is in general *impossible* to establish an acceptable procedure for moving from individual preferences to a single group preference.

We can, however, establish a normative framework if we make some rather strong assumptions about the nature of the individual owners and the markets in which the firm operates. In particular, conditions exist under which the owners would unanimously agree in directing the firm's activities; and under these conditions, our expected utility maximization approach can be interpreted as reflecting the group preferences and beliefs. Furthermore, this can be specialized to the maximization of the firm's present value if additional market assumptions are made. This latter criterion will be useful in considering some cost assessment alternatives in the latter part of the study.

We sketch the requisite conditions and unanimity result below.

3.1 ADDITIONAL ASSUMPTIONS

In this discussion, we characterize the economy as consisting of a set of rational individuals I and a set of firms F. Three significant assumptions are made about this economy. First, it attains an *equilibrium* allocation of resources. Second, all individuals display *nonsatiation* in the sense that they never prefer less to more consumption. Third, all commodities are traded in *perfect markets*.[28] These additional assumptions, coupled with a spanning assumption that is introduced below, provide a setting in which a given firm's owners will unanimously agree in directing their firm's activities. Hence, the preferences of a single owner (for example, a manager or evaluator who owns shares in the firm) will provide the desired characterization of choice behavior.[29]

To provide insight into the implications of these assumptions we now sketch a simple two-period, one-good economy. All decisions are made now ($t = 0$) and returns are realized during the future period ($t = 1$). The single good may be interpreted as a consumption *numéraire,* such as cash. In general, this good will have a time and event characterization. We typically distinguish among dated claims to

---

28. Perfect markets refer to the usual notions of price-taking behavior by all individuals and firms, a costless transaction technology, and convexity.

29. A more thorough analysis would focus on the general notion of cooperative effort in directing the firm's activities, regardless of the market environment. Wilson's (1968, 1969a) work provides a characterization of how divergent the individual owners' preferences and beliefs may be and still allow either unanimity in directing the firm's activities or representation of the ownership *group's* behavior with the expected utility hypothesis. For example, unanimity and group utility and probability functions exist under heterogeneous beliefs if all owners have negative exponential utility functions—provided that Pareto optimality is maintained. Subsequent explorations are available in Rosing (1968), Demski (1972b, 1976), Ross (1973), and Demski and Swieringa (1974).

cash, for example. Similarly, insurance, preferred stocks, prepaid medical plans, and lottery tickets represent event contingent claims to cash.

Regarding the current period as subjectively certain, we therefore speak of current units of the good or future units of the good *if* state $s \in S$ obtains (for example, your future cash flow *if* the state of the economy is $s \in S$). Letting S denote the number of distinct states (as well as the set), we have, effectively, $1 + S$ (time and event) distinct goods.[30]

The productive act of firm $f \in F$ is now interpreted as the provision of some particular commodity schedule. Letting x_{ft}^s denote the net production of firm f at time t if state $s \in S$ obtains, we have $a_f' = (x_{f0}, x_{f1}^1, \ldots, x_{f1}^S)$. Also let A_f denote the firm's technologically feasible set of production schedules.

The outcome relevant to each individual $i \in I$ is his consumption at each point in time. Employing similar indexing, outcome x_{it}^s denotes individual i's consumption at time t if state $s \in S$ obtains and $x_i = (x_{i0}, x_{i1}^1, \ldots, x_{i1}^S)$ is his state-contingent consumption vector. In turn, the set of available consumption vectors is circumscribed by the individual's wealth and market opportunities. His wealth consists of whatever exogenously given goods he possesses, denoted $\bar{x}_i = (\bar{x}_{i0}, \bar{x}_{i1}^1, \ldots, \bar{x}_{i1}^S)$, plus his ownership of the various firms, denoted $\bar{O}_{if}$ (with $\sum_{i \in I} \bar{O}_{if} = 1$, for all $f \in F$). His market opportunities depend on the types of trades he is able to make with the firms and other individuals.

If trading opportunities exist for each element of the individual's consumption vectors, we term the markets *complete*. Conversely, if the trading opportunities are not this rich, we term the markets *incomplete*. For example, trading in our simple economy might be confined to ownership in the various firms and the current consumption good. Such a market regime precludes explicit trading of future period state-contingent consumption among individuals. And it is likely that some types of trades will therefore be unavailable. (To illustrate, if $x_{f1}^1 = x_{f1}^2$ for all $f \in F$, individual trading opportunities would be confined to those for which state 1 and state 2 dependent future period consumption were equal.)[31]

We focus on the complete markets case and let P_1^s denote the current price of a promise to deliver one future unit of the consumption good if state $s \in S$ obtains. For convenience, we normalize the prices so that the price of a current unit of the good is unity. The commodity price vector is then denoted $P = (1, P_1^1, \ldots, P_1^S)$.

Given these prices, the market value of firm f, if it selects production schedule a_f, is

[2.5a] $$V(a_f) = x_{f0} + \sum_{s \in S} P_1^s x_{f1}^s = P \cdot a_f;$$

30. This is an elementary characterization of an Arrow-Debreu (or state preference) economy. See Debreu (1959), Arrow (1964a), and Hirshleifer (1970) for excellent expositions of the system. Also, numerical examples are provided in Appendix 8.3, and we use such an economy in Chapter 8 to explore the question of preference among alternative public financial reporting systems.

31. One such example is provided in Appendix 8.3; and extensive discussion is available in Radner (1968, 1972, 1974).

and the firm's market value maximizing schedule is determined by

[2.5b]
$$V(a_f^*) = \max_{a_f \in A_f} V(a_f).$$

The value of individual i's wealth is $W_i = P \cdot \bar{x}_i' + \sum_{f \in F} \bar{O}_{if} V(a_f^*)$, and he may select any consumption schedule that has a value less than or equal to W_i. That is, his action is $a_i = x_i$ and the set of feasible actions is

$$A_i = \{a_i \mid P \cdot a_i \le W_i\}.$$

Repeating Equation [2.1] with individual indexing we have

[2.6a]
$$E(U_i \mid a_i) = \sum_{s \in S} U_i(p_i(s, a_i)) \phi_i(s)$$

and

[2.6b]
$$E(U_i \mid a_i^*) = \max_{a_i \in A_i} E(U_i \mid a_i)$$

where $x_i = p_i(s, a_i) = (x_{i0}, x_{i1}^s)$.

Finally, our economy is in equilibrium (relative to the price vector P) if the individual and firm actions equate supply and demand:

$$\sum_{i \in I} x_{i0} = \sum_{f \in F} x_{f0} + \sum_{i \in I} \bar{x}_{i0}$$

and

$$\sum_{i \in I} x_{i1}^s = \sum_{f \in F} x_{f1}^s + \sum_{i \in I} \bar{x}_{i1}^s \quad \text{for all } s \in S.$$

We now briefly consider the incomplete markets case. This occurs, recall, whenever there are restrictions on the state-contingent trades that can be consumated. Suppose, for example, that the only available claims to future goods are those obtainable from the firms' distributions to their owners. For individual i we would then have $x_{i1}^s = \sum_{f \in F} O_{if} x_{f1}^s$, where O_{if} is his ownership of firm f after trading in current consumption and ownership shares has taken place. Note that the individual's action is now defined in terms of his current consumption and his ownership of the various firms; and his budget constraint is given by $x_{i0} + \sum_{f \in F} O_{if} P_f \le \bar{x}_{i0} + \sum_{f \in F} \bar{O}_{if} P_f$, where P_f is the current market price of firm f.

The productive schedule selected by firm f is less clear in this case. The market price P_f will depend on that selection, and we could assume that the firm's manager selects that schedule which maximizes the market value. However, this may not be optimal from the owners' point of view, and there are problems in formulating this in that the manager is not necessarily a price taker (as he was in the complete and perfect markets case).[32] In any event, under appropriate conditions an equilibrium exists if we take the firms' productive schedules as given.[33]

---

32. See Ekern and Wilson (1974) and Radner (1974, 1974a) for extensive discussions of these issues.

33. This is not meant to be taken lightly. The question of conditions sufficient to ensure an equilibrium entails much more than the general notion of counting equations and unknowns. For

3.2   Unanimity

Now suppose that our economy is in equilibrium and consider some feasible change in the equilibrium production schedule of firm f. We have the following unanimity result, due to Ekern and Wilson (1974):

Proposition 2.2[34]

The owners of a firm will approve or disapprove unanimously a project that would not alter the set of state distributions of returns available to individuals in the whole economy.

The basic idea is that existing prices can be used to evaluate a proposed small project *if* it provides a set of state-contingent returns that could be obtained (by any individual) from some currently available combination of investments in firms and trades with individuals. This results from the fact that in this case the project's consequences are contained in the space spanned by existing returns and, therefore, can be expressed as a linear combination of the existing returns.

If markets are complete and perfect, this proposition specializes to the familiar prescription of market value maximization. That is, with complete and perfect markets any new proposals will not alter the set of available returns and the

---

example, sluffing off a few minor qualifications, we know that an equilibrium will exist (in the sense that the equilibrium prices will not induce any unsatisfied demand and thus appropriately clear all markets) if (i) individual tastes can be summarized by continuous, convex, and nonsatiating preference relations, (ii) production possibility sets are closed and allow zero production for any firm, and (iii) aggregate production possibilities are convex and irreversible and allow for free disposal of unwanted inputs. See Debreu (1959), Quirk and Saposnik (1968), Radner (1968), Arrow and Hahn (1971), and Intriligator (1971).

34. Proof and further discussion of this proposition are available in Ekern and Wilson (1974), Radner (1974a), and Ekern (1975).

To sketch the basic idea behind the proof, return to the elementary incomplete market economy posed above and, for simplicity, assume that no current goods are involved. Using λ_i as the multiplier on the individual's optimization problem, first-order conditions require

$$\sum_{s \in S} \frac{\partial U_i(\cdot)}{\partial x_{i1}^s} \phi_i(s) x_{f1}^s - \lambda_i P_f = 0.$$

Similarly, at an equilibrium with a_f^* firm f's equilibrium schedule and U_i^* the individual's equilibrium utility, we obtain

$$\left. \frac{\partial U_i^*}{\partial a_f} \right|_{a_f^*} = O_{if} \sum_{s \in S} \frac{\partial U_i(\cdot)}{\partial x_{i1}^s} \phi_i(s) x_{f1}^{s'}.$$

Hence, i prefers an instantaneous alteration in a_f^* if and only if

$$0 < O_{if} \sum_{s \in S} \frac{\partial U_i(\cdot)}{\partial x_{i1}^s} \phi_i(s) x_{f1}^{s'} = O_{if} \sum_{s \in S} \frac{\partial U_i(\cdot)}{\partial x_{i1}^s} \phi_i(s) \sum_{f \in F} \theta_f a_f$$

(where the spanning property gives $x_{f1}^{s'} = \sum_{f \in F} \theta_f a_f$ for some set of weights θ_f, $f \in F$) or

$$O_{if} \sum_{f \in F} \theta_f P_f > 0$$

which has the same sign for every shareholder.

owners will therefore be unanimous in approving or disapproving alterations in the firm's production schedule. Moreover, maximization of the firm's market value is unanimously preferred by the owners in this case. To see this, consider a proposal to switch firm f's action from a_f^1 to a_f^2. If $V(a_f^1) < V(a_f^2)$—that is, the switch will increase firm f's market value—then perfect and complete markets ensure that such an increase is commensurate with increased command over desired objects by each owner, and nonsatiation ensures that such increased command is desirable.[35]

Indeed, we may further interpret this as the firm's owners unanimously desiring maximization of the firm's *present value*. That is, $V(a_f) = x_{i0} + \sum_{s \in S} P_1^s x_{f1}^s$ may be interpreted as the present value of the time and state indexed list of cash flows produced by the firm. For example, with subjective certainty, $V(a_f) = x_{i0} + P_1^{\hat{s}} x_{f1}^{\hat{s}}$ for some $\hat{s} \in S$. Defining $P_1^{\hat{s}} = 1/(1 + \rho)$ we have an objective of maximizing $x_{i0} + x_{f1}^{\hat{s}} (1 + \rho)^{-1}$, the present value of the firm's net cash flows.[36]

Another interesting implication of value maximization in this setting is that the method of firm evaluation of action alternatives is quite distinct from that at the individual level. The firm is assumed to know the state-dependent outcomes of any conceivable action; but it does not know which state will occur. The same holds for the individual; and we view the individual as reflecting consumptive preferences in a utility function, state occurrence possibilities in a subjective state probability function, and rank ordering action alternatives on the basis of their expected utility. The firm, however, does not engage in probability assessment. The state-return-price vector reflects society's collective preference and likelihood opinions. The firm accepts these public prices as given and uses them to evaluate its productive opportunities. This effectively reduces the firm's problem to choice among certain outcomes. The firm should maximize its market value; and the market value effect of any conceivable action is known.

With incomplete markets, however, market value maximization may not be unanimously agreed upon. If a proposed production schedule shift for firm f does not alter the set of returns available to individuals (that is, is consistent with those event-contingent trades that can be made), the firm's owners will unanimously approve or disapprove this shift. However, this unanimity cannot generally be expressed in terms of market value maximization. Ekern and Wilson (1974), for example, show that unanimity always exists in a world where shareholders value

---

35. Appendix 2.2 at the end of this chapter expands on this argument for the special case of subjective certainty.

36. Extension to a horizon of length T is readily accomplished. Further note that inflation and financing concerns are both irrelevant in this formulation. $\sum_{s \in S} P_1^s$, for example, is merely the market rate of exchange between current and future units of the consumption good (or cash), regardless of which state obtains. Similarly, if firm f issues both residual and interest-bearing securities, the latter may be interpreted as an obligation to pay $\hat{x}_{f1}$ in the future period, regardless of the state that obtains. The residual, $x_{f1}^s - \hat{x}_{f1}$, will go to the residual owners. Hence, the market value of the firm will be

$$x_{f0} + \sum_{s \in S} \hat{x}_{f1} P_1^s + \sum_{s \in S} (x_{f1}^s - \hat{x}_{f1}) P_1^s = x_{f0} + \sum_{s \in S} x_{f1}^s P_1^s = V(a_f).$$

only the mean and variance of their portfolios; but, in such a world, the shareholders unanimously prefer that the market price of their firm not be maximized. In fact, they provide an example where the unanimously preferred act produces a market value of zero. The conclusion is that the unanimity conditions extend beyond those that admit to unanimity with respect to market value maximization.

In either case, however, with unanimity present we may characterize the preferences of the firm's owners in terms of those of a *single* owner, and it is this formulation that we shall rely upon throughout much of the study. In particular, we will generally characterize the evaluator as a properly motivated manager (for example, one who holds shares in his firm). Hence, firm f will prefer a_f^1 over a_f^2 if and only if $E(U \mid a_f^1) > E(U \mid a_f^2)$, where the utility computation represents the preferences of the evaluator, or manager, in question. Conversely, where more insight may be gained, as in capital budgeting decisions, we will adopt a present value (or market value) maximization representation simply because this representation underlies much of the normative literature in capital theory. But this should be understood as part of a more general unanimity characterization of firm behavior.

Moreover, the reader should be mindful of the fact that beyond the confines of the assumptions that produce unanimity the theory of the firm is unsettled. We focus on an expected utility (or market value) representation because it is convenient and insightful, but how the firm should behave when unanimity does not obtain is a deep and open question. (See Radner 1974 for an excellent review of problems created by incomplete markets.)

4.0 SUMMARY

We pursue a normative approach to the question of selection among cost assessment alternatives. The basic assumptions that we rely upon are rationality on the part of the evaluator, uncertainty in the basic resource allocation problem, and costless analysis for the evaluator. These assumptions combine to provide the basic statement of the evaluator's problem in Equation [2.4].

APPENDIX 2.1
EXPECTED UTILITY AXIOMS

The purpose of this appendix is to summarize the von Neumann-Morgenstern (1947) expected utility representation.

Recall that the set of outcomes X is finite and may, therefore, be denoted $X = \{x_1, x_2, \ldots, x_N\}$. We now describe an action in terms of the *lottery* it defines over the outcomes. That is, action $a \in A$ may result in outcome x_1 with probability ϕ_{1a}, outcome x_2 with probability ϕ_{2a}, and so on. We denote this

$$L^a = (\phi_{1a}x_1, \phi_{2a}x_2, \ldots, \phi_{Na}x_N)$$

and note that the lottery outcomes are strictly independent. One, and only one, outcome will occur. Also, with $\phi(s)$ assumed known, ϕ_{ja} is merely the sum of the probabilities of all states that, in conjunction with action a, produce outcome x_j:

$$\phi_{ja} = \sum_{\substack{s \in S \\ \text{such that} \\ x_j = p(s,a)}} \phi(s).$$

We now have a situation in which each choice alternative is viewed in terms of producing a known lottery of outcomes. Thus choice among the alternatives is viewed in terms of choice among their respective lotteries; and we naturally assume that the individual regards a choice alternative and its respective lottery as perfect substitutes for each other. Hence, if he prefers one choice alternative to another, he prefers the one lottery to the other, and vice versa.

The von Neumann-Morgenstern axiomatization provides a set of conditions under which an ordering of these lotteries can be represented by the expected value of the utility of the various outcomes. Four axioms are involved. The first requires the ordering that we seek to represent, and the latter three ensure the desired representation.

First, then, we require that the lotteries and outcomes be preferentially ordered and that the ordering be transitive. A straightforward way of viewing this ordering requirement is to momentarily expand the set of available alternatives to include all possible lotteries over X. Denote this expanded set $\hat{A}$; and note in particular that it includes N pure strategies, where pure strategy j produces outcome x_j for certain. That is, denoting the pure strategy j by $\hat{a}^j$, we have $L^{\hat{a}^j} = (0x_1, \ldots, 1x_j, \ldots, 0x_N)$ and $\hat{a}^j \in \hat{A}$. Now consider any $a^1, a^2, a^3 \in \hat{A}$. The ordering component of the axiom states that either L^{a^1} is as desirable as L^{a^2} (denoted $L^{a^1} \succsim L^{a^2}$) or vice versa ($L^{a^2} \succsim L^{a^1}$).[37] Further suppose that the individual ranks a^1, a^2, and a^3 in descending order, $L^{a^1} \succsim L^{a^2} \succsim L^{a^3}$. Then the transitivity component of the axiom requires that in this situation the individual would also regard L^{a^1} as at least as good as L^{a^3}, $L^{a^1} \succsim L^{a^3}$. Further observe that $L^{\hat{a}^i} \succsim L^{\hat{a}^j}$ means that the individual regards outcome x_i as at least as desirable as x_j, which we denote $x_i \succsim x_j$. Without loss of generality, we also assume that the outcomes are indexed in terms of preference—that is, $x_1 \succsim x_2 \succsim \cdots \succsim x_N$.

Second, consider two choice alternatives that involve only the most and least desirable outcomes, x_1 and x_N. Then the individual will prefer the lottery that has the higher probability of producing the more preferred outcome, x_1.

Third, suppose one of the uncertain outcomes of a given choice is itself a set of uncertain outcomes. Then the first uncertain outcome is decomposable, through appropriate use of probability theory, into the more basic outcomes of the second. Howard (1968) refers to this as the "no fun in gambling" axiom.

Fourth, consider any possible outcome x_j and recall by our indexing conven-

---

37. $\succsim$ is a binary relation defined on $\hat{A} \times \hat{A}$. $L^{a^1} \succ L^{a^2}$ denotes strict preference for a^1 over a^2, $L^{a^1} \sim L^{a^2}$ denotes indifference, and $L^{a^1} \succsim L^{a^2}$ denotes strict preference or indifference.

tion that $x_1 \succsim x_N$. There exists a probability $\tilde{\phi}_j$ such that the individual is indifferent between receiving outcome x_j for certain or participating in a lottery where x_1 will obtain with probability $\tilde{\phi}_j$ and x_N with probability $1 - \tilde{\phi}_j$. Moreover, we regard x_j and its $(\tilde{\phi}_j x_1, (1 - \tilde{\phi}_j) x_N)$ lottery as perfect substitutes for each other. The latter may, in particular, be substituted for the former in any lottery.

We formally summarize these axioms in the following manner:

Axiom 1.

For all a^1, a^2, $a^3 \in \hat{A}$, either $L^{a^1} \succsim L^{a^2}$ or $L^{a^2} \succsim L^{a^1}$; and $L^{a^1} \succsim L^{a^2}$ and $L^{a^2} \succsim L^{a^3}$ imply $L^{a^1} \succsim L^{a^3}$.

Axiom 2.

Suppose $L^{a^1} = (\phi_1^1 x_1, (1 - \phi_1^1) x_N)$ and $L^{a^2} = (\phi_1^2 x_1, (1 - \phi_1^2) x_N)$. Then, $L^{a^1} \succsim L^{a^2}$ if and only if $\phi_1^1 \geq \phi_1^2$.

Axiom 3.

Suppose $L^k = (\phi_1^k x_1, \phi_2^k x_2, \ldots, \phi_N^k x_N)$, $k = 1, \ldots, K$. Then $(\phi^1 L^1, \ldots, \phi^k L^k, \ldots, \phi^K L^K) \sim (\phi_1 x_1, \ldots, \phi_N x_N)$ where $\phi_j = \phi^1 \phi_j^1 + \phi^2 \phi_j^2 + \cdots + \phi^K \phi_i^K$.

Axiom 4.

For $j = 1, \ldots, N$ there exists a probability $\tilde{\phi}_j$ such that $x_j \sim (\tilde{\phi}_j x_1, (1 - \tilde{\phi}_j) x_N)$; and the one is substitutable for the other in any lottery.

With this structure it can be shown that there exists a real valued function $U(L^{a^1})$, termed a utility function, such that $U(L^{a^1}) \geq U(L^{a^2})$ if and only if $L^{a^1} \succsim L^{a^2}$. Moreover, this function is defined over the outcomes, and the utility of a choice alternative (or of its equivalent lottery) is equal to the expected utility of its component outcomes. That is,

$$U(L^a) = \sum_{j=1}^{N} U(x_j) \phi_{ja} = \sum_{s \in S} U(p(s, a)) \phi(s) = E(U \mid a).$$

Hence, and this is an important point for our purposes, *the individual can be modeled as if he selected* a* $\in$ A *to maximize his expected utility.* More precisely, we have the von Neumann-Morgenstern representation theorem:

Proposition 2.3:

With X finite and $\phi(s)$ given, Axioms 1, 2, 3, and 4 ensure existence of a function U mapping X into the real line such that $E(U \mid a^1) \geq E(U \mid a^2)$ if and only if $L^{a^1} \succsim L^{a^2}$, for all $a^1, a^2 \in \hat{A}$.

Proof:

The proof is constructive in nature. Quite simply, we define $U(x_1) = 1$, $U(x_N) = 0$ and $U(x_j) = \tilde{\phi}_j$ of Axiom 4 for $1 < j < N$. This provides, for lottery L^{a^1},

$$E(U \mid a^1) = \sum_{j=1}^{N} U(x_j) \phi_j^1 = \phi_1^1 + \sum_{j=2}^{N-1} \tilde{\phi}_j \phi_j^1.$$

For the same lottery now replace each x_j by the $\tilde{\phi}_j$ of Axiom 4. Using Axiom 3 we have

$$L^{a^1} \sim \left(\left[\phi_1^1 + \sum_{j=2}^{N-1} \tilde{\phi}_j \phi_j^1 \right] x_1, \left[1 - \phi_1^1 - \sum_{j=2}^{N-1} \tilde{\phi}_j \phi_j^1 \right] x_N \right).$$

Performing the same reduction for L^{a^2} and, using Axiom 2, we then have $L^{a^1} \succsim L^{a^2}$ if and only if $\phi_1^1 + \sum_{j=2}^{N-1} \tilde{\phi}_j \phi_j^1 \geq \phi_1^2 + \sum_{j=2}^{N-1} \tilde{\phi}_j \phi_j^2$. That is, $a^1 \succsim a^2$ if and only if $E(U \mid a^1) \geq E(U \mid a^2)$.

Further discussion is available in von Neumann and Morgenstern (1947). Excellent elementary expositions are available in Kassouf (1970) and North (1968). More rigorous discussions, in turn, are available in Fishburn (1970) and Luce and Raiffa (1957). Alternative and vastly deeper axiomatizations that relax the requirement of an exogenous probability measure can be found in Savage (1954) and Krantz et al. (1971).

APPENDIX 2.2
THE VALUE OF THE FIRM UNDER CERTAINTY

The purpose of this appendix is to review the firm market value maximization argument in a world of subjective certainty and perfect markets. In such a world, recall, the outcome associated with any conceivable action is known; that is, for some $\hat{s} \in S$, $\phi(\hat{s}) = 1$ and this opinion is shared by all individuals in the society.

To develop the argument, we address the case where only two commodities exist, $x = (x_1, x_2)$, and both are traded in a perfect market. Consider an individual who presently possesses an endowment of $\bar{x}_1$ units of the first commodity and $\bar{x}_2$ units of the second. His market exchange opportunities are reflected by the straight line in Figure 2.2. And, assuming convex indifference curves,[38] his optimal combination would, as indicated, be x_{1m}^* and x_{2m}^*, located through tangency between the (exchange) opportunity curve and the highest indifference curve[39] (where we observe the individual would exchange some x_2 for x_1 to reach his most preferred attainable consumptive position).

In a similar vein, suppose our individual faces only production opportunities. Given an original endowment of $\bar{x}_1$ and $\bar{x}_2$, he can efficiently produce any combination on the concave curve shown in Figure 2.3. Once again, the most preferred position is located through tangency between the (production) opportunity curve and the highest indifference curve.

---

38. An indifference curve is merely the set of all $x \in X$ for which $U(x)$ is equal to some constant.

39. The indifference curve analysis we are expositing here is meant to be reflective of the basic argument and by no means definitive. See Debreu (1959), Hirshleifer (1970), and Intriligator (1971) for excellent discussions.

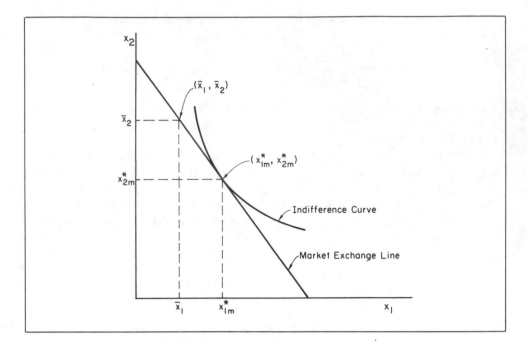

Fig. 2.2. Optimal market exchange.

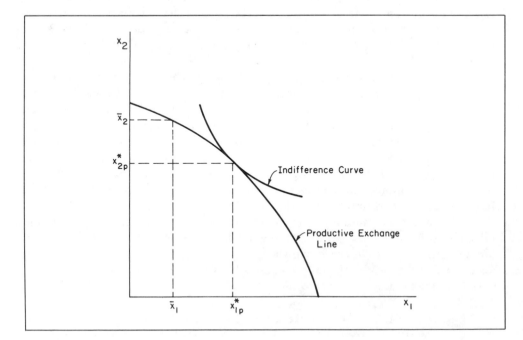

Fig. 2.3. Optimal productive exchange.

An important result is now obtained when we put the two situations together, as in Figure 2.4. The original endownment is again $\bar{x}_1$ and $\bar{x}_2$, and the optimal combination, achieved through both productive and market exchange, is x_1^* and x_2^*. And this optimal pair (x_1^*, x_2^*) can be located by first selecting the production plan with maximum market exchange value and second engaging in market exchange sufficient to obtain a tangency between the altered market exchange opportunity curve and the highest indifference curve. That is, with both production and exchange opportunities, the individual reaches his most preferred consumptive position by first moving to the point of maximum exchange value of production and then engaging in the appropriate market exchange. Moreover, comparison with Figures 2.2 and 2.3 illustrates that combining both productive and market exchange cannot result in a consumptive position less preferred to that attainable under either productive or market exchange alone. Under these circumstances, then, we see that our individual, or for that matter group of individuals, could transfer the original endowments to a productive agent who is instructed to select a production schedule with maximum market value. Subsequent redistribution of the production, coupled with appropriate market exchange transactions at the individual level, results in optimal consumption for each individual.

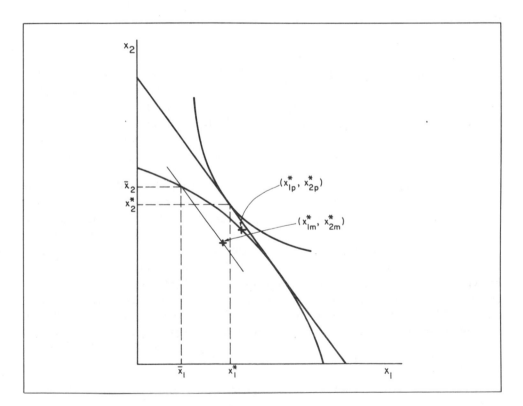

Fig. 2.4. Optimal productive and market exchange.

3

MODIFICATION AND SIMPLIFICATION OF A COMPLETE ANALYSIS

The assumptions discussed in the previous chapter imply that a decision problem is encountered when at least two alternative courses of action are available. In a primitive sense, we view each action as providing a mapping from states into outcomes, or a state-dependent array of possible outcomes. Choice among the possible actions, in turn, becomes a meaningful proposition when the decision maker's preferences are introduced; and we may even go further and, under suitable conditions, represent these preferences via the expected utility hypothesis.

This basic characterization is, in fact, sufficiently rich to offer an extensive study of cost assessment issues. Many cost assessment issues and concepts arise, however, when an analysis other than that described in the preceding chapter is employed. The reasons for departing from, or not following, the normative framework in the preceding chapter are subject to numerous interpretations. Completely specifying and performing the analysis may be simply too expensive, individuals may be incapable of the formulation and preference discriminations called for, or their choice processes may, in some fundamental sense, be incompatible with representation in this manner.[1] Whatever the reasons, we distinguish two types of departures from the complete analysis outlined in the preceding discussion.

---

1. See Demski (1972), Feltham (1972), Marschak and Radner (1972), and Simon (1972) for discussion of these departures from a complete analysis.

The first, termed *modification,* occurs when the complete analysis is altered but identification of the most preferred action is nevertheless guaranteed. The second, termed *simplification,* occurs when an alteration of the complete analysis cannot guarantee identification of the most preferred action. These two classes of alterations are explored in the two major sections of this chapter. Discussion of the cost assessment issues and concepts to which they give rise is deferred to subsequent chapters.

1.0 MODIFICATION OF A COMPLETE ANALYSIS

Modification occurs when we transform some specific choice problem $\{p, S, A, U, \phi\}$ into another choice problem $\{\hat{p}, \hat{S}, \hat{A}, \hat{U}, \hat{\phi}\}$ in a manner such that solution of the latter provides a solution to the original choice problem.[2] There are numerous types of modifications, but we will focus on those that alter the action space under consideration and those that alter the outcome and utility functions. An example of the former is the suppression of action elements of little immediate interest, such as future actions. An example of the latter is the elimination of outcome elements not affected by the action choices considered.

Our discussion of modifications serves three purposes: (i) it provides added insight into the nature of decision analysis; (ii) it provides, as we shall see, added insight into the study of simplification; and (iii) it provides a basis for discussing some cost assessment issues in subsequent chapters.

1.1 ACTION SPACE MODIFICATION

Modification of the set of available actions is a common practice. We can focus explicitly on only some of the choice elements, and implicitly control for the remaining elements. The two parameter capital asset pricing model, for example, focuses on risk and return aspects of investment and relies upon a utility function that implicitly reflects consumption desires and opportunities.[3] Alternatively, we can focus explicitly on "decision variables" rather than actions, as when we formulate a production scheduling problem in terms of the units of each product to be produced rather than the individual productive acts that will produce these units. Finally, we can focus on a single action and question whether pursuing it is "worth its opportunity cost," as in the standard textbook formulation of special order problems. These types of modifications are discussed in turn.

---

2. In an important paper Reiter (1957) discusses this concept and terms the altered or modified problem a surrogate representation of the original problem.

3. See Fama (1970), Fama and Miller (1972), and Fama and MacBeth (1974), for further discussion of the capital asset pricing model and characterization of the derived investment utility function in terms of the properties of the individual's consumption preferences.

1.1.1 SUPPRESSION OF ACTION ELEMENTS

To formulate the suppression of action elements, we partition each action into two sets of elements: $\binom{a}{\mathbf{a}}$. We term $a \in A$ a *primary action* and $\mathbf{a} \in \mathbf{A}(a)$ a *secondary action;* the set of feasible secondary actions $\mathbf{A}(a)$ is expressed as a function of the primary action in order to recognize any interdependencies between the two sets. Primary signal y and secondary signal $\mathbf{y}$ represent the signals produced by system η prior to the selection of the primary and secondary actions. The outcome function, reflecting this partition, is denoted $p\left(s, \binom{a}{\mathbf{a}}, \eta\right)$.

Our goal, now, is to reformulate the problem of selecting an optimal $\binom{a}{\mathbf{a}}$ combination into one of selecting an optimal a. We might, for example, wish to reformulate an admittedly multiperiod production scheduling problem into one of selecting an optimal current period production schedule. This requires, essentially, that we redefine the outcome function to implicitly reflect the relationship between the primary and secondary actions. For example, the outcome function used in compressing a multiperiod scheduling problem would recognize the future period effects of current schedule alternatives.

The key notion in redefining the outcome function is to implicitly recognize the secondary signals that will be received and the secondary action that will be selected upon receipt of that signal. In other words, we must express $\mathbf{y}$ and $\mathbf{a}$ as functions of s, a, y, and η. (This requires, quite naturally, that all uncertainty concerning either secondary signal occurrence or action choice be included in the state definition.)

The simplest situation involving suppression of secondary actions occurs when a single decision maker selects both the primary and secondary actions at the same time. In this case the information available for both decisions is the same (i.e., $y = \mathbf{y}$) and the optimal primary and secondary actions (given signal y from system η) are those which *simultaneously* maximize the conditional expected utility. Denoting these optimal actions $\alpha^*(y, \eta)$ and $\boldsymbol{\alpha}^*(y, \eta)$ we have

$$[3.1a] \qquad E\left(U \,\middle|\, \binom{a}{\mathbf{a}}, y, \eta\right) = \sum_{s \in S} U\left(p\left(s, \binom{a}{\mathbf{a}}, \eta\right)\right)\phi(s \mid y, \eta)$$

and

$$[3.1b] \qquad E\left(U \,\middle|\, \binom{\alpha^*(y, \eta)}{\boldsymbol{\alpha}^*(y, \eta)}, y, \eta\right) = \max_{\substack{a \in A \\ \mathbf{a} \in \mathbf{A}(a)}} E\left(U \,\middle|\, \binom{a}{\mathbf{a}}, y, \eta\right).$$

Suppression of the secondary action is accomplished in the following manner. We let $\alpha(a, y, \eta)$ denote the secondary action that will be selected if primary action a is selected and signal y is received from system η. The modified outcome function is now defined by

$$[3.2] \qquad p(s, a, \eta) = p\left(s, \binom{a}{\alpha(a, \eta(s), \eta)}, \eta\right).$$

and the modified choice problem, following receipt of signal y from system η, is defined by

[3.3a]
$$E(U \mid a, y, \eta) = \sum_{s \in S} U(p(s, a, \eta)) \phi(s \mid y, \eta)$$

and

[3.3b]
$$E(U \mid \alpha^*(y, \eta), y, \eta) = \max_{a \in A} E(U \mid a, y, \eta).$$

Use of this modified analysis will result in selection of the optimal $\binom{a}{a}$ combination, provided that the $\alpha(a, y, \eta)$ function employed in defining the new outcome function selects the optimal secondary action (given receipt of y from η and choice of primary action a). More formally, we have

Proposition 3.1:[4]

Consider the choice problem in [3.1] and let the maximum uniquely exist. Define $\alpha^*(a, y, \eta)$ by

$$E\left(U \,\middle|\, \left(\alpha^*(a, {}^a_{\!}y, \eta)\right), y, \eta\right) = \max_{\mathbf{a} \in A(a)} E\left(U \,\middle|\, \binom{a}{\mathbf{a}}, y, \eta\right) \qquad \text{for all } a \in A.$$

Then use of $\alpha^*(a, y, \eta)$ in [3.2] and optimization of the modified model in [3.3] will identify the optimal primary-secondary action combination.

In some settings the secondary action is selected by a secondary decision maker. His selection may be influenced by the primary action, but it may not be optimal from the primary decision maker's point of view. This occurs in control situations, for example, where the primary decision maker's action includes the establishment of an incentive function and a performance measure for the secondary decision maker.[5] It also occurs when the primary decision maker specifies production plans and the secondary decision maker implements them. In any event, the secondary action is readily suppressed by letting $\alpha(a, y, \eta)$ represent the *predicted* relationship between the primary and secondary actions.[6]

A final example of secondary action suppression occurs when the primary action is selected at the current time and the secondary action is a sequence of

---

4. The proof is straightforward; with the maximum defined and unique, we have

$$E(U \mid \alpha^*(y, \eta), y, \eta) = \max_{a \in A} \left[\sum_{s \in S} U(p(s, a, \eta)) \phi(s \mid y, \eta) \right]$$

$$= \max_{\substack{a \in A \\ \mathbf{a} \in A(a)}} \left[\sum_{s \in S} U\left(p\left(s, \binom{a}{\mathbf{a}}, \eta\right)\right) \phi(s \mid y, \eta) \right].$$

5. See Demski (1972b) for an analysis of a class of multiperson control problems.

6. If there is any uncertainty about this relationship, the domain of $\alpha(\cdot)$ will also include the state variable. The state is also included in the domain if the primary decision maker receives information about the secondary action prior to his decision—the primary action need not influence the secondary action selection. Of course, state dependency may be represented via the primary signal.

actions selected at subsequent times $t = 1, 2, \ldots, T$. That is, $\mathbf{a}'(\mathbf{a}_1, \ldots, \mathbf{a}_t, \ldots, \mathbf{a}_T)$ where $\mathbf{a}_t$ is the action selected at time t. Introducing similar indexing on the secondary information signal, we have $\mathbf{y} = (\mathbf{y}_1, \ldots, \mathbf{y}_t, \ldots, \mathbf{y}_T)$ where $\mathbf{y}_t$ denotes all information available to the decision maker at the time secondary action $\mathbf{a}_t$ is selected. These signals are likely to be influenced by the actions selected prior to time t; consequently, we describe the general process by $\eta_t(a, \mathbf{a}_1, \ldots, \mathbf{a}_{t-1}, s) = \mathbf{y}_t$.

Construction of the modified outcome function is now relatively straightforward. This function and the derivation of the optimal decision rules via dynamic programming are illustrated in Table 3.1 with a three-period case. Extension to other horizons is readily apparent.[7]

TABLE 3.1   MULTIPERIOD MODIFICATION

Outcome Function

$$p(s, a, \eta) = p\left(s, \begin{pmatrix} a \\ \alpha_1(\eta_1(a, s)) \\ \alpha_2(\eta_2(a, \alpha_1(\cdot), s)) \end{pmatrix}, \eta\right)$$

Determination of Optimal Decision Rules

$$E(U \mid a, y, \eta) = \sum_{s \in S} U(p(s, a, \eta)) \phi(s \mid y, \eta)$$

$$= \sum_{\mathbf{y}_1 \in \mathbf{Y}_1} f_1(a, \mathbf{y}_1, \eta) \phi(\mathbf{y}_1 \mid a, y, \eta)$$

$$f_1(a, \mathbf{y}_1, \eta) = \max_{\mathbf{a}_1 \in A_1(a)} \left[\sum_{\mathbf{y}_2 \in \mathbf{Y}_2} f_2(a, \mathbf{a}_1, \mathbf{y}_2, \eta) \phi(\mathbf{y}_2 \mid a, \mathbf{a}_1, \mathbf{y}_1, \eta) \right]$$

$$f_2(a, \mathbf{a}_1, \mathbf{y}_2, \eta) = \max_{\mathbf{a}_2 \in A_2(a, \mathbf{a}_1)} \left[\sum_{s \in S} U\left(p\left(s, \begin{pmatrix} a \\ \mathbf{a}_1 \\ \mathbf{a}_2 \end{pmatrix}, \eta\right)\right) \phi(s \mid a, \mathbf{a}_1, \mathbf{y}_2, \eta) \right]$$

This completes our discussion of secondary action suppression. In subsequent discussions we shall treat our basic notation $\{p, S, A, U, \phi\}$ as reflecting the choice problem at hand, appropriately modified to emphasize the primary problem of interest. In our exploration of cost assessment problems we shall, that is, treat secondary actions as suppressed variables in an appropriately modified statement of the choice problem.

---

7. See Nemhauser (1966) for an extensive treatment of dynamic programming and regularity conditions that are sufficient for this type of decomposition. Also see Feltham (1972) and Long (1972) for extensive treatment of multiperiod models and Porteus (1975) for discussion of the optimality principle.

1.1.2 TRANSFORMATION TO DECISION VARIABLES

A second form of action space modification occurs when we structure the analysis of a choice problem in terms of choice variables other than the actions themselves. An inventory problem, for example, is likely to be structured in terms of the amount to order rather than the detailed order acts (such as requisition verification, payment processing, and source choice) that must be carried out. The key notion in introducing this type of modification is the relationship between these decision variables and the action choices they will induce.

To formulate this modification, we let d denote the decision variable (possibly a vector) and D the set of admissible decision variables. The modified outcome function, now defined over the decision variable representation, is denoted $p(s, d, \eta)$ and the modification of the basic decision problem in [3.3] is stated as

[3.4a] $$E(U \mid d, y, \eta) = \sum_{s \in S} U(p(s, d, \eta)) \phi(s \mid y, \eta)$$

and

[3.4b] $$E(U \mid \alpha_d^*(y, \eta), y, \eta) = \max_{d \in D} E(U \mid d, y, \eta)$$

where $\alpha_d^*(y, \eta)$ denotes the optimal decision, given receipt of y from η.

Although this type of transformation is always available (in the trivial sense of defining $d = a$ and $D = A$), transformation to a decision variable representation cannot necessarily be guaranteed to locate the optimal action. The following conditions are, however, sufficient in this regard:

(i) $A(d)$ defines a nonempty set of feasible actions that are associated with decision variable $d \in D$:

$$A(d) \neq \phi$$

$$\text{all } d \in D$$

$$A(d) \subset A.$$

(ii) The optimal action $\alpha^*(y, \eta)$ is associated with at least one of the decision variables:

$$\alpha^*(y, \eta) \in \bigcup_{d \in D} A(d).$$

(iii) The action induced by decision variable d is the conditionally optimal action associated with d. That is, denoting the action that will be taken, if signal y is received from system η and decision variable d is chosen, by $\alpha(d, y, \eta)$, we require that[8]

$$E(U \mid \alpha(d, y, \eta), y, \eta) = \max_{a \in A(d)} E(U \mid a, y, \eta).$$

---

8. We assume existence of these conditionally optimal choices.

(iv)   The outcome function is modified in a manner consistent with requirement (iii):

$$p(s, d, \eta) = p(s, \alpha(d, \eta(s), \eta), \eta).$$

We now have

Proposition 3.2:[9]
Consider the choice problem in [3.3] and let the maximum exist. Conditions
(i) through (iv) above are sufficient to guarantee that optimization of the modified
model in [3.4] will identify an optimal action in [3.3].

The above are merely illustrative of conditions that ensure that the use of
decision variables results in optimal actions.   Other conditions are, no doubt,
available.[10] However, in many situations the use of decision variables represents
simplifications instead of modifications. Simplifications are discussed later in the
chapter.

1.1.3   DELETION OF ACTION ALTERNATIVES

A third form of action space modification occurs when we delete a number
of feasible alternatives from explicit consideration in the analysis. If we know,
for example, that several feasible alternatives are "dominated" by another, there
is no reason to include the former in our analysis.

To formulate this type of modification we again begin with the basic statement [3.3]. Next, we partition A into those alternatives that will be considered
in the analysis, A_1, and those that will not, A_2.[11] Now let $\alpha_1^*(y, \eta)$ denote the
optimal action in the reduced set A_1 and $\alpha_2^*(y, \eta)$ the optimal action in the
eliminated set A_2. That is,[12]

$$E(U \mid \alpha_1^*(y, \eta), y, \eta) = \max_{a \in A_1} E(U \mid a, y, \eta)$$

and

---

9. *Proof:*
(i), (iii), and (iv) guarantee, with existence assured, that

$$E(U \mid \alpha_d^*(y, \eta), y, \eta) = \max_{d \in D} \left\{ \max_{a \in A(d)} E(U \mid a, y, \eta) \right\}.$$

(ii) guarantees that $\alpha^*(y, \eta) \in A(d)$ for some $d \in D$. Hence [3.3] and [3.4] have the same optimal
values, and $\alpha(\alpha_d^*(y, \eta), y, \eta) = \alpha^*(y, \eta)$. (Note that the economic theory of the firm implicitly assumes that conditions such as (i) through (iv) are satisfied when it uses inputs and outputs as decision variables. See Appendix 5.2 for a brief exploration of the relationship of this theory to our
analysis.)

10. Moreover, this type of transformation can be regarded as a form of action element suppression.

11. That is, $A = A_1 \cup A_2$ and $A_1 \cap A_2 = \phi$.

12. We again assume existence of the indicated maxima.

$$E(U \mid \alpha_2^*(y, \eta), y, \eta) = \max_{a \in A_2} E(U \mid a, y, \eta).$$

We now have

Proposition 3.3:[13]

Consider the choice problem in [3.3] and let the maximum exist. $\alpha_1^*(y, \eta)$ is an optimal choice if, and only if,

$$E(U \mid \alpha_1^*(y, \eta), y, \eta) \geq E(U \mid \alpha_2^*(y, \eta), y, \eta).$$

Corollary:[14]

$\alpha_2^*(y, \eta)$ is an optimal choice if $\alpha_1^*(y, \eta)$ is not an optimal choice.

This form of modification gives rise to the economist's concept of opportunity cost. To illustrate, consider $a \in A$ and let A_1 consist of the single action a. $E(U \mid \alpha_2^*(y, \eta), y, \eta)$ is now the opportunity cost of a, the expected utility from the best alternative use of the available resources. Obviously, a is an optimal choice if it is at least as good as the next best alternative—if its expected utility is not less than its opportunity cost. Quite naturally, opportunity cost is expressed in utility terms that reflect the decision maker's personal beliefs and preferences, a fundamental point eloquently discussed by Buchanan (1969).[15,16]

Illustrations of these various types of action space modifications are contained in succeeding chapters. We now consider modifications that alter the outcome and utility functions.

1.2 OUTCOME AND UTILITY FUNCTION MODIFICATION

Modifications of the outcome and utility functions are also possible. We may, for example, be able to transform the outcome description, as when we eliminate various "irrelevant" outcome elements from the analysis. Alternatively, we may transform the outcome function domain, as when we express the outcome as

---

13. *Proof:*

$$E(U \mid \alpha_1^*(y, \eta), y, \eta) \geq E(U \mid \alpha_2^*(y, \eta), y, \eta)$$

implies

$$E(U \mid \alpha_1^*(y, \eta), y, \eta) = \max \left\{ \max_{a \in A_1} E(U \mid a, y, \eta), \max_{a \in A_2} E(U \mid a, y, \eta) \right\}$$

$$= \max_{a \in A} E(U \mid a, y, \eta).$$

Conversely, $\alpha_1^*(y, \eta) = \alpha^*(y, \eta)$ implies

$$E(U \mid \alpha_1^*(y, \eta), y, \eta) = \max_{a \in A} E(U \mid a, y, \eta) \geq E(U \mid \alpha_2^*(y, \eta), y, \eta).$$

14. *Proof:*
The proof follows immediately from a reversal of A_1 and A_2 in Proposition 3.3.
15. Also see Amey (1968).
16. In a classical production setting in which market value maximization is an acceptable modification of the productive choice problem, the opportunity cost could be stated in market value terms.

a function of the outputs produced and inputs used. Combined transformations of the outcome description and outcome function domain may be employed, but for expositional convenience we discuss them separately.

1.2.1 TRANSFORMATION OF THE OUTCOME DESCRIPTION

Ability to transform the outcome description is related to the fact that the solution to an optimization problem is invariant to strictly increasing transformations of the objective function. For example, maximization of $10z - z^2$ and $(10z - z^2)^3$, $1 \leq z \leq 10$, both occur at $z^* = 5$. More formally,

Definition:
   Let T be a real valued function defined on a subset H of the real line. If for every pair of points h^1 and h^2 in H, $h^1 > h^2$ implies $T(h^1) > T(h^2)$, T is termed a *strictly increasing transformation.*

Proposition 3.4:[17]
   Consider the maximization of some real valued function $Q(z)$ over domain Z. Let the maximum exist and occur at $z^* \in Z$. Then, for any strictly increasing transformation T, the maximum of $T(Q(z))$ exists and occurs at $z^* \in Z$.

Two applicable corollaries are immediately apparent. First, the solution of the general choice problem in [3.3] is invariant to positive linear transformation of the utility function. That is, an arbitrary constant can be added to (or subtracted from) $U(\cdot)$, and $U(\cdot)$ can be multiplied by any positive constant. Second, under subjective certainty, the basic choice problem is invariant to any strictly increasing transformation of the utility function. More formally,

Corollary:[18]
   Consider the choice problem in [3.3] and let $\alpha^*(y, \eta)$ be an optimal choice. $\alpha^*(y, \eta)$ remains an optimal choice for any positive linear transformation of the utility function.

Corollary:[19]
   Consider the choice problem in [3.3] and let $\alpha^*(y, \eta)$ be an optimal choice. Under subjective certainty, $\alpha^*(y, \eta)$ remains an optimal choice for any strictly increasing transformation of the utility function.

---

17. *Proof:*
   Suppose the maximum of $T(Q(z))$ does not occur at z^*. This implies $Q(z) > Q(z^*)$ for some $z \in Z$, which cannot occur. Hence, if the maximum of $T(Q(z))$ exists, it occurs at z^*. Existence, however, is insured by existence of z^*.

18. *Proof:*
   With real $\beta > 0$ and α, $\sum_{s \in S}[\alpha + \beta U(\cdot)]\phi(s \mid y, \eta) = \alpha + \beta E(U \mid a, y, \eta)$ provides a strictly increasing transformation of $E(U \mid a, y, \eta)$; and Proposition 3.4 therefore applies.

19. *Proof:*
   Under subjective certainty, $E(U \mid a, y, \eta) = U(p(\hat{s}, a, \eta))$ for some $\hat{s} \in S$; and Proposition 3.4 readily applies.

Successful transformation of the outcome description is tied to these two corollaries.

In a complete decision analysis, the outcome description must reflect all aspects of the possible action consequences that influence the decision maker's preferences with respect to his alternative choices. In any given decision situation there are alternative consequence descriptions that could be used. The decision maker selects his description when he specifies the outcome function $p(s, a, \eta) = x$ and this selection obviously affects the utility function $U(x)$ that is employed. We will refer to an outcome function $\hat{p}(s, a, \eta) = \hat{x}$ as *payoff adequate* if there exists a utility function $\hat{U}(\hat{x})$ such that $\{\hat{p}, S, A, \hat{U}, \phi\}$ is a modification of $\{p, S, A, U, \phi\}$. More formally,

Definition:

$\hat{p}(s, a, \eta) = \hat{x}$ is a *payoff adequate outcome function* with respect to choice problem $\{p, S, A, U, \phi\}$ if there exists a utility function $\hat{U}(\hat{x})$ and a strictly increasing transformation T such that

$$E(\hat{U} \mid a, y, \eta) = T(E(U \mid a, y, \eta))$$

where

$$E(\hat{U} \mid a, y, \eta) = \sum_{s \in S} \hat{U}(\hat{p}(s, a, \eta)) \phi(s \mid y, \eta).$$

From Proposition 3.4 it is obvious that if $\hat{p}(\cdot)$ is payoff adequate and $\hat{U}(\cdot)$ is appropriately specified, then $\alpha^*(y, \eta)$ remains an optimal choice for $E(\hat{U} \mid a, y, \eta)$.

The decision maker must carefully select his outcome description if it is to be payoff adequate. He can always incorporate more detail than is necessary. For example, he may list the sources and uses of the cash flow at each point in time even though his preferences are only influenced by the net cash flow at each point in time. However, if he aggregates or eliminates outcome components he may be simplifying his decision analysis instead of merely modifying it. The nature of the utility function that reflects his preferences is an important determinant of how he may aggregate and what he may eliminate.

Basically, a decision maker may employ an aggregate description of the components of outcome x provided the aggregation is consistent with the utility function $U(x)$. An obvious extreme example is to let $\hat{p}(s, a, \eta) = U(p(s, a, \eta))$; that is, $\hat{x}$ is the utility measure of the outcome.[20] The acceptability of other aggregations will depend on the specifics of the decision situation. For example, in many decision analyses it is assumed that a sequence of dated cash flows can be aggregated by computing their net present value using an appropriate discount factor. This may be a modification in a world of subjective certainty with perfect markets, but it is likely to be a simplification in a world of uncertainty and incomplete markets.

Elimination of outcome components is a common outcome function transformation. It takes two major forms: the elimination of components that are not influenced by the action choice and the use of incremental analysis.

---

20. $\hat{U}(\hat{x}) = \hat{x}$ is obviously an appropriate utility function for this outcome description.

The first form is illustrated by so-called short-run decisions that consider only current cash flows because future cash flows are the same for all choice alternatives. It is also illustrated by production method decisions that ignore revenues because they are concerned only with how best to produce a specified level of output. These analyses divide the outcome components into two subsets, $x = (\hat{x}, x^0)$, where $\hat{x} = \hat{p}(s, a, \eta)$ and $x^0 = p(s, \eta)$,[21] and only consider $\hat{x}$, the subset affected by the choice alternatives. If such an analysis is to be a modification, and not a simplification, $\hat{p}(s, a, \eta)$ must be payoff adequate. In general, it is *not* payoff adequate, but it may be in some situations.

Incremental analysis is very similar. In that case the decision maker considers only the differences between the outcome for each action choice and the outcome that will result from some base action, $\hat{x} = \hat{p}(s, a, \eta) = p(s, a, \eta) - p(s, a^0, \eta)$, where $a^0 \in A$ is the base action. Observe that the outcome has, in effect, been divided into two components, $x = \hat{x} + x^0$, where $x^0 = p(s, a^0, \eta)$ and $\hat{p}(s, a, \eta)$ must be payoff adequate if the exclusion of x^0 is to be a modification and not a simplification. Again, in general, it is *not* payoff adequate, but it may be in some situations.

A condition sufficient for $\hat{p}(s, a, \eta)$ to be payoff adequate is that the utility function be separable with respect to the two outcome components; that is, $U(x) = \hat{U}(\hat{x}) + U^0(x^0)$.[22] $U(x)$ is separable if it is a linear function of the elements of the vector x, but often is nonseparable if it is a nonlinear function of these elements. The nonlinear, nonseparable case appears to be the commonest. For example, if x is a vector of dated cash flows and $U(x)$ is the present value of those cash flows, $U(x)$ is separable. However, such a utility function probably applies only in a world with complete and perfect markets. In our uncertain, imperfect market world, decision makers are typically risk averse and their preferences must be expressed as nonlinear functions of the cash flows.[23]

In summary, the elimination of outcome elements is a modification if the ele-

---

21. If appropriate changes are made in the definitions of the three vectors, this relationship may be expressed as $x = \hat{x} + x^0$.

22. The sufficiency of the separability condition follows from the first corollary to Proposition 3.4:

$$E(U \mid a, y, \eta) = E(\hat{U} \mid a, y, \eta) + E(U^0 \mid y, \eta)$$

and

$$E(U^0 \mid y, \eta) = \sum_{s \in S} U(p(s, a^0, \eta)) \phi(s \mid y, \eta)$$

is a constant in the incremental analysis case.

23. In a world of subjective certainty $\hat{p}(s, a, \eta)$ will be payoff adequate if $U(x)$ can be expressed as a function of a function, $U(x) = G(g(x))$, such that $g(x) = z$ is a separable function with respect to $\hat{x}$ and x^0, z is a scalar, and $G(z)$ is a strictly increasing function. This follows from the second corollary to Proposition 3.4. This condition is satisfied, for example, if x is a scalar representing the current net cash flow and $U(x)$ is a concave utility function—then $g(x) = x$ and $G(z) = U(z)$. If x is a vector of dated cash flows, the condition is satisfied if $U(x)$ is such that it can be expressed as a strictly increasing function of the present value of those cash flows ($g(x)$ is the present value). There is no reason why this condition will be satisfied in any given situation.

ments not eliminated provide a payoff adequate description of the outcome. In general they are not payoff adequate because of nonlinearities in the utility function. This implies that the elimination of outcome elements is usually a simplification. However, it is more likely to be a modification of a simplified analysis. In particular, it is common to make the simplifying assumption that the utility function is linear with respect to the outcome elements, and then the elimination of invariant outcome elements and the use of incremental analysis just naturally follow.

1.2.2 TRANSFORMATION OF THE OUTCOME FUNCTION DOMAIN

Some outcome function modifications are based on transformations of their domain. In the complete analysis stated in [3.3] the outcome is directly expressed as a function of the action choice (as well as s and η), but in many analyses the action/outcome relationship is indirect. For example, in the theory of the firm an action is typically described in terms of the outputs it produces and the inputs it uses, and the revenues and costs (the outcome) are expressed as functions of these outputs and inputs.

This type of modification may be interpreted as a two-stage procedure for defining the outcome function. In the first stage we identify a set of "factors" that will result from various state-action combinations and that, in turn, can be used to determine the ultimate outcomes these state-action combinations may produce. We refer to this set of factors as a *payoff statistic,* denoted δ. In the second stage, we identify the outcome that will result from each payoff statistic.

We formalize this procedure by expressing the state as consisting of two types of elements and the outcome function as the composite of two functions:

$s = (s_\delta, s_p)$ where $s_\delta \in S_\delta$ denotes those state elements affecting the payoff statistic resulting from an action and $s_p \in S_p$ denotes those state elements affecting the outcome associated with the payoff statistic, $S = S_\delta \times S_p$.

$\delta(s_\delta, a, \eta) = \delta$ the payoff statistic function.

$p_\delta(s_p, \delta, \eta) = x$ the outcome function defined in terms of the payoff statistic.

Quite clearly, then, we have[24]

[3.5] $$p(s, a, \eta) = p_\delta(s_p, \delta(s_\delta, a, \eta), \eta).$$

Two points are readily apparent. First, such a transformation always exists, in the sense of $\delta(s_\delta, a, \eta) = (s, a, \eta)$. Second, use of a payoff statistic requires that the statistic reflect (or represent) the entire influence of the action. That is, if two actions produce the same payoff statistic, they must result in identical outcome lotteries. In this sense the payoff statistic is similar to a sufficient statistic

---

24. We could also define the payoff statistic such that it captures the entire information effect: $p(s, a, \eta) = p_\delta(s_p, \delta)$.

in distribution theory—where the posterior distribution is identical for any pair of outcomes that are described by the same statistic.[25]

We term a payoff statistic that satisfies this essential representation property as *payoff adequate:*[26]

Definition:

A payoff statistic function $\delta(\cdot)$ defines a *payoff adequate statistic* if for any s_δ^1, $s_\delta^2 \in S_\delta, a^1, a^2 \in A, \eta^1, \eta^2 \in H$

$$\delta(s_\delta^1, a^1, \eta^1) = \delta(s_\delta^2, a^2, \eta^2)$$

implies that

$$p((s_\delta^1, s_p), a^1, \eta^1) = p((s_\delta^2, s_p), a^2, \eta^2) \qquad \text{for all } s_p \in S_p.$$

Further note that if this procedure is to provide a nontrivial modification of the outcome function, the payoff statistic will have to incorporate all aspects of the state element s_δ that are useful in predicting which elements of S_p will obtain. Such a payoff statistic is termed *forecast adequate:*

Definition:[27]

A payoff statistic function $\delta(\cdot)$ defines a *forecast adequate statistic* if

$$\phi(s_p \mid s_\delta, y, \eta) = \phi(s_p \mid \delta(s_\delta, a, \eta), y, \eta) \qquad \text{for all } s \in S, a \in A$$
$$y \in Y, \eta \in H.$$

If a payoff statistic is both payoff and forecast adequate, the expected utility for each action may be computed using the expected utility for the statistics that may be generated, denoted $E(U \mid \delta, y, \eta)$. That is,

[3.6a] $$E(U \mid a, y, \eta) = \sum_{s_\delta \in S_\delta} E(U \mid \delta(s_\delta, a, \eta), y, \eta) \phi(s_\delta \mid y, \eta)$$

where

[3.6b] $$E(U \mid \delta, y, \eta) = \sum_{s_p \in S_p} U(p_\delta(s_p, \delta, \eta)) \phi(s_p \mid \delta, y, \eta).$$

More precisely, we have

25. For example, see DeGroot (1970), pp. 155–59.

26. Observe that, in general, a unique payoff adequate partition does not exist. However, the coarsest payoff adequate partition is unique—although the symbols used to denote it are not (Marschak 1963). This latter partition is termed *payoff relevant.*

27. Quite clearly, strict independence between s_p and s_δ ensures a forecast adequate statistic (with independence $\phi(s_p \mid s_\delta, y, \eta) = \phi(s_p \mid y, \eta)$).

Proposition 3.5:[28]

Consider the choice problem in [3.3] and let the maximum exist. If $\delta(s_\delta, a, \eta)$ defines a payoff and forecast adequate statistic, optimization of the modified model in [3.6] will identify an optimal action in [3.3].

This concludes our exploration of modifications of the basic choice problem introduced in the prior chapter. Cost assessment considerations to which these modifications give rise are explored in subsequent chapters. We conclude the present chapter with a discussion of simplification of the basic choice problem.

2.0 SIMPLIFICATION

Simplification occurs, recall, when the basic choice problem is transformed in a manner that cannot be guaranteed to identify the most preferred action. Recognition of analysis cost per se may induce simplification; alternatively, an individual's choice process—even in a costless setting—may only be approximated by the tenets of rationality. Either way, we admit to decision analysis that cannot be guaranteed to identify the action that would be identified by a complete analysis (or its modification).

Two issues emerge. The first concerns the nature of these simplifications and what their presence implies for the interpretation of the decision analysis they are designed to support. The second concerns choice among alternative simplifications, or design of a "good" decision model. These two issues are discussed in turn.

2.1 NATURE AND IMPLICATIONS OF SIMPLIFICATION

Any aspect of the basic choice problem may be simplified: the action or state specifications, as well as the outcome, utility, or probability functions. Our immediate concern is an exploration of the conceptual nature of simplification.[29] Initially we focus on the case where the decision maker selects an action without additional information. The impact of information in a simplified decision analysis is considered later in the section.

---

28. *Proof:*

Since $\delta(\cdot)$ is payoff and forecast adequate we have

$$E(U \mid a, y, \eta) = \sum_{s \in S} U(p(s, a, \eta)) \phi(s \mid y, \eta)$$

$$= \sum_{s_\delta \in S_\delta} \left[\sum_{s_p \in S_p} U(p_\delta(s_p, \delta(s_\delta, a, \eta), \eta)) \phi(s_p \mid \delta(s_\delta, a, \eta), y, \eta) \right] \phi(s_\delta \mid y, \eta)$$

$$= \sum_{s_\delta \in S_\delta} E(U \mid \delta(s_\delta, a, \eta), y, \eta) \phi(s_\delta \mid y, \eta).$$

29. Subsequent chapters contain numerous examples of simplification and alternative discussions are available in Schlaifer (1969), Demski (1972), and Feltham (1972).

Decision makers frequently avoid detailed state and action representations and their associated outcome and utility functions. Instead, a simplified preference function, termed an *objective function,* is defined over alternative sets of *decision variables* and *parameters.* We again denote the decision variables as d, the parameters are denoted θ, and the objective function is $R(\theta, d)$. The parameters may be regarded as uncertain, and we therefore let $\phi(\theta)$ denote the specified probability function over the set of possible parameter values, denoted Θ.

The decision variables are simplified action descriptions, often omitting some action elements altogether and at best implicitly representing many others. No attempt is made to identify the optimal action and utility associated with each decision variable (see section 1.1.2 above). For example, raw material inventory purchases are not explicitly included in the typical product mix model; rather, they are subsequently determined from the activity schedules specified by that model. Other related actions may be selected in a different model by a different decision maker.

In addition, the decision variables are often constrained. One purpose of these constraints is to avoid the cost of evaluating actions that are expected to be undesirable. Another purpose is to facilitate other simplifications. For example, risk considerations may be excluded from the objective function but included in the model by restricting the action set to those maintaining some minimum cash balance. These constraints define the set of "feasible" decision variables, denoted $D(\theta, \phi)$, and are a function of some of the parameters and their predicted values.

The objective function and its parameters typically encompass a multitude of simplifications. The outcome function implicit in the objective function is simplified both by simplifying the outcome description and by simplifying the predicted relationship between the decision variables and the outcome description used. For example, outcome descriptions are often simplified by focusing on the immediate cash flows, ignoring both future cash flows and noncash elements of the outcome. The predicted relationship between the decision variables and the outcome is simplified by using simple functional forms. The frequent use of linear cost functions is an obvious example.

Recognition of all uncontrollable factors influencing the outcome would require a complex outcome function, specification of a large set of possible states, and a complex state probability function. The use of a relatively few parameters simplifies all three. The probability function is further simplified by assuming some parameters are known with certainty, by assuming parameters are independent, and by using standard probability functions, such as the normal, to represent the decision maker's beliefs about those parameters that are treated as uncertain. Moreover, subsequent information processing may be simplified and not done in a Bayesian fashion. It is, for example, difficult to work with standard probability functions and engage in Bayesian revision.

Some parameters may be introduced into the model to facilitate other simplifications. For example, the effect on future period demands of current period inventory stockouts is generally subsumed by specifying a cost function, with appropriate parameters, defined over the stockout possibilities. Similarly, interrelated decisions, such as those requiring the simultaneous use of scarce resources, are often modeled independently by using opportunity cost parameters to reflect the interrelationships.

Another area of simplification is the utility function implicit in the objective function. In particular, most objective functions either ignore the decision maker's attitude toward risk or represent it in a rather simple manner. Risk is ignored, for example, when the objective function is expressed in terms of the expected value of the current profit or discounted cash flow. An example of a simple recognition of risk is provided by those models in the finance literature that focus on the mean and standard deviation of the cash flow distribution.

In sum, simplification of the basic choice problem may result in alteration of the action configurations and possibilities considered in the model, alteration of the state configurations and their probabilities, and approximation of the outcome and utility functions. Collecting the various simplified elements, we obtain the following decision model:

[3.7]
$$E(R \mid d^*) = \max_{d \in D(\theta, \phi)} \left[\sum_{\theta \in \Theta} R(\theta, d) \, \phi(\theta) \right]$$

where $E(R \mid d)$ denotes the expected value of the objective function associated with selecting feasible decision variable d.

To dramatize the conceptual difference between the complete and simplified analysis, we describe the former in terms of actions, states, and outcome and utility functions, and the latter in terms of decision variables, constraints, parameters, and an objective function. Table 3.2 details the various counterparts in this terminology scheme.

TABLE 3.2 COMPLETE AND SIMPLIFIED MODEL REPRESENTATIONS
FOR DECISION MAKER BEFORE INFORMATION RECEIPT

Model Element	Complete Representation	Simplified Representation
Objects of Choice	action: $a' = (a_1, \ldots, a_m)$	decision variable: $d' = (d_1, \ldots, d_n)$
Uncontrollable Phenomena That May Occur	state: $s \in S$	parameter: $\theta \in \Theta$
Probabilities	$\phi(s)$	$\phi(\theta)$
Choice Possibilities	A	$D(\theta, \phi)$
Consequence	$x = p(s, a)$	$R(\theta, d)$
Preference	$U(x)$	(objective function)

Two important points emerge. First, since the choice problem $\{R, \Theta, D, \phi\}$ is a simplification (and not a modification) of the complete analysis choice problem $\{p, S, A, U, \phi\}$, d^* cannot be regarded as reflecting the optimal choice. Consequently, we cannot, strictly speaking, delegate action choice to the arithmetization implied by the simplified model. Decision variable d^* is thus interpreted as information supplied to the decision maker and, as discussed below, evaluation of alternative simplified models is conceptually identical to evaluation of alternative information systems.

Second, since the simplified model does not completely reflect the decision maker's perceptions, it is conceivable that receipt of additional information may alter more than the formal parameter probability assessments. Put another way, with less than complete representation of the basic choice problem, it is *a priori* conceivable that the specification itself may be revised upon receipt of additional information. Indeed, additional information may induce a revision of the objective function or constraint specification—simply because we admit that these representations are simplified. As a result, the simplified counterpart of [3.3] must reflect a general dependency of the simplifications actually employed on the information available. We denote the model elements as[30]

$$M(y, \eta) = \{R(\theta, d \mid y, \eta), \Theta, D(\theta, \phi \mid y, \eta), \phi(\theta \mid y, \eta)\}$$

and let $d(M(y, \eta))$ represent the decision variable selected by that model. That is,

[3.8a]
$$E(R \mid d, y, \eta) = \sum_{\theta \in \Theta} R(\theta, d \mid y, \eta) \phi(\theta \mid y, \eta)$$

and

[3.8b]
$$E(R \mid d(M(y, \eta)), y, \eta) = \max_{d \in D(\theta, \phi \mid y, \eta)} E(R \mid d, y, \eta).$$

We now consider the evaluation of alternative simplifications.

2.2   Evaluation of Alternative Simplifications

In a fundamental sense, the simplified representation may be interpreted as an attempt to analyze the basic choice problem in an economic manner: balancing analysis cost against the possibility of inferior analysis and choice. Numerous simplifications are likely to be available in any particular setting, and the question of which to select therefore arises. Indeed, many cost assessment issues are precisely of this nature.

The key to evaluating alternative simplifications lies in the consequences to which they will give rise. In short, the basic ingredients are the choices that will be induced and the analysis costs that will be incurred. The action choice pri-

---

30. The information may also induce alteration of d or θ but it is notationally convenient to subsume these under R, D, and ϕ alterations. We again note that $\phi(\theta \mid y, \eta)$ is not necessarily processed from prior beliefs in a Bayesian manner.

marily depends on the decision variable selected by the simplified analysis, but it may also be influenced by the method of analysis and the signal received. Consequently, we express the action choice as a function of the decision variable selected, the model used, the signal received, and the system used: $a = \alpha(d(\cdot), M(\cdot), y, \eta)$. We also expand the domain of the outcome function to recognize the cost of analysis: $x = p(s, a, \eta, M(\cdot))$. The expected utility of using model $M(\cdot)$, given receipt of signal y from system η, then becomes

$$[3.9a] \qquad E(U \mid M(y, \eta), y, \eta) = \sum_{s \in S} U(p(s, \alpha(\cdot), \eta, M(\cdot))) \, \phi(s \mid y, \eta).$$

Clearly, given prior receipt of signal y from system η, simplified analysis $M^1(\cdot)$ is as good as $M^2(\cdot)$ if and only if $E(U \mid M^1(\cdot), y, \eta) \geq E(U \mid M^2(\cdot), y, \eta)$. Similarly the expected utility of using model $M(\cdot)$ and system η is

$$[3.9b] \qquad E(U \mid M, \eta) = \sum_{y \in Y} E(U \mid M(y, \eta), y, \eta) \phi(y \mid \eta).$$

In subsequent chapters our examination of the impact of cost assessment alternatives focuses on the action choices induced by those alternatives. Consequently, we often assume, for expositional reasons, that the utility of the action choice consequences can be separated from the "costs" of the information system and the decision analysis. This separability follows naturally, say, in those cases where market value maximization is the criterion. Moreover, in those cases it is often instructive to compute the loss in market value resulting from the use of a simplified analysis instead of a complete analysis. The loss is denoted:

$$[3.10a] \quad L(M(y, \eta), y, \eta) = E(U \mid \alpha^*(y, \eta), y, \eta) - E(U \mid M(y, \eta), y, \eta)$$

and

$$[3.10b] \qquad L(M, \eta) = \sum_{y \in Y} L(M(y, \eta), y, \eta) \phi(y \mid \eta)$$

where $E(U \mid \cdot)$ denotes the market value exclusive of analysis and system costs.

Two related observations conclude our discussion. First, collapsing the M and η notation together reduces [3.9a] to [2.4a]; therefore, the more general question of simplified model design is identical to that of information system design, as depicted in Equation [2.4]. It is in this sense, then, that evaluation of alternative simplifications is equivalent to evaluation of alternative information systems. The two are, in fact, conceptually identical.

Second, the evaluation in [3.9], though developed from a single decision maker's point of view, readily extends to the case of a separate evaluator. In that case, $\alpha(\cdot)$ denotes the evaluator's perception of what the decision maker will do, upon receipt of signal y from system η and use of simplified model $M(\cdot)$. Clearly, the simplification employed by the decision maker will influence the evaluator's choice of information system, and the evaluator's choice will influence the simplification employed. This reciprocal relationship is taken into consideration in the evaluation model described above.

3.0 SUMMARY

The basic choice problem formulated in Chapter 2 provides the necessary framework for identifying and resolving various cost assessment issues. Many of these issues arise, however, when we modify or simplify the basic choice problem. Indeed, design of "cost-effective" or "desirable" simplified cost assessment procedures is a fundamental question in the theory of cost assessment.

If we retain a complete analysis for the accountant or evaluator, a precise meaning can be ascribed to what a "cost-effective" or "desirable" assessment procedure is (Equation [3.9]). If the evaluator operates in the simplified domain, however, we lose the ability to identify a most preferred assessment procedure.

4

COST ASSESSMENT FOR
DECISION MAKING

This chapter explores the general nature of cost assessment for decision making. The first section examines the terms "cost" and "cost assessment." This is followed by a study of the role of cost assessment in facilitating decisions, first under the assumption of complete analysis and then in the context of simplified analysis. The fourth section examines the role of cost assessment in influencing the decisions of subordinates. Each section discusses the nature of cost assessment alternatives within the context being discussed, and the general form of these alternatives is highlighted in the summary at the end of the chapter.

Two central points are maintained throughout the discussion. First, the aspects of a choice problem that we elect to term costs are *conceptually* arbitrary. Second, regardless of the aspects that are termed costs, there are often a number of alternative assessments of those costs. And in these cases the problem of choice among the alternatives is conceptually identical to the question of optimal selection of an information system, as discussed in Chapter 2.

1.0 THE NATURE OF COST ASSESSMENT

"Cost" is a ubiquitous term. We are all familiar with, say, relevant, controllable, fixed, incremental, opportunity, historical, replacement, and standard costs. These and other familiar uses of the term appear to have a common thread: the term cost appears to be reserved for a description of the *sacrifice* associated with some abstract *object*.

This central theme of sacrifice is present in the definitions of cost that have been advanced in the literature. For example, Stigler states:

> ... the cost of any productive service to use A is the maximum amount it would produce elsewhere. [Stigler 1966, p. 105]

And the Committee on Cost Concepts and Standards of the American Accounting Association states:

> For business purposes, cost is a general term for a measured amount of value purposefully released or to be released in the acquisition or creation of economic resources, either tangible or intangible. [*Accounting Review,* April 1956, p. 183]

Chambers, in his discussion of the ends and means of economic activity, suggests:

> Sacrifices for the purpose of production are sacrifices of things valued; they may be described as costs; their object is the production of things more highly valued, not simply other or more things. [Chambers 1966, p. 53]

And Kohler, in his *Dictionary for Accountants,* states that cost is an

> *Expenditure* or outlay of cost, other property, capital stock, or services, or the incurring of a liability therefore, identified with goods or services purchased or with any loss incurred, and measured by the amount of cash paid or payable or the market value of other property, capital stock, or services given in exchange. [Kohler 1970, p. 126]

We use the term *cost assessment* to refer to *both the process* of providing a description of the sacrifice associated with some object *and the description* itself. If, for example, we elect to provide a decision maker with historical cost information, the information system is a form of cost assessment and the resultant description is an assessment of the historical cost. Similarly, the method of predicting total production cost for a product mix decision is a form of cost assessment and the ultimate prediction is an assessment of the cost that will obtain. Observe that in both cases we are describing the sacrifice associated with some object.

Cost assessment consists of three major elements: (i) the object to which cost is assigned; (ii) the type of sacrifice description associated with that object; and (iii) the procedures used to determine that description. We consider some general aspects of each of these elements.

1.1 Cost Objects

The objects to which costs are assigned have three important dimensions: type, time, and quantity. In general, the object may be of any conceivable type: a product, an action, a storm, a production schedule, a conviction, a child, a service center, or an invoice. However, as discussed in section 2 below, the objects must, if cost assessment is to promote decision making, reflect or relate to the action alternatives being evaluated. We often casually suppress this relationship, as when we speak of the cost of a product as opposed to the cost of the actions that produced that product. And the relationship is often oblique, as when we speak of personnel training costs. But the action orientation remains fundamental.[1]

An important aspect of the time dimension is the recognition that objects may relate to either prior or future actions. Most obviously, in selecting among alternative actions, the cost of the various actions is an important *prediction*. However, we also *estimate* the cost of prior actions; knowledge of prior costs may, for example, be useful in predicting future costs.[2]

In addition to distinguishing between past and future objects, it is often important to identify the precise point or interval in time of the object's occurrence. For example, the cost of operating a service department, say a maintenance department, has meaning only if we specify some time interval, say December 1975. Both the *length* of the interval and its *position* relative to current time are important here. Prediction of next month's cost is not likely to be identical to estimation of last month's cost; and estimation of yesterday's cost is not likely to be identical to estimation of last year's cost.

The object description will include a quantity dimension in many situations. For example, the operation of a maintenance department may be described in terms of the number of hours of service provided during a given month. If the object is related to future actions, the quantity will be unknown since it will depend on the actions selected and perhaps the state that occurs. In this situation the cost assessment is a function from the set of possible object quantities to the set of admissible cost descriptions. If the object is related to past actions, the estimated quantity may be a single amount. In this situation the cost assessment is a single ordered pair: the object description and the cost description.[3]

1.2 Cost Descriptions

The second major cost assessment element is the type of sacrifice description. These descriptions typically represent some aspect of the outcome associated with the object. And, if cost assessment is to promote decision making, the descriptions must reflect those aspects of the action outcomes that affect the decision maker's action preferences. Most obviously, in selecting an action the decision maker develops payoff adequate descriptions of the outcomes that may result from his action alternatives—some of the elements of these descriptions may be termed costs.

---

1. Staubus (1971), for example, recognizes this fundamental orientation. Also, in Chapter 5 we shall find it convenient to focus on objects that are outcomes of the action choice. But any action, recall, is a mapping from states into outcomes; hence, this focus on outcomes is but a derivative of the fundamental action orientation.

2. Observe here that we draw a fundamental distinction between retrospective assessment, or *estimation*, and prospective assessment, or *prediction*.

3. The procedure for estimating the object quantity is often part of the cost assessment procedure. For example, specification of the procedure for determining the cost of materials used may include specification of the inventory method (periodic or perpetual) for determining the quantity used.

Observe that future outcomes depend on the state, and thus either the object must reflect the state or the cost description must include a probability function over the set of possible outcomes associated with the object. Also, payoff adequate descriptions of past outcomes may be useful in predicting similar aspects of future outcomes.

In most decision situations the decision maker's preferences are in part a function of the cash flows that occur, and thus the commonest metric (unit of measure) used in cost descriptions is that of the medium of exchange (for example, U.S. dollars). If the decision maker's preferences depend on factors other than the cash flow, other metrics might be used. For example, cost descriptions may be expressed in such diverse units as the number of highway accidents, the number of patient deaths, or the amount of various pollutants in the air or water. Of course, the cost description may well be a vector whose elements are expressed in terms of several different metrics. A vector description may also be used to reflect the time dimension of the outcome—the decision maker's preferences usually depend on *when* an outcome occurs as well as the nature of that outcome.

If a decision maker's choice behavior can be represented by the expected utility hypothesis, a vector of outcome elements can be expressed as a *scalar* such that maximization of the expected value of that scalar will result in the selection of the preferred action.[4] The unit of measure of this scalar is termed utiles and the mapping from the set of possible outcomes to the set of possible scalars is a utility function. Cost descriptions, such as the economist's opportunity cost of an action,[5] that consider all outcome elements may be expressed in utility terms. However, cost descriptions that consider only a subset of the outcome elements in general cannot be expressed in utility terms since the utility function may not be separable with respect to the cost and noncost elements. Consequently, we cannot in general express the cost of an action as a scalar, except in terms of the economist's opportunity cost.[6]

1.3 COST ASSESSMENT PROCEDURES

The third major cost assessment element is the set of procedures used to determine a cost description. The specific form of these procedures and the data upon which they are based will depend on the nature of the object. Cost calculations for past objects are based primarily on observations of past actions and outcomes and on estimates of the outcomes that would have resulted if different actions had been taken. Predictions of future outcomes may also be used if actions affect the outcomes in several periods (for example, depreciation). Cost calculations for future objects are based primarily on predictions of future actions and outcomes. Cost descriptions of past objects are often used in making these predictions.

---

4. See the discussion of decision making in Chapter 2.

5. See section 1.1.3 of Chapter 3 and section 2.1 of this chapter for discussons of this concept.

6. Recall, however, that if market value maximization is a viable modification, separability is present; and the opportunity cost measure will also be measured in monetary units.

Because of the broad range of data and calculations that may be used in determining the cost of an object, we often attempt to communicate the cost assessment procedure to users of the resulting cost description. Indeed, it is this communication issue that gives rise to the numerous cost adjectives with which we are familiar. For example, a person familiar with accounting terminology recognizes that there are significant differences in the data used in calculating the "historical" versus "replacement" cost of using some input. Similarly, he will recognize that there are significant differences in the procedures used to calculate the "direct" versus "full" cost of producing some product.

These adjectives do not, of course, fully describe the complex set of procedures that are involved in most cost assessments. We do not, except in the simplest cases, move directly from the data to a cost description. For example, assessment of the cost of producing some product typically involves separate assessments for direct material, direct labor, and overhead for each stage of production. Furthermore, the assessment of the overhead is likely to be based on the assessment and allocation of service department costs. All these processings must be specified.

Our purpose at this point is not to study the mechanical aspects of cost assessment. Rather, we are presently concerned with its conceptual role and rely on the reader's intuition to appreciate the complexities involved. Some of those specification complexities are considered in Chapter 5, but, for the moment, our focus remains somewhat more abstract.

In summary, a cost assessment is a description of the sacrifice associated with some object. It is also the set of procedures used to generate that sacrifice description. In any given situation there are likely to be alternative cost assessments that could be used. The nature of these alternatives and the basis for selecting from among them depend on the role the cost assessment is to play and the specifics of the situation in which it is to be used. Selection is a question of evaluating means in terms of the desired ends.

In the following sections we explore some of the roles of cost assessment and the general nature of assessment alternatives in those contexts.

2.0 THE ROLE OF COST ASSESSMENT IN A COMPLETE DECISION ANALYSIS

Recall that a complete analysis involves specification of the set of actions and states and the outcome, utility, and probability functions so as to *completely* reflect the decision maker's beliefs and preferences. No conceivable facet of the decision situation has been ignored or overlooked. The decision maker may decide to obtain information prior to his decision, but, *ex ante,* the only conceivable impact of the information will be the revision of the state probability function. If the decision maker does indeed employ a complete decision analysis, cost assessment may play two distinct roles in his analysis. It may form part of his specification of the outcome and utility functions and it may be used to generate information. We discuss these two roles in turn.

2.1 THE OUTCOME AND UTILITY SPECIFICATION ROLE

When evaluating a set of action alternatives, decision makers often separately determine the "benefits" and "costs" that may result from each action, and then select the action with the most preferred set of potential benefits and costs. This approach is consistent with a complete analysis provided the benefit and cost descriptions associated with each action constitute a payoff adequate outcome description and an appropriate utility function is used to evaluate them. Recognize, however, that the benefit/cost distinction is unnecessary. Furthermore, even though an action is a well-defined cost object and the purpose for assessing its cost is well defined, *the cost of an action is not uniquely defined.*

The lack of a unique action cost results from two factors. First, the benefit/cost distinction is arbitrary in the sense that we can refer to any outcome component as either a benefit or a cost, depending on our personal whim. Of course, common usage dictates that only those components viewed as *sacrifices* are termed costs. Second, there are many possible payoff adequate outcome descriptions and the components classified as sacrifices will depend on the description that is used. Variations in the outcome description frequently result from the aggregation of outcome components, the elimination of invariant outcome components, the use of incremental analysis, and the suppression of some action alternatives. We now explore these factors more fully.

2.1.1 ARBITRARINESS OF THE OUTCOME PARTITION

The function $x = p(s, a, \eta)$ is, recall, merely an appropriate representation of the outcome associated with any conceivable state/action pair and the use of system η. That outcome may be divided into a benefit component, denoted x^B, and a cost component, denoted x^C, such that $x = (x^B, x^C)$. Both components will be functions of the state, action, and system: $x^B = p^B(s, a, \eta)$ and $x^C = p^C(s, a, \eta)$.

We term $p^C(s, a, \eta)$ the *outcome cost of action a if state s occurs.*[7] The cost of an action thus depends on the outcome partition and the state. However, state dependence is often suppressed in casual conversation. For example, we often speak of "the" cost (of some action). This may be appropriate in a world of subjective certainty, but in the more general uncertain case the state plays a necessary conditioning role. *Ex ante* assessment of an action's cost is clearly state dependent. Similarly, *ex post* assessment of the cost of an action actually taken depends on the state—the state that actually occurred.

Action cost also depends on the particular partition of the outcome into benefit and cost components. The question we now pose is: What portion of the outcome represents sacrifice? Numerous approaches to this question are possible. For example, in Chapter 5 we characterize a production system in terms of "outputs" and "inputs" and we could elect to regard all payments for "inputs" as

---

7. The outcome cost may be a vector. We do not introduce the utility (as opposed to the outcome) cost of an action since this assumes $U(x^B, x^C) = B(x^B) - C(x^C)$. Such separability does not in general exist (Fishburn 1970; Koopmans 1972). However, as was pointed out in Chapter 3, an action's opportunity (as opposed to outcome) cost is naturally assessed in this manner.

costs. This has some intuitive appeal, but there are numerous examples of common practice that do not conform to that definition. For example, receipts from the sale of by-products are typically treated as reductions in the cost of producing the primary products. Other examples are provided in Chapter 5.

We conclude, then, that partitioning of the outcome function into benefit and cost components does not necessarily follow any "logical" or "natural" pattern. Moreover, the partition is conceptually irrelevant because specification of the outcome function and its use in decision analysis remain completely invariant to whatever partition is imposed. But this should not be a surprising result, because cost, however defined here, is but a subset of the outcome. And myopic focus on cost issues, to the exclusion of their complement, cannot be guaranteed to result in optimal specifications. Cost assessment issues do not exist in a vacuum.

This point is demonstrated by the conditions that must be satisfied if the decision maker is to *separately* develop the benefit and cost components of the outcome function. As was pointed out in Chapter 3, the set of action alternatives explicitly considered by the decision maker typically does not encompass all his actions—secondary actions are suppressed. In a complete analysis the optimal secondary actions must be considered in deriving the outcome function for the primary actions. In general, sufficient conditions for the derivation of the optimal secondary actions require consideration of all outcome elements and the utility function defined over those elements (see Proposition 3.1). However, the optimal secondary actions associated with the benefit and cost component outcome functions can be derived separately *if* the following conditions are satisfied:

(i)   The benefit and cost component outcomes are influenced by different secondary actions;
(ii) The two sets of secondary actions are independent; and
(iii) The utility function is separable with respect to the benefit and cost component outcomes.

These conditions and the separately developed outcome function are formally stated in Table 4.1.

There are a variety of reasons why these conditions may not be satisfied in a given decision situation. For example, if both the benefit and cost component outcomes include future cash flows, it may be impossible to divide future (that is, secondary) actions between those that affect the benefit component and those that affect the cost component. And even if it is possible, the set of "feasible" secondary benefit actions may well depend on the secondary cost action selected (or vice versa). Finally, in a world of uncertainty, risk aversion on the part of the decision maker will preclude satisfaction of the third condition.[8]

These conditions are satisfied, however, by a firm market value maximization

---

8. If the secondary actions are selected by someone other than the primary decision maker, the second and third conditions need not hold. Instead, separate development is possible if the first condition holds and the primary decision maker can separately develop his predictions of the two secondary action components as functions of s, a, and η.

TABLE 4.1 SEPARABLE BENEFIT AND COST OUTCOME FUNCTION

Consider the following separability conditions:

(i) Outcome function separability:

$$p\left(s,\binom{a}{\mathbf{a}},\eta\right) = \left(p^{B}\left(s,\binom{a}{\mathbf{a}_B},\eta\right), p^{C}\left(s,\binom{a}{\mathbf{a}_C},\eta\right)\right)$$

where $\mathbf{a} = \binom{\mathbf{a}_B}{\mathbf{a}_C}$, $\mathbf{a}_B$ is the secondary benefit action, and $\mathbf{a}_C$ is the secondary cost action.

(ii) Secondary action set separability:

$$A(a) = A_B(a) \times A_C(a)$$

where A_B is the set of possible secondary benefit actions and A_C is the set of possible secondary cost actions.

(iii) Utility function separability:[1]

$$U(x) = B(x^B) - C(x^C)$$

where $x = (x^B, x^C)$

and the associated benefit and cost component outcome functions:

$$p^B(s, a, \eta) = p^B\left(s, \left(\alpha_B^*(a, \eta(s), \eta)\right), \eta\right)$$

$$p^C(s, a, \eta) = p^C\left(s, \left(\alpha_C^*(a, \eta(s), \eta)\right), \eta\right)$$

where $\alpha_B^*(a, y, \eta)$ and $\alpha_C^*(a, y, \eta)$ are such that

$$E\left(B \mid \left(\alpha_B^*(a, y, \eta)\right), y, \eta\right) = \max_{\mathbf{a}_B \in A_B(a)} \sum_{s \in S} B\left(p^B\left(s, \binom{a}{\mathbf{a}_B}, \eta\right)\right) \phi(s \mid y, \eta)$$

$$E\left(C \mid \left(\alpha_C^*(a, y, \eta)\right), y, \eta\right) = \min_{\mathbf{a}_C \in A_C(a)} \sum_{s \in S} C\left(p^C\left(s, \binom{a}{\mathbf{a}_C}, \eta\right)\right) \phi(s \mid y, \eta).$$

Proposition 4.1:

Consider the basic problem in Equation [2.2] and let the maximum uniquely exist. The above separability conditions, use of $\alpha_B^*(a, y, \eta)$ and $\alpha_C^*(a, y, \eta)$ to separately construct benefit and cost component functions, and optimization of the following modified model will identify the optimal primary-secondary action combination:

$$E(U \mid a, y, \eta) = E\left(B \mid \left(\alpha_B^*(a, y, \eta)\right), y, \eta\right) - E\left(C \mid \left(\alpha_C^*(a, y, \eta)\right), y, \eta\right).$$

Proof:

From Proposition 3.1 we know that

$$p(s, a, \eta) = p\left(s, \left(\alpha^*(a, y, \eta)\right), \eta\right)$$

---

1. Axiomatization of this separability requirement is available in Fishburn (1970).

Continued on next page

TABLE 4.1 (*Continued*)

provides a modification of the model in Equation [2.2]. Moreover, conditions (i), (ii), and (iii) ensure

$$E\left(U \mid \left(\alpha^*(a, \overset{a}{y}, \eta)\right), y, \eta\right) = \max_{\mathbf{a} \in A(a)} \sum_{s \in S} U\left(p\left(s, \binom{a}{\mathbf{a}}, \eta\right)\right) \phi(s \mid y, \eta)$$

$$= \max_{\mathbf{a}_B \in A_B(a)} \sum_{s \in S} B\left(p^B\left(s, \binom{a}{\mathbf{a}_B}, \eta\right)\right) \phi(s \mid y, \eta)$$

$$- \min_{\mathbf{a}_C \in A_C(a)} \sum_{s \in S} C\left(p^C\left(s, \binom{a}{\mathbf{a}_C}, \eta\right)\right) \phi(s \mid y, \eta)$$

$$= E\left(B \mid \left(\alpha_B^*(a, \overset{a}{y}, \eta)\right), y, \eta\right)$$

$$- E\left(C \mid \left(\alpha_C^*(a, \overset{a}{y}, \eta)\right), y, \eta\right).$$

modification. In that modification, although all actions are suppressed, they are effectively treated as primary actions. That is, the first and second conditions are satisfied merely because there are no secondary actions. Then the third condition is satisfied because the market value is a linear function of the cash flows. (See Appendix 5.2.)

2.1.2 DEPENDENCE OF ACTION COST ON OUTCOME DESCRIPTION

Another major reason why the cost of an action is not unique arises from the fact that many different outcome descriptions may be used. As discussed in Chapter 3 (section 1.2), these descriptions must be payoff adequate if the analysis is to be complete, but there are many such descriptions. In particular, these descriptions may vary considerably as to level of detail and thereby affect the form of the cost description. For example, a set of cash expenditures might be described in detail by type and time period, by totals for each time period, or perhaps by a single amount representing the present value of those expenditures (if the decision maker's preferences are a function of the present value of future cash flows).

Furthermore, differences in the level of detail may result in differences in the set of outcome elements that are incorporated into the cost description. For example, if the cash flows are listed in some detail, receipts from the sale of scrap may be classified as a benefit but may be included in the cost description if we use an aggregate description in which these receipts are deducted from the expenditures for inputs used in production.

If the decision maker's preferences can be represented by a linear function of the outcome elements, he may ignore those outcome elements that are invariant for his set of action alternatives. He may also employ incremental analysis—focusing on the difference between the outcome for each action and the outcome for some base action. Both of these modifications will obviously affect the cost description in that they will result in the exclusion of some elements from that description. Furthermore, incremental analysis may result in changes in classification for some elements. For example, if the base action requires a large expenditure for some input, such as labor, and the other actions require smaller expenditures for that input, then under incremental analysis labor would be a "cost saving" and, hence, likely classified as a benefit instead of a cost.

2.1.3 OPPORTUNITY COST AND THE SUPPRESSION OF ACTION ALTERNATIVES

To this point we have explored partition of the outcome into benefit and cost components and the resulting notion of the outcome cost of an action. This notion, we saw, is dependent on the particular partition itself as well as the manner in which the decision maker structures his thinking. Incremental analysis or elimination of unaffected outcome elements alters, for example, what we mean by the cost of an action, regardless of the outcome partition. Apparently, then, the cost of an action is an elusive concept.

Further variations in the cost of an action are introduced when we consider the suppression of action alternatives and the related concept of opportunity cost. If we explicitly consider all action alternatives in a complete analysis, selection of the optimal action is guaranteed and, therefore, we have no use whatsoever for an explicit expression of what is foregone. The situation drastically changes, however, if we consciously suppress a subset of the action alternatives.

Action space reduction may take place in either of two directions: some actions may be eliminated altogether from explicit analysis or selected elements of all actions may be eliminated. Suppose, for the sake of illustration, that each action alternative is an m element vector and N alternatives are present. Then we would denote the ith action a^i as

$$a^i = \begin{pmatrix} a^i_{1.} \\ a^i_{2.} \\ \vdots \\ a^i_{m.} \end{pmatrix}$$

and the entire action space, A, could be illustrated as

$$A = \left[\begin{array}{ccc|ccc} a^1_{1.} \cdots a^p_{1.} & & a^{p+1}_{1.} \cdots a^N_{1.} \\ \vdots & \vdots & \vdots & \vdots \\ a^1_{l.} \cdots a^p_{l.} & & a^{p+1}_{l.} \cdots a^N_{l.} \\ \hline a^1_{l+1.} \cdots a^p_{l+1.} & & a^{p+1}_{l+1.} \cdots a^N_{l+1.} \\ \vdots & \vdots & \vdots & \vdots \\ a^1_{m.} \cdots a^p_{m.} & & a^{p+1}_{m.} \cdots a^N_{m.} \end{array} \right]$$

Elimination of some actions altogether may be viewed in terms of the vertical partition, eliminating $a^{p+1}, \ldots, a^N$ from explicit consideration. Similarly, elimination of selected elements of all actions may be viewed in terms of the horizontal partition, eliminating

$$\begin{pmatrix} a_{l+1.}^i \\ \vdots \\ a_{m.}^i \end{pmatrix}$$

for all $i = 1, \ldots, N$ from explicit consideration. And, with both forms of elimination employed, the action space is reduced to

$$A_1 = \begin{bmatrix} a_{1.}^1 & \cdots & a_{1.}^p \\ \vdots & & \vdots \\ a_{l.}^1 & \cdots & a_{l.}^p \end{bmatrix}$$

The notion of opportunity cost is both precise and indispensable in the "vertical" elimination scheme. Suppose we eliminate some of the actions. Let A_1 denote those remaining and A_2 those eliminated. Then the opportunity cost of selecting an action from set A_1 is the expected utility associated with the best action from set A_2. From Proposition 3.3 we know that the best action from set A_1 is an optimal action if its expected utility is at least as large as the opportunity cost of selecting an action from that set.

Observe that the opportunity cost of an action is dependent on the definition of A_1. A statement that the opportunity cost is such and such is a meaningless statement unless we explicate the eliminated set of actions. Economists often refer to *the* opportunity cost of action a, implying $A_1 = a$.[9] But this does not reflect the fact that decision makers typically base their decisions on a comparison of the benefits and costs associated with several explicitly considered alternatives.

Also observe that the opportunity cost of an action is naturally expressed in utility as opposed to outcome units.[10] To appreciate this, note that the opportunity cost in this case is used to control for the possibility that the decision maker may prefer the outcome lottery associated with the best action in set A_2 instead of the lottery for the best action in set A_1. Comparison between two lotteries can be reduced to a scalar if we reduce each to its utility equivalent.

Clearly, cost assessment plays an important utility specification role in "vertical" elimination. Opportunity cost is a precise concept for a given set of actions A_1 and it is indispensable in guaranteeing location of the optimal action. The term opportunity cost is often used in connection with "horizontal" elimination as well, but in this case it is neither precise nor indispensable. We will refer

---

9. Indeed, we could modify the choice problem to select the action with the minimum opportunity cost.

10. Again, the natural measure is monetary units in the special case where market value maximization is available.

to this latter cost as an *externality cost* to distinguish it from the more precise opportunity cost associated with vertical elimination.

Under horizontal elimination the vector of action elements is divided into a primary action,

$$a = \begin{pmatrix} a_{1.} \\ \vdots \\ a_{l.} \end{pmatrix},$$

and a secondary action,

$$\mathbf{a} = \begin{pmatrix} a_{l+1.} \\ \vdots \\ a_{m.} \end{pmatrix},$$

and only the alternative primary actions are explicitly evaluated. The secondary action must be selected, but that selection is suppressed in the decision analysis at hand. Proposition 3.1 demonstrates that this approach will result in the selection of the optimal primary and secondary actions if the modified outcome function reflects the optimal secondary action associated with each primary action. (Observe that selection of the optimal action is accomplished without using any notion of an opportunity cost.)

The externality cost associated with the suppression of secondary actions results from dividing the outcome into two components: $x = (x^1, x^2)$, where x^1 is associated with the primary action and x^2 is associated with the secondary action. The externality cost of selecting action a is then the secondary outcome foregone, denoted x^{C2}:

[4.1] $$x^{C2} = p^{C2}(s, a, \eta) = p^2(s, a^0, \eta) - p^2(s, a, \eta)$$

where $p^2(s, a^0, \eta) = x^{2^0}$ is the most preferred secondary outcome (given state s and system η).[11] As in incremental analysis $\hat{x} = (x^1, x^{C2})$ is payoff adequate if the utility function is separable, for example, $U(x) = U^1(x^1) + U^2(x^{2^0}) - C^2(x^{C2})$. In that case, the externality cost can be expressed in utility units as well as outcome units. Observe, however, that the externality cost is imprecise because the primary/secondary outcome division is arbitrary.

The following example is designed to illustrate the cost concepts that we have been discussing.

---

11. The secondary action is suppressed in this exposition:

$$p^2(s, a, \eta) = p^2\left(s, \left(\genfrac{}{}{0pt}{}{a}{\alpha^*(a, \eta(s), \eta)}\right), \eta\right).$$

2.1.4 EXAMPLE

Consider a decision maker who has committed himself to the acquisition of 10 tons of wheat and must decide how to dispose of it. His original intention was to ship it to the island of Alpha or the island of Beta or 5 tons to each. He has made arrangements for, but is not committed to, capacity on airfreight flights that will service both islands. He now realizes that there are other alternatives available to him. First, either 10 or 5 tons of wheat can be sold in the local market. Second, the airfreight capacity reserved for shipment of wheat can be used to ship rice instead; he knows a buyer on the island of Alpha who will take either 5 or 10 tons of rice. These quantities could be acquired in the local market. In addition to the acquisition of the freight capacity and the two products, payments would be required for the acquisition of labor to be used in loading and unloading the airplanes and in shipping wheat to local buyers.

We now construct a complete model for this decision situation. The action that the decision maker will take may be divided into four components: a_1 is the quantity of wheat shipped and sold on the island of Alpha; a_2 is the quantity of wheat shipped and sold on the island of Beta; a_3 is the quantity of wheat shipped and sold in the local market; and a_4 is the quantity of rice purchased locally and shipped and sold on the island of Alpha. There are 10 possible combinations for these action components; they constitute the feasible action set A and are presented in Table 4.2. This table also presents the cash flows associated with each action. We assume that these cash outcomes are viewed as subjectively certain by the decision maker and that he always prefers more to less cash. As a consequence, Proposition 3.4 ensures that we may focus on selection of the action resulting in the maximum net cash flow. From the table we observe that $\alpha^*(y, \eta) = a^4$; that is, the optimal action is to ship $a_1 = 5$ tons of wheat and $a_4 = 5$ tons of rice to the island of Alpha and sell $a_3 = 5$ tons of wheat in the local market. This action will yield a net cash flow of $E(U \mid \alpha^*(\cdot), y, \eta) = \$1,420$.

Suppose we decide to treat cash inflows as benefits and cash outflows as costs. Then the cost of action a^4, from Table 4.2, consists of cash outflows that total \$14,080. This cost is obviously dependent on the definition of $p^C(\hat{s}, a, \eta)$[12] and on how the decision maker elects to analyze his alternatives.

To appreciate this, observe that the cash outflows associated with the acquisition of wheat is invariant to the decision maker's choice of action; he has already committed himself to the acquisition of 10 tons. If we now partition the outcome into action-dependent and action-independent components, $p(\hat{s}, a, \eta) = (\hat{p}(\hat{s}, a, \eta), \hat{p}(\hat{s}, \eta))$, we have $\hat{p}(\hat{s}, \eta) = \$3,000$. Elimination of $\hat{p}(\hat{s}, \eta)$ does not alter the optimal choice in this case, but it does alter the *cost* of an action. For example, with $\hat{p}(\hat{s}, \eta)$ eliminated, the cost of action a^4 now consists of cash outflows that total \$11,080.

The action costs would also be affected by a switch to incremental analysis. To illustrate, let the base action be the cancellation of the delivery arrangements

---

12. Recall that $\hat{s}$ denotes the subjectively certain state.

TABLE 4.2 BASIC DATA FOR COST ASSESSMENT EXAMPLE

Actions:		a^1	a^2	a^3	a^4	a^5	a^6	a^7	a^8	a^9	a^{10}
a_1.	Tons of wheat sold to Alpha.	10	5	0	5	5	0	0	0	0	0
a_2.	Tons of wheat sold to Beta.	0	5	10	0	0	5	5	0	0	0
$a = \ \ a_3$.	Tons of wheat sold locally.	0	0	0	5	5	5	5	10	10	10
a_4.	Tons of rice sold to Alpha.	0	0	0	5	0	5	0	10	5	0
Cash Inflow: $p^B(\hat{s}, a, \eta)$											
	Local sale of wheat	0	0	0	2,000	2,000	2,000	2,000	4,000	4,000	4,000
	Island sale of wheat	9,900	9,900	8,100	5,400	5,400	4,500	4,500	0	0	0
	Island sale of rice	0	0	0	8,100	0	9,000	0	16,200	9,000	0
	Total	9,000	9,900	8,100	15,500	7,400	15,500	6,500	20,200	13,000	4,000
Cash Outflow: $p^C(\hat{s}, a, \eta)$											
	Purchase wheat	3,000	3,000	3,000	3,000	3,000	3,000	3,000	3,000	3,000	3,000
	Purchase rice	0	0	0	5,000	0	5,000	0	10,000	5,000	0
	Delivery										
	Labor	1,900	2,350	1,900	3,080	1,520	3,620	1,430	4,030	2,790	600
	Airfreight	3,000	3,200	3,000	3,000	2,000	3,200	2,000	3,000	2,000	0
	Total delivery	4,900	5,550	4,900	6,080	3,520	6,820	3,430	7,030	4,790	600
	Total	7,900	8,550	7,900	14,080	6,520	14,820	6,430	20,030	12,790	3,600
Net Certain Cash Flow: $E(U \mid a, y, \eta)$		\$1,100	\$1,350	\$ 200	\$ 1,420	\$ 880	\$ 680	\$ 70	\$ 170	\$ 210	\$ 400

and local sale of all 10 tons of wheat, that is, $a^0 = a^{10}$. The resulting incremental outcomes are presented in Table 4.3. The cost of action a^4 now consists of incremental cash outflows that total \$10,480.

Now consider the opportunity cost of the alternative actions. In the economist's view, the opportunity cost of action a^4 is \$1,350, the expected net cash flow for the next best alternative, a^2. The fact that this cost is less than the expected net cash flow for action a^4 indicates that it is the optimal action. The opportunity cost for all other actions is \$1,420.

Opportunity cost may be used to control for the elimination of some alternatives from explicit consideration. Suppose the decision maker explicitly focuses on the sale of wheat in the islands (his original intention) and eliminates all other alternatives. We now have $A_1 = \{a^1, a^2, a^3\}$ and $A_2 = \{a^4, a^5, a^6, a^7, a^8, a^9, a^{10}\}$ and a maximum net cash flow of

$$E(U \mid a^2, y, \eta) = \max_{a \in A_1} E(U \mid a, y, \eta) = \$1,350$$

with an opportunity cost of

$$E(U \mid a^4, y, \eta) = \max_{a \in A_2} E(U \mid a, y, \eta) = \$1,420.$$

The opportunity cost is indispensable here; specifically, since \$1,350 < \$1,420 we know, from the corollary to Proposition 3.3, that a^4 is the optimal action.

The decision maker's focus on the sale of wheat in the islands can also be interpreted in a horizontal elimination format; this gives rise to a different notion of opportunity cost (which we have termed an externality cost). In this context let $a = \begin{pmatrix} a_1. \\ a_2. \end{pmatrix}$ denote the primary action and $\mathbf{a} = \begin{pmatrix} a_3. \\ a_4. \end{pmatrix}$ the secondary action. The set of possible primary actions is

$$A = \left\{ \begin{pmatrix} 10 \\ 0 \end{pmatrix}, \begin{pmatrix} 5 \\ 5 \end{pmatrix}, \begin{pmatrix} 0 \\ 10 \end{pmatrix}, \begin{pmatrix} 5 \\ 0 \end{pmatrix}, \begin{pmatrix} 0 \\ 5 \end{pmatrix}, \begin{pmatrix} 0 \\ 0 \end{pmatrix} \right\}.$$

This set includes every possible shipping combination for wheat. Associated with each primary action is a set of possible secondary actions (the quantity of wheat sold locally and the quantity of rice acquired and shipped) and an optimal secondary action. These sets and actions are

$$\mathbf{A} \begin{pmatrix} 10 \\ 0 \end{pmatrix} = \left\{ \begin{pmatrix} 0 \\ 0 \end{pmatrix} \right\} \qquad \alpha^* \left(\begin{pmatrix} 10 \\ 0 \end{pmatrix}, y, \eta \right) = \begin{pmatrix} 0 \\ 0 \end{pmatrix}$$

$$\mathbf{A} \begin{pmatrix} 5 \\ 5 \end{pmatrix} = \left\{ \begin{pmatrix} 0 \\ 0 \end{pmatrix} \right\} \qquad \alpha^* \left(\begin{pmatrix} 5 \\ 5 \end{pmatrix}, y, \eta \right) = \begin{pmatrix} 0 \\ 0 \end{pmatrix}$$

$$\mathbf{A} \begin{pmatrix} 0 \\ 10 \end{pmatrix} = \left\{ \begin{pmatrix} 0 \\ 0 \end{pmatrix} \right\} \qquad \alpha^* \left(\begin{pmatrix} 0 \\ 10 \end{pmatrix}, y, \eta \right) = \begin{pmatrix} 0 \\ 0 \end{pmatrix}$$

$$\mathbf{A} \begin{pmatrix} 5 \\ 0 \end{pmatrix} = \left\{ \begin{pmatrix} 5 \\ 5 \end{pmatrix}, \begin{pmatrix} 5 \\ 0 \end{pmatrix} \right\} \qquad \alpha^* \left(\begin{pmatrix} 5 \\ 0 \end{pmatrix}, y, \eta \right) = \begin{pmatrix} 5 \\ 5 \end{pmatrix}$$

$$\mathbf{A} \begin{pmatrix} 0 \\ 5 \end{pmatrix} = \left\{ \begin{pmatrix} 5 \\ 5 \end{pmatrix}, \begin{pmatrix} 5 \\ 0 \end{pmatrix} \right\} \qquad \alpha^* \left(\begin{pmatrix} 0 \\ 5 \end{pmatrix}, y, \eta \right) = \begin{pmatrix} 5 \\ 5 \end{pmatrix}$$

TABLE 4.3 INCREMENTAL CASH FLOW DATA: $p(\hat{s}, a, \eta) - p(\hat{s}, a^{10}, \eta)$

	a^1	a^2	a^3	a^4	a^5	a^6	a^7	a^8	a^9	a^{10}
Incremental Cash Inflow										
Local sale of wheat	-4,000	-4,000	-4,000	-2,000	-2,000	-2,000	-2,000	0	0	0
Island sale of wheat	9,000	9,900	8,100	5,400	5,400	4,500	4,500	0	0	0
Island sale of rice	0	0	0	8,100	0	9,000	0	16,200	9,000	0
Total	5,000	5,900	4,100	11,500	3,400	11,500	2,500	16,200	9,000	0
Incremental Cash Outflow										
Purchase wheat	0	0	0	0	0	0	0	0	0	0
Purchase rice	0	0	0	5,000	0	5,000	0	10,000	5,000	0
Delivery	4,300	4,950	4,300	5,480	2,920	6,220	2,830	6,430	4,190	0
Total	4,300	4,950	4,300	10,480	2,920	11,220	2,830	16,430	9,190	0
Net Certain Incremental Cash Flow	$ 700	$ 950	$ -200	$ 1,020	$ 480	$ 280	$ -330	$ -230	$ -190	$0

$$A\begin{pmatrix}0\\0\end{pmatrix} = \left\{\begin{pmatrix}10\\10\end{pmatrix}, \begin{pmatrix}10\\5\end{pmatrix}, \begin{pmatrix}10\\0\end{pmatrix}\right\} \qquad \alpha*\left(\begin{pmatrix}0\\0\end{pmatrix}, y, \eta\right) = \begin{pmatrix}10\\0\end{pmatrix}$$

The modified outcome function is presented in Table 4.4(a). Clearly, the optimal action is $a = \begin{pmatrix}5\\0\end{pmatrix}$ with $\alpha*\left(\begin{pmatrix}5\\0\end{pmatrix}, y, \eta\right) = \begin{pmatrix}5\\5\end{pmatrix}$ and a net cash flow of \$1,420.

If cost of an action is defined to be the cash outflows, the cost of action $a = \begin{pmatrix}5\\0\end{pmatrix}$, for example, consists of cash outflows that total \$14,080. However, the decision maker may find it convenient to allocate the outcome among the primary and secondary actions and then consider the cost of an action to be the primary cash outflows plus the secondary cash flows foregone. There are many possible allocations, but for illustrative purposes suppose we associate the cash inflow from the sale of wheat on the islands with the primary action and the other cash inflows with the secondary action. Similarly, suppose we associate the cash outflow for the acquisition of rice with the secondary action. The other cash outflows present a problem because they are clearly a function of both the primary and the secondary actions; any division will have to be somewhat arbitrary. We adopt the following procedures. Payment for wheat is allocated according to the tons shipped versus the tons sold locally. Payment for the airfreight service is allocated according to the capacity used for wheat versus the capacity used for rice; the labor payment is allocated in a somewhat arbitrary fashion. The results of that division are presented in Table 4.4(b).

The maximum secondary net cash flow is provided by $a^0 = \begin{pmatrix}0\\5\end{pmatrix}$; hence, in applying the externality cost definition of Equation [4.1] we use $p^2(\hat{s}, a^0, \eta) = \$510$. The externality cost is presented in Table 4.4(c), along with the primary cash inflows and outflows. The latter is also viewed as a cost of the primary action and is termed an *outlay cost*. The total cost of action $a = \begin{pmatrix}5\\0\end{pmatrix}$ in this case is \$4,490.

In summary, our simple example has demonstrated that the cost of an action depends on how a decision maker approaches his decision problem. In particular, the cost of selling 5 tons of wheat on island Alpha (selling the remainder locally and shipping 5 tons of rice instead) can quite reasonably be viewed to be \$14,080, \$11,080, \$10,480, \$1,350, or \$4,490. The correct amount depends on the decision analysis that is employed, and the method of analysis is at the discretion of the decision maker.

This finishes our discussion of the role of cost assessment in outcome and utility specification for a complete analysis. In a complete analysis the decision maker must fully specify a payoff adequate description of the outcomes *he believes* will result from his actions. If we view cost assessment as the specification of the cost elements of the outcome, it plays an important role. However, this role is imprecise because the portion of the outcome we elect to term cost is arbitrary and is very likely to depend on which of the many alternative payoff adequate outcome descriptions is used in the analysis.

TABLE 4.4 ALTERNATIVE CASH FLOWS FOR PRIMARY ACTION ALTERNATIVES

Primary Actions

$$a = \begin{pmatrix} a_1 \\ a_2 \end{pmatrix} = \begin{pmatrix} \text{Tons of wheat sold to Alpha.} \\ \text{Tons of wheat sold to Beta.} \end{pmatrix}$$

	$\begin{pmatrix}10\\0\end{pmatrix}$	$\begin{pmatrix}5\\5\end{pmatrix}$	$\begin{pmatrix}0\\10\end{pmatrix}$	$\begin{pmatrix}5\\0\end{pmatrix}$	$\begin{pmatrix}0\\5\end{pmatrix}$	$\begin{pmatrix}0\\0\end{pmatrix}$
(a) Cash Inflows: $p^B(\hat{s},a,\eta)$	9,000	9,900	8,100	15,500	15,500	4,000
Cash Outflows: $p^C(\hat{s},a,\eta)$	7,900	8,550	7,900	14,080	14,820	3,600
Net Cash Flow: $E(U\mid a,y,\eta)$	\$1,100	\$1,350	\$ 200	\$ 1,420	\$ 680	\$ 400
(b) Primary Net Cash Flow: $p^1(\hat{s},a,\eta)$	1,100	1,350	200	1,080	170	0
Secondary Net Cash Flow: $p^2(\hat{s},a,\eta)$	0	0	0	340	510	400
Total	\$1,100	\$1,350	\$ 200	\$ 1,420	\$ 680	\$ 400
(c) Benefits Primary Cash Inflows: $p^{B1}(\hat{s},a,\eta)$	9,000	9,900	8,100	5,400	4,500	0
Costs Outlay Cost (Primary Cash Outflows): $p^{C1}(\hat{s},a,\eta)$	7,900	8,550	7,900	4,320	4,330	0
Externality Cost (Secondary Cash Flows Foregone): $p^{C2}(\hat{s},a,\eta)$	510	510	510	170	0	110
Total	8,410	9,060	8,410	4,490	4,330	110
Modified Outcome $p(\hat{s},a,\eta) - p^2(\hat{s},a^0,\eta)$	\$ 590	\$ 840	\$ -310	\$ 910	\$ 170	\$ -110

Observe that this role cannot be delegated in a complete analysis. Others, such as the accountant, may provide cost predictions, but these predictions are merely information to the decision maker. This information may influence the decision maker's beliefs, but it is his beliefs and tastes that determine the outcome function $p^C(s, a, \eta)$ and the probability function $\phi(s \mid y, \eta)$. We now consider the informative role of cost assessment in a complete analysis.

2.2 The Informative Role

As was discussed in Chapter 2, the role of information in a complete analysis is to improve our probability assessment of the state. If we have divided the outcome function into benefit and cost components, we may, without loss of generality, express the state as $s = (s^B, s^C)$ where s^B consists of those state elements that affect the benefit component and s^C consists of those that affect the cost component:[13]

$$p(s, a, \eta) = (x^B, x^C) = (p^B(s^B, a, \eta), p^C(s^C, a, \eta)).$$

Any information that changes our beliefs about s^C may be termed cost information.

The information that is useful in predicting s^C depends on the nature of its elements and the decision maker's beliefs about their relationship to prior events. Some may be directly observable at the time the decision is made, but most are not. Currently observable state elements include resources, such as inventories and machinery, which the firm has available for use. Examples of elements that are not currently observable include raw material prices, raw material usage rates, lost time due to machine breakdowns, labor production rates, and fixed and variable overhead rates.

Some of the elements that are not currently observable are observable after the fact (*ex post* observable) and the decision maker may find past observations of these elements useful in predicting their future magnitudes. If they are believed to be correlated with other observable phenomena that can be observed prior to the decision, observations of these phenomena will be useful information. For example, the raw material prices for the coming period are not currently observable, but knowledge of the prices during the prior period may be useful. If the raw material is wheat, knowledge of the amount of wheat planted and the weather conditions in wheat growing areas may be useful information in predicting future wheat prices.

Some of the state elements are not directly observable, even after the fact. These elements consist primarily of function coefficients relating various dependent and independent variables. If the dependent and independent variables can be observed after the fact, we often use past observations of these variables to estimate and predict the magnitude of the coefficients. For example, we often

---

13. s^B and s^C are not assumed to be independent and may have common elements (for example, $s = s^B = s^C$ in the limit).

assume that overhead has fixed, variable, and random components and then use past observations of the overhead (the dependent variable) and some activity measure such as direct labor hours (the independent variable) to estimate the fixed overhead, the variable overhead per unit of activity, and the variance of the probability function for the random component.

Observe that some cost information, such as current inventory levels and current weather conditions, does not involve cost assessment. Also observe that in the cost information that does involve cost assessment, the object of costing need not be an action per se. Rather, the object is often some observable aspect of the outcome resulting from prior actions and is an intermediate variable in the link between an action and the cost component.[14] For example, in a report on raw material expenditures, the object of costing is the quantity purchased, and that quantity is the result of many production and acquisition decisions and their consequent actions.

There are *no* cost assessments that *must* be reported *nor* is there a *unique* cost description for a given cost object. The cost assessment procedures used to generate cost information are at the discretion of the decision maker (or the evaluator). Specification of those procedures is a specification of the information system η and evaluation of alternative procedures is equivalent to evaluating alternative systems (as depicted in Equation [2.4]).

In a complete analysis, the decision maker's use of cost assessments for past objects is the same as any other element of the signal y. That is, he specifies the conditional probability of receiving a particular signal (cost object and cost description) from a particular cost assessment procedure, given each possible state, and then uses Bayes's theorem (see Equation [2.2]) to determine his posterior probability function over the possible states. This implies, for example, that Bayesian regression (and not least squares regression) would be used to estimate the fixed overhead, variable overhead per direct labor hour, and the variance of the random cost component, given past observations of the overhead and direct labor hours.[15] These estimates would be in the form of a posterior probability function, and not point estimates.

Most information systems observe basic events such as individual material purchases, material requisitions, and product shipments, and then aggregate, allocate, and otherwise process these observations to arrive at both the object and its cost description. In a complete analysis we assume that the decision maker will process any information *he receives* in a manner consistent with his beliefs. This implies that he would prefer to receive the unprocessed observations unless the system processing is consistent with his beliefs or the processed information is less costly to provide.[16] This ignores the cost of his analysis (and related concepts

---

14. The role of intermediate variables in assessing the cost of actions is explored in Chapter 5, where we refer to them as "cost statistics."

15. See Raiffa and Schlaifer (1961) and Zellner (1971) for discussions of Bayesian regression.

16. The fact that the unprocessed observations are at least as valuable as the processed information follows from Proposition 2.1 (provided that either information is costless or the cost of the information system can be separated from the utility measure associated with the decisions

such as information overload), but to introduce this cost we must move from our complete analysis assumption and recognize both the fact and desirability of simplified decision analysis.

3.0 THE ROLE OF COST ASSESSMENT IN A SIMPLIFIED DECISION ANALYSIS

In section 2 of Chapter 3 we explicitly recognized that a decision maker is likely to select his actions on the basis of simplified analyses (that is, analyses that cannot guarantee selection of an optimal action choice). Each of the model elements may be simplified, and we introduced notation to represent the simplified elements (see Table 3.2). If a simplified analysis is used because it is less costly than a complete analysis, we may consider alternative simplifications and select the one resulting in the highest expected utility. This utility measure, net of analysis and system costs, is characterized by Equation [3.9].

The role of cost assessment in a simplified analysis is similar to that of a complete analysis, but the cost assessment alternatives and their impact are more pervasive. Cost assessment alternatives may represent alternative model specifications, alternative parameter predictions, or alternative information. We examine each of these in turn.

3.1 MODEL SPECIFICATION ROLE

In a simplified analysis, part of the model specification may be viewed as cost assessment. In particular, the objective function may be divided into a benefit component $R^B(\theta, d)$ and a cost component $R^C(\theta, d)$, such that $R(\theta, d) = R^B(\theta, d) - R^C(\theta, d)$; specification of the cost component is a form of cost assessment.

The object of costing is the decision variable d, and it may not fully describe the decision maker's action. For example, d often represents some subset of the action elements or aspects of the action outcome such as input or output quantities. If d represents output quantities, as it frequently does, we term $R^C(\theta, d)$ the cost of output schedule d, given parameter value θ. Fundamentally, the cost refers to the actions necessary to produce the output, but we casually refer to it as the cost of the outputs themselves.

Specification of the cost function $R^C(\cdot)$ implicitly involves specification of a utility function and a cost component outcome function. Both are likely to be simplified. For example, the objective function is often based on the implicit assumption that the decision maker's preferences can be expressed as a linear func-

---

based on the information). The unprocessed observations clearly define a finer partition on the state space than does the processed information.

If y^1 denotes the unprocessed observations, $\eta^2(y^1) = y^2$ the processed information, and z the payoff relevant description of the state, $\eta^2(y^1)$ is a sufficient statistic with respect to y^1 and z if $\phi(z \mid y^1) = \phi(z \mid \eta^2(y^1))$. (See DeGroot 1970.) In that case, η^2 has processed y^1 in accordance with the decision maker's beliefs and will result in the same expected utility.

tion of the discounted cash flow. This ignores risk aversion, but it often greatly simplifies the analysis. The linearity assumption is essential, for example, if linear programming models are to be used. It also allows us to eliminate invariant cash flows and to use incremental analysis without making further simplifying assumptions. Consequently, the costs used in linear programming models include only cash flows that vary with the decision variables.

The cost component outcome function implicit in $R^C(\cdot)$ is often simplified in two ways. First, the outcome description is simplified by excluding some elements that would be necessary to provide a payoff adequate description.[17] For example, future cash flows may be excluded because the decision maker believes that the impact of current production on those cash flows is relatively insignificant. Second, the relationship between the action and the outcome description may be simplified (this usually entails replacement of the state description with a few simple parameters). A common example is the extensive use of linear cost functions that ignore the complex relationship between actions and costs.

Specification of the decision variable and the constraint set is not normally viewed as cost assessment, but we should recognize the link between these specifications and specification of the cost function. In particular, the constraints may exclude "feasible" decisions merely because the decision maker chooses to assume that they are "undesirable"—in a simplified analysis the exclusion of alternatives eliminates the need to specify their cost.[18] For example, the decision maker does not need to specify the cost of operating a second shift if the constraints restrict production to those levels that can be accomplished with one shift.

Alternatively, cost assessment may be made more complex by decision model simplifications that exclude some decision variable elements (that is, horizontal elimination). For example, the back-order cost in inventory models is difficult to assess, as it should reflect the impact of stockouts on the cash flows associated with production and marketing decisions (which have been excluded from the model).

In summary, once we admit to analysis simplification we must recognize that the decision maker faces many cost assessment alternatives in specifying his decision model. He must select the domain of the cost function as well as specify the function. In specifying the function he must select the outcome description to be used, the form of the functional relationship between his decision variable and that outcome, and the utility function defined over the outcome.

3.2 PARAMETER PREDICTION ROLE

In addition to specifying the form of the cost function, the decision maker must predict its parameter values. The prediction is represented by the probability function $\phi(\theta)$ but that function need not fully reflect the decision maker's beliefs.

---

17. As in a complete analysis, the distinction between the benefit and cost component outcome is arbitrary—it is the total outcome description that is important. However, exclusion of some outcome elements from the cost function may mean that they are excluded entirely.

18. In a complete analysis we would control for this vertical elimination by computing an opportunity cost (see section 2.1.3 above).

It too may be simplified. For example, cost parameters are often treated as deterministic even though the decision maker does not believe that he knows them with certainty.

Furthermore, revision of the prediction upon the receipt of information $(\phi(\theta \mid y, \eta))$ need not conform to Bayes's theorem. For example, prediction of the variable overhead rate per hour is often based on the analysis of historical observations of overhead and direct labor hours. This analysis may be as simple as account classification or as complex as least squares regression analysis, but Bayesian regression is seldom employed.

Obviously, once we admit to analysis simplification we must recognize that the decision maker's cost assessment alternatives include alternative methods for predicting cost function parameters. Moreover, the prediction method selected may influence his selection of the form of the cost function. For example, if the decision maker assumes the cost function is linear, account classification is not likely to change that assumption, but regression analysis might result in a change if it indicates the existence of nonlinearities.

3.3 THE INFORMATIVE ROLE

Information system alternatives are an important source of cost assessment alternatives in both complete and simplified analyses. However, the impact of different systems is likely to be more pervasive in a simplified analysis. In addition to influencing the parameter predictions, information may influence the form of the cost function and the constraint set. (This impact is represented by Equation [3.8].)

If the information evaluator and the decision maker are separate individuals, the evaluator's prediction of the action that will result from a particular cost signal will reflect his prediction of the signal's impact on both the decision maker's model and his parameter predictions. This impact will no doubt depend on the decision maker's beliefs about the procedures used to provide a particular signal. Consequently, if he is not selecting the procedure, it may be useful to indicate the cost assessment procedure used in determining a particular cost signal. The accountant's use of adjectives such as "direct," "standard," and "fifo" are obviously attempts to succinctly convey the major aspects of a particular cost assessment procedure.

Moreover, under simplified analysis, alternative processing procedures represent an important source of cost assessment alternatives. In evaluating these alternatives the evaluator must consider the cost of processing by the information system, the cost of analysis by the decision maker, and the outcome that will result from the decision maker's actions. Additional processing of basic data is likely to increase the cost of the information system but may also provide benefits either by reducing the decision maker's cost of analysis or by improving his decisions. Reduction of the cost of analysis will occur if the information system carries out processing the decision maker would have done anyway. Improved decisions may result, for example, if the processed data make it easier for the decision maker to identify and predict the reaction of costs to different action alternatives. If too much detail is reported, the decision maker may simply ignore what is reported; on the other hand, he might give careful consideration to an aggregate description of that detail. Some aggregate descriptions may induce better decisions than others, and the evaluator should evaluate his cost alternatives accordingly.

This completes our general discussion of the role of cost assessment in facilitating decisions. Subsequent chapters more fully examine this role and the evaluation of alternative assessments. We now briefly consider the role of cost assessment in influencing the decisions of subordinates.

4.0 THE ROLE OF COST ASSESSMENT IN INFLUENCING DECISIONS

The influencing role of cost assessment occurs when the decision maker delegates some subset of his action choice problem to a subordinate and then attempts to *influence* what that subordinate does. The classical example of this phenomenon occurs when a departmental manager is given relatively complete autonomy and his superior relies on an incentive system to motivate him in a desired manner. The incentive system is usually based, in part, on a departmental performance measure, and that measure usually includes cost assessment.

A framework for evaluating alternative performance measures is provided by our basic information evaluation model if we explicitly recognize the existence of secondary actions and their selection by a separate manager. In this case, the outcome is a function of the decision maker's action (a) and system (η) choices, and the manager's action choice (**a**). The decision maker's selection of a and η encompasses selection of the manager's performance measure, and the signal received by the manager (**y**) includes information on how his performance will be measured. The manager's action, in turn, is a function of the decision maker's action, the signal received, and the information system ($\mathbf{a} = \alpha(a, \mathbf{y}, \eta)$).

Observe that the influencing role of a performance measure is accomplished by informing the manager prior to his action selection as to how his performance will be measured. It is the manager's anticipation of that measure and its impact on *his* payoff relevant outcome that influences his actual selection.[19] (Of course, the actual performance measure may also confirm to the manager that his performance will be measured in the prescribed manner in the future.)

The impact of the actual performance measure on the decision maker's outcome is reflected in the $p\left(s, \left(\begin{smallmatrix} a \\ \mathbf{a} \end{smallmatrix}\right), \eta\right)$ outcome function. The decision maker's outcome might, for example, consist of the firm's cash flow, net of bonus and salary payments to the manager. However, explicit recognition of the actual performance measure is necessary only if we posit a multiperiod setting. In that context,

---

19. These outcomes may be in the form of tangible rewards, such as salary, or intangibles, such as good relations with his superior.

the actual performance measure provides information that may affect the future decisions of both the decision maker and the manager.[20]

There is *no* unique performance measure for any given situation. The decision maker's preferences are, with our assumptions, represented by his expected utility measure. In determining this measure, however, we recognize that the secondary action is chosen not by the decision maker but by the manager.[21] Thus a need not be chosen in a manner deemed optimal by the decision maker. This, in turn, gives rise to the question of precisely which system and action choices will be made. Cooperative behavior is possible, of course; and Pareto optimality may be observed.[22] Alternatively, noncooperative behavior may be present; indeed informational discrepancies between the decision maker and manager may give rise to "bluffing" or "cheating" behavior.[23]

In any event, cost assessment is often involved both in informing the manager as to how his performance will be measured and in actually measuring it. A common example of the first type is the development of a flexible overhead budget for the manager's department. The budget informs the manager of the expenditures for which he has responsibility (but not necessarily authority!) and the acceptable expenditure level for each possible activity level. An example of the second type is the measurement of "actual" departmental overhead and its comparison to the budgeted overhead.[24]

There are numerous alternative cost assessments that may be used in measuring managerial performance. A basic source of alternatives is the types of costs included in that measure. The accounting literature stresses the need to focus on those costs that are "controllable" by the manager, but the controllable/uncontrollable distinction is often difficult to apply.[25] A second source of alternatives is the method used to assign particular costs to particular departments and their managers. For example, there are many alternative methods for assigning the cost of goods or services obtained from other departments.

Other alternatives arise in the context of developing standards such as the flexible overhead budget. Standards are usually a function of some measure(s) of activity and there are alternative activity measures that can be used. For example, flexible overhead budgets are often expressed as functions of direct labor hours, but other activity measures, such as direct labor cost, machine hours, output produced, and material processed, could be used. The form of the functional rela-

---

20. These issues are explored at length in Demski (1972b).

21. And any uncertainty about the manager's behavior would be reflected in an expanded state variable.

22. This approach is followed by Wilson (1969a). Application of Wilson's framework can be found in Ross (1973) and Demski (1976).

23. See Akerlof (1970), Ponssard and Zamir (1973), Baiman (1974), Groves (1974), and Groves and Loeb (1975).

24. Itami (1975) has recently analyzed some of the behavior pathologies that may be produced by this type of conventional performance measure.

25. Use of this distinction may also lead to nonoptimal decisions because it may preclude beneficial risk sharing between the manager and the decision maker. See Demski (1976).

tionship between the cost and the activity measure constitutes another source of alternatives. Most standards are expressed as simple linear functions consisting of a fixed cost and a variable cost per unit of activity, but other functional forms may be used.[26]

Finally, there are alternative methods for establishing the function and its parameters. Some may be directly specified by the decision maker, perhaps reflecting his personal belief as to how much a department should be allowed to spend in a particular area such as research and development.[27] Others may be based on engineering studies of the products being produced or participatively agreed upon by the decision maker and the manager. Many are based on an analysis of historical data.

In concluding this section we remind the reader that all these cost assessment alternatives may be viewed as information system alternatives. Three implications emerge. First, the most preferred set of alternatives may be expressed as that which has the largest expected utility measure, where that measure reflects both the cost of implementing the selected alternatives and the outcome from both the decision maker's and manager's actions. Second, the manager's actions are a function of his perceptions of the outcomes (that are relevant to his preferences) that will result from his actions; and if these outcomes depend upon the performance measures used, then his actions are likely to be *influenced by* information as to *how that performance will be measured*. Third, although we address the evaluation of alternative cost assessments from the decision maker's (or evaluator's) point of view, the multiperson character of the setting is readily apparent.

5.0   SUMMARY

Cost is a common, popular term denoting the sacrifice associated with some object. We use the term "cost assessment" to refer to both the description of that sacrifice and the procedure used to determine it. Costs are fundamentally the result of actions and we have seen that their assessment may be used both to facilitate and to influence the selection of actions. In both cases, numerous cost assessment alternatives are available; and we have demonstrated that comparison of alternative assessments may be conceptually reduced to a comparison of alternative information systems.

Cost assessment may play three major roles in facilitating decisions, and the availability of alternatives in each role depends on whether the decision analysis is complete or simplified. The first role is the specification of the cost component of the outcome or objective function defined over the action alternatives. In a complete analysis the outcome function must fully reflect the decision maker's

---

26. For example, the budgeted labor cost may be expressed as kz^b (where $k > 0$, $b < 1$, and z is the total output) in order to reflect the "learning" that takes place as more output is produced. See Baloff and Kennelly (1967) for a discussion of the implications of the learning curve phenomenon for accounting.

27. Horngren (1972) refers to these as "discretionary" costs.

beliefs about the outcome elements affecting his preferences. Consequently, although alternative cost assessments may result from alternative outcome descriptions or alternative benefit/cost distinctions, they are effectively identical in that they must all result in the same action selections. On the other hand, if we admit to analysis simplification, we may consider a wide variety of cost functions, some of which may result in widely varying action selections.

The second role of cost assessment concerns the cost information transmitted to the decision maker. This includes both historical cost assessments and other information that may affect the decision maker's prediction of the state or parameters of the cost function specified above. There is no cost information that must be provided, and different information may produce different action selections in the context of both complete and simplified analyses. The impact of these alternatives is likely to be more pervasive if the decision maker's analysis is simplified; if the analysis is simplified the information may affect the form of the cost function and the set of decision variables as well as the parameter predictions.

The third role is the processing of the cost information to obtain the prediction of the cost function state or parameters. There are no alternatives in a complete analysis, the processing must be in accordance with Bayes's theorem. On the other hand, many processing alternatives may be considered within the context of a simplified analysis.

To gain further insight into the conceptual nature of these cost assessment alternatives, consider the viable assessment possibilities as we move between use of complete or simplified analysis in a world of subjective certainty to one of uncertainty. If, in a subjectively certain setting, the decision maker's model is completely specified, there can be no cost assessment (or information) alternatives whatever. The unique consequence of every action is known, and the only problem is one of computation. Suppose, however, that the model is simplified to ease the computational burden. This moves us to the case of a simplified model under conditions of subjective certainty. Cost assessment alternatives may appear here, but they will be limited to alternative cost functions. Information and prediction are not issues in a certain world.

It is only with movement to the uncertain case that we encounter a role for historical measures and processing methods. If the analysis is complete, variations in cost information provide cost assessment alternatives through their impact on the state probabilities. But cost function or prediction alternatives do not exist because the model is completely specified, including the method for assimilating information. However, simplification of the uncertain model opens up the possibility of variation in all three facets. Thus, in the decision-facilitating case, cost assessment alternatives are potentially most numerous in a simplified uncertain situation. Table 4.5 summarizes the cases.

A number of cost assessment alternatives also exist in decision-influencing contexts. They are similar to those in decision facilitating but have a different focus in that cost assessment is used here to influence a subordinate's actions. This is accomplished by providing information to the subordinate that affects his beliefs about the outcomes (relevant to him) that will result from his actions. This information may take the form of performance standards, descriptions of mea-

TABLE 4.5 SOURCES OF COST ASSESSMENT ALTERNATIVES
          FOR FACILITATING DECISIONS

| | | Method of Decision Analysis | |
		Complete	Simplified
State	Certain	None	Cost Function
	Uncertain	Cost Information	Cost Function Prediction Method Cost Information

sures to be used in evaluating his performance, and past performance measures. Cost function and prediction method alternatives arise in the context of specifying standards. Alternative historical cost assessment procedures arise in specifying how a subordinate's performance will be measured and in specifying the information that will be used in developing standards.

5

INPUT AND OUTPUT COST FUNCTIONS

This chapter extends our general discussion of the assessment of the cost of actions to the assessment of the cost of inputs and outputs. The basic choice problem (expressed in the state-action-outcome paradigm) is modified so that specification of the action cost calls for the construction of input and output cost functions. This provides a basis for considering issues that arise in product costing.

The role of inputs and outputs in cost assessment is often that of intermediate variables. For example, prediction of the cost of an action is often based on a prediction of the inputs required to carry out that action and a prediction of the cost of those inputs. We term these intermediate variables *cost statistics* and in section 1 we develop conditions sufficient to permit construction of action cost functions based on separately determined functions relating actions to cost statistics and cost statistics to cost component outcomes.

In section 2 we consider the use of inputs as cost statistics. This provides a basis for discussing the familiar direct/indirect cost distinctions, as well as the nature of material, labor, and equipment usage costs. The exploration is then extended, in section 3, to the use of outputs as objects of costing. We consider output both as a cost statistic and as an object of choice (as in the classical theory of the firm). Finally, in section 4 we consider cost statistics, such as those associated with learning effects, that are neither inputs nor outputs.

Throughout the chapter we focus on general production decisions. Appendix 5.1 elaborates on the nature of these decisions, and Appendix 5.2 briefly relates our analysis to the analysis of production decisions in microeconomic theory.

1.0   COST STATISTICS

Although the basic discussion of cost assessment in Chapter 4 underlies our approach to choice among cost assessment alternatives, it does not explicitly reflect many of the cost assessments with which we are familiar. Rather than abstract notions of action costs, we are more familiar with the costs of inputs (for example, direct materials) and outputs (for example, finished goods). A basis for discussing input and output costs is provided by appropriately modifying our basic choice problem.

If the utility measure associated with the action alternatives is divided into benefit and cost components, specification of the cost component may be viewed as a two-stage process. The first stage is the prediction of the *cost statistics* (for example, the inputs used or outputs produced) that will result from each action. The second stage is the prediction of the cost (component outcome) of those cost statistics.

This two-stage process is a modification of our basic decision problem if appropriate separability conditions are satisfied and the cost statistic reflects all aspects of the primary action that affect the cost component outcome. These requirements essentially combine those assumed in Propositions 4.1 and 3.5. Proposition 4.1 provides a set of separability conditions that permit expression of the expected utility measure as the difference between an expected benefit and an expected cost. Proposition 3.5 establishes that a payoff and forecast adequate statistic may be used as an intermediate variable in the development of an action's utility measure.

In combining these requirements we must recognize that some suppressed secondary actions, such as input acquisition activities, affect the cost of the cost statistic. Consequently, in a complete analysis the cost statistic must reflect those aspects of the primary action that affect the set of feasible secondary actions incorporated in the cost of that statistic. A cost statistic that reflects these aspects and is both payoff and forecast adequate is termed a *sufficient cost statistic*. (A sufficient benefit statistic may be defined in an analogous manner.) Details are summarized in Table 5.1 and Figure 5.1.

We now consider the input and output cost functions to which this type of modification gives rise.

2.0   INPUT COST FUNCTIONS

Inputs are productive factors consumed by the production process. They are important objects of costing, since many decision analyses determine the costs of alternative production activities by focusing on the costs of the inputs used in that production. From our discussion in section 1 we know that, given the appropriate separability conditions, such modifications are possible if the inputs provide a sufficient cost statistic for that action (and the input cost function is determined in the manner specified in Table 5.1). In this section we explore the nature of input cost functions under these assumptions.

In the discussion that follows, we first use the cost statistic notion to differ-

TABLE 5.1   SUPPRESSION OF SECONDARY ACTIONS IN THE
CONSTRUCTION OF SEPARABLE COST FUNCTIONS

Consider the following separability conditions:

(i)   Outcome function separability:

$$p\left(s,\binom{a}{a},\eta\right) = (x^B, x^C) = p^B\left((s_\delta, s_B),\binom{a}{a_B},\eta\right), p^C\left((s_\delta, s_C),\binom{a}{a_C},\eta\right)$$

where a_B is the secondary benefit action,

a_C is the secondary cost action, and

$s = (s_\delta, s_B, s_C)$, and $S = S_\delta \times S_B \times S_C$;

(ii)   Secondary action set separability:

$$A(a) = A_B(a) \times A_C(a); \text{ and}$$

(iii)   Utility function separability:

$$U(x) = B(x^B) - C(x^C).$$

Further divide the secondary cost action into two components $a_C = \binom{a_{C1}}{a_{C2}}$ such that a_{C1} affects the level of cost statistic δ_C associated with the primary action and a_{C2} affects the cost of that cost statistic. (These relationships are depicted in Figure 5.1.) $\delta_C\left(s_\delta, \binom{a}{a_{C1}}, .\right)$ defines a *sufficient cost statistic* if it is

(iv)   Payoff adequate for $x^{C:}$[1]

$$p^C\left((s_\delta, s_C),\binom{a}{a_C},\eta\right) = p^C(s_C, \delta_C(\cdot), a_{C2}, \eta);$$

(v)   Forecast adequate for s_C:[1]

$$\phi(s_C \mid s_\delta, y, \eta) = \phi(s_C \mid \delta_C(\cdot), y, \eta); \text{ and}$$

(vi)   Circumscribes the set of feasible secondary actions:

$$A_{C2}\binom{a}{a_{C1}} = \left\{a_{C2} \mid \binom{a_{C1}}{a_{C2}} \in A_C(a)\right\}$$
$$= A_{C2}(\delta_C(\cdot)).$$

We now construct:

$$E(C \mid \delta_C, y, \eta) = \min_{a_{C2} \in A_{C2}(\delta_C)} \left[\sum_{s_C \in S_C} C(p^C(s_C, \delta_C, a_{C2}, \eta))\, \phi(s_C \mid \delta_C, y, \eta)\right]$$

and

$$E(C \mid a, y, \eta) = \min_{a_{C1} \in A_{C1}(a)} \left[\sum_{s_\delta \in S_\delta} E\left(C \mid \delta_C\left(s_\delta, \binom{a}{a_{C1}}, \eta\right), y, \eta\right) \phi(s_\delta \mid y, \eta)\right]$$

where

$$A_{C1}(a) = \left\{a_{C1} \mid \binom{a_{C1}}{a_{C2}} \in A_C(a), \text{ any } a_{C2}\right\}.$$

1. Defined in Chapter 3.

Continued on next page

TABLE 5.1 *(Continued)*

Proposition 5.1:

Consider the basic choice problem in Equation [2.2] and let the maximum uniquely exist. The above separability conditions, coupled with a sufficient cost statistic known at the time a_{C2} is selected, will allow optimization of the following modified model to identify the optimal action:

$$E(U \mid a, y, \eta) = E(B \mid a, y, \eta) - E(C \mid a, y, \eta)$$

where $E(C \mid a, y, \eta)$ is constructed in the indicated manner.

Proof:

From conditions (i) to (iii) and Proposition 4.1 we have

$$E(U \mid a, y, \eta) = E(B \mid a, y, \eta) - E(C \mid a, y, \eta)$$

with

$E(C \mid a, y, \eta)$

$$= \min_{a_C \in A_C(a)} \left[\sum_{(s_\delta, s_C) \in S_\delta \times S_C} C\left(p^C\left((s_\delta, s_C), \binom{a}{a_C} \right), \eta \right) \phi(s_C \mid s_\delta, y, \eta) \phi(s_\delta \mid y, \eta) \right]$$

$$= \min_{a_{C1} \in A_{C1}(a)} \left[\sum_{s_\delta \in S_\delta} \left\{ \min_{a_{C2} \in A_{C2}\binom{a}{a_{C1}}} \left(\sum_{s_C \in S_C} C\left(p^C\left((s_\delta, s_C), \binom{a}{a_{C1}}{a_{C2}} \right), \eta \right) \cdot \right. \right. \right.$$
$$\left. \left. \left. \phi(s_C \mid s_\delta, y, \eta) \right) \right\} \phi(s_\delta \mid y, \eta) \right]$$

$$= \min_{a_{C1} \in A_{C1}(a)} \left[\sum_{s_\delta \in S_\delta} E\left(C \mid \delta_C\left(s_\delta, \binom{a}{a_{C1}} \right), \eta \right), y, \eta \right) \phi(s_\delta \mid y, \eta) \right]$$

by sufficiency of $\delta_C(\cdot)$ and Propositions 3.1 and 3.5.

---

entiate between direct and indirect inputs. This is followed by development of an input cost framework that separates the cost of an input into outlay and externality cost components. This framework is then used to explore some of the important factors that underlie determination of the cost of material, labor, and machine hours in appropriately modified analyses.

2.1 DIRECT AND INDIRECT INPUTS

Most firms use a wide variety of externally acquired and internally produced inputs, and that usage is influenced by many of the firm's production decisions. However, the cost statistic for a particular production decision need not include every input whose usage or acquisition the decision affects. Rather, an input need be included only if it is necessary for describing the impact of the primary action

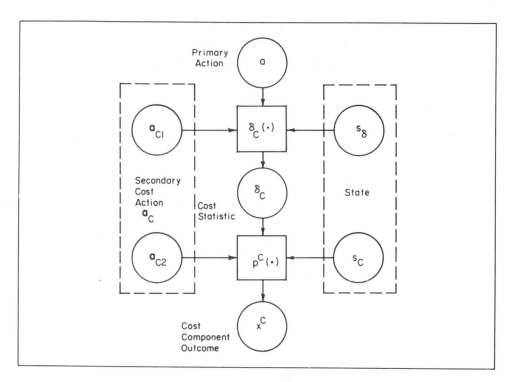

Fig. 5.1. Elements of a separable cost statistic cost function.

on the cost component outcome or the set of feasible secondary actions. We define the *direct inputs* to be those inputs that are included in the cost statistic of a particular analysis. Those excluded from the cost statistic are termed *indirect inputs*.[1]

Since the cost statistic for a particular analysis is not unique, this direct/indirect distinction is not unique. Furthermore, the types of inputs classified as direct are likely to differ from one decision situation to another. For example, the inputs classified as direct in a personnel department decision might be classified as indirect in many production decisions.

In exploring the cost of direct inputs in subsequent sections, we make three additional assumptions to facilitate exposition. First, we ignore other possible statistic elements and assume that the direct inputs provide a sufficient cost statistic. Second, although, in general, use of inputs as a sufficient cost statistic might call for a variety of representation forms, we assume that the direct inputs can be represented by a finite vector of nonnegative real numbers: $q = (q_1, \ldots, q_m)$, where q_j is the quantity used of input j. Finally, extending the separability conditions in Proposition 5.1 to each of the direct inputs, we assume that the input

---

1. Observe that this definition merely discriminates between input categories. In the extreme, all inputs might be classified as indirect because the cost statistic contains no elements that we would care to call an input. On the other hand, all acquired inputs are treated as direct in the classical microeconomic model (see Appendix 5.2).

TABLE 5.2   SEPARABLE DIRECT INPUT COST FUNCTIONS

Assume that the antecedents to Proposition 5.1 are satisfied and that m direct inputs, $(q_1, \ldots, q_m)$, provide a sufficient cost statistic. Further assume that the cost component outcome and secondary cost component actions are separable with respect to these m statistics:

$$p^C(s_C, q, \mathbf{a}_{C2}, \eta) = (x^{C1}, \ldots, x^{Cm}) = (p^{C1}(s_{C1}, q_1, \mathbf{a}_{21}, \eta), \ldots, p^{Cm}(s_{Cm}, q_m, \mathbf{a}_{2m}, \eta))$$

and

$$A_{C2}(q) = A_{21}(q_1) \times \cdots \times A_{2m}(q_m)$$

where $s_C = (s_{C1}, \ldots, s_{Cm})$ and $\mathbf{a}_{C2} = \begin{pmatrix} \mathbf{a}_{21} \\ \vdots \\ \mathbf{a}_{2m} \end{pmatrix}$.

If, in addition, the cost function is separable by inputs,

$$C(x^C) = \sum_{j=1}^{m} C_j(x^{Cj}),$$

repeated application of Proposition 5.1 provides an input cost function that is the sum of m *separately determined direct input cost functions*:

$$E(C_j \mid q_j, y, \eta) = \min_{\mathbf{a}_{2j} \in A_{2j}(q_j)} \left[\sum_{s_{Cj} \in S_{Cj}} C_j(p^{Cj}(s_{Cj}, q_j, \mathbf{a}_{2j}, \eta)) \phi(s_{Cj} \mid q_j, y, \eta) \right]$$

and

$$E(C \mid q, y, \eta) = \sum_{j=1}^{m} E(C_j \mid q_j, y, \eta).$$

cost function can be expressed as the sum of m separately constructed functions, one for each direct input. Details are summarized in Table 5.2.

2.2   AN INPUT COST FRAMEWORK

The cost of inputs used represents the impact of input usage on all elements of the cost component outcome. In assessing this cost, however, we divide it into two parts. The first includes any expenditures required to acquire (or produce) the inputs used; and the second includes any "side effect" of that usage. We refer to the first as the *outlay cost* and, employing the terminology in Equation [4.1], the second as the *externality cost* (or benefit). For example, the price paid to purchase an input is an outlay cost, while the impact of using an input from inventory is an externality cost.[2]

---

2. Coase (1968) stresses these two aspects in his discussion of the nature of cost; and further discussion is available in Arrow (1971) and Starrett (1972). Also note that, contrary to the development in Equation [4.1], we have not yet stated the externality component in incremental terms. This is accomplished in Equation [5.2] where we modify the input cost development to an incremental format.

To explore the nature of these two costs we consider a single direct input category and divide both the cost component outcome (x^C) and the input cost activities (denoted $\mathbf{a}_{C2}$ in Figure 5.1) into outlay and externality subcomponents $\left(\text{that is, } x^C = (x^{C1}, x^{C2}) \text{ and } \mathbf{a}_{C2} = \begin{pmatrix} \mathbf{a}_{21} \\ \mathbf{a}_{22} \end{pmatrix}\right)$. The outlay component outcome (x^{C1}) represents those elements associated with input acquisitions induced by direct input usage. The input cost activities associated with that outcome are termed *primary input activities* ($\mathbf{a}_{21}$). Similarly, the externality component outcome (x^{C2}) represents those elements associated with production and marketing of secondary outputs during current and future periods. The input cost activities associated with that outcome are termed *secondary activities* ($\mathbf{a}_{22}$).

We now formulate a *sufficient secondary cost statistic* (denoted δ_2) that reflects those aspects of direct input usage affecting the externality cost. These include both input availability and acquisition effects. The input availability effect arises because inputs not used in primary production may be used in secondary production. For some inputs, such as electrical power and labor services, that availability is restricted to the current period in that they cannot be stored in any ordinary sense. Other inputs, such as raw materials, may be stored, so that those not used in primary production are available for either current or future secondary production.

Acquisition effects are essentially of two types. First, primary acquisition activities may affect the prices paid for secondary inputs. For example, a supplier may offer quantity discounts based on the volume of inputs acquired during a time interval that covers more than the current acquisition period. Second, primary acquisition activities may affect the inputs used in carrying out secondary acquisition activities. For example, while labor services must be acquired each period, the activities of the personnel department will be lessened if an individual was hired in some prior period or for some other use. Similarly, more purchasing department effort may be required in the acquisition of new rather than previously acquired types of materials.

Table 5.3 and Figure 5.2 present the modification that produces this outlay-

TABLE 5.3 INPUT COST MODEL

Assume that the antecedents to Proposition 5.1 are satisfied with q a sufficient cost statistic. Further assume that

    (i)   the cost component outcome function is divided into outlay and externality components,

$$x^C = (x^{C1}, x^{C2}) = p^C(s_C, q, \mathbf{a}_{C2}, \eta)$$

$$= \left(p^{C1}(s_{C1}, q, \mathbf{a}_{21}, \eta), p^{C2}\left((s_{C1}, s_{C2}), q, \begin{pmatrix} \mathbf{a}_{21} \\ \mathbf{a}_{22} \end{pmatrix}, \eta \right) \right)$$

where $s_C = (s_{C1}, s_{C2})$ and $\mathbf{a}_{C2} = \begin{pmatrix} \mathbf{a}_{21} \\ \mathbf{a}_{22} \end{pmatrix}$;

Continued on next page

TABLE 5.3 *(Continued)*

(ii) the cost function is separable,

$$C(x^C) = C_1(x^{C1}) + C_2(x^{C2});$$

(iii) $\delta_2(s_{C1}, q, \mathbf{a}_{21}, \eta)$ defines a sufficient secondary cost statistic,

$$p^{C2}\left((s_{C1}, s_{C2}), q, \binom{\mathbf{a}_{21}}{\mathbf{a}_{22}}, \eta\right) = p^{C2}(s_{C2}, \delta_2(\cdot), \mathbf{a}_{22}, \eta)$$

$$\phi(s_{C2} \mid s_{C1}, y, \eta) = \phi(s_{C2} \mid \delta_2(\cdot), y, \eta)$$

$$\left\{\mathbf{a}_{22} \mid \binom{\mathbf{a}_{21}}{\mathbf{a}_{22}} \in A_{C2}(q)\right\} = A_{22}(\delta_2(\cdot)).$$

Then Proposition 5.1 provides that a modified input cost function may be expressed as the sum of outlay and externality costs, provided $\delta_2(\cdot)$ is known when $\mathbf{a}_{22}$ is selected:

$$E(C \mid q, y, \eta) = E(C_1 \mid q, y, \eta) + E(C_2 \mid q, y, \eta)$$

where the *outlay cost* is

$$E(C_1 \mid q, y, \eta) = \sum_{s_{C1} \in S_{C1}} C_1(p^{C1}(s_{C1}, q, \alpha_{21}(q, y, \eta), \eta)) \phi(s_{C1} \mid \dot{q}, y, \eta)$$

and the *externality cost* is

$$E(C_2 \mid q, y, \eta) = \sum_{s_{C1} \in S_{C1}} E(C_2 \mid \delta_2(s_{C1}, q, \alpha_{21}(q, y, \eta), \eta), y, \eta) \phi(s_{C1} \mid q, y, \eta)$$

with

$$E(C_2 \mid \delta_2, y, \eta) = \sum_{s_{C2} \in S_{C2}} C_2(p^{C2}(s_{C2}, \delta_2, \alpha_{22}(\delta_2, y, \eta), \eta)) \phi(s_{C2} \mid \delta_2, y, \eta)$$

where $\alpha_{22}(\delta_2, y, \eta)$ is the secondary activity that satisfies,

$$E(C_2 \mid \delta_2, y, \eta) = \min_{\mathbf{a}_{22} \in A_{22}(\delta_2)} \left[\sum_{s_{C2} \in S_{C2}} C_2(p^{C2}(s_{C2}, \delta_2, \mathbf{a}_{22}, \eta)) \phi(s_{C2} \mid \delta_2, y, \eta)\right]$$

and $\alpha_{21}(q, y, \eta)$ is the primary input activity that satisfies,

$$E(C \mid q, y, \eta) = \min_{\mathbf{a}_{21} \in A_{21}(q)} \left[\sum_{s_{C1} \in S_{C1}} \left\{C_1(p^{C1}(s_{C1}, q, \mathbf{a}_{21}, \eta)) \right.\right.$$
$$\left.\left. + E(C_2 \mid \delta_2(s_{C1}, q, \mathbf{a}_{21}, \eta), y, \eta)\right\} \phi(s_{C1} \mid q, y, \eta)\right]$$

with $A_{21}(q) = \left\{\mathbf{a}_{21} \mid \binom{\mathbf{a}_{21}}{\mathbf{a}_{22}} \in A_{C2}(q), \text{ any } \mathbf{a}_{22}\right\}.$

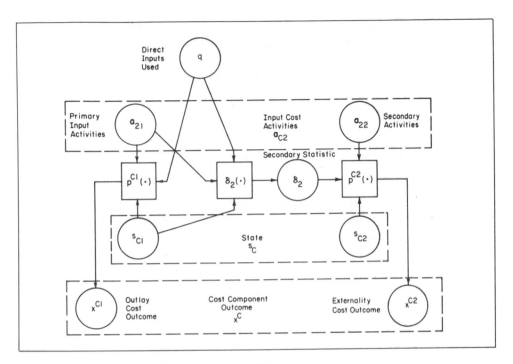

Fig. 5.2. Major elements of the input cost model.

externality cost paradigm. Observe that the secondary activities do not directly affect the outlay cost; rather, their effect is indirect via the effect of the primary input activities on the externality cost and feasible secondary activities.[3]

In applying this framework to specific input categories, we adopt the additional assumption that the cost component outcome is a vector of date and state indexed cash outflows[4] and that the input cost function is merely the market value (present value) of those cash outflows. As noted in Chapter 3, this modification (when available) requires that only incremental cash flows need be considered. This allows us to conveniently exclude all irrelevant cost component elements by letting the (modified) cost component outcome equal the difference between the gross cost component cash outflows for a given input level and the gross cost component cash outflows for the *least cost* input level (denoted q^0 with associated secondary action $\mathbf{a}_{C2}^0$). That is, if $\hat{p}^C(\cdot)$ denotes the gross cost component cash outflows, then

[5.1] $$p^C(s_C, q, \mathbf{a}_{C2}, \eta) = \hat{p}^C(s_C, q, \mathbf{a}_{C2}, \eta) - \hat{p}^C(s_C, q^0, \mathbf{a}_{C2}^0, \eta)$$

---

3. This is a very reasonable assumption if all secondary activities occur in the future but may be somewhat restrictive if some secondary activities occur during the current period. If the secondary activities have a direct effect on the outlay cost, there is no point is dividing the input cost activities into subcomponents, and the approach in Table 5.1 should be used.

4. Inflows are negative outflows.

where q^0 is the least cost input level in a set of feasible inputs Q:

$$E(C \mid q^0, y, \eta) = \min_{q \in Q} E(C \mid q, y, \eta).$$

We now explore the cost of three common types of direct inputs: material, labor, and machine hours.[5]

2.3 DIRECT MATERIAL

A key element in determining cost of direct materials is construction of a material input description that constitutes (part of) a sufficient cost statistic. This is not a straightforward task.

In the cost accounting literature, *traceability* is often considered to be the basis on which one decides whether particular inputs are direct or indirect:

> The first step in production is the transfer of direct materials from a storeroom to a production center. Direct materials are all materials, parts, and subassemblies that are used in one particular job order. Indirect materials or supplies, on the other hand, are issued for general factory use and not for the specific benefit of any one job.

> These definitions are based on the traceability of the costs and not necessarily on the physical incorporation of the specific input into the end-product. Thus direct material costs of a large order for precision-ground lenses would include the costs of grinding materials that are used directly on the job, even though they are not physically incorporated in the finished product. They should be treated as overhead only if they cost too little to justify the clerical expense of tracing them to jobs. [Shillinglaw 1972, p. 92]

It appears that a particular type of material is considered to be traceable if the quantity of material associated with a particular object can be observed *ex post,* and it is worthwhile to do so.

The traceability criterion may be consistent with our definition of a direct input, but it probably does not go far enough. We require that the direct inputs include at least those input categories that are required, *ex ante,* to describe the impact of the primary action on the secondary actions and cash flows. This requirement is likely to result in more types of materials being classified as direct than the traceability criterion would select. For example, miscellaneous supplies, such as those used in machine maintenance, might be classified as indirect by the traceability criterion when they should be classified as direct inputs because their acquisition is affected by production differences not reflected by other elements of the cost statistic.

Another difficulty with the traceability criterion is that while it may indicate that some general type of input should be classified as direct, it does not indicate what categories should be used in describing that input. On the other hand, the cost statistic requirements do specify a minimal set of input categories. For

---

5. For a similar analysis of input costs see Schoenfeld (1974) for a discussion of Edmund Heinen's work in this area. Also see the AAA Committee on Cost Concepts and Standards (1956).

example, quality differences must be recognized if such differences affect the price paid for the materials and the amount of spoilage that occurs in production.

Once the requisite material input description has been established, we divide the direct material cost into two components: an incremental outlay cost and an externality cost (or benefit).

The Incremental Outlay Cost. A key element in the calculation of the incremental outlay cost is the identification of those indirect inputs whose acquisition is a function of the direct materials used. This indirect category is likely to include inputs acquired in order to accomplish the procurement, storage, and issuance of direct materials, that is, inputs used to operate the material inventory system.[6] Recognition of these costs in calculating the incremental outlay cost for material is illustrated by the following simple example.

A Direct Material Inventory Example. We assume that primary production uses a single type of material, that all the material for the current production period will be acquired during that period (there are no opening or closing inventories), and that subjective certainty prevails. The material is used at a constant rate over the production period and thus it is sufficient to know the total quantity that will be used during the period; this quantity is denoted q and the primary production may require between 0 and 1,000 units of that material, $Q = \{q \mid 0 \leq q \leq 1,000\}$.

The current acquisition activities include procurement, storage, and issuance activities and the alternative procurement procedures are represented by the number of orders that are placed during the production period. There are three alternatives: (i) acquire the entire period's requirements at the start of the period; (ii) acquire half the requirements at the start and the remainder half way through the period; and (iii) place four orders at equally spaced intervals throughout the period. Table 5.4 presents the incremental cash outflows associated with the procurement, storage,[7] and issuance activities and the present value of those cash outflows that would result from each of the three procurement procedures for a given level of input. The cost of providing input q (which is equivalent to the incremental outlay cost in this example) is the *minimum* of these three present values. Figure 5.3 depicts the cost function.

The Impact of Externalities. The above example assumes that all material purchased in the current period is used in primary production. This assumption (plus the absence of other externalities) means that the material cost is equivalent to the incremental outlay cost. The cost calculation becomes somewhat more complex if we admit the existence of other uses for currently acquired materials.

---

6. Optimal, cost minimizing, inventory policies are discussed in a number of texts; for example, see Hadley and Whitin (1963) and Buffa (1968).

7. Many inventory models, such as the traditional economic order quantity model, include the cost of "capital tied up in inventory" as part of the storage cost. However, in a complete analysis, there is no need to introduce a special cost for this item; it is taken into consideration by the fact that we evaluate all cash flows in terms of their present value and earlier acquisition results in earlier payments for these materials.

TABLE 5.4 DIRECT MATERIAL INVENTORY EXAMPLE

Alternative Primary Input Quantities:

$A_{21}(q) = \{q, q/2, q/4\}$, where a_{21} denotes the order quantity.

Cash Flows:

Procurement: Purchase price, transportation, order processing, receiving, and payment processing (payable at the time the order is received) ..... $150.00 per order ; $10.50 per unit

Storage: Warehouse rental (payable now) ..... $80.00 per 100 units of capacity

Heat, light, etc. (1/4 payable at the end of each quarter period) ..... $40.00 per 100 units of capacity

Issuance: Requisition processing (payable at the end of each quarter period) ..... $0.80 per unit

Outcome Function:[1]

$$p^{C1}(\hat{s}_{C1}, q, a_{21}, \eta) = (x_0^{C1}, x_1^{C1}, x_2^{C1}, x_3^{C1}, x_4^{C1})$$

where x_t^{C1} is the cash flow at time t ($t = 0$ is now and $t = 1, 2, 3, 4$ is the end of each quarter period).

a_{21}	q	$q/2$	$q/4$
x_0^{C1}	$150 + 10.5q + 80\,I(q/100)$	$150 + 5.25q + 80\,I(q/200)$	$150 + 2.625q + 80\,I(q/400)$
x_1^{C1}	$10\,I(q/100) + 0.2q$	$10\,I(q/200) + 0.2q$	$10\,I(q/400) + 2.825q + 150$
x_2^{C1}	same as x_1^{C1}	$10\,I(q/200) + 5.45q + 150$	same as x_1^{C1}
x_3^{C1}	same as x_1^{C1}	same as x_1^{C1}	same as x_1^{C1}

x_4^{C1}	same as x_1^{C1}	same as x_1^{C1}	$10\,I(q/400) + 0.2q$

Cost Function:

$$C_1(x^{C1}) = x_0^{C1} + 0.98x_1^{C1} + 0.96x_2^{C1} + 0.94x_3^{C1} + 0.92x_4^{C1}$$

(for example, 0.96 is the discount factor for cash paid at end of second quarter)

$$E(C\,|\,q, y, \eta) = \min_{\mathbf{a}_{21}\in A_{21}(q)}\ [C_1(p^{C1}(\pounds_{C1}, q, \mathbf{a}_{21}, \eta))]$$

$$= \min\begin{cases} 0 & \text{for} \quad q = 0 \\[4pt] \left\{\begin{array}{l} 150 + 11.26q + (118)I(q/100) \\ 294 + 11.05q + (118)I(q/200) \\ 582 + 10.945q + (118)I(q/400) \end{array}\right\} & \text{for} \quad 0 < q \le 1{,}000 \end{cases}$$

$$= \begin{cases} 0 & \text{for} \quad q = 0 \\ 150 + 11.26q + (118)I(q/100) & \text{for} \quad 0 < q \le 123 \\ 294 + 11.05q + (118)I(q/200) & \text{for} \quad 124 \le q \le 600 \\ 582 + 10.945q + (118)I(q/400) & \text{for} \quad 600 < q \le 1{,}000 \end{cases}$$

Optimal Procurement Decision:

$$\alpha_{21}(q, y, \eta) = \begin{cases} 0 & \text{for} \quad q = 0 \\ q & \text{for} \quad 0 < q \le 123 \\ q/2 & \text{for} \quad 124 \le q \le 600 \\ q/4 & \text{for} \quad 600 < q \le 1{,}000 \end{cases}$$

1. $I(k)$ denotes the smallest integer larger than or equal to k.

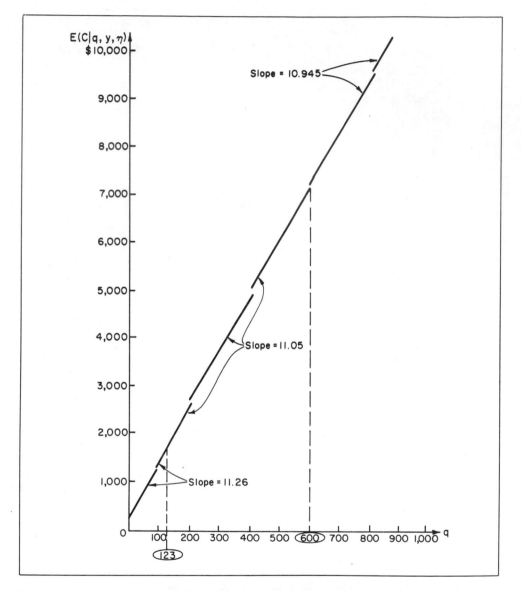

Fig. 5.3. Direct material cost. The different slopes correspond to different procurement procedures and the "steps" occur when it becomes necessary to increase warehouse capacity.

We now examine the impact of those possibilities and also explicitly recognize the possibility of opening inventories.

There are four basic responses the firm may make to the use of materials in primary production: increase current acquisitions, increase future acquisitions, reduce secondary production, or decrease disposals.

The first response, *increase current acquisitions,* affects the acquisition cash outflows and results in a material cost equivalent to the incremental outlay cost. This is the situation depicted in our example except that the acquisitions for use in primary production may be in addition to materials acquired for use in secondary production. For example, in Figure 5.3 the cost of acquiring 600 units of material is \$7,278, but that cost becomes \$6,931 if the firm plans to acquire 400 units of that material for use in current secondary production and will increase acquisitions to 1,000 units in order to supply 600 units for primary production.

The second response, *increase future acquisitions,* implies that current acquisitions are unaffected by primary production, and any unused material is stored and used in some subsequent period. Consequently, if material is used in current production, the firm must either increase future acquisitions or reduce future production. If future acquisitions are increased, the cost consists primarily of the discounted incremental cash outflows required to acquire the additional units in future periods.

The third response, *reduce secondary production,* implies that current acquisitions are unaffected by primary production and unused material is either used in current secondary production or stored and used in some subsequent period. The latter case is very similar to the second response, but now we assume that if the material is not carried over to the subsequent periods the production in those periods is reduced. In this case, the material cost primarily consists of the decrease in discounted cash flows resulting from the reduction in production.

The fourth response, *decrease disposals,* could be classified as a special case of the third, but we have stated it separately because accountants often think of the disposal price as the minimum cost of using materials.[8] That is, if you have material in inventory or are committed to the acquisition of some material, the cost of that material is *at least* the discounted incremental cash flow that would result from selling it instead of using it in some production. In most situations the material cost is somewhat greater than this because it would be better to use the material in some current or future secondary production.

Although we have discussed the above responses as if only one would be employed, the optimal response may be a mix of these. If material is used in primary production, the optimal response may be to increase current acquisitions and decrease current secondary production, or to increase future acquisitions and decrease future production.

2.4 DIRECT LABOR

As with direct material, construction of a direct labor cost function requires specification of a labor input description that constitutes (part of) a sufficient cost statistic. This will require use of separate categories for skill differences that affect the wage rates paid. Daily categories may be required to recognize the payment of overtime or shift differentials. And even if that is not necessary, labor

---

8. Some accounting authors, such as Chambers (1966) and Sterling (1970), suggest that the disposal price ("exit values") should be used in reporting inventories on balance sheets. As the above discussion indicates, however, this price may not be the amount of interest to the decision maker.

will have to be categorized by pay period since that will affect the timing of the amounts paid.

The Incremental Outlay Cost.   The major element in the incremental outlay cost is the amount paid for the labor used.   Labor cannot be stored, so any amounts used in the current period must be acquired during that period.   The payment for labor takes two familiar forms: direct wage payments and fringe benefits.

Another element of the incremental outlay cost is the payment for indirect inputs whose acquisition is a function of the direct labor hours used.   Examples include the inputs used in hiring and releasing employees and the inputs used in maintaining employee records and paying their wages.   Supervisory personnel may also be classified as indirect inputs, but this will be a simplification if the additional supervisory personnel employed are dependent on aspects of the production decision that are not depicted by the direct labor used.

The Impact of Externalities.   There are two common and important types of externalities associated with direct labor.   First, there may be alternative uses for the labor, but unlike direct materials these alternative uses can occur only in the current period.   Second, the size and composition of the work force employed during the current period often determines the work force existing at the start of the following period and thereby may affect future cash flows.

There are three basic responses the firm may make to a decision to use labor in primary production: reduce current secondary production, increase the labor obtained from the existing work force, or increase the work force.   The first type of response was discussed in conjunction with direct materials; the labor cost is the decrease in discounted cash flows resulting from the change in secondary production.   The second and third responses are somewhat different from the responses considered in the direct material case.

The second response, *increase the labor obtained from the work force,* may affect the wage payments and the record-keeping activity but will not affect the hiring and releasing activities.   The increased wage payments will be at regular rates if the additional labor is obtained by more fully using part-time employees. If the additional labor is obtained by having employees work overtime, the increased wage payments will include overtime premiums.   However, there will be no increase in wage payments if the additional labor is obtained from employees who would otherwise have been idle.   This latter situation may occur, for example, when employment contracts contain a guaranteed wage clause.

The third response, *increase the work force,* will affect the wage payments, the record-keeping activity, and either the hiring or releasing activities.[9]   The labor cost in this case is the present value of the incremental cash flows required by the acquisition of the additional labor plus any future effects of the size of the current work force.

These future effects may be either positive or negative.   For example, a decision to increase the current work force will decrease future hiring costs if the

9. The releasing activity is affected if the use of more employees in the current period is accomplished by releasing fewer than would have been released otherwise.

additional employees would have been hired anyway in the subsequent period. On the other hand, an increase in the current work force will increase future releasing costs if these additional employees are released at the start of that period. Moreover, there may be differences in levels of future production. These elements of the direct labor cost are illustrated in the following example.

Two-Period Work-Force Example.   In this example the direct labor cost is dependent upon the size of work force used to provide the number of hours required by primary production. Selection of the work force implicitly determines the number of employees that must be either hired or released and the number of idle or overtime hours worked by that work force. Each employee is paid a basic weekly wage that is independent of his number of hours worked, and he receives overtime pay for his hours worked in excess of forty per week. The cash outflows resulting from each of these factors are given in Table 5.5. We again assume subjective certainty.

TABLE 5.5   TWO-PERIOD WORK-FORCE EXAMPLE

Notation:

$$q = q_1 \qquad \mathbf{a}_{21} = w_1 \qquad \mathbf{a}_{22} = (z_2, w_2, q_2)$$

where

q_t = labor hours used in period t, $t = 1, 2$
w_t = workers employed during period t, $t = 1, 2$
z_2 = output produced in period 2
δ_t = workers in the work force at the start of period t, $t = 1, 2$

$$w_t - \delta_t = \begin{cases} \text{workers hired at start of period } t & w_t \geq \delta_t \\ \text{workers released at start of period } t & w_t \leq \delta_t \end{cases}$$

$$40w_t - q_t = \begin{cases} \text{idle hours in period } t & 40w_t \geq q_t \\ \text{overtime hours in period } t & 40w_t \leq q_t \end{cases}$$

Alternative Input Cost Activities:

$$A_{21}(q_1) = \{w_1 \mid w_1 \text{ integer}, 60w_1 \geq q_1\}$$
$$A_{22}(\delta_2) = \{(z_2, w_2, q_2) \mid w_2 \text{ integer}, 2z_2 = q_2, 60w_2 \geq q_2\}$$

The maximum number of hours each employee will work, including overtime, is 60 hours. Each unit produced in period 2 requires 2 hours of labor.

Cash Flows:
Hiring and Releasing:[1] $\$10(w_t - \delta_t)^2$
Wage Payments and Record Keeping:
  Regular Wages   \$200 per worker
  Overtime   \$8   per hour
Period 2 Operating Cash Inflows (not including labor costs): $\$(40z_2 - 0.05z_2^2)$

---

1. The quadratic cost function for hiring and releasing is essentially the same as that used in a number of production scheduling models based on the pioneering work by Holt et al. (1960).

Continued on next page

TABLE 5.5 *(Continued)*

Outcome Function:

Incremental Outlay Cash Outflow

$$p^{C1}(\hat{s}_{C1}, q, a_{21}, \eta) = \begin{cases} 10(w_1 - \delta_1)^2 + 200w_1 - \hat{p}^{C1}(\hat{s}_{C1}, 0, \eta) & q_1 \leq 40w_1 \\ 10(w_1 - \delta_1)^2 + 200w_1 + 8(q_1 - 40w_1) \\ \quad - \hat{p}^{C1}(\hat{s}_{C1}, 0, \eta) & q_1 \geq 40w_1 \end{cases}$$

where $\hat{p}^{C1}(\hat{s}_{C1}, 0, \eta)$ is the outlay cash outflow that would occur if there were δ_1 workers in the work force at the start of period 1, q equaled zero, and δ_1 is an element of the subjectively certain state $\hat{s}_C$.[1]

Incremental Externality Cash Outflow

$$p^{C2}(\hat{s}_{C2}, \delta_2, a_{22}, \eta) = \begin{cases} 10(w_2 - \delta_2)^2 + 200w_2 - \hat{p}^{C2}(\hat{s}_{C2}, \delta_2^0, \eta) \\ \quad - (40z_2 - 0.05z_2^2) & q_2 \leq 40w_2 \\ 10(w_2 - \delta_2)^2 + 200w_2 - \hat{p}^{C2}(\hat{s}_{C2}, \delta_2^0, \eta) \\ \quad - (40z_2 - 0.05z_2^2) + 8(q_2 - 40w_2) & q_2 \geq 40w_2 \end{cases}$$

where $\hat{p}^{C2}(\hat{s}_{C2}, \delta_2^0, \eta)$ is the net cash outflow in period 2 that would occur if there were δ_2^0 workers in the work force at the start of period 2 and δ_2^0 is the number that would be in that work force if there were δ_1 in the work force at the start of period 1 and q equaled zero.[1]

Cost Function:[2]

$$C(x^C) = x^C = x^{C1} + x^{C2} \quad \text{(no discounting)}$$

$$E(C \mid q, y, \eta) = \min_{w_1 \in A_{21}(q)} [10(w_1 - \delta_1)^2 + 200w_1 + 8 \max\{q - 40w_1, 0\}$$

$$- \hat{p}^{C1}(\hat{s}_{C1}, 0, \eta) + E(C_2 \mid w_1, y, \eta)]$$

$$E(C_2 \mid \delta_2, y, \eta) = \min_{\substack{(z_2, q_2, w_2) \\ \in A_{22}(\delta_2)}} [10(w_2 - \delta_2)^2 + 200w_2 + 8 \max\{q_2 - 40w_2, 0\}$$

$$- \hat{p}^{C2}(\hat{s}_{C2}, \delta_2^0, \eta) - (40z_2 - 0.05z_2^2)]$$

1.

δ_1	0	15	30
$\hat{p}^{C1}(\hat{s}_{C1}, 0, \eta)$	0	2,160	5,040
$\hat{p}^{C2}(\hat{s}_{C2}, \delta_2^0, \eta)$	$-3,200$	$-4,260$	$-4,440$

These amounts are deducted to convert the gross cash flows to incremental cash flows and thereby more sharply focus on the costs incurred in using direct labor in primary production. See Equation [5.1]; $q^0 = 0$.

2. Observe that the initial work force δ_1 may be viewed as an element of the signal y.

Table 5.5 also specifies the cash flows that will occur in the period following primary production. These predictions are required in calculating the cost of the labor used because the size of the work force used in primary production determines the work force available at the start of the second period. If that work force is larger than desired, employees will be released in the second period; if that work force is smaller than desired, employees will be hired in the second period. In addition, the size of the second period production may be changed if the work force at the start of the period is not at the desired level. In our example, the second period cash flow is largest if the work force at the start of that period is fifteen. (A complete analysis would consider periods subsequent to period two, but two periods are sufficient to demonstrate the nature of the process.)

The direct labor cost is depicted in Figure 5.4 for three different initial work-force sizes. There is only one decision variable in the first period, the number em-

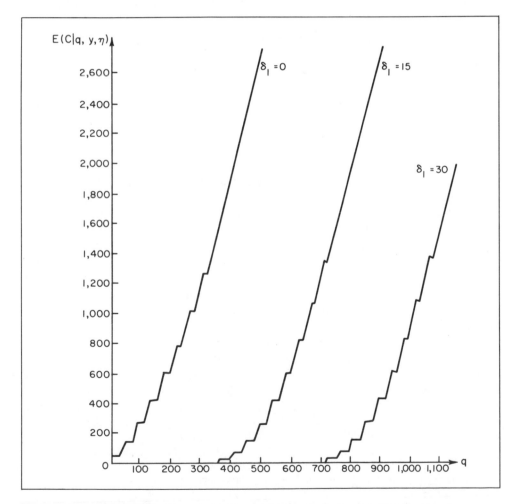

Fig. 5.4. Direct labor cost.

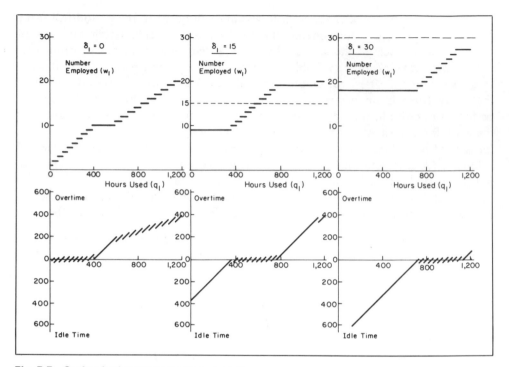

Fig. 5.5. Optimal primary production work force.

ployed ($\mathbf{a}_{21} = w_1$). The optimal number is presented in Figure 5.5 (this number is dependent on the hours required and the initial work force). This figure also presents the idle hours and the overtime hours that will be associated with each number of labor hours used.

Figures 5.4 and 5.5 show that the labor cost and the decision variables are greatly affected by the size of the initial work force. If the initial work force is zero, there is little idle time or overtime at the low end of the range of hours used, but there is considerable overtime in the upper two-thirds of the range and there would be even more at the high end if employees would work more than sixty hours per week. If the initial work force is fifteen, idle time is prevalent at the low end of the range as workers are retained for use in period two, and overtime is prevalent at the high end of the range as additional workers are not hired because they would only be released at the start of period two. If the initial work force is thirty, there is little overtime at any level, but there is considerable idle time at the low end of the range as some employees are needed in period two and it is too costly to release everyone simultaneously. The plateaus in the labor cost function occur when excess employees exist and additional labor is obtained by reducing the idle time; the slope between plateaus is equal to the overtime rate of $8 per hour.

To compute the above results we had to calculate the second-period cash flows for each possible work-force size that could exist at the start of period two; the results of these calculations are presented in Figure 5.6. Three decision vari-

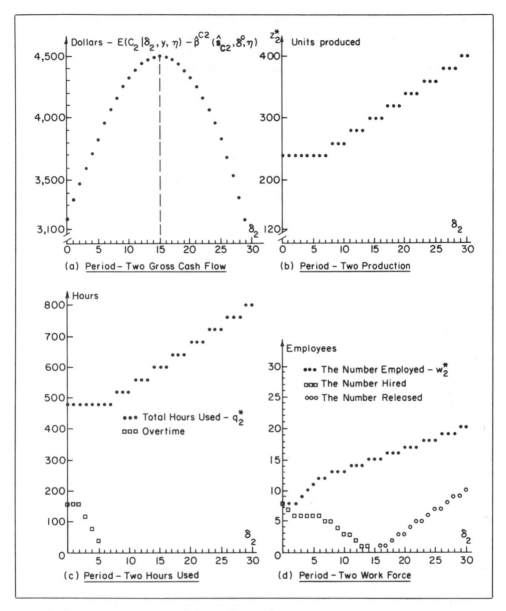

Fig. 5.6. Optimal period-two cash flow and work force.

ables had to be determined in calculating those cash flows: the number of units produced (z_2), the number employed (w_2), and the number of hours used (q_2). (Thus $\mathbf{a}_{22} = (z_2, w_2, q_2)$).

The optimal values for each of these decision variables, plus the overtime and the number hired and released, are depicted in Figure 5.6 for each possible work-force size. The largest second-period cash flow occurs for an initial period-two work force of fifteen. If the work force is less than fifteen, the number of units produced is less and some employees are hired. At the very low levels some overtime will be used. If the initial period-two work force exceeds fifteen, the number of units produced is greater and some employees will be released.

2.5 MACHINE HOURS

The cost accounting literature usually focuses its discussion of direct inputs on material and labor, as we have done in the two preceding sections.[10] Other inputs may be treated as direct, but in most cost accounting systems these inputs are "allocated" to one or more "overhead" categories and then the amount in each category is "allocated" to the firm's outputs and departments on the basis of some activity measure, such as direct labor cost, direct labor hours, or machine hours.

These activity measures are essentially used as elements of a cost statistic, and many of them could be called direct inputs. The inclusion of machine hours in the cost statistic is warranted if the impact of primary production decisions on some cash flows can be expressed as a function of that activity measure. This may be possible (indeed essential) since there are several inputs that are acquired to facilitate the operation of machines and the more a machine is used in primary production the less time there is available for current secondary production. Furthermore, current usage may increase the maintenance that must be performed now or in the future and may also affect the economic life of the machine.

The Incremental Outlay Cost.   There are three major classes of activities associated with machine use that cause primary cash outflows: acquisition, operation, and maintenance. All three may vary as current machine usage varies. Of course, machine acquisition outflows are likely to increase in jumps as, say, increased usage forces the firm to acquire additional machines.[11]

The Impact of Externalities.   Two major types of externalities may result from machine usage. First, there may be alternative current uses for machine hours. Second, the number and condition of the machines under the firm's control at the end of the primary production period may be affected by the machine usage in primary production. Differences in the number and condition of the machines may affect future production as well as future machine acquisitions, disposals, and maintenance.

There are three basic responses the firm may make to a decision to use machines in primary production: increase the machines available, increase the usage of machines, or reduce current secondary production. Both the first and second

---

10. For example, see Horngren (1972) and Shillinglaw (1972).

11. The machines available are often taken as given in production decisions because the decision maker considers it to be too costly to acquire additional machines quickly. However, a complete analysis would recognize that such acquisitions are possible. It would include the current acquisition payments as part of the outlay cost of any production activities requiring additional acquisitions.

responses will result in increased machine usage; this will probably lead to an increase in the operating and maintenance cash outflows during the current period. However, the other elements of the machine usage cost differ somewhat for the two responses.

The first response, *increase the machines available,* will require a change in the acquisition activities and will also affect future activities. The machine usage cost will include the present value of the differences in acquisition cash outflows and future cash flows. The latter may take several forms. For example, the availability of these machines may induce the firm to increase future production; in that case, future cash flows will be increased by the additional production and the eventual disposal of these machines. Alternatively, the availability of these machines may induce the firm to reduce future machine acquisitions; in that case, the change in future cash flows will be the acquisition outflows avoided and any differences in the operations, maintenance, and acquisition cash flows that follow. These latter cash flows are likely to differ because there will be a difference in the ages of the machines that are acquired in the current period and those that would have been acquired in the future.

The second response, *increase the usage of machines,* is only possible if there is idle capacity. The machine usage cost is the present value of the increase in current operating and maintenance cash outflows plus the increase in future cash outflows resulting from the increased use of the machines during the current period. For example, increased use may result in increased maintenance activity in the future or it may shorten the economic life of the machine.

The third response, *reduce current secondary production,* has no impact on future cash flows nor on current operating and maintenance cash outflows; current acquisitions and machine usage are unaffected by primary usage. Instead, the machine usage cost is the present value of the net cash inflows foregone as a result of reducing current secondary production to provide the machine hours required by primary production. This situation is illustrated in the following example.

A Two-Product Machine Usage Example. In this example the number of machines available for use is specified and we do not consider the possibility of acquiring additional machines for current production. The primary input activities are not explicitly considered, but there are some primary cash outflows associated with the use of the machines in primary production. These constitute the incremental outlay cost. The data are given in Table 5.6.

An externality cost arises from the fact that the machines in question can be used to produce another product. (We assume that there are no other externalities; for example, the amount the machines are used does not affect future maintenance or disposals.) The decision maker is not directly concerned with determining the secondary output, but that decision must be included in the cost calculation. The machine hours available for secondary production constitute the secondary statistic, and that amount is dependent upon the number of machines available and the machine hours used in primary production. The firm faces a downward sloping demand curve with respect to the secondary product

TABLE 5.6 TWO-PRODUCT MACHINE USAGE EXAMPLE

Notation:

$$q = q_1 \qquad \mathbf{a}_{21} = \text{none} \qquad \mathbf{a}_{22} = (z_2, q_2)$$

where
q_i = machine hours used in product, $i, i = 1, 2$
z_2 = quantity of output 2 produced
δ_1 = machine hours available for use in primary and secondary production
δ_2 = machine hours available for use in secondary production

$$\delta_2(\delta_1, q_1) = \delta_1 - q_1$$

Alternative Secondary Activities:

$$\mathbf{A}_{22}(\delta_2) = \{(z_2, q_2) \mid 2z_2 = q_2, q_2 \leq \delta_2\}$$

Each unit of product 2 output requires 2 machine hours and the machine hours used cannot exceed hours available.

Cash Flows:

Machine Operations:	\$10 per hour
Net Cash Inflows from Production and Sale of Product 2 (excluding the machine cost):	$\$(288z_2 - 0.5z_2^2)$

Outcome Function:

Incremental Outlay Cash Outflow

$$p^{C1}(\hat{s}_{C1}, q, \mathbf{a}_{21}, \eta) = 10q_1$$

Incremental Externality Cash Outflow[1]

$$p^{C2}(\hat{s}_{C2}, \delta_2, \mathbf{a}_{22}, \eta) = 10q_2 - (288z_2 - 0.5z_2^2) - \hat{p}^{C2}(\hat{s}_{C2}, \delta_2^0, \eta)$$

where $\hat{p}^{C2}(\hat{s}_{C2}, \delta_2^0, \eta)$ is the net cash outflow that would occur if there were $\delta_2^0 = \delta_1$ machine hours available for secondary production.

Cost Function:

$$C(x^C) = x^C = x^{C1} + x^{C2}$$

$$E(C \mid q, y, \eta) = 10q + E(C_2 \mid \delta_1 - q, y, \eta) \qquad\qquad 0 \leq q \leq \delta_1$$

$$E(C_2 \mid \delta_2, y, \eta) = \min_{\substack{(z_2, q_2) \\ \in A_{22}(\delta_2)}} [10q_2 - (288z_2 - 0.5z_2^2) - \hat{p}^{C2}(\hat{s}_{C2}, \delta_2^0, \eta)]$$

$$= \begin{cases} -\hat{p}^{C2}(\hat{s}_{C2}, \delta_2^0, \eta) - 134\delta_2 + 0.125\delta_2^2 & 0 \leq \delta_2 \leq 536 \\ -\hat{p}^{C2}(\hat{s}_{C2}, \delta_2^0, \eta) - 35,912 & 536 \leq \delta_2 \end{cases}$$

Continued on next page

TABLE 5.6 *(Continued)*

Therefore[1]

$$E(C \mid q, y, \eta) = 10q + \begin{cases} 134q + 0.125q^2 - 0.25\delta_1 q & 0 \le \delta_1 \le 536 \\ 35{,}912 - 134(\delta_1 - q) \\ \quad + 0.125(\delta_1 - q)^2 & \delta_1 - q \le 536 \le \delta_1 \\ 0 & 536 \le \delta_1 - q \le \delta_1 \end{cases}$$

1.
$$-\hat{p}^{C2}(\hat{s}_{C2}, \delta_2^0, \eta) = \begin{cases} 134\delta_1 - 0.125\delta_1^2 & 0 \le \delta_1 \le 536 \\ 35{,}912 & 536 \le \delta_1 \end{cases}$$

See Equation [5.1]; $q^0 = 0$.

and, if enough hours are available (536), the firm will set the price such that the maximum secondary cash flows are achieved. However, if the hours available are insufficient to achieve that output, the firm will charge a higher price such that the demand for the secondary output is equivalent to the quantity that can be produced with the available hours. The externality cost arises if the use of machine hours in primary production forces the firm to reduce the amount of secondary output produced and sold. A formal statement of the calculation of these amounts is presented in Table 5.6 and the amounts are depicted in Figure 5.7.

In Figure 5.7 the externality cost is the difference between the machine hour cost curves and the incremental outlay cost. Observe that the externality cost is incurred at all levels of usage when there are either one or three machines available; this is because the firm will fully use those machines in secondary production even if no hours are used in primary production. On the other hand, when five or eight machines are available, there are no externality costs if the number of hours used in primary production is small; this is because there is enough capacity to produce both the primary output and the optimal secondary output.

3.0 OUTPUT COST FUNCTIONS

Output is often used as an object of costing in production decisions. In those decisions, output cost functions are developed either because the output is the object of choice or because the action alternatives influence the output and the output is assumed to be a sufficient cost statistic. We now briefly discuss these two output roles, as well as the general nature of output cost functions.

3.1 OUTPUT AS AN OBJECT OF CHOICE

Treating output as an object of choice is a special case of the decision variable modification discussed in Chapter 3. Sufficient conditions for such modifications are provided in Proposition 3.2.

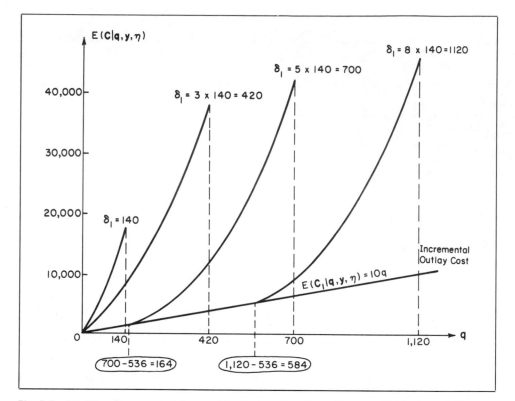

Fig. 5.7. Machine-hour cost. δ_1 is equal to the number of machines available times 140 hours per machine.

The output is an outcome of the selected action, and its use as the object of choice is straightforward if we are subjectively certain as to the output that will result from each action alternative. In that case, the outcome associated with a particular output is the outcome associated with the most preferred action that will result in that output. This approach can also be extended to the uncertain output case by including the output level for each state as part of the output description.

Appendix 5.2 provides a brief discussion of the relationship of the above approach to the development of output cost functions in the classical economic theory of the firm. Development of output cost functions is further illustrated by the examples in Chapter 6 (see, for example, section 3.2.).

3.2 OUTPUT AS A COST STATISTIC

To provide a sufficient cost statistic, the output description must be forecast and payoff adequate for the cost component outcome, as well as provide a basis for specifying the feasible set of secondary cost activities (see Table 5.1). Clearly, the nature of the primary action and the cost component outcome elements are important determinants of the factors that must be reflected in that description.

If the primary action consists of activities that determine the quantity of output[12] and the cost component outcome includes the cost of inputs used in production, the output description must obviously include some measure of the quantity produced. Furthermore, that description must reflect any possible differences in the output characteristics that will influence the cost of inputs used in production.

Similarly, if the primary action consists of activities that determine the method of production,[13] the output description must reflect any differences in the production method selection that will influence the cost of inputs used. For example, consider a situation in which we select production rates prior to knowing the demand, and later make special arrangements to produce additional units for any demand in excess of planned production. In that situation, if output is to be the cost statistic, the description of that output must indicate both the quantity produced as a result of the initial plans and the quantity produced on the basis of special arrangements (the total quantity produced would not likely be sufficient).

3.3   The General Nature of Output Cost Functions

Use of a separately determined output cost function presumes that some appropriate separability conditions are satisfied. Proposition 5.1, recall, provides a set of sufficient conditions for the case where output is used as a cost statistic. Similar conditions can be specified for the case where output is used as the object of choice. The only difference is that all actions would be secondary and treated as functions of the output selected.[14]

Many analyses develop the output cost function from the cost of the direct inputs used to achieve the output in question. Direct inputs, recall, include all inputs required to provide a sufficient cost statistic. Further observe that the input description required to satisfy this requirement depends on the division between input usage activities (a_{C1}) and input cost activities (a_{C2}). This division is arbitrary. Consequently, the direct/indirect distinction is an inherently fickle concept when applied to the inputs used to produce some output.

There is no such distinction in the classical economic theory approach. In that approach, all outputs are considered simultaneously and the direct inputs include *all* externally acquired resources. Internally produced inputs are ignored, as is the timing of input usage. Moreover, all secondary cost activities are implicitly treated as input usage activities (that is, $a_C = a_{C1}$). Appendix 5.2 briefly outlines this approach.

However, input acquisition quantities are not likely to provide a sufficient cost statistic in those analyses in which we focus on a subset of the output (the

---

12. See Appendix 5.1 (section 2.1) for a discussion of the nature of decisions that influence output quantity.

13. See Appendix 5.1 (section 2.2) for a discussion of the nature of production method decisions.

14. This may be interpreted as an application of Proposition 3.2 to the present setting of Proposition 5.1.

primary output). Input usage is likely to be more appropriate here.[15] Furthermore, factors other than input usage also may need to be considered. We briefly
discuss some of those other factors in the following section.

4.0 OTHER COST STATISTIC ELEMENTS

In this section we briefly consider two particular types of noninput cost statistics: secondary outputs and learning effects. Both may need to be considered in
developing some output cost functions. We readily adopt the input cost framework to these statistics by replacing input q with the primary cost statistic δ_C.

4.1 SECONDARY OUTPUT FROM PRIMARY PRODUCTION

In many situations the primary output represents only a portion of the output
produced by primary production activities. This may be the case, for example,
when there are joint products or output inventories.

Joint products occur when production activities, such as the refining of crude
oil, simultaneously produce several outputs. If our analysis focuses on some subset of the joint products, the impact of the secondary products may be recognized
by including them in the cost statistic. In that case, the cost of the primary output
will include the cost of the inputs used to produce the primary output *less* the value
of the secondary output that results from that production.

The value of the secondary output will depend upon how it is used. If it is
sold directly, and if a present value modification is available, the value is the
present value of the additional net cash inflows resulting from that sale. If the
secondary output is processed further, the value is the present value of the additional cash inflows resulting from the sale of the final product less the additional
cash outflows resulting from the inputs used in the additional processing activities.
If that output is an input into another process and reduces the external acquisitions of such inputs, the value is the present value of the reduction in cash outflows
resulting from the reduced acquisitions (See Jensen 1974).

The output inventories (finished or in process) on hand at the end of the primary production period represent another important type of secondary output. If
there are no joint products, the minimum cost primary output level will probably
be zero. If this is the case, any initial output inventories will be included in the
cost and secondary statistics. In addition, it may be desirable to produce some
output for future sales, but this will depend on the situation. For example, if zero
output would result in an idle work force, it may be desirable to use that work
force to produce outputs for future sale. In that case, the least-cost cost statistic
(δ_C^0) would contain the optimal output inventory and any inputs used in producing
that inventory.

If output is to be sold, the firm could either increase current production or decrease the ending output inventory. In the first case, the cost of the primary output is the cost of the additional inputs used to achieve the additional output. In

---

15. This point is illustrated in the detailed discussion of input costs in section 2.

the second case, the cost of the primary output is the reduction in the value of the ending output inventory, and that value depends upon whether changes in inventory result in changes in future sales or future production.

A somewhat opposite situation occurs when inputs are required to "start up" the production process for an individual output and thus, if no output is required for current use, it is best to produce nothing. If the primary output comes from the initial inventory, the cost of that output is again the decrease in the value of the ending inventory, less the reduction in the cost of the inputs used in storing inventories. If the primary output is produced, the cost of that output is the cost of the inputs used in that production *less* the value of any output produced in excess of current requirements. Additional units may be produced because once the "start-up costs" have been incurred it is optimal to produce a large batch and retain the unsold output for future sales.

4.2 LEARNING EFFECTS

The accounting literature on cost behavior frequently points out that the amount of input required to produce a given quantity of output decreases as the firm gains experience in producing that output.[16] The airframe industry is the most frequently used example of this "learning effect," but it is a rather general phenomenon.[17]

Learning effects have two cost assessment implications. First, these effects must be recognized in the construction of the cost component outcome. Second, when learning effects exist, the inputs used may not satisfy the cost statistic requirements. For example, some description of the work force's experience with various tasks and products may be required to depict the impact of current production on future outcomes.

In this type of situation, the cost of producing a given quantity of primary output is the cost of the inputs used in that production *less* the value of the experience gained by the work force in producing that output. If the experience results in more future output from the same labor input, the value of the experience is the cash inflow resulting from the additional sales less the cash outflows resulting from any additional inputs used to produce and sell that output. On the other hand, if that experience results in the use of fewer inputs to produce the same output, the value of the experience is the resulting reduction in cash outflows. (And, with a present value modification, these various cash flows may be stated in present value terms.)

5.0 SUMMARY

This chapter has explored the nature of input and output cost functions in a production decision context under the assumption of costless analysis. Separate development of these cost functions rests, it must be recalled, on some rather strong separability conditions.

---

16. For example, see Bierman and Dyckman (1971) and Dopuch et al. (1974).

17. It has been found in both labor and machine intensive industries. See Baloff (1966).

Of particular significance is the requirement that the input or output description must constitute a sufficient cost statistic if it is used as an intermediate variable in the development of an action cost function. To satisfy this requirement, the descriptions must reflect all aspects of the primary action that will directly or indirectly affect the cost component outcome.

An important factor affecting the cost component outcome associated with a particular primary action is the secondary (cost) action selection it induces. Consequently, development of input or output cost functions requires determination of the optimal secondary action associated with each input or output level. Our discussion has illustrated the complexity of that determination and of its incorporation into the cost function calculation.

Given that we do not operate in a world of costless analysis, the lack of separability conditions and the complexity of the analysis usually forces us to employ simplified cost functions. The cost functions discussed in this chapter represent an ideal that we may consider in evaluating alternative simplified functions. The following chapter explores the nature and impact of cost function simplifications in a short-run production decision context and Chapter 7 extends this to investment decisions.

APPENDIX 5.1
THE GENERAL NATURE OF PRODUCTION ACTIVITIES
AND THE DECISIONS THAT INFLUENCE THEM

Production, or exchange with "nature," refers to those entity activities involved in acquiring commodities, converting them into other commodities, and transferring the latter to other entities.[18] The entity may be a firm or a subunit of a firm. The commodities may be goods or services; those acquired are called inputs and those transferred out are called outputs. The following discussion first describes the general nature of production systems and then briefly describes some decisions affecting production activities.[19] Note especially that the term *production activities* is used in the broadest sense; that is, manufacturing activities are only one type of production activity.

1.0 THE PRODUCTION SYSTEM
Figure 5.8 depicts the basic elements of the production system. The entity acquires inputs from its suppliers, including its employees, to obtain the services

---

18. For a discussion of the nature of commodities in economic theory, see Debreu (1959), Hirshleifer (1970), Arrow and Hahn (1971), and Intriligator (1971).

19. For a more complete discussion of the nature of production activities and decisions, the reader is referred to texts on the subject, such as Buffa (1966, 1968).

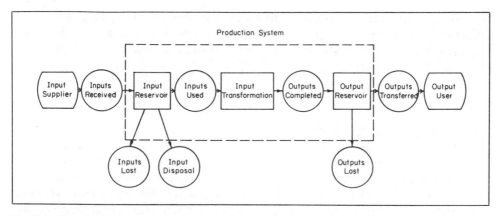

Fig. 5.8. The production system.

that these inputs provide. The services are not always used at the time of acquisition and, therefore, the inputs are depicted as entering a "reservoir" of input services. Occasionally the rights to some input services are sold (disposed of) to persons external to the entity, but in most situations the services are either used in one of the many production system activities or lost through nonuse. The central production activity is that which transforms input services into outputs.

The inputs acquired by an entity take a variety of forms. They include raw materials, secretarial and janitorial supplies, buildings, equipment, labor services of various skill types, transportation services, electrical power, telephone service, postal service, and so on. Production management, particularly those involved in acquisition activities such as purchasing and personnel, must make a variety of acquisition decisions. They must decide on the type and quantity of inputs to acquire, and where and when to acquire them. These decisions will usually depend on the predicted input service requirements for the system's activities. Some inputs, such as labor and electric power, are simultaneously received and used, but other inputs, such as raw materials and equipment, may be received in advance of their use.

The input reservoir represents the set of input services, such as raw material inventory and equipment services, held by the entity at any point in time. During any given time interval the reservoir may be increased by acquisitions and decreased by use, disposal, or loss.

The pattern of input usage will depend on the activities of the production system. Major decisions affecting these activities include selection of the outputs and quantities to be produced, plus the timing and methods of production. In these selections, the decision maker will probably consider (among other things) the current output reservoir level, the predicted customer demand, the input services currently available, and the impact on cash flows of acquiring additional input services prior to production.

The output produced may not be transferred immediately upon its completion, and thus we introduce the notion of an output reservoir. The major element of this reservoir is finished goods inventory. During a given time interval the reservoir may be increased by production and decreased by sale or loss of outputs. Losses may occur because of pilferage, breakage, obsolescence, and so on. The amount transferred will depend on user demands and the availability of the outputs demanded by users.

2.0   PRODUCTION DECISIONS

There are obviously a broad range of decisions that must be made in operating a production system, and they may be categorized in a variety of ways. In our discussion of input cost functions we distinguish between those that affect input usage and those that affect input cost. In our discussion of output cost functions it is instructive to distinguish between output and production method decisions. Some of the decisions in these latter two categories are outlined below.

2.1   OUTPUT DECISIONS

Output decisions are those decisions that influence the type, quantity, or timing of the output produced by the entity of interest. Illustrative examples include:

Selection of the products to be produced. Decisions to introduce new products or to drop old products obviously influence the entity's output. The acceptance or rejection of a customer's order is a similar type of decision.

Selection of the production level and schedule for one or more products. These decisions often influence the outputs transferred to customers in that they affect the quantity available and the timing of that availability.

Selection of prices for one or more products. A pricing decision is an output decision if the price influences customer demand and demand affects the output produced by the entity.

2.2   PRODUCTION METHOD DECISIONS

Production method decisions are those decisions that influence how a particular output is achieved. Illustrative examples include:

Output and component specifications. An important first step in the selection of production methods is the specification of what constitutes a particular product and the materials and parts that will be used to achieve those specifications. Differences in the type and quality of the components will affect the inputs that are acquired and may affect the production procedures that are employed.

Procedure specifications. Specification of the various steps that are to be taken in transforming the inputs into outputs will largely define the types of labor skills and machines that will be used in the production process.

Production scheduling. Production scheduling decisions take place at several levels within the production system. Some of these decisions may specify the general level at which various production departments are to operate during the forthcoming period, while other decisions specify the sequence of job assignments for particular machines and personnel within a department. These decisions greatly influence the amount and timing of the inputs used in production and the amount and timing of the outputs completed. If the output can be stored, the latter will influence the finished goods inventory carried by the firm. These inventories may be carried because of uncertainties in demand, the desirability of batch processing, or because it is desirable to produce in excess of demand during periods of temporarily low demand.

Input acquisition decisions. These decisions include the selection of the types of inputs and the quantities to be acquired, plus the source and timing of those acquisitions. The types, quantities, and timing of the inputs used are often determined by the production decisions described above and the decision maker here is primarily concerned with the source and timing of the acquisitions. However, in some cases, such as in the acquisition of machines and buildings, the acquisition decision effectively determines the availability of some input and the other production decisions are made given that constraint. Storable inputs may be acquired in advance of use because of usage uncertainties, the desirability of batch acquisitions, or the availability of temporarily low prices. Excess employees may be retained during periods of temporarily low production and the employees may work overtime during periods of temporarily high production.

Make-or-buy decisions. A make-or-buy decision may arise with respect to some output sold by the firm, or some input that the firm uses. Both decisions may materially affect the inputs acquired and used in the production system.

Selection of plant layout. The physical location of the machines and operating departments within the plant will influence the production activities. This decision is likely to be made in conjunction with the selection of the machines and buildings that are to be acquired for the production process.

APPENDIX 5.2
THE ECONOMIC THEORY OF THE FIRM

Microeconomic theory includes among its areas of analysis the characteristics of a firm's optimal input/output combinations. While the microeconomic literature has explored a wide variety of situations,[20] there is one type of analysis that forms the core of most microeconomic texts.[21] We briefly explore this analysis to indicate its relationship to the material in Chapter 5.

Intriligator summarizes the basic problem posed in the theory of the firm as follows:

The neoclassical theory of the firm postulates that the objective of the firm is that of maximizing profits by choice of inputs, given the production function and given output

---

20. For examples of the extent of this analysis see Dano (1966), Lancaster (1968), Shepard (1970), and Intriligator (1971).

21. For examples of this core analysis see Samuelson (1965) and Intriligator (1971).

> price ... and input prices (wages).... Profits ... equal revenue ... less cost of production, ... where revenue is output price times output ... and cost of production is the total payments to all inputs.... In the *problem of the firm in the long run* the firm is free to choose any input vector in input space.... By contrast to the *long run*, in which all inputs can be freely varied, in the *short run* there are restrictions on the choice of inputs such as, for example, lower limits on certain inputs because of contractual obligations. In the *problem of the firm in a short run* the firm must choose a vector of inputs from a given subset of input space. [Intriligator 1971, pp. 189–190]

The basic problem assumes a world of certainty and focuses on a single output. More general discussions consider uncertainty[22] and several interrelated outputs.[23] The comments below relate the general case to our analysis.

The economic model suppresses all actions and uses the inputs acquired and outputs sold as the objects of choice. If there is uncertainty, the input and output descriptions must be state indexed.[24] That is, if there are S possible states, then $q = (q_1, \ldots, q_S)$ and $z = (z_1, \ldots, z_S)$ where q_s and z_s are the vectors of inputs and outputs that will occur if state s occurs.

Given state indexing, we may express the inputs and outputs as functions of actions. These functions may then be used to specify the set $Q(z)$, all $z \in Z$, that contains all input vectors that can be used to achieve output z; that is,

$$Q(z) = \{q \mid q(a) = q, z(a) = z, \text{ and } a \in A\}$$

where $z(a)$ is the output that will result from action a and $q(a)$ is the input that is used as a result of that action. Most economic analyses assume that it never costs less to use more inputs and that more revenue never results from the production of fewer outputs. These are rather unrestrictive assumptions if all current outputs are considered simultaneously and there are no interperiod effects. The advantage of these exclusions is that they allow us to immediately exclude a large number of feasible input/output combinations from consideration. In particular, we need only consider the set of *efficient input/output combinations* Δ^* where $\Delta^* = \{(q, z) \mid z \in Z, q \in Q(z)$, there is no $q^1 \in Q(z)$ such that $q^1 \leq q$, and there is no $z^1 \geq z$ such that $q \in Q(z^1)\}$. That is, an input/output combination is excluded from consideration if there is another combination that produces the same output vector but uses less of at least one input and no more of all other inputs, *or* if the same input vector can be used to produce more of at least one output and no less of all other outputs. It is the set of efficient input/output combinations Δ^* that constitutes the production function.

Most economic analyses assume that the profit function can be separated into a revenue (benefit) function over the outputs and a cost function over the inputs.[25]

---

22. See McCall (1971) for a discussion of the need for more work in this area and a partial review of what has been done.

23. See Samuelson (1965) for an extensive analysis of the multiple output case in a world of certainty.

24. If more than one period is considered, they must be time indexed as well.

25. This separability immediately follows if the usual market value maximization and complete and perfect market assumptions are made.

These analyses then approach determination of the optimal input/output combination, $(q*, z*)$, as a two-stage process.

In the first stage we determine the minimum cost input for each efficient output $z \in Z* = \{z \mid (q, z) \in \Delta*, \text{ any } q\}$. The minimum cost input for efficient output $z \in Z*$ is denoted $q(z)$ and this function describes what is commonly called the *expansion path*. This function can then be used to determine the cost function over the outputs produced, denoted $E(C \mid z)$. For example, if we assume market value maximization in a world of complete and perfect markets, where P^s is the current market value of one dollar in state s and c_{sj} is the purchase price of input j in state s, then the input cost function is

$$E(C \mid q) = \sum_{s=1}^{S} P^s \left(\sum_{j=1}^{m} c_{sj} q_{sj} \right),$$

$q(z)$ is defined to be such that

$$E(C \mid q(z)) = \min_{\substack{q \\ \text{such that} \\ (q,z) \in \Delta^*}} E(C \mid q)$$

and

$$E(C \mid z) = E(C \mid q(z)) \qquad \text{for all } z \in Z.*$$

In the second stage we determine the optimal output by maximizing the profit function, denoted $E(U \mid z)$, which is the difference between the output revenue function, denoted $E(B \mid z)$, and the cost function calculated in stage one. That is, continuing our example, if b_{si} is the selling price of output i in state s, then

$$E(B \mid z) = \sum_{s=1}^{S} P^s \left(\sum_{i=1}^{n} b_{si} z_{si} \right)$$

and $z*$ is defined to be such that

$$E(U \mid z*) = \max_{z \in Z*} [E(B \mid z) - E(C \mid z)].$$

To determine the characteristics of the expansion path and the optimal input/output combination, most economic analyses make various assumptions about the nature of the production function, the revenue function, and the cost function. We will not explore those assumptions and their related solution characteristics.

6

ANALYSIS OF COST ASSESSMENT ALTERNATIVES IN A SHORT-RUN DECISION CONTEXT

This chapter explores a number of cost assessment alternatives in a short-run decision context. As discussed in Chapter 4, cost assessment includes the cost function used in the decision model, the methods used to predict the parameters of that function, and the information used by the decision maker.

In a complete analysis, information alternatives are the only source of cost assessment alternatives, and these exist only if we admit uncertainty. Modifications of the complete analysis outcome function may, as explored in Chapters 4 and 5, result in a variety of cost functions; and we may, in the limited context of complete analysis, view these modifications as cost assessment alternatives. Otherwise, alternative cost functions exist only if we admit to simplification. Simplification also introduces the possibility of alternative methods for predicting the cost function parameters. The cost assessment alternatives explored in this chapter take the form of cost function simplifications and the methods used to predict their parameters.

The evaluation of cost assessment alternatives was also discussed in Chapter 4. All cost assessment alternatives, recall, may be interpreted as information system alternatives; hence, the basic evaluation model is the expected utility associated with a particular information system (see Equations [2.4] and [3.9]).

For expositional reasons, we adopt the simplifying assumption that the utility measure can be separated from the "costs" of the information system and the decision analysis. Moreover, much of our analysis assumes market value (or profit) maximization; and, in those cases where model simplifications are considered, we cast the analysis in terms of the loss resulting from use of a simplified as opposed to a complete analysis. (Formal statement of that loss is provided by Equation [3.10].)

Finally, to focus on cost issues, we must presume that the decision maker's objective function is divided into benefit and cost components. And to keep the focus as specific as possible, we further assume that the evaluator's utility function is separable and that his benefit component is equivalent to that of the decision maker. The decision maker's cost component, on the other hand, may be simplified.

The simplifications we explore fall into three broad classes. The first encompasses those that simplify the domain of the cost functions. This type of simplification often results from either imposing constraints on "feasible" input usage or by aggregating input categories. The second encompasses those that simplify the form of the cost functions. Accountants frequently do this by using linear approximations to nonlinear cost functions. The third encompasses those that use cost allocation as a basis for decomposing decision problems into a number of separate components.

1.0 SIMPLIFICATION OF THE COST FUNCTION DOMAIN

In many decision analyses the costs of alternative actions are determined by first predicting various consequences (including the inputs used) of each action and then predicting the cost of those consequences. This can constitute a complete analysis if, as explored in Chapter 5, the consequence description constitutes a sufficient cost statistic, but that is seldom the case. Instead, the descriptions are typically simplified to reduce the cost of analysis. Two types of simplification are particularly prevalent: cost statistic constraints and cost statistic aggregation.

1.1 COST STATISTIC CONSTRAINTS

The set of decision variables $D(\theta, \phi \mid y, \eta)$ is typically defined by a set of constraints on the magnitude of the vector of decision variable d. Some constraints are necessary; these include those that specify the technical relationships among the decision variable components and those that specify limitations that in fact exist. Other constraints are imposed on the decision maker by his superiors. Those constraints that are neither necessary nor externally imposed are usually included to simplify the analysis. Quite simply, restricting the decision variable limits the domain over which the benefit and cost functions must be defined. This will reduce the effort required in determining these functions and may also reduce the effort required to search for the "optimal" decision. The effort required in determining the cost function is further reduced if the constraint is used in place of a cost function over some element of the cost statistic; for example, the model may limit unsatisfied demand instead of specifying the cost of various levels of unsatisfied demand.

Section 1.1.1 considers the case where the cost function per se is not simplified, but the inputs used are restricted. Section 1.1.2 considers the case where a constraint is used instead of specifying the cost function over some cost statistic.

1.1.1 INPUT USAGE CONSTRAINTS

Many decision models contain constraints that limit the quantities of inputs that may be used (see Dorfman et al. 1958; Dano 1966). These limitations are often far less than the quantity that could be obtained and usually exclude input usage that the decision maker believes would be "too costly" to acquire. For example, he may limit the machine hours used to the capacity of the machines currently on the firm's premises because he considers it "too costly" to expedite the acquisition of additional machines. Similarly, he may limit the labor hours used to those that can be supplied by the current work force, because he considers it "too costly" to hire additional employees to satisfy a short-run increase in production; furthermore, in calculating the capacity of the work force, he may exclude the possibility of overtime because he also considers it to be "too costly." Obviously, deciding what is "too costly" is an important part of the analysis.

From Proposition 3.2 we know that the optimal action will be selected if the benefit and cost functions are equivalent to those for a complete analysis and the decision variable associated with the optimal action is included in the set of feasible decision variables. If, however, the decision associated with the optimal action is excluded from the set of feasible decision variables, the selected action will be nonoptimal and the loss (in utility) will be strictly positive. Conversely, formal use of the vertical elimination procedures discussed in Chapter 3 will—at a cost—preclude such an event.

The set of feasible decision variables is dependent on the parameters of the constraint functions. Some of these parameters may be the upper limits on the inputs used. If the vector of upper limits on the inputs used, denoted θ_q, is greater than or equal to the optimal usage, denoted q^*, the action selected by an otherwise complete analysis will be the optimal action. Presumably, the decision maker attempts to select input limits so that they are greater than or equal to the optimal usages, but he does not know the optimal usages at the time he selects the limits and he may, in fact, select limits such that $\theta_q \ngeq q^*$. In that case, the action selected by the simplified analysis will be nonoptimal and the resulting utility measure will be less than that which would have resulted from a complete analysis.[1]

---

1. As a check on the impact of the limits he has selected, the decision maker may employ sensitivity analysis. This involves calculation of the increase in the objective function measure that would result if the limits on a particular set of inputs were increased.

Many optimization procedures, such as linear and nonlinear programming algorithms, automatically provide the rate of increase in the objective function associated with an increase in each input limit. These rates of increase are often called *shadow prices* or the *opportunity cost of not increasing the inputs available for use*. If the opportunity cost of not increasing an input is greater than the cost of increasing it, the increase should take place. However, the range of increase over which these rates apply may be extremely small and seldom apply for all increases; if the input must be acquired in discrete units, such as the acquisition of an entire machine instead of a few hours of use, the analysis would have to be extended to determine the impact of *unit* increases in the input available.

1.1.2 SUBSTITUTION OF CONSTRAINTS FOR COST FUNCTIONS

In the previous section we assumed that the decision model cost function was equivalent to that of a complete analysis. The use of constraints merely limited the domain over which this function had to be specified. We now briefly consider those models that eliminate the portion of the cost function attributable to some cost statistic element and replace it with a constraint.

A cost statistic constraint may specify either a specific quantity or a range of "feasible" quantities.[2] An example of the first case is a model specifying the level of ending inventory instead of including the value of alternative inventory levels in the calculation of the cost function. Examples of the second case include the use of upper limits on the level of unsatisfied demand or the number of machine hours used. In general, we expect these constraints to result in the selection of nonoptimal actions, but there are some conditions under which the selected action will be optimal.

The action selection will be optimal in the first case if the cost (or value) of the restricted cost statistic element is separable from the cost of the other elements and the specified quantity is optimal.[3] A similar result applies in the second case; the action selection will be optimal if the upper bound is greater than or equal to the optimal quantity and the cost of the optimal quantity is no less than all other feasible quantities.[4] These conditions will be satisfied, for example, if the cost function is strictly increasing and the upper bound is equal to the optimal quantity.

The loss from using these types of constraints will depend on the situation but

---

In general, we cannot add shadow prices to determine the impact of simultaneously increasing several limits. Simultaneous changes can be considered in parametric analysis, but it may be very costly to evaluate all possible combinations of increase. If only a few combinations are evaluated, the analysis may not uncover those input increases that are required if the optimal action is to be selected. Consequently, the use of input limits followed by the use of sensitivity analysis may be quite costly, or it may result in a nonoptimal decision.

See Chapter 7 (Footnote 30 and Table 7.11) for one example of this type of analysis. Also, for more complete discussions of sensitivity analysis procedures in these contexts, see Hadley (1962), Rappaport (1967), and Wagner (1969); see Demski (1968) for a general discussion of the limitations of sensitivity analysis.

2. The quantity or range must be state indexed if the cost statistic resulting from each action is uncertain.

3. More formally, consider cost statistic $\delta_C = (\delta_u, \delta_r)$, where δ_u denotes the unrestricted elements and δ_r the restricted elements. The specified level of δ_r given state s_δ is denoted $\theta_r(s_\delta)$.

Then
$$\alpha^*(y, \eta) = \alpha(d(\cdot), M(\cdot), y, \eta)$$
if
$$E(C \mid \delta, y, \eta) = E(C_u \mid \delta_u, y, \eta) + E(C_r \mid \delta_r, y, \eta)$$
$$E(R^B \mid d, y, \eta) = E(B \mid \alpha(d, M(\cdot), y, \eta), y, \eta)$$
$$E(R^C \mid d, y, \eta) = \sum_{s_\delta \in S_\delta} E(C_u \mid \delta_u(s_\delta, d, \eta), y, \eta) \, \phi(s_\delta \mid y, \eta),$$
$$D(\theta, \phi \mid y, \eta) = \{d \mid d = a \in A \text{ and } \delta_r(s_\delta, d, \eta) = \theta_r(s_\delta), \text{ all } s_\delta \in S_\delta\},$$
and
$$\theta_r(s_\delta) = \delta_r(s_\delta, \alpha^*(y, \eta), \eta).$$

4. The formal statement of this is analogous to the preceding footnote. The last two requirements are replaced with $D(\theta, \phi \mid y, \eta) = \{d \mid d = a \in A \text{ and } \delta_r(s_\delta, a, \eta) \leq \theta_r(s_\delta), \text{ all } s_\delta \in S_\delta\}$, and $\theta_r(s_\delta) \geq \delta_r(s_\delta, \alpha^*(y, \eta), \eta) = \delta_r^*(s_\delta)$. In addition, we require that $E(C_r \mid \delta_r^*(s_\delta), y, \eta) \geq E(C_r \mid \delta_r, y, \eta)$ for all $\delta_r \leq \theta_r(s_\delta)$ and each $s_\delta \in S_\delta$.

may be relatively small if the specified level or the upper limit is close to the optimal quantity. Of course, the decision maker will not know the optimal quantity when he specifies his restrictions, and he can only attempt to develop procedures that will yield restrictions close to those optimal quantities. Periodic determination of the losses induced by his procedures may help in selecting them.

1.2   Cost Statistic Aggregation

In section 2 of Chapter 5 we stated that any set of input categories that could be used to satisfy the sufficient cost statistic requirements may be used as the set of direct inputs. This raises two basic issues. First, which inputs can be classified as indirect? This was explored to some extent in section 2, where we concluded that, in a complete analysis, an input may be classified as indirect if its cost can be expressed as a function of the direct inputs used or any other elements of the cost statistic. However, this criterion is not satisfied by many of the inputs typically classified as indirect, and thus this represents a form of simplification.

Second, how many categories should be used to describe those inputs that are classified as direct? Essentially, each input category in a complete analysis must be defined such that the cost of using the inputs is a function of only the quantities used of each category. Consequently, if two inputs are placed in the same direct input category, we assume that the costs of two actions are the same if they differ only as to which of the two inputs they use. However, this criterion is not satisfied by many of the inputs placed in the same categories, and thus this represents a form of simplification.

Both of the above simplifications result in a reduction of the number of direct input categories and we refer to them as *input aggregation*. The following subsections explore the nature of this aggregation and its evaluation.

1.2.1   THE GENERAL NATURE OF INPUT AGGREGATION

In this discussion we assume that the cost statistic consists entirely of direct inputs and the cost function is separable with respect to those inputs.[5] For the complete analysis, the vector of direct input categories is $q = (q_1, \ldots, q_m)$; the vector of simplified input categories is $\hat{q} = (\hat{q}_1, \ldots, \hat{q}_{\hat{m}})$. We also assume that each direct input is used in one, and only one, of the simplified input categories and let J_h denote the index set of direct input categories used in determining the cost of simplified input category h.[6]

The decision maker must make four types of aggregation decisions in the process of constructing this type of simplified analysis. In particular, he must select

(i)   the number of input categories: $\hat{m}$;

---

5. See Table 5.2 for assumptions and notation associated with separable direct input cost functions.

6. That is, $J_1 \cup J_2 \cup \cdots \cup J_{\hat{m}} = \{1, \ldots, m\}$, $J_{h^1} \cap J_{h^2} = \emptyset$ for all $h^1, h^2, h^1 \neq h^2$.

(ii)   the set of direct input categories to be used in determining the cost of each simplified input category: $J_1, \ldots, J_{\hat{m}}$;

(iii) the unit of measure that will be used to specify the quantity of each simplified input: $\hat{q}_1, \ldots, \hat{q}_{\hat{m}}$; and

(iv)   the cost function for each simplified input category, including the parameter predictions: $\hat{C}_1(\theta_1, \hat{q}_1), \ldots, \hat{C}_{\hat{m}}(\theta_{\hat{m}}, \hat{q}_{\hat{m}})$, and $\phi(\theta_1), \ldots, \phi(\theta_{\hat{m}})$.[7]

These selections may be made consciously by the decision maker or they may be induced by the cost information he receives. And in the latter case, the aggregation alternatives of interest are those of the accountant. For example, if the costs of inputs used in the past are observable, the accountant's aggregation alternatives may be viewed in terms of specifying

(i)   the number of aggregate cost categories to be reported: $\hat{m}$;

(ii)   the set of direct input costs to be used in determining the cost of each aggregate cost category: $J_1, \ldots, J_{\hat{m}}$; and

(iii) the activity measure to be reported in period t with each aggregate cost category: $\hat{q}_{t1}, \ldots, \hat{q}_{t\hat{m}}$.

The cost description for aggregate cost category h in period t will be $\hat{C}_{th} = \sum_{j \in J_h} C_{tj}$, where C_{tj} denotes the total cost incurred for direct input j in period t.

To provide insight into the nature of these aggregation decisions, we briefly consider two basic forms of aggregation. One occurs when a number of direct inputs have similar physical characteristics and are combined into a single simplified input category whose quantity is merely the sum of the direct inputs:

$$\hat{q}_h = \sum_{j \in J_h} q_j.$$

This form of aggregation is used, for example, when we combine various types of labor into a single labor category. The quantity of that input is then the total labor, of all types, that is used.

Observe that decision (iii), the selection of an input measure, is immediately resolved by a decision to use this form of aggregation. However, the other decisions remain to be made. For example, the number of labor categories must be selected, as well as the types of labor to be placed in each category. And once this has been done, the decision maker must also select the form and parameters of the simplified cost functions.

If the direct input cost functions are linear, the simplified cost functions will no doubt be linear. The major decision will be that of selecting the slope and intercept of each function. The slope for simplified input h will likely be a weighted average of the slopes of the cost functions for the set of direct inputs J_h; the intercept would then be the sum of the intercepts for those same input cost functions. That is, if

[6.1a] $E(C_j \mid q_j, y, \eta) = f_j + v_j q_j \qquad j \in J_h$

---

7. In this discussion, $E(\hat{C}_h \mid \hat{q}_h, y, \eta) = \sum_{\theta_h \in \Theta_h} \hat{C}_h(\theta_h, \hat{q}_h) \phi(\theta_h), \quad h = 1, \ldots, \hat{m}$.

we would then have

[6.1b] $$E(\hat{C}_h \mid \hat{q}_h, y, \eta) = \hat{f}_h + \hat{v}_h \hat{q}_h$$

where $E(\theta_h \mid y, \eta) = (\hat{f}_h, \hat{v}_h)$, $\hat{f}_h = \sum_{j \in J_h} f_j$, $\hat{v}_h = \sum_{j \in J_h} \lambda_j v_j$, and λ_j is the percentage of input h that is attributed to direct input j ($\sum_{j \in J_h} \lambda_j = 1$). The weights ($\lambda_j$) may be consciously selected by the decision maker, but in most situations he is likely to accept the weights implicit in the aggregate cost information used in predicting the cost function parameters.

A second basic form of aggregation occurs when a single direct input is used as the input measure for several direct input categories. That is, $\hat{q}_h = q_{j_h}$, where j_h is the direct input used to measure simplified input h and J_h includes all direct inputs associated with that one direct input. This form of aggregation is used when the costs of several secondary inputs are expressed as a function of some primary input[8] and when a number of miscellaneous inputs are combined into a single overhead category. In the first case the simplified input measure is the primary input, but in the overhead case the decision maker must determine an appropriate measure. An example of the first case is the inclusion of freight and material handling costs in the cost of material used. Another example is the inclusion of fringe benefits in the cost of labor used. Direct labor hours and machine hours are common examples of the input measures used in the overhead case.

Observe that the set of secondary inputs to be associated with each primary input, the number of overhead categories, the set of inputs to be associated with each overhead category, and the input measure for each overhead category must be specified in this case. Again, these selections may be made consciously by the decision maker, but in most situations they follow directly from the aggregations employed in the cost information he receives.

The form and parameters of the simplified cost functions must also be specified. As in the first form of aggregation, the simplified cost functions will no doubt be linear if the direct input cost functions are linear. The relationship in [6.1] again applies except that the weights (λ_j) now represent the quantity of input $j \in J_h$ that is expected to be used if one unit of input j_h is used.

1.2.2 EVALUATION OF INPUT AGGREGATION ALTERNATIVES[9]

One set of aggregation decisions is preferred to another if the expected utility measure (net of analysis and information costs) for the former is greater than for the latter. Unfortunately, such evaluation requires specification of the complete analysis cost function. Yet a major motivation for aggregation is to avoid the cost of doing this. Thus it would not be desirable to compute the expected utility associated with either alternative aggregate decision models or alternative aggregate

---

8. As we discussed in Chapter 5, some of these secondary inputs may be indirect inputs, and then it would not be a simplification to aggregate them.

9. See Feltham (1975) for a more extensive discussion of the evaluation of aggregation alternatives.

cost information each time a selection is to be made. On the other hand, periodic evaluation of such alternatives might provide useful information; and it may be possible to develop less costly, yet effective, surrogate evaluation procedures.

Ideally, a surrogate evaluation procedure results in the same model or system selections as the complete analysis evaluation models. However, it is effective if the expected loss due to nonoptimal selections is less than the reduction in the cost of evaluation.[10] This trade-off could be expressed formally, but it could not be calculated each time a selection is to be made (the loss would be known only if the complete analysis selections were determined).[11]

Accountants are constantly faced with selecting from among aggregation alternatives, yet there is little discussion in the accounting literature of evaluation procedures. *Homogeneity* is the main criterion that is advanced:

> For management purposes, the data in each account should be *homogeneous*. This means that the costs assigned to a particular account should exhibit the same pattern of response to the various determinants of cost behavior. [Shillinglaw 1972, p. 77]

> If the number of cost pools is small, there is a strong probability that dissimilar services and their costs are being averaged. The idea of using a "blanket overhead" pool from which assignments are made to all departments for general service charges is only satisfactory when such services are homogeneous. Every cost pool should refer to some specific activity or service; non-homogeneous services and costs can be averaged together only by sacrifice of validity.
> One important problem of cost analysis arises in this connection. There is no way to be certain that costs and services are in fact homogeneous and thus amenable to averaging, except to examine the data in detail—not only from the cost side, but also from the viewpoint of the nature of the services that flow from given cost centers. This is a basic reason why some people think that cost analysis is bound to be somewhat arbitrary, because it is inherently a matter of compromise between accuracy and expediency. Of course, there is a limit to the degree of homogeneity that can be achieved, and such efforts do take time and effort, which themselves produce costs. [Vatter 1969, pp. 34–35]

The literature provides little specific guidance as to how to implement this criterion, but regression analysis provides a surrogate evaluation procedure that is similar in spirit.[12] Given a set of observed costs $(\hat{C}_{1h}, \ldots, \hat{C}_{Th})$ and input levels $(\hat{q}_{1h}, \ldots, \hat{q}_{Th})$, classical regression analysis may be used to determine the input cost function parameters that minimize the sum of the square of the difference between the observed costs and the estimated costs given the input levels:

---

10. The expected gain from evaluating alternatives (instead of intuitive selection) must exceed the cost of evaluation—otherwise, intuition is the better evaluation procedure.

11. However, periodic assessment of the selection errors of surrogate evaluation procedures and research into the factors that cause these errors may provide useful information for deciding which procedures to employ. See Demski and Feltham (1972).

12. For a discussion of the use of regression analysis in cost prediction see Benston (1966), Horngren (1972), or Dopuch et al. (1974).

$$\min_{\hat{f}_h, \hat{v}_h} \left[\sum_{t=1}^{T} (\hat{C}_{th} - \hat{f}_h - \hat{v}_h \hat{q}_{th})^2 \right].$$

The coefficient of determination (commonly denoted r^2) then measures the percentage variation in $\hat{C}_{th}$ that is explained by variations in $\hat{q}_{th}$.[13] If alternative input measures are being considered, the evaluator may select that measure which explains the greatest percentage variation in past costs.[14] Alternatively, if the available input measures do not explain a "satisfactory" percentage of the variation, category h may be subdivided and different input measures considered for each subcategory.

1.2.3 AN INPUT AGGREGATION EXAMPLE

The following example illustrates the process of aggregation and the calculations of the loss resulting from that aggregation. For simplicity we assume that the evaluation is performed from the point of view of the decision maker and that he is subjectively certain as to the state that will occur.[15] The form of aggregation is of the first type mentioned above—the quantity of the simplified input is equal to the sum of the quantities of the complete analysis inputs.

The decision maker is concerned with the production of one product and must select the output level and the method of production for the next period. The demand is downward sloping, and thus revenue is a nonlinear function of the output to be sold. This function and other basic relationships are presented in Table 6.1. The action consists of three different processes that may be used to produce the output; one unit of activity for a given process will result in the production of one unit of output. These processes use three direct inputs: (i) material, (ii) skilled labor, and (iii) unskilled labor. All three are linear functions of the levels at which the three processes are operated. The inputs are the only elements of the cost statistic and the cost of the primary action is a linear function of the quantities used of each of these inputs.

The decision maker has decided to aggregate the skilled and unskilled labor into a single labor category. The total hours worked will be the input measure,

---

13.
$$r^2 = \frac{\sum_{t=1}^{T} (\overline{C}_h - \hat{f}_h - \hat{v}_h \hat{q}_{th})^2}{\sum_{t=1}^{T} (\overline{C}_h - \hat{C}_{th})^2}$$

where $\overline{C}_h = (1/\mathrm{T}) \sum_{t=1}^{T} \hat{C}_{th}$.

14. Other information, such as the results of specification analysis, may also be taken into consideration in this selection. But focus on the explained variation is sufficient for our purpose. See Benston (1966), Horngren (1972), and Johnston (1972) for further discussion.

15. Chapter 1 presents another simple aggregation example. That example recognizes uncertainty, and the evaluation is performed from the point of view of the accountant. See Feltham (1975) for further examples that recognize uncertainty.

TABLE 6.1 INPUT AGGREGATION EXAMPLE: BASIC ELEMENTS

Action:

$a = (a_1, a_2, a_3)$ where a_i denotes the units produced in process i

$z = a_1 + a_2 + a_3$ is the total output

Benefit Function:

$$\bar{E}(B \mid a, y, \eta) = E(R^B \mid a, y, \eta) = 11z - 0.0005z^2$$

Inputs Used:

$q_1(a) = 0.15a_1 + 0.3a_2 + 0.5a_3$ material

$q_2(a) = 0.25a_1 + 0.09a_2 + 0.12a_3$ skilled labor

$q_3(a) = 0.25a_1 + 0.27a_2 + 0.04a_3$ unskilled labor

Simplified Input Measures:

$\hat{q}_1(a) = q_1(a)$ material

$\hat{q}_2(a) = q_2(a) + q_3(a) = 0.5a_1 + 0.36a_2 + 0.16a_3$ labor

Labor Cost Function:

$E(C_2 \mid q_2, y, \eta) = 7q_2$ $E(C_2 \mid a, y, \eta) = 1.75a_1 + 0.63a_2 + 0.84a_3$

$E(C_3 \mid q_3, y, \eta) = 3q_3$ $E(C_3 \mid a, y, \eta) = 0.75a_1 + 0.81a_2 + 0.12a_3$

Simplified Labor Cost Function:

$E(\hat{C}_2 \mid \hat{q}_2, y, \eta) = [0.5(7) + 0.5(3)]\hat{q}_2 = 5\hat{q}_2$ $E(\hat{C}_2 \mid a, y, \eta) = 2.5a_1 + 1.8a_2 + 0.8a_3$

---

and the simplified cost function is based on the assumption that the two types of labor will be used in equal quantities (that is, $\lambda_2 = \lambda_3 = 0.5$).

Table 6.2 analyzes the impact of this aggregation for three different material costs. In the first case the actual and simplified cost functions differ, but both analyses select process one as the production method and their output cost functions are the same. Consequently, there is no loss of profit[16]—the selected output and production method are optimal. This is a result of the fact that process one uses a 50–50 mix of skilled and unskilled labor and the material and labor costs are such that process one is selected by both analyses.

In the second case the complete analysis selects process two and the simplified analysis selects process one. This leads to different cost functions over the output and the selection of different output levels. Consequently, there is a loss in profit. But the predicted profit is the same as the actual profit because the sumplified analysis selects process one, which uses the 50–50 mix of labor.

In the third case both analyses select process three, but the output cost functions are not the same. This again leads to the selection of different output levels

---

16. Profit (Revenue-Cost) is our utility measure in this and subsequent examples.

TABLE 6.2 INPUT AGGREGATION EXAMPLE: LOSS CALCULATIONS

	Case 1	Case 2	Case 3
Material Cost:			
$E(C_1 \mid q_1, y, \eta) = E(\hat{C}_1 \mid \hat{q}_1, y, \eta)$	$10q_1$	$6q_1$	$2q_1$
$E(C_1 \mid a, y, \eta) = E(\hat{C}_1 \mid a, y, \eta)$	$1.5a_1 + 3a_2 + 5a_3$	$0.9a_1 + 1.8a_2 + 3a_3$	$0.3a_1 + 0.6a_2 + 1.0a_3$
Complete Analysis:			
Action Cost:			
$E(C \mid a, y, \eta)$	$4a_1 + 4.44a_2 + 5.96a_3$	$3.4a_1 + 3.24a_2 + 3.96a_3$	$2.8a_1 + 2.04a_2 + 1.96a_3$
Optimal Production			
Method: $\alpha^*(z, y, \eta)$	$(z, 0, 0)$	$(0, z, 0)$	$(0, 0, z)$
Optimal Output			
Level: $z^*(y, \eta)$	7,000	7,760	9,040
Optimal Profit:			
$E(U \mid \alpha^*(y, \eta), y, \eta)$	\$24,500.00	\$30,108.80	\$40,860.80
Simplified Analysis:			
Action Cost:			
$E(R^c \mid a, y, \eta)$	$4a_1 + 4.8a_2 + 5.8a_3$	$3.4a_1 + 3.6a_2 + 3.8a_3$	$2.8a_1 + 2.4a_2 + 1.8a_3$
Selected Production			
Method: $\alpha(z, M(\cdot), y, \eta)$	$(z, 0, 0)$	$(z, 0, 0)$	$(0, 0, z)$
Selected Output			
Level: $z(M(\cdot))$	7,000	7,600	9,200
Predicted Profit:			
$E(R \mid \alpha(\cdot), y, \eta)$	\$24,500.00	\$28,880.00	\$42,320.00
Evaluation:			
Actual Profit:			
$E(U \mid M(\cdot), y, \eta)$	\$24,500.00	\$28,880.00	\$40,848.00
Loss in Profit:			
$L(M(\cdot), y, \eta) = E(U \mid \alpha^*(\cdot), y, \eta)$			
$ - E(U \mid M(\cdot), y, \eta)$	\$0	\$ 1,228.80	\$ 12.80

and a loss in profit. In this case the actual profit and the predicted profit also differ; process three does not use a 50–50 mix of labor.

2.0 SIMPLIFICATION OF THE FORM OF THE COST FUNCTION

There are two basic reasons for simplifying the form of a cost function. First, complete analysis functions are usually very complex, and thus it is costly to precisely specify them. Second, the irregularity of those functions would often make it difficult to determine which action would result in the maximum utility measure. The simplified cost and benefit functions that are commonly employed have mathematical characteristics that permit the use of efficient algorithms for locating the "optimal" action. Of course, the "optimal" action based on the simplified function will probably not be the action that would be selected on the basis of a complete analysis.

The linear function is the commonest form of simplified function, and it is particularly prevalent in accounting. Consequently, we focus on linear approximations in this section, first discussing their general nature and impact and then discussing the impact of linear approximations to step functions.[17]

2.1 LINEAR APPROXIMATIONS TO NONLINEAR COST FUNCTIONS

The following discussion considers the general nature of linear approximations and provides an example to illustrate the loss that may result from using three specific approximation methods.

2.1.1 THE GENERAL NATURE OF LINEAR APPROXIMATIONS

We will refer to a cost function as being linear if it takes the following form:

[6.2]
$$E(\hat{C} \mid z, y, \eta) = \hat{f} + \hat{v}z$$

where z is the object of costing (for example, outputs, inputs, or production activities) and $\hat{f}$ and $\hat{v}$ are constants.[18] Two linear output cost functions are depicted in Figure 6.1; in (a) the set of feasible output levels is the set of nonnegative real numbers and in (b) the output is restricted to the set of nonnegative integers.

As illustrated in Chapter 5, complete analysis cost functions are seldom

---

17. We will not discuss other approximations, although they certainly exist. For example, quadratic cost functions are often used in aggregate production-scheduling models so that calculus may be used to derive a linear decision rule. See Holt et al. (1960) and Buffa (1968). Hanssman and Hess (1960) formulate a linear programming model of the same decision and, of course, use linear cost functions.

18. Our use of the term "linear" is consistent with its popular usage, but in mathematics literature the term linear is often restricted to functions in which $\hat{f}$ is zero. For example, see Rudin (1964), p. 184, and Luenberger (1969), p. 104.

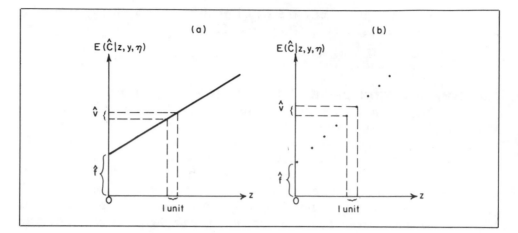

Fig. 6.1. Linear output cost functions.

linear. Yet linear functions are frequently used because of their simplicity and the widely held belief that such functions provide satisfactory approximations. In fact, if a linear function provides a close approximation to the complete function, we know that the loss due to simplification will be relatively small. This point is illustrated by the following proposition:

Proposition 6.1: [19]

$$L(M(\cdot), y, \eta) \leq k^+ + k^-$$

where

$$k^+ = \max_{a \in A} [E(U \mid a, y, \eta) - E(R \mid a, y, \eta)]$$

$$k^- = \max_{a \in A} [E(R \mid a, y, \eta) - E(U \mid a, y, \eta)]$$

and $d = a.$

That is, the loss will not be any greater than the sum of the largest understatement plus the largest overstatement of the expected utility measure.[20]

---

19. *Proof:*

$$E(R \mid d(M(y, \eta)), y, \eta) - E(R \mid \alpha^*(y, \eta), y, \eta) \geq 0$$
$$[E(U \mid d(M(y, \eta)), y, \eta) + k^-] - [E(U \mid \alpha^*(y, \eta), y, \eta) - k^+] \geq 0$$
$$E(U \mid d(M(y, \eta)), y, \eta) - E(U \mid \alpha^*(y, \eta), y, \eta) \geq -k^- - k^+$$
$$E(U \mid \alpha^*(y, \eta), y, \eta) - E(U \mid d(M(y, \eta)), y, \eta) \leq k^+ + k^-$$
$$L(M(\cdot), y, \eta) \leq k^+ + k^-$$

20. If the decision maker is "certain" that the optimal action and the action selected by the simplified analysis will belong to a particular subset of A, then k^+ and k^- may be determined using that subset. In accounting terminology, that subset is the "relevant range." Moreover, after the simplified

A desirable aspect of the above upper bound is that it is the same for any two simplified models that only differ by a constant (that is, $E(R^1 \mid a, y, \eta) - E(R^2 \mid a, y, \eta) = k$, for all $a \in A$). These two simplified models will result in the selection of the same action. This means that differences in the intercept have no impact on the loss. Consequently, the crucial aspect of a linear cost function is its slope.[21]

Many procedures commonly used to determine the slope (and intercept) of linear cost functions are based on rather simple analyses of historical data.[22] Three such procedures are illustrated in the following example.[23] The first (account classification) treats the cost of each input as either strictly variable or strictly fixed. For the former the slope is equal to the average cost per unit, and for the latter it is zero. The second (high-low points method) determines the slope from two representative observations, one "high" and one "low." The third

---

analysis has been completed, the bound may be restated as

$$L(M(\cdot), y, \eta) \leq k^+ + k^1$$

where

$$k^1 = E(R \mid d(M(y, \eta)), y, \eta) - E(U \mid d(M(y, \eta)), y, \eta).$$

Both of these changes will improve the upper bound in that it will not be further from the actual loss. In general, however, we will not know how close it is.

21. The importance of the slope is further illustrated by the following:

If (i) $E(U \mid z^*) = \max_{z \geq 0} [E(B \mid z) - E(C \mid z)]$,

   (ii) $E(B \mid z)$ is strictly concave and differentiable,
   (iii) $E(C \mid z)$ is convex and differentiable, and
   (iv) $E(R \mid z) = [E(B \mid z) - \hat{v}^*z]$

where

$$\hat{v}^* = \frac{d\,E(C \mid z)}{dz}\bigg|_{z = z^*}$$

then

$$E(R \mid z^*) = \max_{z \geq 0} [E(R \mid z)].$$

That is, under the appropriate conditions, a linear approximation will result in the selection of the optimal output if the slope of the linear function is equal to the marginal cost of the optimal output. Furthermore, under these conditions, if the slope of one approximating function is closer to $\hat{v}^*$ than the slope of another function, the loss resulting from the use of the former will be less than the loss resulting from the latter. (This statement applies only if both slopes understate or overstate $\hat{v}^*$.)

Similar results can be obtained for the multiple output case or for decision variables other than output, including production activities and inputs used. These results can also be extended to the case where the set of feasible outputs is the set of nonnegative integers; in that case the desired slope of the linear cost function is $E(C \mid z^* + 1) - E(C \mid z^*)$. However, these results depend critically on the convexity and strict concavity conditions of the cost and revenue functions.

22. An exception is the use of engineering studies to predict the material, labor, and machine hours that will be used in producing various outputs, particularly for new products.

23. See Horngren (1972) and Dopuch et al. (1974) for discussions of these procedures.

TABLE 6.3 LINEAR APPROXIMATION EXAMPLE: BASIC RELATIONSHIPS
AND THE COMPLETE ANALYSIS

Action:

$$a = (a_1, a_2, a_3) \qquad \text{where } a_i \text{ is the units produced in process } i$$
$$z = a_1 + a_2 + a_3 \qquad \text{is the total output}$$

Benefit Function:

$$E(B \mid a, y, \eta) = E(R^B \mid a, y, \eta) = 11z - 0.0005z^2$$

Inputs Used:

$$q_1(a) = \hat{q}_1(a) = 0.06a_1 + 0.3a_2 + 0.5a_3$$
$$q_2(a) = \hat{q}_2(a) = 0.5a_1 + 0.3a_2 + 0.2a_3$$

Input Cost Functions:

$$E(C_1 \mid q_1, y, \eta) = 10q_1$$
$$E(C_2 \mid q_2, y, \eta) = 10{,}000 + 0.008(q_2)^2$$

Action Cost Function:

$$E(C \mid a, y, \eta) = E(C_1 \mid q_1(a), y, \eta) + E(C_2 \mid q_2(a), y, \eta)$$
$$= 10{,}000 + 0.6a_1 + 3.0a_2 + 5.0a_3$$
$$+ 0.008[0.5a_1 + 0.3a_2 + 0.2a_3]^2$$

Optimal Production Method:

$$\alpha^*(z, y, \eta) = \begin{cases} (z, 0, 0) & 0 \le z \le 1{,}500 \\ (3{,}750 - 1.5z, 2.5z - 3{,}750, 0) & 1{,}500 \le z \le 2{,}500 \\ (0, z, 0) & 2{,}500 \le z \le 4{,}167 \\ (0, 12{,}500 - 2z, 3z - 12{,}500) & 4{,}167 \le z \le 6{,}250 \\ (0, 0, z) & 6{,}250 \le z < \infty \end{cases}$$

Optimal Output and Production Activities:

$$z^*(y, \eta) = 3{,}279 \qquad \alpha^*(y, \eta) = (0, 3{,}279, 0)$$

Optimal Profit:

$$E(U \mid \alpha^*(y, \eta), y, \eta) = E(B \mid \alpha^*(y, \eta), y, \eta) - E(C \mid \alpha^*(y, \eta), y, \eta)$$
$$= \$3{,}115$$

(regression analysis) uses all the representative observations available, and selects the slope and intercept so as to minimize the sum of the square of the differences between the simplified cost function and the observed costs.

2.1.2 A LINEAR APPROXIMATION EXAMPLE

Consider a decision maker who must select the output level and production method for a single product. As before, we have a downward sloping demand

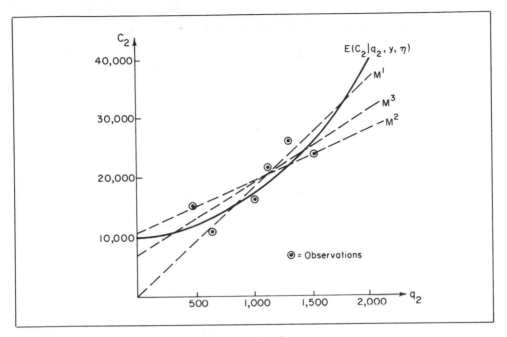

Fig. 6.2. The input cost function and its approximations.

curve and three production processes. Two direct inputs are employed; the cost function is linear for one and nonlinear for the other. Table 6.3 presents the basic model elements and its complete solution.

The complete analysis is fairly complex, largely because the nonlinearity of the second input cost function causes the optimal production method to vary over the set of possible output levels. If, however, we assume that the decision maker simplifies his analysis by using a linear cost function for the second input, one production method will appear to be optimal for all output levels. Further assume that six "representative" periods of cost and input level observations are available (these observations are included in y and are encompassed in the complete analysis cost prediction):

t	1	2	3	4	5	6
C_{t2}	16,000	11,000	26,000	15,000	22,000	24,000
q_{t2}	1,000	600	1,300	500	1,100	1,500

These observations, the complete analysis cost function, and three approximations are plotted in Figure 6.2. The losses resulting from the three approximations are computed in Table 6.4.

The cost of the second input clearly varies with the level of input, and thus it would no doubt be classified as variable under the account classification method (denoted M^1). The average cost per unit over the past six periods has been \$19.

TABLE 6.4 LINEAR APPROXIMATION EXAMPLE: LOSS CALCULATIONS

	M^1: Account Classification	M^2: High-Low Points Method	M^3: Regression Analysis
Simplified Analysis:			
Input Cost Functions: $E(\hat{C}_1 \mid \hat{q}_1, y, \eta)$ $E(\hat{C}_2 \mid \hat{q}_2, y, \eta)$	$10q_1$ $19q_2$	$10q_1$ $10{,}500 + 9q_2$	$10q_1$ $5{,}710 + 13.29q_2$
Action Cost: $E(R^C \mid a, y, \eta)$	$10.1a_1 + 8.7a_2 + 8.8a_3$	$10{,}500 + 5.1a_1 + 5.7a_2 + 6.8a_3$	$5{,}710 + 7.25a_1 + 6.99a_2 + 7.66a_3$
Selected Production Method: $\alpha(z, M(\cdot), y, \eta)$	$(0, z, 0)$	$(z, 0, 0)$	$(0, z, 0)$
Selected Output Level: $z(M(\cdot))$	$2{,}300$	$5{,}900$	$4{,}010$
Predicted Profit: $E(R \mid \alpha(\cdot), y, \eta)$	$\$2{,}645$	$\$6{,}905$	$\$2{,}330$
Evaluation:			
Actual Profit: $E(U \mid M(\cdot), y, \eta)$	$\$1{,}946$	$\$-35{,}665$	$\$2{,}462$
Loss in Profit: $L(M(\cdot), y, \eta)$ $= E(U \mid \alpha^*(\cdot), y, \eta)$ $\quad - E(U \mid M(\cdot), y, \eta)$	$\underline{\underline{\$1{,}169}}$	$\underline{\underline{\$\ 38{,}780}}$	$\underline{\underline{\$\ \ 653}}$

Use of this average as the predicted cost overstates the relevant marginal cost of the input.[24] Consequently, the selected output level is too small and there is a loss of $1,169. Observe, however, that the optimal production method is selected despite this overstatement.

Use of the high-low points method (denoted M^2) results in a predicted variable cost per unit of $9. This understates the relevant marginal cost of the input and results in the selection of both a nonoptimal production method and an output level that is too large. The resulting loss is $38,780.[25]

Finally, regression analysis (denoted M^3) provides a predicted variable cost per unit of $13.29. This slightly understates the relevant marginal cost of the input but is closer than either of the other two approximations. The optimal production method is selected, but the selected output level is too large. The resulting loss is $653.[26]

Before leaving this example, consider the bound developed in Proposition 6.1. A crucial factor in computing that bound is the set of possible actions that are considered. We consider those that result in the use of 0 to 3,000 units of the second input. The upper bounds for the three approximations are

	k^+	k^-	$k^+ + k^-$
M^1	1,281	25,000	26,281
M^2	3,031	44,500	47,531
M^3	1,230	36,420	37,650

The upper bound for M^2 is somewhat indicative of the loss that occurs, but the upper bounds are much greater than the actual losses for the other two cases. This is because they greatly understate the cost function at $q_2 = 3,000$, while the decisions based on those approximations do not use anywhere near that quantity. A smaller range of input quantities would be more appropriate for M^1 and M^3.[27]

---

24. This decision context satisfies the conditions outlined in Footnote 21. Consequently, the following variable cost per unit for input 2 will result in selection of both the optimal production method and the optimal output level:

$$\hat{v}_2^* = \left.\frac{dE(C_2 \mid q_2, y, \eta)}{dq_2}\right|_{q_2 = q_2(\alpha^*(y, \eta))} = 0.016 q_2 \Big|_{q_2 = 0.3(3279)} = 15.74.$$

25. Observe that providing a very good prediction of the fixed cost is of no value. It is the slope that is important.

26. The coefficient of determination (r^2) is 0.78 for this sample of points. The lack of fit, however, is due largely to random cost factors and not the nonlinearity of the complete analysis cost function. In fact, the percentage variation in the observed costs "explained" by the latter is only 0.74. This is lower than for the linear approximation because the complete analysis function reflects all information available to the decision maker—not just the six observations.

27. Alternatively, we can use the bound developed in Footnote 20.

	k^+	k^1	$k^+ + k^1$
M^1	1,281	699	1,980
M^2	3,031	42,570	45,601
M^3	1,230	−120	1,110

where k^1 is the difference between the "actual" and the "predicted" cost of input 2 at the input level selected by the simplified analysis.

2.2   LINEAR APPROXIMATIONS TO STEP FUNCTIONS

A step function is nonlinear, and thus the general discussion in the preceding section applies to this type of function. This section specializes our discussion to the step function case. There are two reasons for doing this. First, the step function is very prominent in the accounting literature; it is often listed as a fourth cost category, along with fixed, variable, and semivariable (see Horngren 1972; Dopuch et al. 1974). Second, the special structure of this function allows us to make more specific comments than can be made for nonlinear functions in general.

2.2.1   THE GENERAL NATURE OF STEP FUNCTION COSTS

A basic step function is depicted in Figure 6.3; it is characterized by intermittent jumps (steps) in the cost function. A common cause of these steps is the inability of the firm to acquire fractional quantities of an input despite the fact that fractional quantities can be used. For example, employees must usually be hired (or at least paid) for some minimum period of time such as a day, week, or month, even if the firm wishes to use them for only some fraction of that period. (Many raw materials, such as manufactured parts, cannot be acquired in fractional units, but this does not create a step function unless fractional units are used.)

Although the basic acquisition prices for many inputs are applicable only for the acquisition of "whole" units, it is often possible to obtain fractional quantities by paying premium prices. This situation is depicted in Figure 6.4; the slope of the cost function between steps is the premium price that must be paid. Once the total premium is equal to the regular cost of a whole unit, an additional unit will be acquired and some portion will merely be unused. For example, rather than hire an employee to work only a fraction of his time, those employees who are to work full time might be asked to work overtime. If too much overtime is required, it will be cheaper to hire an additional employee and allow him to have some idle time. This was illustrated in the work-force example in section 2.4 of Chapter 5.

In the discussions that follow we focus on the two types of input cost functions depicted in Figures 6.3 and 6.4. In the first case, there is no possibility of

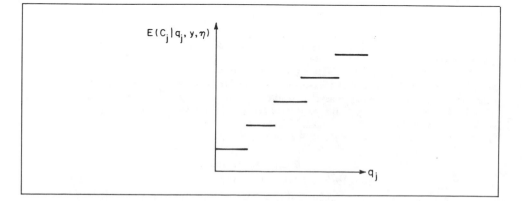

Fig. 6.3. Basic step function.

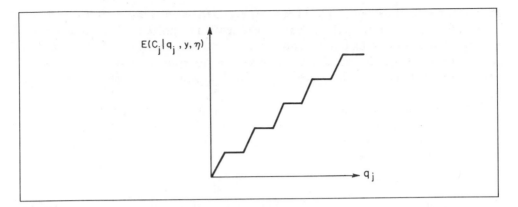

Fig. 6.4. Fractional acquisition at premium rates.

fractional acquisitions and the cost of the inputs used is constant between steps. This input cost function is defined as

[6.3] $$E(C_j \mid q_j, y, \eta) = v_j I(q_j)$$

where $I(q_j)$ denotes the smallest integer that is greater than or equal to q_j and v_j denotes the expected cost of one unit of input j.

In the second case fractional units can be acquired at a premium rate. This input cost is defined as

[6.4] $$E(C_j \mid q_j, y, \eta) = \begin{cases} v_j I(q_j) & q_j - I'(q_j) \geq v_j/v_j' \\ v_j I'(q_j) + v_j'[q_j - I'(q_j)] & q_j - I'(q_j) \leq v_j/v_j' \end{cases}$$

where v_j' is the expected premium rate and $I'(q_j)$ denotes the largest integer that is less than or equal to q_j. Observe that the cost function reflects the fact that it is less costly to acquire fractional units at a rate of v_j' if the fractional quantity required is less than v_j/v_j'. If the fractional quantity required exceeds that amount, it is less costly to acquire a whole unit at the regular price and leave a portion unused.

2.2.2 STEP FUNCTION APPROXIMATIONS

The existence of step function costs makes it difficult to determine the optimal output and production methods. A mathematical programming model would have to contain integer variables and these usually make the solution costly to obtain. Consequently, simplified functions are commonly used, unless the decision maker considers the step function to be an important part of the analysis.

These issues lead to two basic questions: (i) when should step functions be simplified and (ii) what form should the simplifications take? The accounting literature typically suggests rather *ad hoc* procedures at this point. If the steps are relatively small, they are ignored and the cost is classified as variable. If the steps are relatively large and the relevant range is contained within one step, the appropriate step is classified as a fixed cost. If more than one large step is contained within the relevant range, the steps are explicitly recognized. This approach is perhaps a reasonable one, but it is rather vague in that no reference is made to the consequences of the simplifications involved. Furthermore, it is not clear what constitutes a relatively small or large step. The following analysis sheds some light on these issues.

We first consider the suggestion that the step function be approximated by a linear function if the steps are small. We assume that this is accomplished by letting the regular cost per unit, v_j, become the slope of the linear cost function. That is, $\hat{v}_j = v_j$ and the simplified cost function is

[6.5] $$E(\hat{C}_j \mid q_j, y, \eta) = v_j q_j.$$

with an intercept, $\hat{f}$, equal to zero. This simplified cost function is depicted in Figure 6.5.

From Proposition 6.1 we know that the loss resulting from the use of an approximating function will not exceed the sum of the maximum overstatement plus the maximum understatement of the complete analysis cost function. From Figure 6.5 we see that this linear approximation never overstates the complete analysis cost function. However, it understates the actual cost function at all points except those corresponding to whole units.

If, then, the linear function given in [6.5] is used to approximate the basic step function given in [6.3], the understatement is less than v_j for all values of q_j. It approaches this amount for values of q_j that are slightly greater than $I'(q_j)$.[28] Consequently, in the basic case $k_j^+ + k_j^- = v_j$; and the loss will not exceed the cost of one unit of input.[29]

Similarly, if the linear function given in [6.5] is used to approximate the input cost function given in [6.4], the maximum understatement is $(v_j' - v_j)(v_j/v_j')$. This amount occurs at the point where the decision maker is indifferent between obtaining fractional quantities at the premium price v_j' or acquiring a whole unit at the regular price v_j. Consequently, $k_j^+ + k_j^- = (v_j' - v_j)(v_j/v_j') < (v_j' - v_j)$; that is, the loss will not exceed the difference between the premium and regular price.[30]

---

28. In this particular case, the maximum used to define k^- does not exist and we must use the supremum instead.

29. From Footnote 20, we know that after the simplified analysis has been completed we can replace k_j^- with

$$k_j^1 = E(C_j \mid q_j(\alpha(\cdot)), y, \eta) - E(\hat{C}_j \mid q_j(\alpha(\cdot)), y, \eta)$$

where $q_j(\alpha(\cdot))$ is the amount of input j that will be used if the action is selected by the simplified model. In the basic step function case

$$k_j^1 = v_j[I(q_j(\alpha(\cdot))) - q_j(\alpha(\cdot))].$$

That is, the loss will not exceed the "variable" cost of the fraction of any unit that is acquired but not used.

30. In the fractional acquisition case,

$$k_j^1 = \begin{cases} v_j[I(q_j(\alpha(\cdot))) - q_j(\alpha(\cdot))] & q_j(\cdot) - I'(\cdot) \geq v_j/v_j' \\ (v_j' - v_j)[q_j(\alpha(\cdot)) - I'(q_j(\alpha(\cdot)))] & q_j(\cdot) - I'(\cdot) \leq v_j/v_j'. \end{cases}$$

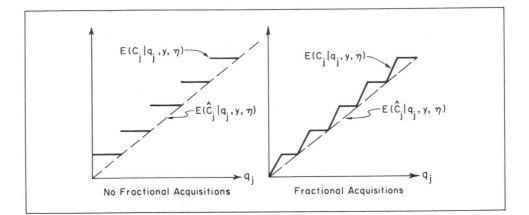

Fig. 6.5. Step function approximations.

Now consider the suggestion that the step function be treated as a fixed cost—a linear function with zero slope—if the steps are large. This assumes that the resulting input usage will be within some expected range; and most discussions are rather vague as to what happens if the selected action would result in the use of more inputs than expected. One possible approach is to assume that the decision maker (or his superior) has selected the quantity that will be acquired and the action selected will not require input usage in excess of the quantity to be acquired. This, in effect, replaces the cost function with a constraint and is an example of the situation discussed in section 1.1.

If, on the other hand, there are no constraints, this implies that the firm intends to acquire all inputs required by the selected action. This may result in the selection of the optimal action, but only if the step function cost has no effect on the decision. Further investigation might indicate some conditions under which the step function has no effect.

2.2.3 STEP FUNCTION APPROXIMATION EXAMPLES

We now consider three examples of approximating step functions with linear functions. The first two are the same except that the second admits the possibility of hiring employees to work overtime. Both examples assume that there is only one production method and that the decision is concerned with selecting the output to be produced. The third example is similar to the examples in sections 1.2 and 2.1 in that there are three alternative production methods for producing a single output.

Examples One and Two: The basic elements and complete analyses for the first two examples are presented in Table 6.5. A downward sloping demand curve provides a strictly concave revenue function. There are three inputs: labor, machines, and material. The material cost is a linear function. The machine cost is a step function—the firm must lease a machine for an entire month or not at all. In example one, the labor cost is a step function—an employee must be hired for an

TABLE 6.5 BASIC ELEMENTS AND COMPLETE ANALYSIS FOR STEP FUNCTION EXAMPLES ONE AND TWO

Action: $a = z$ is the total output produced

Benefit Function:

$$E(B \mid a, y, \eta) = E(R^B \mid z, y, \eta) = 160z - 0.1z^2$$

Inputs Used:

$$q_1(a) = \hat{q}_1(a) = 0.03125z \quad \text{labor}$$
$$q_2(a) = \hat{q}_2(a) = 0.008z \quad \text{machines}$$
$$q_3(a) = \hat{q}_3(a) = 30z \quad \text{material}$$

Example One	Example Two
Input Cost Functions: $E(C_1 \mid q_1, y, \eta) = 480\, I(q_1)$ $E(C_2 \mid q_2, y, \eta) = 750\, I(q_2)$ $E(C_3 \mid q_3, y, \eta) = 0.4q_3$	$E(C_1 \mid q_1, y, \eta) = \min \begin{cases} 480\, I(q_1) \\ 480\, I'(q_1) + 800(q_1 - I'(q_1)) \end{cases}$ $E(C_2 \mid q_2, y, \eta) = 750\, I(q_2)$ $E(C_3 \mid q_3, y, \eta) = 0.4q_3$
Action (Output) Cost Function: $E(C \mid z, y, \eta) = 480I(0.03125z) + 750I(0.008z) + 12z$	$E(C \mid z, y, \eta) = \min \begin{cases} 480I(0.03125z) + 750I(0.008z) + 12z \\ 480I'(0.03125z) + 750I(0.008z) + 12z \\ \qquad + 800(0.03125z - I'(0.03125z)) \end{cases}$
Optimal Output: $z^* = \alpha^*(y, \eta) = 608$	$z^* = \alpha^*(y, \eta) = 615$
Optimal Profit: $E(U \mid \alpha^*(y, \eta), y, \eta) = \$40{,}148$	$E(U \mid \alpha^*(y, \eta), y, \eta) = \$40{,}153$

TABLE 6.6 LOSS CALCULATIONS FOR STEP FUNCTION EXAMPLES ONE AND TWO

Simplified Analysis:
  Input Cost Function:

$$E(\hat{C}_1 \mid \hat{q}_1, y, \eta) = 480\hat{q}_1$$
$$E(\hat{C}_2 \mid \hat{q}_2, y, \eta) = 750\hat{q}_2$$
$$E(\hat{C}_3 \mid \hat{q}_3, y, \eta) = 0.4\hat{q}_3$$

Action (Output) Cost Function:

$$E(R^C \mid z, y, \eta) = 33z$$

Selected Output:

$$z(M(\cdot)) = 635$$

Predicted Profit:

$$E(R \mid z(M(\cdot)), y, \eta) = \$40{,}323$$

Evaluation:

Example One	Example Two
Actual Profit: $E(U \mid M(\cdot), y, \eta) = \$39{,}558$	$E(U \mid M(\cdot), y, \eta) = \$39{,}558$
Loss in Profit: $L(M(\cdot), y, \eta) = E(U \mid \alpha^*(\cdot), y, \eta)$ $\qquad - E(U \mid M(\cdot), y, \eta) = \underline{\underline{\$590}}$	$L(M(\cdot), y, \eta) = \underline{\underline{\$595}}$

entire month (\$3 per hour for 160 hours) and there is no possibility of having employees work overtime. The second example admits the possibility of overtime at the rate of \$5 per hour.[31]

Prior to conducting either a simplified or complete analysis, we can compute the loss upper bound described above. This computation reveals that the loss in example one will not exceed \$1,230 and in example two it will not exceed \$942.[32]

---

31. Note that overtime cannot be used to expand the machine capacity.

32. These upper bounds are calculated as follows:

$$v_1 + v_2 = 480 + 750 = 1{,}230$$
$$(v_1' - v_1)(v_1/v_1') + v_2 = (800 - 480)(480/800) + 750$$
$$= 192 + 750 = 942.$$

After the simplified analysis has been completed, the upper bound for examples one and two can be

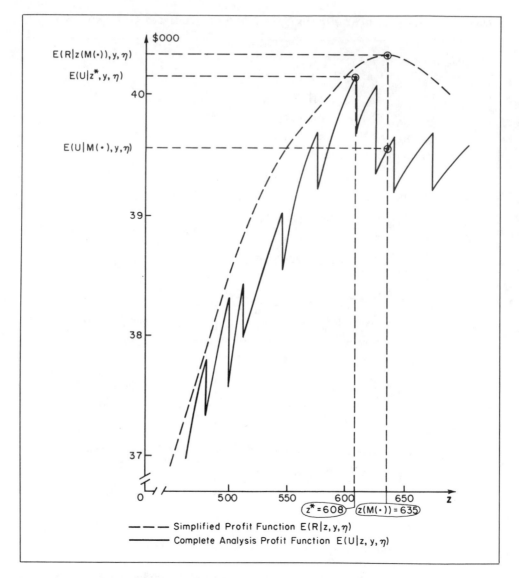

Fig. 6.6. Profit function with step function costs.

recomputed:

$$v_1\left[I(q_1(\alpha(\cdot))) - q_1(\alpha(\cdot))\right] + v_2\left[I(q_2(\alpha(\cdot))) - q_2(\alpha(\cdot))\right] = 480[20 - 19.84] + 750[6 - 5.08]$$
$$= 77 + 690$$
$$= 767.$$

This bound is the same in both examples because the selected output does not involve the use of overtime.

Table 6.6 presents the simplified analysis and its evaluation, revealing actual losses of $590 in example one and $595 in example two.

Figures 6.6 and 6.7 depict the complete and simplified analysis profit functions for the two examples. From these figures we see that the loss in profit is due in part to underutilization of resources. If the twentieth man were used to capacity, the actual profit would have increased to $39,660. Also, if another man had been hired and fully used, so as to more fully use the sixth machine, the profit would have been increased to $39,668. On the other hand, we see that it is best to acquire only five machines and nineteen men. In case one, the nineteen men are used to capacity and the fifth machine is slightly underutilized. In case two, the nineteen men are required to work a few hours of overtime but not enough to fully use the fifth machine.

In summary, we see that there are two types of causes of the loss in profit that may result from the use of a simplified cost function. First, the production plan selected may lead to the acquisition of the wrong quantity of inputs. Second, even if the correct input quantities are acquired, they may not be used optimally.

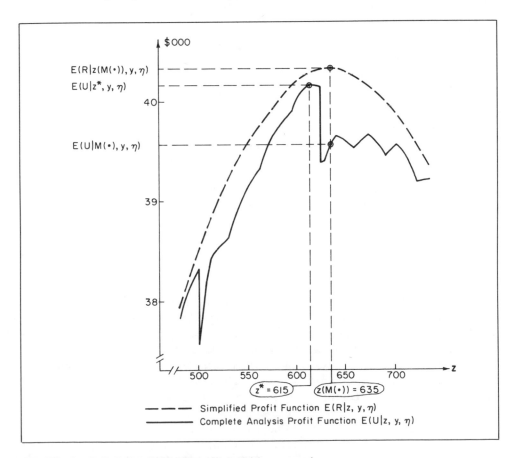

Fig. 6.7. Profit function for fractional acquisition example.

TABLE 6.7 BASIC ELEMENTS AND COMPLETE ANALYSIS
FOR STEP FUNCTION EXAMPLE THREE

Action:

$$a = (a_1, a_2, a_3) \qquad \text{where } a_i \text{ is the units produced in process } i$$
$$z = a_1 + a_2 + a_3 \qquad \text{is the total output}$$

Benefit Function:

$$E(B \mid a, y, \eta) = E(R^B \mid a, y, \eta) = 11z - 0.0005z^2$$

Inputs Used:

$$q_1(a) = \hat{q}_1(a) = 0.5a_1 + 0.33a_2 + 0.25a_3$$
$$q_2(a) = \hat{q}_2(a) = 0.0015a_1 + 0.003a_2 + 0.005a_3$$

Input Cost Functions:

$$E(C_1 \mid q_1, y, \eta) = 5q_1$$
$$E(C_2 \mid q_2, y, \eta) = 1,000 \, I(q_2)$$

Action Cost Function:

$$E(C \mid a, y, \eta) = 2.5a_1 + 1.65a_2 + 1.25a_3$$
$$+ 1,000 \, I(0.0015a_1 + 0.003a_2 + 0.005a_3)$$

Optimal Production Method:

$$\alpha^*(z, y, \eta) = \begin{cases} (0, 0, z) & 0 \le z \le 200 \\ (0, 2.5z - 500, 500 - 1.5z) & 200 \le z \le 333 \\ (2z - 666 \, I(0.0015z), 666 \, I(0.0015z) - z, 0) & 333 \le z < \infty \end{cases}$$

Optimal Output and Production Activities:

$$z^*(y, \eta) = 7,333 \text{ or } 6,666 \qquad \alpha^*(y, \eta) = (7,333, 0, 0) \text{ or } (6,666, 0, 0)$$

Optimal Profit:

$$E(U \mid \alpha^*(y, \eta), y, \eta) = \underline{\underline{\$24,444}}$$

Example Three: The basic elements and complete analysis for the third example are given in Table 6.7. A downward sloping demand curve again provides a
strictly concave revenue function; there are three production methods and two
inputs. The cost of the first is linear, but the second is a step function.

The step function cost results in a rather complex relationship between the
output and the optimal production method. The optimal production method, for
most output levels, is a combination of process one and process two. Furthermore, except at very low output levels, the optimal production method fully
utilizes any units of the second input that are acquired.

Prior to conducting either a simplified or complete analysis, we know that the
loss from using a linear approximation will not exceed $1,000—the cost of one unit

TABLE 6.8   LOSS CALCULATIONS FOR STEP FUNCTION EXAMPLE THREE

Simplified Analysis:

Input Cost Functions:

$$E(\hat{C}_1 \mid \hat{q}_1, y, \eta) = 5\hat{q}_1$$
$$E(\hat{C}_2 \mid \hat{q}_2, y, \eta) = 1,000\hat{q}_2$$

Action Cost:

$$E(R^C \mid a, y, \eta) = 4a_1 + 4.65a_2 + 6.25a_3$$

Selected Production Method:

$$\alpha(z, M(\cdot), y, \eta) = (z, 0, 0)$$

Selected Output Level:

$$z(M(\cdot)) = 7,000$$

Predicted Profit:

$$E(R \mid \alpha(\cdot), y, \eta) = \$24,500$$

Evaluation:

Actual profit:

$$E(U \mid M(\cdot), y, \eta) = \$24,000$$

Loss in Profit:

$$L(M(\cdot), y, \eta) = E(U \mid \alpha^*(\cdot), y, \eta) - E(U \mid M(\cdot), y, \eta)$$
$$= \underline{\underline{\$444}}$$

---

of input two.[33] Evaluation of the simplified analysis reveals a loss of $444 (see Table 6.8). Insight into the reasons for this loss is provided by Figure 6.8, which presents the profit as a function of the selected output. Three profit functions are depicted. The simplified profit function assumes that the cost of the second input is linear and thus process one is used to produce all output levels. The second profit function presents the actual (complete analysis) profit, given that process one is used to produce all output levels; it is much less than the first due to the nonlinearity of the input cost. The third profit function presents the optimal profit for each output level. The simplified analysis selects a nonoptimal output level and further compounds this error by selecting a nonoptimal production

---

33. After the simplified analysis is completed we know that the loss cannot exceed $500; that is, from Footnote 20 we compute the upper bound

$$k^+ + k^1 = 1,000[I(0.0015 \times 7,000) - 0.0015 \times 7,000]$$
$$= 1,000[11 - 10.5]$$
$$= 500.$$

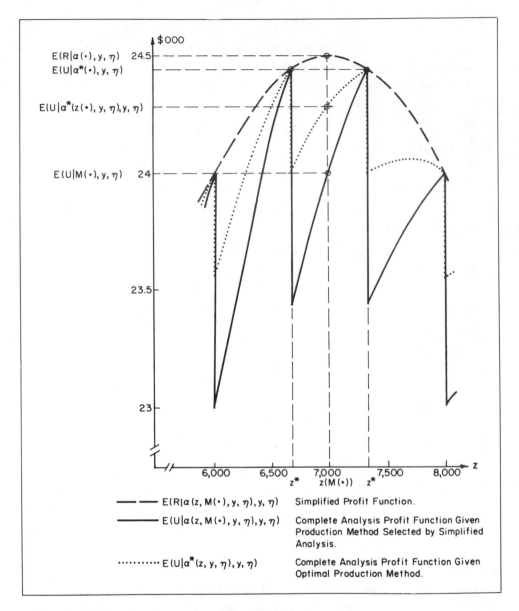

Fig. 6.8. Profit functions for step function example three.

method. The quantity of the second input acquired (11 units) is optimal, but it is underutilized.

3.0 DECISION DECOMPOSITION AND COST ALLOCATION

In this section we explore the use of cost allocation to facilitate separate selection of subcomponents of the action vector. To simplify the discussion, we assume that the subcomponents are independent except for the fact that they use common inputs.

The analysis applies to at least two major types of situations. The first arises when the decision maker has a number of activities to select and, for whatever reason, separately selects subsets of these activities instead of selecting them simultaneously. One common example is the use of separate inventory models for each type of material handled by a purchasing department.

The second situation arises when the decision maker divides his operations into a number of departments and then delegates authority, over some elements of departmental operations, to departmental managers. Cost allocations are used to construct departmental performance measures that the decision maker then uses to influence the action selections of his managers. Arrow refers to this as organizational *control* and points out that "it divides itself naturally into two parts: the choice of *operating rules* instructing the members of the organization how to act, and the choice of *enforcement rules* to persuade or compel them to act in accordance with the operating rules" (Arrow 1964, p. 393). We focus on operating rules in this discussion and essentially ignore the enforcement rules.[34]

Prior to discussing specific allocations we specify the complete analysis problem facing the decision maker. This model is then used to analyze the allocation of both predicted and sunk costs.

3.1 THE DECOMPOSED DECISION PROBLEM

We assume that the decision maker has divided his decision into n components and let a_i denote the activities that constitute component i. (Alternatively, a_i denotes the activities of department i.) To facilitate our analysis we adopt the following additional assumptions:

  (i)   The benefit function is separable with respect to the action components;
  (ii) The inputs used are known, separable functions of the action components; and
  (iii) The inputs used are the only cost statistic elements and the cost function is separable with respect to the input categories (observe that we do *not* assume that the cost function is separable with respect to the action components).

In our discussion of the allocation of predicted costs, we also assume that

  (iv) The sets of feasible activities for each component are independent. (This implies that all required common inputs can be acquired; of course, the cost may become very large for requirements in excess of some quantity.)

---

34. In effect, we assume that the decision maker has costless enforcement rules that will result in the selection of the optimal action if the departmental performance is appropriately specified. The general discussion of the decision-influencing role of cost assessment in Chapter 4 recognizes these costs. Also see Wilson (1969a) and Demski (1972b, 1976).

TABLE 6.9 DECOMPOSED DECISION MODEL ASSUMPTIONS AND NOTATION

(i) $E(B \mid a, y, \eta) = \sum_{i=1}^{n} E(B_i \mid a_i, y, \eta)$

where $E(B_i \mid a_i, y, \eta)$ is the expected benefit for component i.

(ii) $q_j(a) = \sum_{i=1}^{n} q_{ij}(a_i)$

where $q_{ij}(a_i)$ is the quantity of input j used by component i if action a_i is selected.

(iii) $E(C \mid a, y, \eta) = \sum_{j=1}^{m} E(C_j \mid q_j(a), y, \eta)$

where $E(C_j \mid q_j, y, \eta)$ is the expected cost of input j.

(iv) $A = A_1 \times \cdots \times A_n$

where A_i is the set of feasible component i actions.

These assumptions are formally stated in Table 6.9 and the resulting complete analysis is

$$E(U \mid \alpha^*(y, \eta), y, \eta) = \max_{a \in A} \left[\sum_{i=1}^{n} E(B_i \mid a_i, y, \eta) - \sum_{j=1}^{m} E\left(C_j \mid \sum_{i=1}^{n} q_{ij}(a_i), y, \eta\right) \right]$$
[6.6]

where $a' = (a_1, \ldots, a_n)$.

We view the construction of separate decision models for each component as a simplification and let $E(R_i \mid a_i, y, \eta)$ denote the performance measure for component i.[35] We assume that the benefit function used in specifying the performance measure is $E(B_i \mid a_i, y, \eta)$ and that A_i is the set of actions considered for that component; that is, these elements are the same as in the complete analysis. The cost function, however, is simplified and is denoted $E(R_i^C \mid a_i, y, \eta)$. The resulting decision problem for component i is

[6.7] $E(R_i \mid \alpha_i(M(\cdot), y, \eta), y, \eta) = \max_{a_i \in A_i} [E(B_i \mid a_i, y, \eta) - E(R_i^C \mid a_i, y, \eta)].$

The loss from using these action selections is specified by Equation [3.10], where $\alpha(\cdot)' = (\alpha_1(\cdot), \ldots, \alpha_n(\cdot))$.

We now consider some procedures for generating the separate cost functions.

---

35. The separate models need not be simplified. Each component could be treated as the primary action and all other components suppressed as secondary actions. Proposition 3.1 then guarantees that the resulting action selections are optimal. However, that approach would effectively require solution of the complete analysis n times. Recognition of the cost of analysis obviously precludes such an approach.

3.2 ALLOCATION OF THE PREDICTED INPUT COSTS

In this section we focus on the direct use of the expected input cost functions, $E(C_j \mid q_j, y, \eta)$, in specifying the separate action component cost functions. We have assumed that input usage is a separable function of the action components; consequently, separate action costs can be developed from separate input cost functions for the inputs used by each component. And, if the cost function for the inputs used in component i reflects the *incremental cost* of that usage over the total optimal usage in all other components, the selected action will be optimal. That is, letting $i = 1$,

Proposition 6.2:[36]

If

$$E(R_1^c \mid a_1, y, \eta) = \sum_{j=1}^{m} E(C_{1j} \mid q_{1j}(a_1), y, \eta)$$

where

$$E(C_{1j} \mid q_{1j}, y, \eta) = E(C_j \mid q_{1j} + q_j^{**}(y, \eta), y, \eta) - E(C_j \mid q_j^{**}(y, \eta), y, \eta)$$

is the incremental cost of input j and $q_j^{**}(y, \eta) = \sum_{i=2}^{n} q_{ij}(\alpha_i^*(y, \eta))$, then

$$E(R_1 \mid \alpha_1^*(y, \eta), y, \eta) \geq E(R_1 \mid a_1, y, \eta) \quad \text{all } a_1 \in A_1.$$

The input cost function specified in Proposition 6.2 is, in some sense, the cost function the decision maker would like to use in his separate decision models. Observe, however, that in general this cost function depends on the optimal input usage for all other components ($\sum_{i=2}^{m} q_{ij}(\alpha_i^*(\cdot))$).[37] This requirement does not present a problem if the input cost function is linear but does make specification of the optimal component cost function impractical if the input cost function is nonlinear. We now consider these two cases in more detail.

   Linear Cost Functions: The most straightforward case occurs when the input

---

36. *Proof:*
By definition of $\alpha^*(y, \eta)$,

$$E(U \mid \alpha^*(\cdot), y, \eta) \geq E(B_1 \mid a_1, y, \eta) + \sum_{i=2}^{n} E(B_i \mid \alpha_i^*(\cdot), y, \eta) - E(C \mid (a_1, \alpha_2^*(\cdot), \ldots, \alpha_n^*(\cdot)), y, \eta)$$

$$\text{all } a_1 \in A_1.$$

Subtracting $\sum_{i=2}^{n} E(B_i \mid \alpha_i^*(\cdot), y, \eta)$ and $-\sum_{j=1}^{m} E(C_j \mid q_j^{**}(\cdot), y, \eta)$ from both sides

$$E(B_1 \mid \alpha_1^*(\cdot), y, \eta) - \sum_{j=1}^{m} E(C_{1j} \mid q_{1j}(\alpha_1^*(\cdot)), y, \eta) = E(R_1 \mid \alpha_1^*(\cdot), y, \eta)$$

$$\geq E(B_1 \mid a_1, y, \eta) - \sum_{j=1}^{m} E(C_{1j} \mid q_{1j}(a_1), y, \eta)$$

$$\text{all } a_1 \in A_1$$

$$= E(R_1 \mid a_1, y, \eta).$$

37. If input usage is uncertain, this function would also depend on the events that influence input usage of all components (s_δ).

cost function is linear:

$$E(C_j \mid q_j, y, \eta) = f_j + v_j q_j.$$

In this case, the incremental cost of inputs used in component i is merely the variable cost of those inputs; that is,[38]

$$E(C_{ij} \mid q_{ij}, y, \eta) = v_j q_{ij}.$$

Observe that this function is independent of the optimal input quantities for the other components.

This cost function is consistent with what accountants call direct or variable costing. No portion of the intercept (f_j) is included in the separate cost functions. That intercept has no impact on the decisions and there is no apparent reason for "allocating" it to the components. If the decision maker desires to make such an allocation, he may do so in any manner he desires, *provided* the allocation does not affect the actions selected, as in Kaplan and Thompson (1971) and Kaplan and Welam (1974).

Nonlinear Cost Functions: If an input cost function is not linear, it is not separable with respect to the action components except in the special case where only one component uses that input. Proposition 6.2 provides a cost function that will result in selection of the optimal actions, but it is of little use because it requires knowledge of the optimal action. However, the decision maker could use a similar approach by replacing the optimal action with some selected action a_i^0 for each component; the resulting cost function would be

$$[6.8] \quad E(\hat{C}_{1j} \mid q_{1j}, y, \eta) = E\left(C_j \mid q_{1j} + \sum_{i=2}^{n} q_{ij}(a_i^0), y, \eta\right) - E\left(C_j \mid \sum_{i=2}^{n} q_{ij}(a_i^0), y, \eta\right).$$

The effectiveness of this approach would no doubt depend on the form of the input cost function and the "closeness" of the selected action components to their optimal values.

An alternative approach is to construct a linear approximation of the input cost function, and then use the resulting slope as the slope of a linear cost function for each component. That is, if

$$E(\hat{C}_j \mid q_j, y, \eta) = \hat{f}_j + \hat{v}_j q_j$$

is a linear approximation of $E(C_j \mid q_j, y, \eta)$, then

$$E(\hat{C}_{1j} \mid q_{1j}, y, \eta) = \hat{v}_j q_{1j}.$$

Any of the approximating procedures discussed in section 2 could be employed and the general comments in that section apply here as well.[39]

---

38. $E(C_j \mid q_{1j} + q_j^{**}(\cdot), y, \eta) - E(C_j \mid q_j^{**}(\cdot), y, \eta) = [f_j + v_j(q_{1j} + q_j^{**}(\cdot))] - [f_j + v_j q_j^{**}(\cdot)]$
$$= v_j q_{1j}.$$

39. For example, if the benefit functions are differentiable and strictly concave and the cost functions are differentiable and convex, the separate decision models will select the optimal actions if the slopes of their cost functions are equal to the marginal costs of the optimal inputs. This is, in fact, a familiar result in the transfer-pricing literature. See Hirshleifer (1956) and Jennergren (1971).

TABLE 6.10 BASIC ELEMENTS AND COMPLETE ANALYSIS:
COST ALLOCATION EXAMPLE

Input Costs:	
$$E(C_1 \mid q_1, y, \eta) = 10q_1$$ $$E(C_2 \mid q_2, y, \eta) = 2q_2 + 0.001q_2^2$$	
Component One	**Component Two**
Actions: a_1 = output of product 1 $A_1 = \{a_1 \mid a_1 \geq 0\}$ Inputs Used: $q_{11}(a_1) = 0.2a_1$ $q_{12}(a_1) = a_1$ Benefit Functions: $E(B_1 \mid a_1, y, \eta) = 10a_1 - 0.001a_1^2$	Actions: a_2 = output of product 2 $A_2 = \{a_2 \mid a_2 \geq 0\}$ Inputs Used: $q_{21}(a_2) = 0.5a_2$ $q_{22}(a_2) = 2.0a_2$ Benefit Functions: $E(B_2 \mid a_2, y, \eta) = 19a_2 - 0.006a_2^2$
Complete Analysis Profit Function: $$E(U \mid a, y, \eta) = (10a_1 - 0.001a_1^2) + (19a_2 - 0.006a_2^2) - (2a_1 + 5a_2)$$ $$- (2a_1 + 4a_2 + 0.001(a_1 + 2a_2)^2)$$	
Optimal Action: $\alpha_1^*(y, \eta) = \underline{1,250}$	Optimal Action: $\alpha_2^*(y, \eta) = \underline{250}$
Optimal Profit: $$E(U \mid \alpha^*(y, \eta), y, \eta) = \underline{\$5,000}$$	

A Cost Allocation Example: To illustrate decomposition via allocation, consider the example presented in Table 6.10. There are two products, each of which use two common inputs. The cost of the first input is linear, but the cost of the second is nonlinear. The complete analysis simultaneously considers both products; the optimal actions and profit for this analysis are presented in Table 6.10.

Decomposed models for the two products are presented in Table 6.11. The first section of that table presents incremental cost functions developed in ac-

Table 6.11   Decomposed Models: Cost Allocation Example

Component One	Component Two
(i) Incremental Input Cost Based on Optimal Actions, $\alpha^*(y, \eta) = (1,250, 250)$	
$E(C_{11} \mid q_{11}, y, \eta) = 10q_{11}$ $E(C_{12} \mid q_{12}, y, \eta) = 3q_{12} + 0.001q_{12}^2$ $E(R_1^C \mid a_1, y, \eta) = 5a_1 + 0.001a_1^2$	$E(C_{21} \mid q_{21}, y, \eta) = 10q_{21}$ $E(C_{22} \mid q_{22}, y, \eta) = 4.5q_{22} + 0.001q_2^2$ $E(R_2^C \mid a_2, y, \eta) = 14a_2 + 0.004a_2^2$
(ii) Incremental Input Cost Based on $a^0 = (1,000, 500)$: $M^1(\cdot)$	
$E(\hat{C}_{11} \mid q_{11}, y, \eta) = 10q_{11}$ $E(\hat{C}_{12} \mid q_{12}, y, \eta) = 4q_{12} + 0.001q_{12}^2$ $E(R_1^C \mid a_1, y, \eta) = 6a_1 + 0.001a_1^2$ $E(R_1 \mid a_1, y, \eta) = 4a_1 - 0.002a_1^2$ $\alpha_1(M^1(\cdot), y, \eta) = 1,000$	$E(\hat{C}_{21} \mid q_{21}, y, \eta) = 10q_{21}$ $E(\hat{C}_{22} \mid q_{22}, y, \eta) = 4q_{22} + 0.001q_{22}^2$ $E(R_2^C \mid a_2, y, \eta) = 13a_2 + 0.004a_2^2$ $E(R_2 \mid a_2, y, \eta) = 6a_2 - 0.01a_2^2$ $\alpha_2(M^1(\cdot), y, \eta) = 300$
$E(U \mid M^1(\cdot), y, \eta) = \$4,900$ $L(M^1(\cdot), y, \eta) = \underline{\underline{\$\ \ 100}}$	
(iii) Decomposed Input Cost Based on Linear Approximation: $M^2(\cdot)$	
$E(\hat{C}_{11} \mid q_{11}, y, \eta) = 10q_{11}$ $E(\hat{C}_{12} \mid q_{12}, y, \eta) = 6q_{12}$ $E(R_1^C \mid a_1, y, \eta) = 8a_1$ $E(R_1 \mid a_1, y, \eta) = 2a_1 - 0.001a_1^2$ $\alpha_1(M^2(\cdot), y, \eta) = 1,000$	$E(\hat{C}_{21} \mid q_{21}, y, \eta) = 10q_{21}$ $E(\hat{C}_{22} \mid q_{22}, y, \eta) = 6q_{22}$ $E(R_2^C \mid a_2, y, \eta) = 17a_2$ $E(R_2 \mid a_2, y, \eta) = 2a_2 - 0.006a_2^2$ $\alpha_2(M^2(\cdot), y, \eta) = 167$
$E(U \mid M^2(\cdot), y, \eta) = \$4,723$ $L(M^2(\cdot), y, \eta) = \underline{\underline{\$\ \ 277}}$	

cordance with Proposition 6.2. Use of these cost functions will result in the optimal decisions, but knowledge of the optimal decisions is required to obtain them.

The second section presents a simplified model, denoted $M^1(\cdot)$, based on incremental cost functions developed using Equation [6.8]. The selected action (a^0) is too low for product one and too high for product two. Consequently, the resultant decisions are nonoptimal and a loss of $100 is incurred. A comparison of the two sets of incremental cost functions is provided by Figure 6.9.

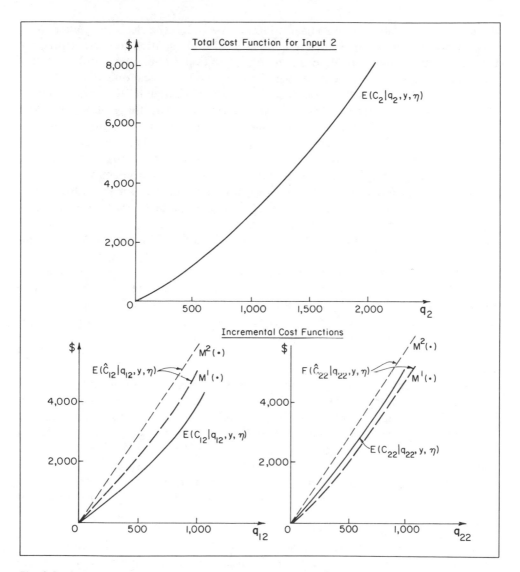

Fig. 6.9. A comparison of the two sets of incremental cost functions.

The third section of Table 6.11 presents a simplified model, denoted $M^2(\cdot)$, based on a linear approximation. The slope of that approximation is equivalent to the slope of the total cost function at $q_2 = 2,000$ (the quantity that would be used by the selected action a^0). This slope is too high $(q_2(\alpha^*(y, \eta)) = 1,750)$. Consequently, the decisions are again nonoptimal and a loss of \$277 is incurred.

3.3 ALLOCATION OF SUNK COSTS

"Sunk costs" are costs that arise from *prior* input acquisition decisions. We are particularly interested in inputs for which it would be "very" costly to increase the amounts available for current production, or which the decision maker must take as given. For example, the equipment and buildings used in current production are usually the result of prior actions; additional equipment and buildings could be obtained, but it might be "very" costly to obtain them quickly.

In many situations these types of costs are allocated to the products and departments that use the inputs that were acquired. And these allocated costs are often considered in making production decisions even though the accounting literature frequently recommends that they be ignored. There are two general types of arguments given for using these allocations. One is that "in the long run all costs are variable." Although expenditures for this input may not change immediately, current decisions may affect future expenditures for that input. The second argument is that if the firm is operating at capacity the allocated sunk costs may provide a rough approximation to the externality (opportunity) cost of using some of that capacity in one product instead of in some other alternative.[40]

Obviously, if a complete analysis is used, there is no reason to allocate sunk costs. The future implications of current decisions are encompassed in a multiperiod model and the implications of allocating capacity to a particular product are encompassed in a multiproduct model. Alternatively, these multiperiod and multiproduct considerations can be recognized in an appropriately modified single-period, single-product analysis in the manner outlined in Chapters 3 and 5.

We now focus on the second reason for sunk cost allocation and essentially consider the question: Is sunk cost allocation a "good" method to use in approximating the externality cost of the inputs used by the various components?[41] This will, of course, depend on the situation, but we can gain some insight by examining the process by which the sunk costs arise and their relationship to the production decisions. In this examination we first consider the case where the prior input acquisitions benefit only the current production period and then consider the case where they benefit subsequent periods as well. An example of the first case is the leasing of equipment for the next month; the second case is illustrated by the purchase of equipment.

For purposes of this analysis we make two changes in the conditions underlying the complete analysis presented in [6.6]. First, and most important, we introduce another input (or vector of inputs), denoted q_0, that has been acquired prior to the production decision. The amount acquired is denoted q_0^0, and we assume that it is either impossible or too costly to acquire additional quantities for use in current production. Second, we assume that the cost functions for inputs 1 through m are separable with respect to the inputs used in each component. This latter assumption simplifies the discussion, but the analysis can easily be

40. See Devine (1950) for a discussion of this type of argument.

41. In our discussion, "good" means that the cost of analysis plus the loss resulting from the selection of nonoptimal actions is less than for alternative approximation methods.

extended to the more general case considered in [6.6]. We now have[42]

$$E(U \mid \alpha^*(q_0^0, y, \eta), y, \eta) = \max_{a \in A} \sum_{i=1}^{n} \left[E(B_i \mid a_i, y, \eta) - \sum_{j=1}^{m} E(C_{ij} \mid q_{ij}(a_i), y, \eta) \right]$$

[6.9]

subject to

$$\sum_{i=1}^{n} q_{i0}(a_i) \leq q_0^0$$

where $\alpha^*(q_0^0, y, \eta)$ denotes the optimal component actions given that q_0^0 units of input 0 are available for use and $E(C_{ij} \mid q_{ij}, y, \eta)$ is the expected cost of using q_{ij} units of input j in component i.

Assume that the decision maker decomposes his decision problem by replacing the input constraint with a linear cost function. The cost of input 0 used in component i is set equal to $\hat{v}_0 q_{i0}$, where $\hat{v}_0 = C_0(q_0^0) \div q_0^0$ is the average cost per unit of input 0 acquired and $C_0(q_0^0)$ is the total historical cost of that input. The resulting decomposed decision models are

$$E(R_i \mid \alpha_i(\cdot), y, \eta) = \max_{a_i \in A_i} \left[E(B_i \mid a_i, y, \eta) - \sum_{j=1}^{m} E(C_{ij} \mid q_{ij}(a_i), y, \eta) - \hat{v}_0 q_{i0}(a_i) \right]$$

[6.10] $i = 1, \ldots, n.$

Calculation of the loss resulting from the use of the decomposed models requires calculation of the expected utility associated with the actions selected by those models. This latter calculation is relatively straightforward if the selected action requires fewer units of input 0 than are available, but problems occur if the required quantity exceeds the quantity available. The calculation must reflect what will happen. For example, if the firm feels that it must meet its commitments, the necessary inputs might be acquired at the required high cost. Alternatively, the selected actions may not be implemented as planned. For example, if jobs arrive sequentially, the last jobs that arrive might be rejected even though they are more desirable than some accepted earlier.[43]

To further explore the relationship between the complete analysis and the simplified models we must consider the decision problem that was facing the purchaser who acquired the q_0^0 units of input 0. We first consider the case where the acquired inputs may be used only in current production.

Single Period Acquisitions: Assume that there is no uncertainty with respect to the acquisition costs, and let $E(C_0 \mid q_0, y, \eta) = C_0(q_0)$. If the purchaser uses a

---

42. This model is very dependent upon the assumption that the amount of input required by the selected action is known. If there is uncertainty about that usage, the model must reflect the fact that planned production may be "infeasible" and some adjustment must be made during the period.

43. This issue is further explored in Chapter 7, where we consider alternative uses of a fixed facility.

complete analysis and predicts that the production decisions will be optimal, his decision problem is

[6.11] $E(U_0 \mid q_0^0, y, \eta) = \max_{q_0 \in Q_0} [E(U \mid \alpha^*(q_0, y, \eta), y, \eta) - C_0(q_0)]$

where Q_0 is the set of possible acquisition quantities.

When the production decision model uses a sunk cost per unit instead of the appropriate constraint, the production decision maker is, in effect, repeating the above decision using a linear approximation to $C_0(q_0)$.[44] Observe that if $C_0(q_0)$ is a linear function of the form $C_0(q_0) = v_0 q_0$ and $Q_0 = \{q_0 \mid q_0 \geq 0\}$, then $\hat{v}_0 = v_0$ and we have a modification of the purchaser's decision model. Consequently, in that case the simplified decision model will result in the selection of the optimal production activities. In all other situations the simplified model is likely to result in a loss because it employs a linear function to approximate a nonlinear function. The comments in section 2 apply here. For example, if the cost function is linear, but only integer quantities can be acquired, use of the above procedure cannot have a loss of more than the cost of one unit (v_0).

Multiple Period Acquisition: Now consider the case where the input acquisition will benefit T production periods. To simplify the discussion, assume that the inputs available in each period are constant and unaffected by prior production activities. Further assume that the production activities and their utility evaluations are separable with respect to the production periods and let $E(U_t \mid a_t, y, \eta)$ denote the expected utility function for production period t, given that the action in that period is a_t, $t = 1, \ldots, T$. The purchaser's decision problem in this case is

[6.12] $E(U_0 \mid q_0^0, y, \eta) = \max_{q_0 \in Q_0} \left\{ \sum_{t=1}^{T} E(U_t \mid \alpha_t^*(q_0, y, \eta), y, \eta) - C_0(q_0) \right\}$

where q_0 is the input quantity available in each period.

The simplified decision model for a given production period again uses some allocation of the acquisition cost $C_0(q_0)$. This allocation, however, must be made both with respect to the periods and the production within those periods. For example, if $C_0(q_0)$ consists of only an initial outlay and the allocation is based on straight-line depreciation, the amount allocated to each production period is $C_0(q_0^0) \div T$ and the slope of the simplified cost function is $[C_0(q_0^0) \div T] \div q_0^0$.

The loss resulting from the use of any allocation procedure will, of course, depend upon the situation. There is, however, at least one set of conditions that are sufficient for the simplified models to result in optimal production decisions.

---

44. If the purchaser recognizes that the production decision model will use this sunk cost per unit, his decision model should be

$$E(U_0 \mid q_0^0, y, \eta) = \max_{q_0 \in Q_0} [E(U \mid \alpha(\cdot), y, \eta) - C_0(q_0)]$$

where $\alpha(\cdot)$ is the action that will be selected if a varible cost per unit of $C_0(q_0) \div q_0$ is used in a simplified model.

These conditions are[45]

    (i)   The acquisition cost function is linear, with zero intercept:

$$C_0(q_0) = v_0 q_0.$$

    (ii)   Any level of input can be acquired:

$$Q_0 = \{q_0 \mid q_0 \geq 0\}.$$

    (iii)   The production alternatives are the same for each period and the utility measures differ only by a per-period discount factor $1/(1 + \rho), \rho > 0$:

$$A = A_1 = \cdots = A_T$$
$$E(U_t \mid a_t, y, \eta) = (1 + \rho)^{-t} E(U \mid a_t, y, \eta) \quad t = 1, \ldots, T$$

where $E(U \mid a_t, y, \eta)$ is the expected cash flow in period t if a_t is selected. (Note that $\alpha_t^*(q_0, y, \eta)$ is the same for all $t = 1, \ldots, T$.)

    (iv)   The slope of the simplified cost function is equal to the cost per unit of capacity adjusted by the discount factor:

$$\hat{v}_0 = \beta v_0$$

where

$$\beta = 1 \div \left(\sum_{t=1}^{T} (1 + \rho)^{-t} \right) = \rho / (1 - (1 + \rho)^{-T}).$$

Observe that $\beta v_0 q_0$ is equal to the periodic cash flow that is required to recover the cost of the input, including interest.[46]

Additional research might find other conditions and depreciation methods that are sufficient for sunk cost allocation to result in optimal decisions, but in most situations sunk cost allocation will result in nonoptimal actions. That does not mean that sunk cost allocation should not be used. The decision maker will

---

45. The sufficiency of these conditions can be seen by considering the resulting decision problem for the purchaser

$$E(U_0 \mid q_0^0, y, \eta) = \max_{q_0 \geq 0} \left\{ \sum_{t=1}^{T} (1 + \rho)^{-t} E(U \mid \alpha^*(q_0, y, \eta), y, \eta) - v_0 q_0 \right\}.$$

From the corollary to Proposition 3.4, we can multiply both sides by $\beta > 0$ without affecting the solution; thus

$$\beta E(U_0 \mid q_0^0, y, \eta) = \max_{q_0 \geq 0} \left\{ E(U \mid \alpha^*(q_0, y, \eta), y, \eta) - \beta v_0 q_0 \right\}$$

provides the desired modification.

46. This is equivalent to the depreciation charge made under the compound interest (or annuity) method of depreciation plus the interest charged to the period. See Horngren (1972) for a discussion of this depreciation method.

TABLE 6.12   BASIC ELEMENTS OF MULTIPLE PERIOD EXAMPLE

Actions:

$$a = (a_1, a_2) = \text{output of products 1 and 2}$$
$$A = \{(a_1, a_2) \mid a_1 \geq 0, a_2 \geq 0\}$$

Inputs Used:

$$q_0(a) = a_1 + 2a_2$$

Input Cost (10-year life):

$$C_0(q_0) = 50q_0 \qquad Q_0 = \{q_0 \mid 0 \leq q_0 \leq 10{,}000\}$$

Annual Cash Flow:

$$E(U \mid a, y, \eta) = 10a_1 - 0.001a_1^2 + 25a_2 - 0.005a_2^2$$

Optimal Production Decision:

$$\alpha^*(q_0, y, \eta) = \begin{cases} (0, q_0/2) & 0 \leq q_0 \leq 1{,}000 \\ ((5q_0 - 5{,}000)/9, (2q_0 + 2{,}500)/9) & 1{,}000 \leq q_0 \leq 10{,}000 \end{cases}$$

Optimal Annual Cash Flow:

$$E(U \mid \alpha^*(q_0, y, \eta), y, \eta) = \begin{cases} 12.5q_0 - 0.00125q_0^2 & 0 \leq q_0 \leq 1{,}000 \\ (100q_0 - 0.005q_0^2 \\ \qquad +6{,}250)/9 & 1{,}000 \leq q_0 \leq 10{,}000 \end{cases}$$

Optimal Input Acquisition ($\rho = 0.10$):

$$q_0^0 = \underline{\underline{2{,}676}} \qquad \alpha^*(q_0^0, y, \eta) = (931, 872)$$

Optimal Discounted Cash Flow:

$$E(U_0 \mid q_0^0, y, \eta) = \underline{\underline{\$28{,}718}} \qquad E(U \mid \alpha^*(q_0^0, y, \eta), y, \eta) = \underline{\underline{\$26{,}449}}$$

want to use that method of analysis minimizing the cost of analysis plus the loss resulting from the selection of nonoptimal actions.

A Multiple Period Example: This example illustrates the impact of using depreciation based on the straightline method instead of the compound interest method. The basic elements of the example and the complete analysis are presented in Table 6.12. There are two products and a single common input. The input is to be acquired now and has an expected economic life of 10 years. The cost of capital ρ is 0.10.

The decomposed models based on the use of a depreciation charge are presented in Table 6.13. A depreciation and interest charge of $8.14 per unit (based on the compound interest method) will induce the optimal production decisions. The straightline depreciation charge of $5 per unit is too small and induces planned production that requires more input than is available. In determining the actual

TABLE 6.13   DECOMPOSED MODELS: MULTIPLE PERIOD EXAMPLE ($q_0^0 = 2,676$)

Product One	Product Two
(i) Input Cost Based on Compound Interest Method of Depreciation: $\beta = 0.162745$ $\hat{v}_0 = (0.162745)(50) = 8.13725$	
$E(R_1 \mid a_1, y, \eta) = 10a_1 - 0.001a_1^2$ $\qquad - 8.13725a_1$	$E(R_2 \mid a_2, y, \eta) = 25a_2 - 0.005a_2^2$ $\qquad - 16.2745a_2$
(ii) Input Cost Based on Straightline Method of Depreciation, $M(\cdot)$: $\hat{v}_0 = 50/10 = 5$	
$E(R_1 \mid d_1, y, \eta) = 10d_1 - 0.001d_1^2$ $\qquad - 5d_1$ $d_1(M(\cdot)) = 2,500$ $\alpha_1(\cdot) = 1,216$	$E(R_2 \mid d_2, y, \eta) = 25d_2 - 0.005d_2^2$ $\qquad - 10d_2$ $d_2(M(\cdot)) = 1,500$ $\alpha_2(\cdot) = 730$
$E(U \mid M(\cdot), y, \eta) = \$26,267$ $L(M(\cdot), y, \eta) = \underline{\$\quad 182}$	

production in that case, we have proportionately reduced the plans to a feasible level. The resulting annual loss is $182.

4.0 SUMMARY

We have examined a few of the numerous cost assessment alternatives that arise in the typical short-run production context. Our intention has been to consider some specific types of alternatives and in each case to point out the basic issues to be considered in evaluating those alternatives. In some cases we have developed general results, but the major thrust has been to illustrate the impact and evaluation of alternatives in specific contexts.

In each instance we moved from a consideration of the decision that would be induced by a particular cost assessment alternative to the utility measure associated with that decision's outcome. No "correct" cost assessment methods were put forth. Selection of a particular alternative must be based on the circumstances at hand.

7

ANALYSIS OF COST ASSESSMENT ALTERNATIVES IN A LONG-RUN DECISION CONTEXT

The purpose of this chapter is to explore a number of cost assessment alternatives in a long-run production decision context. As such, the chapter is a natural extension of the discussion in Chapter 6: we address the same types of issues, but in a setting where the decision maker finds it useful *not* to suppress the multiperiod flavor of the decisions at hand. In particular, we consider decisions involving the acquisition of resources that will provide inputs for several periods; these are commonly termed capital budgeting decisions.

There is a vast literature on capital budgeting decisions. The bulk of it, as well as our basic familiarity with the problem, is based on a setting in which the market value maximization rule is assumed to be operative.[1] For this reason, we structure our analysis in terms of the market value rule. (As noted in Chapter 4, this naturally provides the separability conditions employed in most of our abstract discussions of cost.)

The particular simplifications explored again fall into the three broad categories of simplifying the form or domain of the cost function and of using allocation as a basis for decomposing complex problems into separate subcomponents. Since the general nature of these simplifications was discussed in Chapter 6, we concentrate on exploring their nature and effect in a long-run decision context.

We maintain the expositionally convenient assumption used throughout Chapter 6 that the utility measure can be separated from the "costs" of the infor-

---

1. Additional discussion is available in Weingartner (1967), Morris (1968), Bernhard (1969), Mao (1969), Hirshleifer (1970), Demski (1972), and Van Horne (1974).

mation system and decision analysis. And in calculating the loss resulting from simplified cost analysis by the decision maker, we continue to assume that the decision maker and evaluator perceive equivalent benefit functions.

The discussion is divided into four major sections. The first discusses the capital budgeting decision context we shall consider. The remaining three then explore cost function form, domain, and decomposition simplifications.

1.0 A COMPLETE STATEMENT OF THE CHOICE PROBLEM

In this initial section we describe the *specific* capital budgeting choice situation that is employed throughout the chapter. Since most of the normative capital budgeting literature assumes market value maximization as the firm's objective, we explicitly employ the market value characterization of firm behavior. (Recall from Chapter 2 that this entails equilibria in an economy with nonsatiating rational individuals and perfect and complete markets.)

Under this characterization, the outcome of interest is the state-dependent sequence of cash flows to the firm's owners; and the utility measure of that sequence is its current market value.[2] Extending the notation of Chapter 2, section 3, the market value of cash flow sequence $x = (x_0, x_1, \ldots, x_T)$ is

$$V(x) = \sum_{t=0}^{T} \sum_{s_t \in S_t} x_t^{s_t} P_t^{s_t}$$

where $x_t = (x_t^1, \ldots, x_t^{S_t})$, $x_t^{s_t}$ is the cash flow in period t *if* state s_t occurs, and $P_t^{s_t}$ is the current price of a promise to deliver \$1 in future period t *if* state s_t occurs.

Now consider a decision maker who is motivated to maximize the firm's market value. He must select an action now, denoted a, as well as a policy for selecting future actions. The outcome will be a dated sequence of state-dependent and action-dependent cash flows. Supressing explicit reference to future actions, we have[3,4]

$$x_t^{s_t} = p_t(s_t, a, \eta).$$

Hence, the decision maker's choice problem may be stated as

[7.1a]
$$E(U \mid a, y, \eta) = \sum_{t=0}^{T} \sum_{s_t \in S_t} p_t(s_t, a, \eta) P_t^{s_t}$$

---

2. We assume cash-mediated transactions so that the firm's outcome function can be described in terms of net cash flow. Restriction to cash as opposed to general commodity flows is, recall, unnecessary but convenient.

3. We suppress explicit reference to future actions by assuming that either the current action alternatives encompass alternative policies for selecting future actions or an optimal policy for selecting them is implicit in the cash flow function $p_t(\cdot)$. See Chapter 3, section 1.1.1, for a formal statement of the latter form of suppression; also see Godfrey (1969) for one such example.

4. The outcome is likely to depend on the state (and action) history up to and including period t; that state history is reflected in s_t. See Debreu (1959), Chapter 7.

and

[7.1b] $$E(U \mid \alpha^*(y, \eta), y, \eta) = \max_{a \in A} E(U \mid a, y, \eta).$$

Within this framework we now focus on the direct input cost function developed in Chapter 5, Table 5.2. In particular, we focus on the selection of input acquisition activities ($\mathbf{a}_{C2}$), given a particular pattern of input usage, $q = (q_0, q_1, \ldots, q_T)$, where q is a sufficient cost statistic and q_t denotes input usage in period t. (q_t can, of course, be a state-dependent vector.)[5]

In this context, the decision maker's objective is to minimize the cost of providing the specified input. We denote that cost

[7.2a] $$E(C \mid q, \mathbf{a}_{C2}, y, \eta) = \sum_{t=0}^{T} \sum_{s_t \in S_t} p_t^C(s_t, q, \mathbf{a}_{C2}, \eta) P_t^{s_t}$$

and

[7.2b] $$E(C \mid q, y, \eta) = \min_{\mathbf{a}_{C2} \in A_{C2}(q)} E(C \mid q, \mathbf{a}_{C2}, y, \eta),$$

where $p_t^C(s_t, q, \mathbf{a}_{C2}, \eta)$ denotes the cost component cash flow in period t and $A_{C2}(q)$ is the set of acquisition alternatives that will provide input pattern q.

Both [7.1] and [7.2] are general statements of capital budgeting problems. Indeed, each may be described in present value terms. This is somewhat more obvious if we consider a subjectively certain world in which $P_{t+1}/P_t = 1/(1 + \rho)$ for all $t = 0, \ldots, T - 1$. (With no state indexing in a subjectively certain world, P_t is merely the current price of a dollar to be received in period t.) We then interpret the market price as representing a constant cost of capital, $P_t = (1 + \rho)^{-t}$, and this provides the familiar discounted present value characterization. For example, if the alternatives are to either accept ($a = 1$) or reject ($a = 0$) a project, the project will be accepted if and only if

$$\sum_{t=0}^{T} [p_t(\hat{s}_t, 1, \eta) - p_t(\hat{s}_t, 0, \eta)](1 + \rho)^{-t} \geq 0$$

where $\hat{s}_t$ is the subjectively certain state. That is, we accept the project if and only if its incremental present value, at the firm's cost of capital, is nonnegative.[6]

This last statement, as well as those in [7.1] and [7.2], presume that the proj-

---

5. Recall that $q = \delta_C\left(s_\delta, \begin{pmatrix} a \\ \mathbf{a}_{C1} \end{pmatrix}, \eta\right)$.

6. Similarly, an input acquisition project ($\mathbf{a}_{C2} = 1$) is at least as desirable as rejection ($\mathbf{a}_{C2} = 0$) if and only if

$$\sum_{t=0}^{T} [p_t^C(\hat{s}_t, q, 1, \eta) - p_t^C(\hat{s}_t, q, 0, \eta)](1 + \rho)^{-t} \leq 0.$$

That is, with cash flows expressed as expenditures, their incremental present value must be *nonpositive* for acceptance.

ects are evaluated by a complete analysis.[7] Recognizing the cost of such analysis naturally raises questions of simplification. Some of these simplifications are explored in the following sections.

2.0 SIMPLIFICATION OF THE FORM OF THE COST FUNCTION

Our general expression for the cost of providing q units of input throughout the horizon is provided in [7.2]. The motive for simplifying the form of this cost function is to effect computational economies in determining and using such a function. The use of average cost functions and the familiar payback criterion may, with suitable assumptions, be interpreted in this manner. We discuss them in turn.

2.1 LONG-RUN AVERAGE COST FUNCTIONS

Short-run decisions often focus on the cash flows of a single period. Extension of this type of analysis to a long-run decision may lead to a focus on the *average* cash flows over the periods influenced by the decision in question. This appears to be particularly prevalent in decisions that involve the periodic acquisition of inputs that are constantly being used in production. In these contexts, decision makers often select acquisition frequencies that minimize the "average cost" of providing the inputs instead of those that minimize the present value of the cash outflows involved.

These acquisition frequency decisions typically affect the level of expenditures both at the time of acquisition and during the interval between acquisitions. The average of the former is usually increased and the latter decreased if the acquisition frequency is increased. Therefore, minimization of the average cost involves determination of the appropriate trade-off between these two types of expenditures. For example, in inventory decisions the trade-off is between the costs of placing and receiving orders and the costs of storing inventories. Simi-

---

7. We must recognize, of course, that in a complete analysis any accept/reject decision presumes that we are comparing the best possible accept alternative with the best possible reject alternative. For example, consider a situation in which a decision maker must decide whether to purchase a building to provide warehouse space (q) required by his production activities. If there are a number of possible ways that he can purchase and operate the building (denoted $A_{C2}^1(q)$), and a number of possible ways that he can supply the required space without purchasing the building (denoted $A_{C2}^0(q)$), the accept alternative must be such that

$$E(C \mid q, a_{C2} = 1, y, \eta) = \min_{a_{C2} \in A_{C2}^1(q)} E(C \mid q, a_{C2}, y, \eta)$$

and the reject alternative must be such that

$$E(C \mid q, a_{C2} = 0, y, \eta) = \min_{a_{C2} \in A_{C2}^0(q)} E(C \mid q, a_{C2}, y, \eta).$$

We thus characterize a capital budgeting decision in terms of choice between conditionally optimal cash flow sequences. See Proposition 3.3.

larly, in machine replacement decisions the trade-off is between the costs of machine acquisition and the costs of machine maintenance.

In general, if average cost models ignore the "cost of capital," we would expect the selected actions to require either larger or more frequent acquisitions than is optimal. This is because these models ignore timing considerations and treat the expenditure of $1 now as equivalent to the expenditure of $1 at time t (but this is not the case in the complete analysis cost function). However, the biases of some average cost models are not so clear in that they give limited recognition to timing considerations. In particular, these models often include the average cost of capital "tied up" in acquisitions as part of the interval costs. For example, inventory models usually include the cost of capital tied up in average inventories as part of the storage costs, and the cost of the capital required by machine acquisition and retention may be included in the cost of operating a machine. However, since these models only recognize timing considerations for a fraction of the cost components, they are still simplifications of the complete analysis and, therefore, may result in the selection of nonoptimal actions.

We now present two examples to illustrate the evaluation of average cost models. The first is an inventory model and the second a machine replacement model.

2.1.1   AN INVENTORY EXAMPLE

In Chapter 5, section 2.3, we presented an inventory example to illustrate the determination of direct material costs in a complete analysis. We now return to that example and use it to illustrate the impact of using average cost models.

The basic elements and the complete analysis cost function are presented in Table 5.4. Observe that the one-year decision horizon is divided into four quarters (periods) and that the input usage rate is a constant q units per year. The acquisition frequencies considered are once, twice, and four times a year; and the optimal frequency depends on the input usage rate.

Three types of cash flows are involved: those that vary with the number of orders placed, those that vary with the number of units acquired, and those that vary with the storage capacity required. The complete analysis identifies the size and timing of these expenditures and determines their present value. This analysis is considerably simplified if we ignore cash flow timing considerations and minimize the average expenditures instead of the present values.[8] In this simplified analysis, denoted M^1, we ignore those expenditures that vary with the number of units purchased since our decision affects the timing but not the total of those expenditures. Table 7.1 presents the simplified (average) cost function for this

---

8. In this simple example we could consider the total cost instead of the average, but in actual practice inventory models use the concept of a long-run average cost. The decision horizon in these models is assumed to be infinite and any order frequency is considered. This allows calculus to be used to derive the optimal order frequency. See Horngren (1972) or Dopuch et al. (1974).

TABLE 7.1 AVERAGE COST INVENTORY MODELS

	M^1 (Cost of Capital Ignored)	M^2 (Cost of Capital on Average Inventory)
Simplified Cost Models ($0 < q \leq 1,000$):[1] $$E(\hat{C} \mid q, \mathbf{a}_{C2}, y, \eta) \text{ for } \begin{cases} \mathbf{a}_{C2} = q \\ \mathbf{a}_{C2} = q/2 \\ \mathbf{a}_{C2} = q/4 \end{cases}$$	$37.50 + 30I(q/100)$ $75 + 30I(q/200)$ $150 + 30I(q/400)$	$37.50 + 30I(q/100) + 0.105q$ $75 + 30I(q/200) + 0.0525q$ $150 + 30I(q/400) + 0.02625q$
Selected Order Quantities: $$\alpha_{C2}(q, M(\cdot), y, \eta)$$	$\begin{cases} q & \text{for } 0 \leq q \leq 300 \\ q/2 & \text{for } 300 < q \leq 1,000 \end{cases}$	$\begin{cases} q & \text{for } 0 \leq q \leq 142 \\ q/2 & \text{for } 142 < q \leq 600 \\ q/4 & \text{for } 600 < q \end{cases}$
Loss Due to Simplification: (Increase in Present Value of Cash Outflows) $$L(q, M(\cdot), y, \eta)$$ $$= E(C \mid q, M(\cdot), y, \eta)$$ $$- E(C \mid q, y, \eta)$$	$\begin{cases} 0 & \text{for } 0 \leq q \leq 123 \\ & \text{and } 300 < q \leq 600 \\ -144 + 0.21q \\ \quad + 118[I(q/100) - I(q/200)] & \text{for } 123 < q \leq 300 \\ -288 + 0.105q \\ \quad + 118[I(q/200) - I(q/400)] & \text{for } 600 < q \leq 1,000 \end{cases}$	$\begin{cases} 0 & \text{for } 0 \leq q \leq 123 \\ & \text{and } 142 < q \leq 1,000 \\ -144 + 0.21q \\ \quad + 118[I(q/100) - I(q/200)] & \text{for } 123 < q \leq 142 \end{cases}$

Note: See Table 5.4 for the basic elements and complete analysis of this example. The capital cost parameter used in Model M^2 is 0.02 per quarter, for example, $(0.02)(10.5)(q/2) = 0.105q$. (The prices in Table 5.4 do not imply a constant cost of capital.) Also recall that $\mathbf{a}_{C2}$ and $\mathbf{a}_{21}$ are equivalent in this example.

1. $I(k)$ denotes the smallest integer larger than or equal to k.

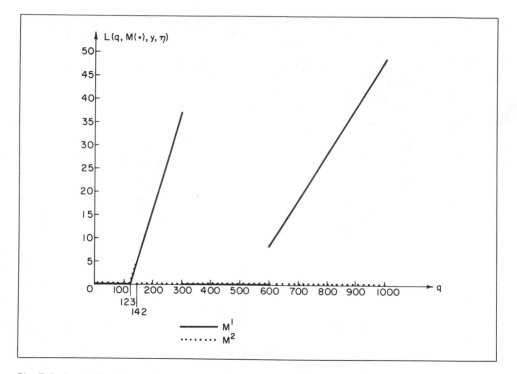

Fig. 7.1. Loss due to use of average cost inventory models.

model, as well as the selected order quantity and the resulting loss from non-optimal decisions. Observe that for some input levels the order quantities are optimal, but for others they are too large (that is, orders are not placed frequently enough). The losses are plotted in Figure 7.1.

Partial recognition of the cash flow timing considerations can be introduced into the average cost model by including an amount equal to the acquisition cost of the average inventory times the cost of capital.[9] Table 7.1 presents the simplified cost function for this model (denoted M^2), as well as the selected order quantity and the loss from nonoptimal decisions. Observe that this model selects the optimal order quantity for all but a small range of input levels. The losses incurred in that range are also plotted in Figure 7.1.

2.1.2 A MACHINE REPLACEMENT EXAMPLE

In a machine replacement setting the relevant question is one of *when* to replace equipment that provides the input in question. The outcome in each period will in general depend on uncertain events, the age of the existing equipment, and when it was acquired (to account for possible technological change).

---

9. This is typically an important cost in inventory models such as the traditional economic order quantity model. See Horngren (1972) or Dopuch et al. (1974).

Indeed, the replacement activities themselves are likely to be quite rich. For example, the equipment may display varying levels of performance and some alternatives may involve investigation and restoration of the equipment to a preferred operating level (see Jorgenson et al. 1967; Kaplan 1975).

Quite naturally, with this level of complexity we consider simplifying the complete analysis. To explore this theme and the use of average cost models we focus on a specific, elementary replacement setting, again assuming subjective certainty. No technological change is present; existing and all new equipment are identical in all respects (including price and post acquisition cash flow patterns). The equipment can be replaced at any given instant for a net cash outflow b. (This reflects a constant salvage value assumption, for example, zero.) Finally, end of period maintenance or operating cash flows increase linearly with the equipment's age. We denote the constant rate of increase z.

Table 7.2 presents the complete analysis cost function for this setting, assuming a constant cost of capital and an infinite horizon. Under these conditions the optimal policy is *periodic* in nature, calling for replacement precisely every d periods.[10] The difference conditions that characterize that optimal replacement period are also presented in Table 7.2. These conditions effectively state that you should not replace if the long-run average cost of replacing at the current age exceeds or equals the marginal maintenance cost of continuing with the existing equipment. Rather, replacement should occur at the first period in which the long-run average cost does not exceed the marginal maintenance cost. Of course, definition of the long-run average cost is crucial; in this context it is the constant amount per period that would provide the same present value as the cash flows resulting from the replacement policy in question.[11] For example, the minimum long-run average cost for the numerical example in Table 7.2 is

$$\rho E(C \mid q, d = 6, y, \eta) = 0.25(25,026) = \$6,257$$

and this is less than the marginal maintenance cost of[12]

$$1,000(6 + 1) = \$7,000.$$

Now consider simplifying the form of the cost function. One approach is to ignore completely the cost of capital and to minimize the average cost per period.[13] Table 7.3 presents the cost function for this model, denoted M^1, as well as the

---

10. See Taussig (1964) and Jorgenson et al. (1967). Capitalizing on the periodic nature of the optimal replacement sequence, we modify the problem in terms of finding an optimal replacement interval (or decision variable) d. See Proposition 3.2.

11. The present value of receiving an amount θ every period for an infinite number of periods is

$$PV = \sum_{t=1}^{\infty} \theta(1 + \rho)^{-t} = \theta/\rho$$

Therefore, the amount θ required to provide a given present value is $\rho(PV)$.

12. On the other hand, the long-run average cost for $d = 5$ is $\rho E(C \mid q, d = 5, y, \eta) = 0.25(25,126) = \$6,282$, which is greater than the marginal maintenance cost of $1,000(5 + 1) = \$6,000$.

13. This model is discussed in Taussig (1964).

TABLE 7.2 BASIC ELEMENTS AND COMPLETE ANALYSIS
FOR MACHINE REPLACEMENT EXAMPLE

Decision Variable:

$$D(q) = \{1, 2, \ldots\}$$

where d is the number of periods between replacements and q specifies that one machine will be used in each period.

Input Cost Function:

$$E(C \mid q, d, y, \eta) = b + \sum_{t=1}^{d} zt(1 + \rho)^{-t}$$

$$+ b(1 + \rho)^{-d} + \sum_{t=1}^{d} zt(1 + \rho)^{-t-d} + \cdots$$

$$= \left(b + \sum_{t=1}^{d} zt(1 + \rho)^{-t}\right) \bigg/ \left(1 - (1 + \rho)^{-d}\right)$$

where b = acquisition price (net)
z = maintenance cost parameter
ρ = cost of capital

Characterization of Optimal Replacement Interval:

(i) $\rho E(C \mid q, d^*, y, \eta) \leq z(d^* + 1)$
(ii) $\rho E(C \mid q, d^* - 1, y, \eta) \geq zd^*$

Cost of Various Replacement Policies (for b = \$10,000, z = \$1,000, ρ = 0.25):

d	$E(C \mid q, d, y, \eta)$	$\rho E(C \mid q, d, y, \eta)$
1	\$54,000	\$13,500
2	33,556	8,389
3	27,902	6,975
4	25,837	6,459
5	25,126	6,282
d^* = 6	25,026	6,257
7	25,223	6,306
8	25,565	6,391
9	25,969	6,492
10	26,391	6,598

$$E(C \mid q, y, \eta) = 25,026$$

---

difference conditions that characterize the "optimal" replacement period. Observe that these conditions are the same as in the complete analysis except that the average cost definitions differ. As illustrated by the numerical example, this model results in replacing the machine too frequently.

A major cause of the decision error in this model is failure to recognize the cost of capital on the funds required to acquire a replacement. One of numerous possible *ad hoc* recognitions of this cost is to incorporate into the model a periodic charge for the cost of capital based on the start of period market value of the equipment used during each period. In this particular example that market value is zero except at the time of acquisition, in which case it is b. Table 7.3 presents this model, denoted M^2, including the difference conditions that characterize the "optimal" replacement period. These conditions are again the same as in the complete analysis except for the average cost definition. In the numerical example, the selected replacement period is closer to the optimum than for model M^1, but the decision is still not optimal.

Observe that model M^1 is in some sense a natural one for a decision maker who desires to minimize the costs charged against his department by a traditional accounting system. And model M^2 is a natural one if the accounting system introduces an interest charge based on the "exit" value of the equipment used.[14]

2.2 PAYBACK

Use of the payback criterion may also be interpreted as a simplification of the form of the cost function in that no attempt is made to explicitly recognize cash flow timing considerations. Instead, the predicted incremental cash flows are compared to the initial investment to determine the number of periods required to recover that investment; if that number does not exceed some (exogenous) cutoff level, the project is accepted.

The payback criterion is generally criticized for completely ignoring the situation's economic structure. On the other hand, it is often employed as a crude "risk" control device;[15] and, with uniform receipts over a sufficiently long horizon, its reciprocal approximates the internal rate of return (see Gordon 1955; Weingartner 1969).

To explore this latter theme, consider a situation where two methods of acquiring q units of some input over a T period horizon are available. One (denoted $\mathbf{a}_{C2} = 0$) entails annual purchase in the local spot market, paying z dollars at the end of each and every period. The second (denoted $\mathbf{a}_{C2} = 1$) entails a purchase contract, paying b dollars immediately and nothing thereafter. For convenience, we assume subjective certainty and a constant cost of capital, denoted ρ. The cost function is therefore given by

$$E(C \mid q, y, \eta) = \min\left\{\sum_{t=1}^{T} z(1 + \rho)^{-t}, b\right\}$$

which reflects the familiar present value rule. That is, the contract should be

---

14. If the interest charge is based on either the replacement cost or the average book value (based on straight-line depreciated cost), the decision will be the same as for model M^1. In the replacement cost case there will be an annual charge of ρb in each period, irrespective of the replacement interval; and in the book value case there will be an average periodic charge of $\rho(b/2)$.

15. This amounts to use of a constraint to simplify the cost function domain. Analysis of this type of simplification is illustrated in Appendix 7.1.

TABLE 7.3 AVERAGE COST MODELS AND RESULTING LOSSES IN MACHINE REPLACEMENT EXAMPLE

	M^1 (Cost of Capital Ignored)	M^2 (Cost of Capital on Average Investment)
Simplified Cost Models: $E(\hat{C} \mid q, d, y, \eta)$	$\dfrac{1}{d}\left[b + \displaystyle\sum_{t=1}^{d} zt\right]$	$\dfrac{1}{d}\left[b + \displaystyle\sum_{t=1}^{d} zt + bp\right]$
Characterization of "Optimal" Replacement Interval:	$\dfrac{1}{\hat{d}^*}\left[b + \displaystyle\sum_{t=1}^{\hat{d}^*} zt\right] \le z(\hat{d}^* + 1)$ $\dfrac{1}{\hat{d}^* - 1}\left[b + \displaystyle\sum_{t=1}^{\hat{d}^*-1} zt\right] \ge z\hat{d}^*$	$\dfrac{1}{\hat{d}^*}\left[b + \displaystyle\sum_{t=1}^{\hat{d}^*} zt + bp\right] \le z(\hat{d}^* + 1)$ $\dfrac{1}{\hat{d}^* - 1}\left[b + \displaystyle\sum_{t=1}^{\hat{d}^*-1} zt + bp\right] \ge z\hat{d}^*$

Average Costs for Alternative Replacement Intervals: ($b = \$10,000$, $z = \$1,000$, $\rho = 0.25$)		
$d =$ 1	$11,000	$13,500
2	6,500	7,750
3	5,333	6,167
4	5,000	5,625
5	5,000	5,500
6	5,167	5,583
7	5,429	5,786
8	5,750	6,063
9	6,111	6,389
10	6,500	6,750
Selected Decision Interval: $\hat{d}^*$	4 or 5	5
Loss (Increase in Present Value of Expenditures): $L(q, M(\cdot), y, \eta) = E(C \mid q, M(\cdot), y, \eta) - E(C \mid q, y, \eta)$	$811 or $100	$100

TABLE 7.4   PAYBACK SIMPLIFICATION ($\rho = 0.20; b = \$10,000$)

$E(C \mid q, y, \eta)$:						
$z =$	2,000	2,200	2,400	2,600	2,800	3,000
$T = 5$	5,981	6,579	7,177	7,776	8,374	8,972
10	8,385	9,223	10,000	10,000	10,000	10,000
15	9,351	10,000	10,000	10,000	10,000	10,000
20	9,739	10,000	10,000	10,000	10,000	10,000

$L(q, M(\cdot), y, \eta)$:[1]						
$z =$	2,000	2,200	2,400	2,600	2,800	3,000
$T = 5$	4,019	3,421	2,823	2,224	1,626	1,028
10	1,615	777	0	0	0	0
15	649	0	0	0	0	0
20	261	0	0	0	0	0

1. A payback criterion of $1/\rho = 5$ is employed, implying acceptance with $z \geq \$2,000$, regardless of the horizon.

employed if and only if

$$b \leq \sum_{t=1}^{T} z(1 + \rho)^{-t}.$$

An alternative modification here is based on the internal rate of return associated with the contract. We determine the internal rate of return, denoted r^*, by equating the present value of the two alternatives:

$$b = \sum_{t=1}^{T} z(1 + r^*)^{-t}.$$

And the contract is employed if and only if $r^* \geq \rho$.[16]

Expanding, we have

$$b = z \sum_{t=1}^{T} (1 + r^*)^{-t} = z \left(\frac{1 - \left(\frac{1}{1 + r^*} \right)^{T}}{r^*} \right)$$

$$= \frac{z}{r^*} - \frac{z}{r^*} \left(\frac{1}{1 + r^*} \right)^{T}$$

$$\simeq z/r^*.$$

16. Observe that although no problems arise in our elementary setting, in the general case r^* is not necessarily unique. Also, this method is generally regarded as inferior to the net present value method if subjective certainty and perfect capital markets are present. See Hirshleifer (1970).

This amounts to allowing T to grow without bound to obtain a simplified form of the cost equation.

In any event, we now have $r^* \cong z/b$; or, in terms of payback, $b/z \cong 1/r^*$. And the contract should be employed if and only if the payback period is less than or equal to $1/\rho$.

Precisely how well this simplification works naturally depends on the setting. One specific situation is illustrated in Table 7.4. For example, with $T = 10$, $b = \$10,000$, $z = \$2,200$, and $\rho = 0.20$, the optimal action is to reject the contract, implying $E(C \mid q, y, \eta) = \$9,223$. The payback simplification, however, results in acceptance of the contract, with a loss of $L(q, M(\cdot), y, \eta) = \$10,000 - \$9,223 = \$777$.

3.0 SIMPLIFICATION OF THE COST FUNCTION DOMAIN

In Chapter 6, section 1.0, we examined the impact on short-run production decisions of simplifying the domain of the input cost functions. In this section we extend the discussion of domain simplification to consider its impact on long-run input acquisition decisions.

Two familiar examples of domain simplification are explored. The first concerns suppression of uncertainty through the use of expected values in the domain of the cost function. The second concerns aggregation of the decision variables associated with several types of inputs.

3.1 UNCERTAINTY SUPPRESSION

Simplifying the cost function domain in the face of uncertainty is a common practice. Some simplifications, such as adjusting the expected present value by a factor proportional to the standard deviation of the possible values or the use of expected values with a payback constraint, provide partial recognition of uncertainty.[17] Here, however, we consider only the extreme case of suppressing uncertainty altogether.[18]

Suppression of uncertainty simplifies the analysis in that it eliminates the necessity of predicting the cash flow for each state; instead, only a single cash flow prediction is provided for each action (and period). This prediction could, for example, be the expected cash flow or the cash flow associated with some "representative" state. In any event, the analysis is simplified and may result in the selection of a nonoptimal action.

For example, a short-run decision based on the expected cash flows ignores aversion to risk and may, if risk and expected return are positively correlated, lead

17. Analysis of both simplifications is illustrated in Appendix 7.1, and Van Horne (1974) and Magee (1975) provide additional discussion of simplified means of recognizing uncertainty.

18. Alternatively, we might limit the domain to mean and variance measures. See Jensen (1969), Hirshleifer (1970), and Howard (1971).

to selection of actions with more diverse and uncertain cash flows than is optimal.[19] On the other hand, the loss from selecting nonoptimal actions is likely to be negligible if the possible cash variations are relatively small. This is perhaps the case in many short-run production decisions. Similar comments apply to uncertainty suppression in long-run, capital-budgeting decisions, though we suspect that possible cash flow variations are relatively larger in this case.

In our market value setting, the decision maker's personal aversion to risk does not play any role in the analysis. Instead, risk considerations are reflected in the state and date indexed market prices. This raises a subtle question of what prices the decision maker employs if he suppresses uncertainty by specifying a single dated sequence of cash flows for each action, and evaluates them *as if* they will occur no matter what the state. We assume that he will use the prices for certain amounts for each period,

$$P_t = \sum_{s_t \in S_t} P_t^{s_t}.$$

Note that this approach introduces a bias in favor of projects that provide larger cash returns in favorable as opposed to unfavorable states. By favorable states we mean those in which the economy produces relatively larger returns and values them, at the margin, relatively lower. For example, with state-independent preferences and diminishing marginal utility we would expect the marginal value (and price) of another dollar in a favorable state to be less than that in an unfavorable state.[20] And it is this type of distinction that is unrecognized in this type of uncertainty suppression.

A Machine Replacement Example: To illustrate these general comments we extend our previous machine replacement example (Table 7.2) to uncertainty and then determine the impact of suppressing that uncertainty in the selection of a replacement policy.

The specific state and price structures used in this example are detailed in Table 7.5. Observe that the market price consists of four components. The first ($e^{-0.3s}$) has different "values" for different states reflecting the favorableness of the states from the economy's point of view; for example, $e^{-0.3s}$ is largest for $s = -3$ since it is the least favorable state. The second component ($\phi(s)$) also has different "values" for different states, but these reflect the market's assessment of the states' likelihoods. The third component ($(1 + \rho)^{-t}$) differs only as to the time period and reflects a conventional discounting structure. The fourth component (k) is a normalizing constant that makes the price of a certain amount at time zero equal to unity.

---

19. See Van Horne (1974) and Magee (1975) for further discussion. Also note that internalizing risk-taking incentives is a fairly common difficulty in the design of performance evaluation measures. See Demski (1972b, 1976) and Itami (1975).

20. In making price comparisons we must remember that they reflect the likelihood of the state occurring as well as their desirability. Returns dependent on less likely states will have lower prices, other things equal.

TABLE 7.5   COMPLETE ANALYSIS COST FUNCTION FOR
UNCERTAIN MACHINE REPLACEMENT EXAMPLE

Decision Variable:

$$D(q) = \{1, 2, \ldots\}$$

where d is the number of periods between replacements and q specifies that one machine will be used each period.

Market Prices:

$$P_t^{s_t} = e^{-0.3s_t}\phi(s_t)(1 + \rho)^{-t}k \quad \text{where } k = \left[\sum_{s_t \in S_t} e^{-0.3s_t}\phi(s_t)\right]^{-1} = 0.8758$$

and

$s_t =$	-3	-2	-1	0	1	2	3	all $t = 0, 1, \ldots, T.$
$\phi(s_t) =$	0.10	0.10	0.20	0.20	0.20	0.10	0.10	

Input Cost Function:

$$E(C \mid q, d, y, \eta) = b \sum_{s_0 \in S_0} P_0^{s_0} + \sum_{t=1}^{d} \sum_{s_t \in S_t} z(s_t)tP_t^{s_t}$$

$$+ b \sum_{s_d \in S_d} P_d^{s_d} + \sum_{t=d+1}^{2d} \sum_{s_t \in S_t} z(s_t)(t - d)P_t^{s_t} + \cdots$$

$$= b + \sum_{t=1}^{d} \hat{z}t(1 + \rho)^{-t}$$

$$+ b(1 + \rho)^{-d} + \sum_{t=d+1}^{2d} \hat{z}(t - d)(1 + \rho)^{-t} + \cdots$$

$$= \left(b + \sum_{t=1}^{d} \hat{z}t(1 + \rho)^{-t}\right)\bigg/\left(1 - (1 + \rho)^{-d}\right)$$

where b = acquisition price (certain)

$z(s_t)$ = state-dependent maintenance cost parameter

$$\hat{z} = \sum_{s_t \in S_t} z(s_t)e^{-0.3s_t}\phi(s_t)k.$$

Within this economy-wide structure we consider a replacement situation identical to that in Table 7.2, with the single exception that the maintenance cost variable, z, is now uncertain and hence state dependent. Observe that the input cost expression $E(C \mid q, d, y, \eta)$ is the same as in Table 7.2 except that z is replaced by $\hat{z}$; $\hat{z}$ may be interpreted as the certainty equivalent of the state-dependent distribution $z(s)$.

In Table 7.6 we determine the input cost for two slightly different cases. In case 1, the large maintenance expenditures occur in the least favorable states,

TABLE 7.6 IMPACT OF UNCERTAINTY SUPPRESSION IN UNCERTAIN MACHINE
REPLACEMENT EXAMPLE (b = $10,000 and ρ = 0.25)

	Case 1	Case 2
Maintenance Cost Parameter: State-dependent Function:		
$z(s_t)$	1,000 − 250s_t	1,000 + 250s_t
Certainty Equivalent:		
z	1,217.27	782.72
Simplified Prediction:		
z	1,000	1,000
Input Cost for Alternative Replacement Policies: $(E(C \mid q, d, y, \eta))$		
d = 1	$54,869	$53,131
2	34,811	32,300
3	29,512	26,292
4	27,771	23,904
5	27,354 (d^*)	22,899
6 ($\hat{d}^*$)	27,519	22,533
7	27,954	22,492 (d^*)
8	28,509	22,621
9	29,102	22,836
10	29,691	23,091
$E(C \mid q, y, \eta)$	$27,354	$22,492
$E(C \mid q, M(\cdot), y, \eta)$	27,519	22,533
Loss:		
$L(q, M(\cdot), y, \eta)$	$ 165	$ 41

while in case 2 they occur in the most favorable states; the optimal replacement
period is 5 for case 1 and 7 for case 2. However, if we suppress uncertainty by
using the "expected" maintenance cost ($1,000) we would select a replacement
period of 6 in both cases (see Table 7.2).[21] A nonoptimal decision is made in

---

21. Observe that $P_t = \sum_{s_t \in S_t} P_t^{s_t} = (1 + \rho)^{-t} k \sum_{s_t \in S_t} e^{-0.3s_t} \phi(s_t) = (1 + \rho)^{-t}$. Therefore, the
model in Table 7.2 is the simplified model for our example here.

both cases, but the direction of the error is different. In case 1, we want to avoid the increasing and uncertain maintenance costs because the larger amounts occur when the economy has the least resources. In case 2, on the other hand, the uncertainty is less of a deterrent since the large expenditures will occur when the economy's resources are relatively plentiful.

3.2 DECISION VARIABLE AGGREGATION

In Chapter 6, section 1.2, we explored the impact on short-run production decisions of aggregating the costs of the inputs used in that production. In this section we extend that discussion to consider the impact of aggregating the decision variables that determine the cost of those inputs. That is, we consider the case where the acquisition decision variables for several inputs ($d' = (d_1, \ldots, d_m)$) are replaced by a single decision variable ($\hat{d}$). This simplifies the analysis by reducing the number of alternative decisions that must be considered both in developing cost predictions and in identifying the "optimal" decision.

To focus exclusively on the aggregation issue, we assume that the cost associated with decision variable $\hat{d}$ is that associated with the action d that will be taken if $\hat{d}$ is selected. That is, if $\alpha(\hat{d}) = d$ specifies the action d that will be taken if decision variable $\hat{d}$ is selected, then

$$E(\hat{C} \mid q, \hat{d}, y, \eta) = E(C \mid q, \alpha(\hat{d}), y, \eta).$$

For example, if d_j denotes the frequency with which direct material j is ordered and $\hat{d}$ denotes a common frequency for materials 1 through m, then

$$\alpha(\hat{d})' = (\hat{d}, \ldots, \hat{d})$$

and $E(\hat{C} \mid q, \hat{d}, y, \eta)$ is the cost of ordering all these materials with the same frequency $\hat{d}$.

As in input aggregation (see Chapter 6), unless analysis costs are relevant, such aggregation can never be strictly desirable. At best, it will not interfere with determination of the optimal input acquisition activities. From Proposition 3.2, we know that the latter will occur if

$$d^* \in D(M(\cdot), q) = \{d \mid \alpha(\hat{d}) = d \text{ and } \hat{d} \in \hat{D}(q)\}$$

where $\hat{D}(q)$ is the set of aggregate decision variables to be considered. Obviously, $D(M(\cdot), q)$ is a subset of $D(q)$ (provided that $\alpha(\hat{d}) \in D(q)$ if $\hat{d} \in \hat{D}(q)$) and thus the optimal decision may not be a member of the former.

With analysis costs, however, use of aggregate decision variables may be a worthwhile simplification. This is particularly likely if the decision maker can identify groups of inputs whose optima are likely to be similar or for which the selection of nonoptimal actions is of little consequence. ABC inventory systems are illustrations of attempts to do the latter (see Horngren 1972; Dopuch et al. 1974).

A Machine Replacement Example: We now extend our original machine replacement example to illustrate the impact of decision variable aggregation.[22]

---

22. See Trippi and Khumawala (1975) for an example of a more complex renewal situation.

TABLE 7.7   MACHINE REPLACEMENT EXAMPLE OF
            DECISION VARIABLE AGGREGATION ($\rho = 0.25$)

Complete Analysis:	Input 1	Input 2	Input 3
Cost Parameters:			
b_j	$10,000	$9,000	$5,000
z_j	$1,000	$1,000	$300
Optimal Replacement Policy:			
d_j^*	6	5	8
Minimum Input Cost:			
$E(C_j \mid q_j, y, \eta)$	$25,026	$23,639	$10,073
$E(C \mid q, y, \eta)$		$58,738	
Simplified Analysis:			
Aggregate Cost Parameters:			
$\hat{b} = b_1 + b_2 + b_3 = \$24,000$			
$\hat{z} = z_1 + z_2 + z_3 = \quad 2,300$			
Selected Replacement Policy:			
$\hat{d}^* = 6 \ \therefore \ \alpha_j(\hat{d}^*) =$	6	6	6
Actual Cost:			
$E(C_j \mid q_j, M(\cdot), y, \eta)$	$25,026	$23,671	$10,218
$E(C \mid q, M(\cdot), y, \eta)$		$58,915	
Loss:			
$L_j(q_j, M(\cdot), y, \eta)$	0	$32	$145
$L(q, M(\cdot), y, \eta)$		$177	

The prior assumptions of subjective certainty, constant salvage values, constant net replacement price, and no technological change are maintained for each input. There are three inputs, and the first is the same as in Table 7.2. Pertinent data are displayed in Table 7.7.

We assume that the three inputs are completely independent and thus there are no savings to be gained by replacing them at the same time. Consequently, since their optimal replacement policies differ, aggregation of the decision variables is bound to lead to a loss. In Table 7.7 we see that the selected policy is optimal for input 1 but not for the other two. These nonoptimal policies result in a loss of $177.[23]

4.0 DECISION DECOMPOSITION AND COST ALLOCATION

In general, the consequences of a firm's production and input acquisition activities are highly interrelated and identification of the optimal activities requires complex analyses that, in effect, simultaneously consider all such activities. The costliness of these complex analyses induces the construction of separate models for selecting the various activities. In Chapter 6, section 3, we explored the use of cost allocation as a means of constructing models for separately determining various production activities. In this section we first explore the use of cost allocation in constructing models for separately determining long-run input acquisition activities and then explore the impact of fixed cost allocation on the selection of projects that use a common scarce resource.

4.1 DECOMPOSED INPUT ACQUISITION DECISIONS

In our previous discussions we have viewed input acquisition activities as secondary, and their selection has been conditioned on the input usage required by the selected production activities.[24] We now consider separate determination of the input acquisition activities and view their selection as *determining* the inputs available for use.

There are two types of interactions that should be considered in the development of separate input acquisition models. First, if the input usage is not specified, selection of the input acquisition activities may affect both the benefit and cost component cash flows. If so, both components should be considered in constructing an input acquisition cost function. This will require specification of the production activities associated with each input acquisition activity; and if selection of the latter is to be optimal, the specified relationship must be optimal.

The second type of interaction arises because, in general, the optimal cash flow is not a separable function of the acquisition activities for the various inputs. Consequently, development of separate acquisition models usually requires the use of some simplified allocation procedure.[25]

To illustrate these general comments, we consider a specific example, again involving machine replacement.

---

23. A perhaps more interesting variant of this theme occurs when cost information, as opposed to decision variable, aggregation is involved. For example, we might consider a situation where the maintenance parameters are uncertain and recent historical outcomes are available for analysis. Aggregation of these costs would give rise to allocation questions.

24. Selection of the optimal production activities depends, in part, on the acquisition costs of the input usage levels associated with the alternative production activities. See Proposition 5.1.

25. See Chapter 6, section 3.2, for a discussion of these allocations.

TABLE 7.8   MACHINE REPLACEMENT EXAMPLE WITH AN INTERINPUT EXTERNALITY

Primary Actions:

$$a' = (a_1, \ldots, a_T)$$

where $a_t = (a_{t1}, a_{t2}, a_{t3})$ and a_{ti} is the quantity of product i produced in period t.

$$A = A_1 \times \cdots \times A_T$$

where $A_t = \{a_t \mid a_{t1} + a_{t2} + 2a_{t3} \leq 300; 2a_{t1} + a_{t2} + a_{t3} \leq 400; a_{ti} \geq 0, i = 1, 2, 3\}$.

Secondary Actions:

$$\mathbf{a}'_{C2} = (\mathbf{a}_1, \ldots, \mathbf{a}_T)$$

where $\mathbf{a}_t = (\mathbf{a}_{t1}, \mathbf{a}_{t2})$ and $\mathbf{a}_{tj} = 1$ (or 0) denotes replacement (or nonreplacement) of machine j at the end of period t.

Cost Statistic:

$$q = (q_1, \ldots, q_T)$$

where $q_t = (q_{t1}, q_{t2})$ and q_{tj} is a measure of machine j usage during period t:

$$q_{t1} = 0.1(a_{t1} + a_{t2} + a_{t3}) \text{ and } q_{t2} = 0.2(a_{t1} + a_{t2} + a_{t3}).$$

Cash Flows:

$$p_t^B(\hat{s}, a, \eta) = 8a_{t1} + 6a_{t2} + 5a_{t3}$$
$$p_t^C(\hat{s}, q, \mathbf{a}_{C2}, \eta) = b_1\mathbf{a}_{t1} + b_2\mathbf{a}_{t2} + (5\theta_{t1})q_{t1} + (2.5\theta_{t2})q_{t2}$$

where b_j is the cost of replacing machine j and $\theta_{t,j}$ is the age of machine j used during period t.

Optimal Production Decisions:
  (as a function of machine age)

$$E(\hat{U}_t \mid \alpha_t^*(\theta_t, y, \eta), \theta_t, y, \eta) = \max_{a_t \in A_t} \; [(8 - 0.5(\theta_{t1} + \theta_{t2}))a_{t1}$$
$$+ (6 - 0.5(\theta_{t1} + \theta_{t2}))a_{t2} + (5 - 0.5(\theta_{t1} + \theta_{t2}))a_{t3}]$$

$$= \begin{cases} 2{,}000 - 150(\theta_{t1} + \theta_{t2}) & 0 < \theta_{t1} + \theta_{t2} \leq 8 \\ 1{,}600 - 100(\theta_{t1} + \theta_{t2}) & 8 < \theta_{t1} + \theta_{t2} \leq 16 \\ 0 & 16 < \theta_{t1} + \theta_{t2} \end{cases}$$

"Maintenance" Cost:
  (as a function of machine age)

$$\hat{p}_t^C(\theta_t, \eta) = 2{,}000 - E(\hat{U}_t \mid \alpha_t^*(\cdot), \theta_t, y, \eta)$$

$$= \begin{cases} 150(\theta_{t1} + \theta_{t2}) & 0 < \theta_{t1} + \theta_{t2} \leq 8 \\ 400 + 100(\theta_{t1} + \theta_{t2}) & 8 < \theta_{t1} + \theta_{t2} \leq 16 \\ 2{,}000 & 16 < \theta_{t1} + \theta_{t2} \end{cases}$$

Continued on next page

TABLE 7.8 *(Continued)*

Optimal Replacement Policy:

$E(\hat{C} \mid \alpha^*_{C2}(\cdot), y, \eta) = f_1((1, 1), y, \eta)$ (assuming new machines at time $t = 0$)

$f_t(\theta_t, y, \eta) = \min_{a_{t1}, a_{t2} \in \{0,1\}} [(1 + \rho)^{-1}(b_1 a_{t1} + b_2 a_{t2} + \hat{p}^C_t(\theta_t, \eta)$

$$+ f_{t+1}((\theta_{t1}(1 - a_{t1}) + 1, \theta_{t2}(1 - a_{t2}) + 1), y, \eta)]$$

$$1 \leq t \leq T$$

$f_{T+1}(\theta_{T+1}, y, \eta) = 0$

A Machine Replacement Example: In this example two machines are used in the production of three products. The number of machines is fixed, but the decision maker must determine the replacement policies for the two machines and the production level for each product for each period. The cost component cash flows are affected by both the level of production and the age of the machines, and thus the production and replacement policies are determined jointly.

For convenience, we assume subjective certainty, with the firm's cost of capital again denoted ρ. No technological change is present, and replacement cash flows are again assumed independent of the age of the replaced equipment.

The benefit component cash flows depend only on the current production levels, but the cost component depends on current production levels, end of period replacements, and prior replacements (since these determine the age of the machines used during the current period). The production levels are restricted by the capacity of the two machines.[26] These elements are all specified in Table 7.8.

We could approach the problem in the manner outlined in Table 5.1. That would involve determining the optimal replacement policy for each possible sequence of machine usage levels (the cost statistic) and then using the derived cost function to determine the optimal sequence of production levels. Our computations are more straightforward, however, if we develop a replacement cost model that reflects the optimal production levels for the inputs made available.

The production level in any given period affects only what might be termed the operating cash flows of that period (that is, all cash flows except those associated with replacement acquisitions). Furthermore, the effect on those cash flows is the same in each period except for differences caused by variations in the ages of the machines used. Consequently, we can determine both the optimal production level and optimal operating cash flows for any given period as functions of only the machine ages for that period. This is done in Table 7.8.

Note that, with the specific data assumed, the operating cash flow varies between $2,000 and $0, depending on the combined ages of the machines. We

---

26. Capacity additions are assumed to be uneconomic. The only investment issue is when to replace the existing equipment with identical but new counterparts.

interpret this dependence on machine age as a form of "maintenance" cost, and define a short-run maintenance cost function as the difference between the maximum possible operating cash flow with zero aged machines ($2,000) and the actual maximum possible given a specific pair of ages. See Table 7.8.

The optimal replacement policy can now be determined with a straight-forward dynamic programming model. The cash flow in any given period depends on the age of the machines used during that period and the end of period replacement decision. If machine j is replaced at the end of period t, its age statistic for the following period is reset to $\theta_{t+1,j} = 1$; otherwise, $\theta_{t+1,j} = \theta_{tj} + 1$. Details of the model are presented in Table 7.8.

Solution of this model requires fairly complex calculations despite the modifications we have made; consequently, we again consider simplification. One approach is to develop approximations of the maintenance cost function $\hat{p}_t^C(\theta_t, \eta)$ that express this cost as a separable function of each machine's age. The simplest approximation of this type is a linear function:[27]

$$\hat{p}_t^C(\theta_t, \eta) = z_1\theta_{t1} + z_2\theta_{t2}.$$

This provides a basis for independently determining the replacement policy for each machine using the elementary replacement model in Table 7.2.

The only question is one of determining the (z_1, z_2) parameters. In a sense, this amounts to allocating the total cost between the two inputs. Observe that in the first region $(0 < \theta_{t1} + \theta_{t2} \leq 8)$ the cost increases at the rate of $150 per unit increase in age for either machine. Similarly, in the second region $(8 < \theta_{t1} + \theta_{t2} \leq 16)$ the rate is $100 per unit increase in age. Hence we might assume that maintenance costs increase at the rate of either $150 or $100 per unit increase in age. Alternatively, a simple arithmetic average would be $125 per unit increase in age. Finally, another expression of the average relationship can be obtained by fitting a linear regression through the first two segments of the cost curve. Using a random sample of points results in an average increase in maintenance cost of $120 per unit increase in age.

Table 7.9 displays the policies induced by each of these parameter predictions, in a specific numerical example. In each case we determine the policy by employing the respective prediction of z_j in the model in Table 7.2 (with $\rho = 0.20$ and the added simplifying assumption of an infinite horizon).[28]

Finally, observe that separate determination of the optimal replacement policies is possible with appropriate modification. Following Proposition 3.1, we could insert, say, the optimal policy for the second machine into $f_t(\theta_t, y, \eta)$ in Table 7.8. We are then faced with the problem of separately determining the

---

27. A constant term could be included in this linear approximation, but it would have no effect in the resulting decisions.

28. The cost and loss calculations in Table 7.9 are, recall, based on a horizon of $T = 40$. In making these calculations it was assumed that all machines were costlessly disposed of at the end of the last period. $T = 40$ is, however, a sufficiently long horizon to make this particular assumption inconsequential.

TABLE 7.9 COSTS AND POLICIES ASSOCIATED WITH
VARIOUS AVERAGE MAINTENANCE COST SIMPLIFICATIONS

Parameters:

$$b_1 = \$2{,}917 \qquad b_2 = \$3{,}333$$
$$T = 40 \qquad \rho = 0.20$$

Optimal Replacement Cost:[1]

$$E(\hat{C} \mid \alpha^*_{C2}(\cdot), y, \eta) = \underline{\underline{\$6{,}151}}$$

Simplified Models and the Resulting Losses:

Average Maintenance Cost: $z_1 = z_2$	Selected Replacement Policy:[2] $\alpha_{C2}(\cdot)$ Machine 1	Machine 2	Actual Replacement Cost:[3] $E(\hat{C} \mid M(\cdot), y, \eta)$	Loss $L(M(\cdot), y, \eta)$
$120	$d_1 = 9$	$d_2 = 10$	$6,742	$591
125	9	10	6,742	591
150	8	9	6,860	709
100	11	11	6,525	374

1. This is a somewhat pathological example in that the optimal policy is never to replace the machines. However, it provides us with a simple example to illustrate the impact of simplification in this context.

2. The selected replacement policy is of the form: replace machine j ($\mathbf{a}_{tj} = 1$) if $\theta_{tj} \geq d_j$ and do not replace ($\mathbf{a}_{tj} = 0$) if $\theta_{tj} < d_j$.

3. This cost is obtained by using the selected replacement policy instead of the optimal policy in the replacement cost model formulated in Table 7.8.

policy for the first machine. This modification requires, however, knowledge of the optimal policy, a calculation we seek to avoid with the allocation procedures.

4.2 DECOMPOSED PROJECT SELECTION

Our second exploration of simplified decomposition procedures is a direct extension of the cost allocation analysis in Chapter 6, section 3.3. The decision context considered here involves a previously acquired facility, such as a building, with excess capacity and m proposals for using that capacity. For example, if the facility is a department store, the proposals may be alternative additional departments. We allow for the possibility of acquiring additional capacity at the time the proposals are selected, and any future excess demand for capacity may be satisfied by making acquisitions in a local spot market (for example, temporarily renting space).

We let $a_i \in \{0, 1\}$, $i = 1, \ldots, m$, denote rejection or acceptance of the respective proposals. The net cash flows, exclusive of the incremental costs of supplying the input in question, are assumed to be additive across the proposals: [29]

$$x_t^B = \sum_{i=1}^{m} p_{ti}^B(s_t, a_i, \eta)$$

Capacity, or input, usage is assumed for convenience to be proportional to the individual benefit component outcomes. With h_i denoting the proportionality constant for project i, the total input required in state s_t of period t is therefore

$$q_t = \delta_{Ct}(s_t, a, \eta) = \sum_{i=1}^{m} h_i p_{ti}^B(s_t, a_i, \eta).$$

The existing available capacity is denoted q^0 and the number of units of capacity acquired at time $t = 0$ is denoted $\mathbf{a}_{C2}$. The immediate cash outflow associated with acquiring additional capacity is C^0 dollars per unit of capacity and the cash outflow required to satisfy excess demand for capacity in any future period is C^1 dollars per unit of capacity:

$$p_0^C(s_0, \mathbf{a}_{C2}, \eta) = C^0 \mathbf{a}_{C2}$$
$$p_t^C(s_t, q_t, \mathbf{a}_{C2}, \eta) = [q_t - q^0 - \mathbf{a}_{C2}]^+ C^1 \quad 1 \leq t \leq T$$

where the "+" denotes the fact that this cost is incurred only if the input demand exceeds available supply. These elements and the resulting decision model are summarized in Table 7.10.

Now consider methods for simplifying this model. We might, for example, suppress uncertainty and reformulate the problem in terms of maximizing the expected present value (given some cost of capital) subject to a capacity limitation. The resulting model is an integer programming problem. And subsequent parametric analysis of the capacity constraint will provide a basis for deciding whether to acquire additional capacity. [30]

---

29. With an incremental modification, we naturally have $p_{ti}^B(s_t, 0, \eta) = 0$.

30. Assuming a cost of capital of ρ, we define the expected present value of project i by

$$PV(\rho)_i = E\left(\sum_{t=1}^{T} (1 + \rho)^{-t} p_{ti}^B(s_t, 1, \eta)\right)$$

and define the average capacity demand by

$$\bar{q}_i = \frac{1}{T} E\left(\sum_{t=1}^{T} h_i p_{ti}^B(s_t, 1, \eta)\right).$$

(Note that with homogeneous expectations there would be no difficulty in assessing these expectations.) The basic integer programming problem is

$$E(\hat{U} \mid q^0, d^*(\cdot), y, \eta) = \max_{d' = (d_1, \ldots, d_m)} \sum_{i=1}^{m} PV(\rho)_i d_i$$

subject to

$$\sum_{i=1}^{m} \bar{q}_i d_i \leq q^0$$
$$d_i \in \{0, 1\}.$$

TABLE 7.10 PROJECT SELECTION EXAMPLE

Actions:

$$a' = (a_1, \ldots, a_m)$$

with $a_i \in \{0, 1\}$ denoting rejection or acceptance of project i and

$$\mathbf{a}_{C2} \in \mathbf{A}_{C2}$$

denoting the number of units of additional capacity acquired at $t = 0$.

Benefit Component Cash Flow:

$$x_t^B = \sum_{i=1}^{m} p_{ti}^B(s_t, a_i, \eta) \qquad t = 1, \ldots, T$$

Cost Component Cash Flow:

$$q_t = \delta_{Ct}(s_t, a, \eta) = \sum_{i=1}^{m} h_i p_{ti}^B(s_t, a_i, \eta) \qquad t = 1, \ldots, T$$

$$x_0^C = p_0^C(s_0, \mathbf{a}_{C2}, \eta) = C^0 \mathbf{a}_{C2}$$

$$x_t^C = p_t^C(s_t, q_t, \mathbf{a}_{C2}, \eta) = [q_t - q^0 - \mathbf{a}_{C2}]^+ C^1 \qquad t = 1, \ldots, T$$

Benefit Function:

$$E(B \mid a, y, \eta) = \sum_{t=1}^{T} \sum_{s_t \in S_t} \left(\sum_{i=1}^{m} p_{ti}^B(s_t, a_i, \eta) \right) P_t^{s_t}$$

Cost Function:

$$E(C \mid a, y, \eta) = \min_{\mathbf{a}_{C2} \in \mathbf{A}_{C2}} \left\{ \sum_{s_0 \in S_0} (C^0 \mathbf{a}_{C2}) P_0^{s_0} \right.$$

$$\left. + \sum_{t=1}^{T} \sum_{s_t \in S_t} ([\delta_{Ct}(s_t, a, \eta) - q^0 - \mathbf{a}_{C2}]^+ C^1) P_t^{s_t} \right\}$$

Optimal Choice:

$$E(U \mid \alpha^*(\cdot), y, \eta) = \max_{a \in A} [E(B \mid a, y, \eta) - E(C \mid a, y, \eta)]$$

Alternatively, we might decompose the project selection decision into m separate individual project decisions. Of particular concern here is the externality cost (see Table 5.3) associated with the common input. One conceivable approach, as discussed in Chapter 6, is to allocate the sunk cost of that imput. We might, for example, accept any individual project that has an expected present value in excess of the allocated sunk cost of the average capacity it requires. Besides suppressing uncertainty, then, this entails using the sunk cost allocation as a (crude) surrogate

---

The maximum present value associated with a capacity increase of $\mathbf{a}_{C2}$ is determined in the same manner except that q^0 is replaced by $q^0 + \mathbf{a}_{C2}$. The capacity increase would then be considered desirable if $E(\hat{U} \mid q^0 + \mathbf{a}_{C2}, d^*(\cdot), y, \eta) - E(\hat{U} \mid q^0, d^*(\cdot), y, \eta) \geq C^0 \mathbf{a}_{C2}$.

TABLE 7.11 SIMPLIFICATIONS OF PROJECT SELECTION EXAMPLE

Parameters:

$$P_t^{s_t} = e^{-0.1 s_t}(1 + \rho)^{-t}\phi(s_t)$$

where

$s_t =$	-3	-2	-1	0	1	2	3
$\phi(s_t) =$	0.01	0.06	0.24	0.38	0.24	0.06	0.01

$\rho = 0.20$ $m = 5$ $T = 10$

$q^0 = 25{,}000$ $C^0 = \$0.4$ $C^1 = \$0.24$ $A_{C2} = \{0; 20{,}000; 40{,}000; 60{,}000\}$

Project Descriptions:

	Case A	Case B	Case C	Case D
Project 1				
$PV(0.20)_1$	54	5,245	5,836	7,912
$\bar{q}_1$	8,213	10,487	10,966	10,692
Project 2				
$PV(0.20)_2$	5,174	4,316	3,453	3,265
$\bar{q}_2$	10,748	9,120	10,763	11,597
Project 3				
$PV(0.20)_3$	9,247	7,768	3,277	685
$\bar{q}_3$	10,737	12,193	10,379	10,798
Project 4				
$PV(0.20)_4$	4,013	5,147	5,819	4,330
$\bar{q}_4$	12,492	9,956	9,756	10,280
Project 5				
$PV(0.20)_5$	4,370	6,425	6,834	5,896
$\bar{q}_5$	12,040	11,762	10,039	10,632

Continued on next page

for the externality cost of the inputs used to implement the project. Of course, we could ignore the externality altogether and merely accept any project with a nonnegative expected present value.

Table 7.11 presents specific numerical results for several simplified procedures in one particular setting. The event and price structure is similar to that in Table

Table 7.11 *(Continued)*

	Case A	Case B	Case C	Case D
Complete Analysis:				
$E(U \mid \alpha^*(\cdot), y, \eta)$	14,088	12,374	12,266	13,196
$\alpha^*(\cdot)'$	(0, 1, 1, 0, 0)	(1, 1, 1, 0, 1)	(1, 1, 0, 1, 1)	(1, 0, 0, 0, 1)
$\alpha^*_{C2}(\cdot)$	0	20,000	20,000	0
Simplification Results:				
M^1: Integer programming with capacity constraint and separate expansion analysis				
$E(U \mid M^1(\cdot), y, \eta)$	14,088	12,310	12,266	13,196
$L(M^1(\cdot), y, \eta)$	0	64	0	0
$\alpha(\cdot)'$	(0, 1, 1, 0, 0)	(1, 0, 1, 1, 1)	(1, 1, 0, 1, 1)	(1, 0, 0, 0, 1)
$\alpha_{C2}(\cdot)$	0	20,000	20,000	0
M^2: Present value analysis with allocated sunk cost (of $\overline{q}_i C^0$) and separate expansion analysis				
$E(U \mid M^2(\cdot), y, \eta)$	14,088	11,870	10,467	10,433
$L(M^2(\cdot), y, \eta)$	0	504	1,799	2,763
$\alpha(\cdot)'$	(0, 1, 1, 0, 0)	(1, 1, 1, 1, 1)	(1, 0, 0, 1, 1)	(1, 0, 0, 1, 1)
$\alpha_{C2}(\cdot)$	0	40,000	0	0
M^3: Myopic present value analysis and separate expansion analysis				
$E(U \mid M^3(\cdot), y, \eta)$	5,908	11,870	6,478	5,116
$L(M^3(\cdot), y, \eta)$	8,180	504	5,788	8,080
$\alpha(\cdot)'$	(1, 1, 1, 1, 1)	(1, 1, 1, 1, 1)	(1, 1, 1, 1, 1)	(1, 1, 1, 1, 1)
$\alpha_{C2}(\cdot)$	40,000	40,000	20,000	40,000

7.5. Also, since the results are likely to depend on the idiosyncratic nature of the projects themselves, four separate random samples of projects were taken from the same underlying population.[31]

Three types of simplified analyses are considered. The first, M^1, selects projects on the basis of an integer programming model with a capacity constraint. The second, M^2, selects projects on the basis of a simple *ad hoc* present value analysis with proration of the excess capacity's sunk cost. And the third, M^3, uses a simple present value analysis that ignores the externalities created by the limited capacity. All three analyses suppress uncertainty and carry out a separate analysis to determine the size of any expansion. The losses resulting from the use of the first analysis are minimal, they are somewhat greater for the second, and much greater for the third. That is, in this context we obtain distinctly inferior results when we ignore the externality created by capacity limitations.

5.0 SUMMARY

In conclusion, we have seen that simplified cost functions are familiar phenomena in long-run decision problems. The various examples presented have, however, been too complex and diverse to permit meaningful summarization at this point. We therefore conclude by repeating two familiar observations.

First, our focus has been on the analysis of cost assessment alternatives, but we have not made any specific recommendations. Cost concepts or methods of assessment provide neither true nor false, useful nor not useful assessments in and of themselves. They are inherently contextual. What works well in one setting need not and may not work well in another.

Second, in examining the fundamental question of what appears to work well in some particular setting, we found it necessary to resort to a level of analysis that the decision maker was attempting to avoid. Otherwise, definitive analysis would not be attainable. That is, each case required a determination of the decision that would be induced by a given simplification and subsequent reflection of these decisions in terms of change in the firm's market value. While we could afford the luxury of such a complete analysis given our assumption of costless analysis by the evaluator,[32] it is apparent that resolution of these issues is costly. More will be said about this in Chapter 9.

---

31. In generating these projects we assumed

$$p_{ti}^B(s_t, 1, \eta) = f_{ti} + g_{ti}(100 + 4s_t) \qquad t = 1, \ldots, 10$$

with g_{ti} normally distributed with a mean of 100 and a standard deviation of 33 and f_{ti} with a mean of 1,000 and a standard deviation of 100, $i = 1, \ldots, 5$ and $t = 1, \ldots, 10$. In addition, each h_i is normally distributed with a mean of 1 and a standard deviation of 0.1.

32. Noncost to the evaluator should, however, not be construed in terms of implying noncost to the authors.

APPENDIX 7.1
SIMPLIFICATION INTERACTIONS

The purpose of this appendix is to provide an example of the possible inter-actions between cost assessment alternatives and the particular type of simplified model employed by the decision maker. This question is examined in a setting where the decision maker must decide which subset of a group of $m = 25$ invest-ment projects to accept. Each project can be analyzed independently (in the sense of Proposition 6.2).

A $T = 10$ period horizon is recognized. Individual project benefit cash flows, in turn, are described by

$$p_{ti}^{B}(s_t, 1, \eta) = f_{ti} + g_{ti}(100 + 4s_t) \qquad \begin{matrix} i = 1, \ldots, m \\ t = 1, \ldots, T \end{matrix}$$

where $p_{ti}^{B}(\cdot)$ is the cash flow in period t for project i and $a_i = 1$ denotes ac-ceptance of that project (0 denotes rejection). The state and price structure are the same as characterized in Table 7.11, except that $\rho = 0.10$. Also, each f_{ti} is drawn from a normal distribution with a mean of \$1,100 and a standard deviation of \$110[33] and each g_{ti} from a normal distribution with a mean of \$100 and a stan-dard deviation of \$33 for $i = 1, \ldots, m$ and $t = 1, \ldots, T$.[34] In addition, the ini-tial investment required for each project, $p_0^{C}(S_0, 1, \eta)$, is drawn from a normal distribution with a mean equal to 60% of its total undiscounted expected cash flow and a standard deviation of 6% of this undiscounted flow.

Fourteen simplified decision models are examined: a simple payback model with a 5- or 7-period payback parameter, a simple expected present value model with a cost of capital of 0.08, 0.10, or 0.12,[35] and the three present value models with a 7-period payback constraint, and the three present value models with a standard deviation constraint requiring that the expected present value of the project less either two or three times the project present value's standard deviation be nonnegative. Observe that all of the models except those with a standard deviation constraint suppress all recognition of project flow uncertainty.

Finally, the cost assessment alternatives considered relate to alternative methods of predicting the incremental overhead (cash outflow) incurred by a com-

---

33. This description relates to the population of projects showing neither expected growth nor decline over the horizon. However, in most sets of projects we assumed that one-third would display no expected change in the level of cash flows from period to period, another one-third would display an expected increase from period to period, and the remaining third an expected decrease. Thus projects with growth or decline in the resource flow patterns are drawn from a population identical to that described, except f_{ti} is drawn from a normal distribution with a mean of $1,000 \pm 100t$ and a standard deviation equal to $100(1 \pm 0.1t)$.

34. An independent, zero mean random error term was also employed in the cash flow model. This has no effect whatever, except in calculating the variance of the net present value distribution.

35. That is, in two cases (0.08 and 0.12) we use a cost of capital other than that implicit in the price structure.

mon service facility that will be used by all the selected projects. The level of service used by a project in each period is assumed to be proportional to the benefit cash flow components associated with that project in each period; that is,

$$q_t = \delta_t(s_t, a, \eta) = \sum_{i=1}^{m} [h_{i1}f_{ti} + h_{i2}g_{ti}(100 + 4s_t)]a_i \qquad t = 1, \ldots, T$$

where q_t is a measure of service used in period t and h_{i1} and h_{i2} are the proportionality constants for project i.[36] Furthermore, the service department overhead is assumed to be a linear function of the level of service used:

$$p_t^C(s_t, q_t, \eta) = f + vq_t + \epsilon_t \qquad t = 1, \ldots, T$$

where f (fixed) and v (variable) are appropriate constants and ϵ_t is a zero mean, constant variance random error term.[37] The cost assessment alternatives center around alternative methods of predicting the (variable) overhead parameter v.

In the analysis we assume that the actual value of v is \$10 and then consider five alternative predictions (which we denote $\hat{v}$). The first (Case 1), with $\hat{v} =$ \$10.64, is a typical prediction obtained from estimating the past relationship with regression techniques and a random sample of data generated with the posited relationship. Two other more biased predictions of $\hat{v} =$ \$12 (Case 2) and $\hat{v} =$ \$8 (Case 3) are examined to provide a basis for assessing whether a preference for a biased prediction exists. The actual relationship (Case 4), $\hat{v} =$ \$10, is examined to see how well simplified models perform with perfect predictions. Finally, a full cost version (Case 4f) is analyzed, based on a fixed cost allocation of \$10 per unit of q_t. That is, the overhead allocated to a given project under Case 4f will be precisely double that under Case 4.[38]

There is no intrinsic reason for including the full cost allocation in the analysis, except that it provides a method of biasing the anticipated returns downward. The bias occurs because all the projects require the service, and if we overstate its cost, we understate the individual project's cash flows. This is similar to such heuristic practices as increasing the required rate of return or scaling the predicted cash flows in an uncertain return situation.

Thus five alternative parameter predictions are considered, one being the actual value (Case 4) and the others ranging from 80% (Case 3) to 200% (Case 4f) of the actual value. The method of analysis should be very familiar at this point. For a given set of projects and a given overhead prediction method we determine the set of predicted cash flows the decision maker would produce and then, with knowledge of his decision model, determine the projects he would

---

36. h_{i1} and h_{i2} are each drawn from a normal distribution with a mean of 1.5 and a standard deviation of 0.48.

37. In a complete embracing of the state preference formulation, ϵ_t would be state dependent.

38. Comparable full cost figures for Cases 1, 2, and 3 were not examined because the effect of deliberately moving to a full cost allocation of this general magnitude can be readily assessed with the single case.

actually implement. Then, using the posited overhead relationship and the state preference characterization in Table 7.11 (with $\rho = 0.10$), we determine the market value effect of the decisions induced by the specific overhead prediction method and model, given the set of projects. Results are displayed in Table 7.12.

Consider the results obtained with project set A, a randomly generated set of $m = 25$ projects, as described above. Optimal selection among the projects using the market value maximization criterion would result in a market value increase of \$106,255; and the various overhead parameter and model combinations approach this with varying degrees of success. Reliance on the expected present value model with a cost of capital equal to the time preference factor embedded in the price structure, $\rho = 0.10$, coupled with an overhead parameter that closely or exactly equals the actual value of 10, $\hat{v} = 10.64$ or $\hat{v} = 10$, produces the most desirable result. Thus, for this specific situation, the present value model with $\rho = 0.10$ and an accurate overhead parameter provide an excellent simplification; and we can interpret the other model-parameter prediction combinations as deviations from this approximate ideal that may be either reinforcing or counterbalancing.

For example, if we continue to suppress the risk information and rely on an expected value analysis, lowering the required cost of capital would probably result in acceptance of undesirable projects, thereby producing less of an increase (or even a decrease) in the firm's market value. The present value model with $\rho = 0.08$ (column [c] in Table 7.12) illustrates this phenomenon. If we also understate the project returns in this model, we should experience some offsetting of the downward biased cost of capital. Thus, if we move from $\hat{v} = 10$ to $\hat{v} = 12$, thereby downward biasing project returns, we improve the performance of the model.

Similarly, since both the 7-period payback and present value model with $\rho = 0.08$ tend to accept uneconomic projects, we should be able to improve their performance by appending a constraint designed to filter out marginal projects. For example, if we require that the expected return (with $\rho = 0.08$) less two or three times the return distribution's standard deviation be nonnegative for acceptance, we will probably eliminate some of the marginal projects. Movement from model (c) to either model (i) or model (l) should, therefore, tend to improve performance, regardless of the overhead parameter employed. And this is precisely the case. For the same reason, adding a payback constraint to the present value model with $\rho = 0.08$ should improve its performance, regardless of the overhead parameter. This is also demonstrated by the results in Table 7.12 (model [b] or [c] and model [f]). Conversely, if the cost of capital is overstated in the present value model, as in model (e) with $\rho = 0.12$, downward biasing the return or adding either a payback or return variability constraint should lessen its performance. Results for models (e), (k), and (n) confirm this; and overstating the return through use of $\hat{v} = 8$ improves the performance of model (e).

Thus, the preferred overhead parameter prediction, given the actual overhead relationship posited and project set A, is dependent on the model employed by the decision maker. The next question is how dependent are these results on the

TABLE 7.12 MARKET VALUE EFFECTS FOR ALTERNATIVE OVERHEAD PREDICTION METHODS AND DECISION MODEL COMBINATIONS

	5-Period Payback	7-Period Payback	NPV(0.08)[1]	NPV(0.10)[1]	NPV(0.12)	NPV(0.08) and (b)	NPV(0.10) and (b)	NPV(0.12) and (b)	NPV(0.08)[2] $-2\sigma \geq 0$	NPV(0.10) $-2\sigma \geq 0$	NPV(0.12) $-2\sigma \geq 0$	NPV(0.08) $-3\sigma \geq 0$	NPV(0.10) $-3\sigma \geq 0$	NPV(0.12) $-3\sigma \geq 0$
	(a)	(b)	(c)	(d)	(e)	(f)	(g)	(h)	(i)	(j)	(k)	(l)	(m)	(n)
Project Set A (maximum increase = 106,255)														
(1) $\hat{v} = 10.64$	55,759	77,678	88,155	106,253	93,198	96,562	106,253	93,197	94,169	103,564	72,831	100,984	101,019	65,073
(2) $\hat{\theta} = 12$	42,691	78,939	94,169	103,564	78,596	100,833	103,564	78,596	100,985	101,019	65,073	100,985	93,198	65,073
(3) $\hat{\theta} = 8$	66,436	77,875	79,884	100,985	97,451	83,483	100,985	97,457	88,155	106,253	93,198	88,155	106,253	93,198
(4) $\hat{\theta} = 10$	55,759	77,678	88,155	106,253	93,198	93,562	106,253	93,197	94,169	103,564	86,355	94,169	101,019	65,073
(4f) $\hat{\theta} = 20$	0	101,364	93,198	65,073	30,546	93,198	65,073	30,546	93,198	54,396	16,763	93,198	43,614	16,763
Project Set B (maximum increase = 97,621)														
(1)	48,861	81,382	77,081	97,250	56,373	87,159	97,250	56,373	91,483	91,553	56,373	95,061	91,553	48,861
(2)	48,861	91,666	91,484	95,590	56,373	95,061	95,590	56,373	95,061	88,117	48,861	95,061	79,246	48,861
(3)	53,749	74,881	71,304	95,061	84,134	74,881	95,061	84,134	77,081	97,618	74,552	77,081	97,249	56,373
(4)	48,861	74,881	77,081	97,618	74,552	80,658	97,618	74,552	88,092	93,674	56,373	95,061	91,554	56,373
(4f)	34,592	95,001	86,653	48,861	48,861	86,653	48,861	48,861	69,652	48,861	34,592	63,513	48,861	18,885
Project Set C (maximum increase = 73,769)														
(1)	43,771	22,612	33,341	71,933	70,790	43,456	71,933	70,790	25,926	14,425	0	0	0	0
(2)	33,557	26,275	42,275	73,768	61,018	56,046	73,768	61,018	25,926	0	0	0	0	0
(3)	51,856	18,442	22,384	54,067	72,377	28,326	54,067	72,377	44,225	25,926	0	0	0	0
(4)	43,771	22,612	33,341	71,933	70,791	43,456	71,933	70,791	25,926	14,425	0	0	0	0
(4f)	0	71,853	70,791	52,505	25,926	70,791	52,505	25,926	0	0	0	0	0	0

Project Set D (maximum increase = 4,491)

	1	2	3	4	5	6	7	8	9	10	11	12	13	14
(1)	0	1,036	1,036	1,130	1,130	1,036	1,130	0	1,036	0	0	1,036	0	0
(2)	0	1,036	1,036	0	0	1,036	0	0	1,036	0	0	1,036	0	0
(3)	485	1,036	1,036	1,036	1,036	1,036	1,036	0	1,036	3,442	0	1,036	1,485	0
(4)	0	1,036	1,036	4,076	4,076	1,036	4,076	0	1,036	0	0	1,036	0	0
(4f)	0	1,529	0	0	0	0	0	0	0	0	0	0	0	0

Project Set E (maximum increase = 105,615)

	1	2	3	4	5	6	7	8	9	10	11	12	13	14
(1)	24,533	70,298	92,640	90,727	105,062	98,049	105,062	90,727	97,994	98,574	77,204	101,593	85,342	77,204
(2)	1,363	71,562	97,996	84,069	103,701	104,661	103,701	84,069	101,597	95,343	67,083	101,593	90,727	56,205
(3)	67,689	68,492	76,760	95,342	103,395	80,357	103,395	95,342	92,640	105,611	90,726	92,640	105,062	90,726
(4)	54,865	70,302	92,643	90,727	105,063	98,052	105,063	90,727	97,996	103,701	90,726	97,996	98,574	72,704
(4f)	0	105,612	93,459	17,878	56,205	93,459	56,205	17,878	90,727	56,205	17,878	77,204	56,205	17,878

Project Set F (maximum increase = 49,212)

	1	2	3	4	5	6	7	8	9	10	11	12	13	14
(1)	14,630	11,588	26,756	31,038	48,344	26,756	48,344	31,038	40,179	48,344	18,244	43,469	48,344	18,244
(2)	5,031	11,588	40,179	18,244	48,344	40,179	48,344	18,244	46,349	48,344	18,244	48,152	36,070	9,598
(3)	13,143	5,338	-2,796	44,273	45,272	5,338	45,272	44,273	26,756	49,072	36,069	26,756	48,962	25,530
(4)	14,630	11,588	26,757	36,070	49,181	26,757	49,181	36,070	36,780	48,344	18,244	40,179	48,344	18,244
(4f)	0	43,692	40,140	0	9,598	40,140	9,598	0	25,530	0	0	25,530	0	0

Project Set G (maximum increase = 55,550)

	1	2	3	4	5	6	7	8	9	10	11	12	13	14
(1)	11,117	34,782	34,782	37,455	55,550	34,782	55,550	37,445	45,685	51,414	37,445	49,462	48,779	37,445
(2)	0	35,962	42,749	37,445	53,463	42,749	53,463	37,445	51,470	48,779	37,445	53,015	48,779	37,445
(3)	11,117	11,716	11,716	48,778	51,006	11,716	51,006	48,778	19,487	55,515	37,445	25,714	55,550	37,445
(4)	11,117	25,715	25,715	37,445	55,550	25,715	55,550	37,445	30,723	53,501	37,445	49,462	51,414	37,445
(4f)	0	52,039	50,828	0	37,445	50,828	37,445	0	48,779	37,445	0	42,689	26,328	0

1. NPV (0.08) denotes acceptance of project i if and only if the expected present value with $\rho = 0.08$ is greater than or equal to zero.

2. NPV (0.08) – 2σ denotes acceptance of project i if and only if the expected present value with $\rho = 0.08$ less 2 times the standard deviation of the present value distribution is greater than or equal to zero.

posited set of projects.[39] A second set of projects, project set B in Table 7.12, was randomly selected from the identical population; and we observe, essentially, the same characteristics.

Next, variability was increased by using

$$p_{ti}^{B}(s_t, 1, \eta) = f_{ti} + g_{ti}(100 + 40s_t)$$

to alter the cash flow data in project set A. The results are presented as project set C in Table 7.12. Observe that the parameter-decision model effects remain. But use of the standard deviation constraints to improve the performance of models that tend to accept marginal projects is no longer advisable, apparently because the variability associated with all projects has increased to a point where the two or three standard deviation limits are too tight.

Four other project sets of varying characteristics were also examined and the same types of results were obtained. Project set D is composed of 25 marginal projects. Here we observe an increase in the sensitivity of predicting the overhead parameter to obtain near-optimal results with the present value model (with $\rho = 0.10$). In project set E, on the other hand, half of the projects have g_{ti} terms that are negative, resulting in state-dependent returns that vary inversely with the state variable. And, finally, all the projects in project set F have expected net cash flows that decline through time and all those in project set G increase with time.

Taken together, these results suggest that preference for the overhead parameter may depend on both the model used and project types analyzed by the decision maker.[40]

---

39. The results are obviously dependent on how much service (and hence overhead) is demanded by each of the projects. If the average amounts are larger than in A, the tolerable and/or useful biases will be altered, but the direction of the effects remains. Similarly, if the average amounts are sufficiently small, the evaluation of alternative overhead prediction methods becomes trivial because the cash flow prediction errors will be insignificant.

40. This observation is consistent with the results obtained in another simulation reported by Sundem (1974).

8

INTERORGANIZATION REPORTING OF COST ASSESSMENTS

The purpose of this chapter is to extend our analysis to cost assessments that are reported to decision makers external to the organization. Two obvious examples of this type of setting are public financial reporting and cost measurement in "cost-plus" procurement contracts. Although we emphasize these two specific settings (along with the corresponding roles of the Financial and Cost Accounting Standards Boards), it will become evident that the same principles are involved in the design of performance measures for responsibility centers and in the reporting of cost assessments to either regulatory agencies or the makers of governmental policies.

Analysis of cost assessment alternatives in these settings proceeds in the same fashion as in the intraorganization settings examined in prior chapters. That is, we evaluate the alternatives in terms of the consequences of the decision makers' actions they induce. The only addition to our basic description is the inherent complexity of the settings.

This complexity is, however, a fundamental addition. The consequences of a particular cost assessment procedure will now depend on how it affects the actions of decision makers both internal *and* external to the organization; and the desirability of those consequences will depend on whose preferences we consider in the evaluation. That is, we now face a multiperson setting; and generalization from the single-person to the multiperson setting is not readily accomplished. For example, it is never rational, assuming complete analysis, to pay scarce resources to suppress absolutely free information in a single-person setting (Proposition 2.1). Yet such payment may be rational if others also receive the information and their acts might have an unfavorable impact on the person in question. (Specific examples are provided in Appendices 8.2 and 8.3.)[1]

A more disconcerting aspect of multiperson complexity is Arrow's Impossibility Theorem.[2] The single-person focus in earlier chapters was considerably aided by assuming consistent behavior that admits to an expected utility representation. But no such convenient representation is generally available if we wish to consider the preferences of all those involved in a multiperson setting.[3]

The first section discusses the interorganization reporting setting and sets the stage for subsequent discussion. Financial reporting considerations and the role of the Financial Accounting Standards Board are discussed in the second section. Cost-based procurement considerations and the role of the Cost Accounting Standards Board are discussed in the third section.

1.0 THE GENERAL NATURE OF INTERORGANIZATION REPORTING

In previous chapters we considered systems (including simplified analysis) that provide information for decision makers internal to the firm. These systems are costly, yet they are often desirable, from the point of view of the firm's owners or management, in that they improve operating decisions by an amount sufficient to justify their cost. Similarly, the firm may be motivated to provide information to those external to it. Of course, the underlying incentives are somewhat different than in the internal reporting case.

Many reports, for example, are provided to the government and the public in order to conform to legal regulations. Presumably, these reports are provided because failure to do so would be illegal and could possibly result in fines or loss of the right to carry on business. Furthermore, though some reporting requirements are imposed on essentially all firms (for example, tax reports), others are imposed only on those in particular types of business (for example, utilities, railways, household movers) or those that have particular legal structures (for example, public corporations). Thus the cost of satisfying some external reporting requirements may be viewed as part of the cost of entering a particular industry or of employing a particular legal structure.

---

1. Also see Marshall (1974), Baiman (1975), Ho and Chu (1975) and Ng (1975) for additional examples and discussions.

2. We summarize Arrow's theorem in Proposition 8.5. Proof and extensive discussion are available in Luce and Raiffa (1957), Arrow (1963), Quirk and Saposnik (1968), and Sen (1970).

3. Wilson (1968) identifies conditions under which group preferences admit to an expected utility representation provided there is Pareto optimal sharing of the consequences of the actions. For example, the representation exists if all individual utility functions are of the form

$$\frac{U_i'(\cdot)}{U_i''(\cdot)} = \alpha_i + \beta x_i$$

where i indexes the individuals in the group and x_i denotes individual i's outcome. Application of Wilson's result is contained in Wilson (1969a), Demski (1973a, 1976), and Rubinstein (1974).

Alternatively, we find reports provided to external parties in order to transact some form of business with them. Some are provided voluntarily, without any direct impetus from the user. For example, reports (such as prospectuses) are often provided to potential investors (for example, venture capitalists) to assist in persuading them to provide capital for the firm.[4] Other reports are bilaterally agreed upon by the firm and an external party. For example, we find cost reports used in negotiating and consumating sales that are priced on a "cost-plus" basis. That is, a "cost-plus" contract requires some assessment of cost, just as a more conventional insurance contract rests upon observability of the insured event. In any case, we presume the firm expects to gain some benefit from these transactions with external parties; and the cost of providing the external reports is merely one of the costs of obtaining these benefits.

The motivation behind some external reports is, however, less clear. Consider, for example, the nonrequired information contained in annual financial reports and the information elicited by financial analysts. Of course, if information is favorable and not yet known externally, the firm may be motivated to release it to increase the market value of its shares earlier than would otherwise be the case. However, the objective of many external reports appears less obvious than that and is bound up in some vague notion of increasing the firm's goodwill by, perhaps, signaling "integrity" or "quality." The benefits of such reports may manifest themselves in such diverse ways as increasing sales, reducing the likelihood of governmental regulation, or improving the firm's ability to obtain funds in the future.[5]

Further observe that in many instances external organizations prescribe the type of external report to be provided by the firm. However, these prescriptions are hardly ever so detailed as to precisely specify the system to be used. Instead, they may be viewed as prescribing a set of acceptable systems, and the particular selection is left to the firm. We let $\bar{H}$ denote the prescribed set.

Also note that auditing often plays a key role in verifying that the selected system is, in fact, within the acceptable set. That is, those who prescribe the acceptable set often require the firm to permit an external "independent" auditor to conduct such tests as are considered necessary to verify that an appropriate system has been used. (Alternatively, the firm itself may be motivated to have the report audited to provide a signal of its "quality.") The audit costs may be borne by the external organization (for example, governmental auditors) or by the firm. In the latter case, the audit costs are part of the firm's information system costs.

In evaluating cost assessment alternatives in these external reporting contexts, we must clearly identify from whose point of view the evaluation is being conducted. We could, for example, consider the choices to be made by the firm's management, assuming that their preferences differ or are congruent with those of the owners. In either case, their selection may be constrained by any prescriptions

---

4. Indeed, advertising provides a rich set of examples at this point.

5. Conceivably, the firm could benefit from external reports by selling them to those that want them. However, this is seldom done, for reasons that we will discuss later.

imposed by external organizations, and the consequences of any system will depend upon the actions of both management and external users of the reports provided.

Alternatively, we could consider the choices to be made by external organizations that, when acting in their own self-interests, prescribe the information that they are to receive from the firm. It is the external organization's preferences that are directly relevant here; but the preferences of the firm's management must also be considered in that the ultimate consequences will depend on the actions of both the firm and the external organization. This is clearly the case, for example, when external organizations purchase goods on a "cost-plus" basis and specify the cost information that they are to receive from the firm. Another example is the request for information by banks when a loan is being negotiated.[6]

Finally, we could consider the choices to be made by external organizations that, when acting in the interests of the public, prescribe information that is to be reported either to themselves or to the public. Evaluation in this context requires the development of a concept of public preference, as well as prediction of the actions of the firm, the public, and the external organization (if relevant). The Securities and Exchange Commission (SEC) and the Financial Accounting Standards Board (FASB) are examples of organizations that impose reporting requirements that are designed to facilitate decisions by the public, while regulatory agencies impose reporting requirements that are designed to facilitate their own decisions.

2.0 FINANCIAL REPORTING AND THE FASB

We now address the question of optimal cost assessment in a financial reporting context. Cost assessment issues are pervasive here. Questions of inventory valuation, depreciation policy, and research and development capitalization provide illustrations. We approach these issues by concentrating on the broader question of determining the firm's optimal financial reporting system.

The key element in placing these issues within our framework is to recognize that financial reports provide information to numerous, heterogeneous decision makers. We face a multiperson problem. And, as illustrated in Appendix 8.3, alternative financial reporting systems may result in different prices and different allocations of resources in the economy as a whole. Accordingly, we do not approach the problem from the firm's or the direct users' points of view per se. Rather, we take a more global, social view of the consequences that follow from adopting one financial reporting policy as opposed to another.

Once again, however, the evaluation concept remains intact. We evaluate the alternatives in terms of the consequences they induce. In the first subsection we sketch a general equilibrium model of the consequences of a given set of external reporting systems and then briefly discuss conditions under which a laissez faire

---

6. Yet another example is provided by the multinational firm, where central headquarters prescribes reporting policies for the various divisions.

solution will provide an efficient allocation of resources. The second subsection discusses some characteristics of information that may induce inefficient or undesirable resource allocations and, thereby, motivate intervention by collective choice agencies such as the FASB. In the final subsection we discuss the problems inherent in any attempt to select reporting systems in accordance with the preferences of the individuals in the economy and then relate this to the role of the FASB.

2.1   A GENERAL EQUILIBRIUM MODEL OF CONSEQUENCES

A key element in our evaluation of alternative reporting systems is the predicted consequences of each system. Assuming that an individual's preferences are a function of the goods he consumes, the consequences of interest are the state- and date-indexed consumption schedules of each of the individuals within the economy. Those consumption schedules will depend on a variety of factors, including the beliefs, preferences, and endowments of the individuals and the prices of commodities and investments (which are direct or indirect state-contingent claims to future commodities). Of course, these prices are themselves influenced by the beliefs, preferences, and endowments of the individuals.

The beliefs of each individual will depend, in part, on the information he receives. Consequently, in predicting the consequences of alternative information systems we must predict how the alternatives affect the information that is received by the various individuals and how that information affects their beliefs. We must then relate those beliefs to the resulting market prices and, finally, to the resulting consumption schedules.

To provide some insight into the above relationships, we draw on the models in general equilibrium theory (Debreu 1959; Quirk and Saposnik 1968; Radner 1968, 1972; Arrow and Hahn 1971; Wilson 1974) and expand the Chapter 2, section 3 specific (2 period, S state) economy model to include acquisition of information by the various individuals. This is followed by a brief discussion of the existence and efficiency of an equilibrium in this context.

2.1.1   THE MODEL

Recall that a set of individuals I and a set of firms F are present in the example economy. A consumption plan for individual i is denoted

$$a_i' = (x_{i0}, x_{i1}^1, \ldots, x_{i1}^s, \ldots, x_{i1}^S),$$

where x_{i0} denotes certain current period cash flow and x_{i1}^s future period cash flow *if* state s obtains. The individual's wealth is equal to the market value of his exogenously specified endowments, consisting of prior claims to cash ($\bar{x}_{i0}, \bar{x}_{i1}^1, \ldots, \bar{x}_{i1}^S$) and ownership of various firms ($\bar{O}_{if}, f \in F$). That is, with a price vector $P = (1, P_1^1, P_1^2, \ldots, P_1^S)$, his wealth is equal to

$$W_i = \bar{x}_{i0} + \sum_{s \in S} P_1^s \bar{x}_{i1}^s + \sum_{f \in F} \bar{O}_{if} V(a_f^*),$$

where the value of firm f, $V(a_f^*)$, is defined in Equation [2.5].

To introduce financial reporting considerations, we now recognize that firms produce information as well as commodities and distribute this information to various individuals. We interpret such information as financial reports, and let $\eta = (\eta_1, \ldots, \eta_F)$ denote the reporting alternatives used by the F firms and $\gamma_f(\eta_f)$ the cost to firm f of using alternative η_f. The set of reports received by individual i is denoted y_i, with $y = (y_1, \ldots, y_I)$, and the direct cost to him is $\gamma_i(\eta)$.[7] Observe that a firm's information costs are indirectly costs to its owners in that such costs reduce the value of the firm. Also, for expositional convenience, we assume that the information becomes available before any trades or productive acts are consummated.[8]

Under these conditions, production and dissemination of information affects individual consumption decisions in two basic ways. First, and most obviously, the posterior belief measure of individual i, denoted $\phi_i(s \mid y_i, \eta)$, is a function of the information he receives.[9] This follows directly from our discussion of rational individual choice in Chapter 2. Second, the set of consumption alternatives available to individual i, denoted $A_i(y, \eta)$, is a function of the systems used by each firm and the information received by each individual. This follows from the fact that equilibrium prices[10] may depend on the information individuals receive; and both firms and individuals may incur costs in providing and obtaining information. More formally,

$$A_i(y, \eta) = \{a_i \mid P(y, \eta) \cdot a_i \le W_i(y, \eta)\}$$

where $P(y, \eta)$ denotes the posterior equilibrium price vector, $W_i(y, \eta)$ is i's posterior wealth (net of information costs),

$$W_i(y, \eta) = \bar{x}_{i0} - \gamma_i(\eta) + \sum_{s \in S} P_1^s(y, \eta) \bar{x}_{i1}^s + \sum_{f \in F} \bar{O}_{if} V(\alpha_f^*(y, \eta), y, \eta),$$

and $V(\alpha_f^*(\cdot), y, \eta)$ is the posterior value of firm f (net of information costs),[11]

$$V(\alpha_f^*(y, \eta), y, \eta) = \max_{a_f \in A_f} [P(y, \eta) \cdot a_f - \gamma_f(\eta)].$$

The consumption decision, following Equation [2.6], is then given by

7. If this cost includes payments to firm f, then $\gamma_f(\eta_f)$ may be viewed as being net of any receipts firm f receives for the information it provides. Also observe that we view y_i as a vector, $y_i = (y_{i1}, \ldots, y_{iF})$ where y_{if} is the report received by individual i from firm f.

8. Alternatively, we could describe a situation in which trades and productive acts are consummated with knowledge of η_i but before y_i is observed. This, in turn, would allow for signal contingent trades (with the information systems providing the event determinations on which event contingent trading is based). See Appendix 8.3 and Radner (1968).

9. The posterior beliefs will be a function of the information received by all individuals if individual i is able to infer the information received by others from the prices that prevail. See Kihlstrom and Mirman (1975).

10. The economy is in equilibrium, recall, if the firm and individual actions, given prices, equate supply and demand for each commodity.

11. The information costs could also affect the action alternatives available to the firm, but for expositional convenience we exclude that possibility.

[8.1a]
$$E(U_i \mid a_i, y, \eta) = \sum_{s \in S} U_i(p_i(s, a_i, \eta))\phi_i(s \mid y_i, \eta)$$

and

[8.1b]
$$E(U_i \mid \alpha_i^*(y, \eta), y, \eta) = \max_{a_i \in A_i(y, \eta)} E(U_i \mid a_i, y, \eta)$$

where, recall, $x_i = p_i(s, a_i, \eta) = (x_{i0}, x_{i1}^s)$. In turn, individual utility evaluation of information alternative η is a direct application of Equation [2.3a],

[8.2]
$$E(U_i \mid \alpha_i^*(\eta), \eta) = \sum_{y \in Y} \phi_i(y \mid \eta) E(U_i \mid \alpha_i^*(y, \eta), y, \eta).$$

Numerical examples are provided in Appendix 8.3.

We could embellish this description in a number of directions. But introduction of information in an idealized economy is sufficient for our immediate purpose of sketching a model of the *consequences* that will follow from adopting one set of financial reporting policies as opposed to another.

In essence, this model of consequences focuses on equilibrium resource allocations in the economy. However, technical considerations arise in this use of equilibrium actions. Existence and efficiency considerations are briefly reviewed below.

2.1.2 EQUILIBRIUM EXISTENCE AND PARETO OPTIMALITY

Mere existence of a set of equilibrium prices is hardly an issue in a simple example (such as the numerical illustrations in Appendices 8.1 and 8.3). But as complexity is introduced, the existence question becomes critical.

Existence of a set of equilibrium prices has, in fact, been established under fairly broad conditions. For example, and somewhat casually, we have

Proposition 8.1:

In a competitive economy where (i) individual tastes can be summarized by continuous, convex, and nonsatiating preference relations, (ii) individual production possibility sets are closed and allow zero production by any firm, and (iii) aggregate production possibilities are convex, irreversible, and allow for free disposal of unwanted inputs, an equilibrium set of prices does exist.[12,13]

---

12. Briefly, a preference relation is continuous if, when one consumption schedule is strictly preferred to another, this strict preference continues to hold when one of the schedules is slightly altered. Nonsatiation, of course, means the individual never prefers less to more of a desirable commodity. Convexity of the preference relation means that for any set of consumption schedules lying on a line segment, one of the endpoint schedules is least preferred. Finally, a production possibility set is closed if any production schedule that can be approximated arbitrarily closely by feasible schedules is itself feasible.

13. We are, at this point, ignoring some minor qualifications. See Debreu (1959), Quirk and Saposnik (1968), and Arrow and Hahn (1971) for discussion of the various assumptions and proof of the existence theorem under a variety of similar conditions. Intriligator (1971) provides a summary of the central features of these results.

Note that we say nothing about whether the prices are unique, whether the resulting equilibrium is stable, or how it could be achieved. We merely state a set of production and consumption conditions *sufficient* to ensure existence of a set of equilibrium prices.

More important for our purposes, however, are two welfare propositions that also follow from these assumptions. Both are concerned with the Pareto optimality of the resulting allocations.

Proposition 8.2:

Given the conditions in Proposition 8.1, the resulting equilibrium achieves a Pareto optimal distribution of resources.

Proposition 8.3:

Given the conditions in Proposition 8.2, any arbitrary Pareto optimal distribution of the economy's resources can be achieved as an equilibrium distribution of resources through an appropriate redistribution of the initial endowments.

That is, the equilibrium ensured by our assumptions produces a distribution of resources such that no single individual can be made better off without offending at least one other individual. Furthermore, any feasible Pareto optimal distribution of commodities can be achieved by appropriate redistribution of the initial endowments.[14] (Both propositions are illustrated by the first simple example in Appendix 8.1.)

The implication is that, if appropriate conditions exist, we can rely on market forces to determine a Pareto optimal level of financial reporting. We term this the laissez faire approach. It is characterized by information production, transmission, and use policies that are determined by the firms and individuals pursuing their respective private interests. Information, then, is treated in a manner identical to, say, a conventional durable commodity.[15]

Intervention, on the other hand, occurs when some collective choice agency restricts the set of reporting systems that may be used by firms.[16] And the obvious question is whether there is any compelling reason to suspect that intervention is likely to be desirable. We address this question in the following section.

2.2 THE IMPETUS FOR INTERVENTION

We clearly have intervention in financial reporting, as witnessed by the activities of the FASB and SEC (not to mention the Federal Aviation Agency, Federal

---

14. Again, these conditions are sufficient conditions. We do not, for example, assert that pure competition is necessary for Pareto optimality. In fact, Proposition 8.2 holds in the absence of convexity; and all three propositions are approximately true under weaker convexity conditions. The references cited in the previous footnote contain numerous discussions of these theorems. Radner (1968) in particular discusses information system conditions that guarantee these theorems in the absence of complete state-contingent markets.

15. Indeed, we could construct a demand function for information, as in Kihlstrom (1974).

16. A closely related form of intervention is to restrict the actions that may be taken by those possessing some information, for example, restrictions on insider trading.

Communications Commission, Federal Power Commission, and so on). Indeed, a regulatory view is so common here that we are unaccustomed to formulating the setting in alternative terms.[17]

Under the appropriate conditions (see Proposition 8.2), a laissez faire approach in a market economy will result in a Pareto optimal allocation of resources. And, from Proposition 8.3, we know that any legitimate (that is, feasible) dissatisfaction with the resulting resource allocation can, in principle, be reduced to dissatisfaction with the initial allocation of endowments. While redistribution considerations are certainly significant, there is no reason to suspect judicious design of financial reporting systems will be a particularly adept policy vehicle in this regard. Hence, efficiency considerations appear to provide the major impetus for considering intervention in the determination of financial reporting policies.

Viewed in this light, the intervention question takes the form of whether significant *market failure* possibilities are likely to exist. Is there reason to suspect that, without intervention, Pareto optimality will not be achieved?

We initially observe that information is a somewhat atypical commodity. Unlike pretzels and automobiles, it is not necessarily destroyed or even altered through private consumption by one individual. For example, a newspaper (or this book) may be read by a number of individuals; that is, it may provide useful information to more than one individual (scratch the parenthetical example). This characteristic may induce market failure.

In particular, if those who do not pay for information cannot be excluded from using it and if the information is valuable to these "free riders," then information is a public good.[18] That is, under these circumstances, production of information by any single individual or firm will costlessly make that information available to all. A conventional market solution, in turn, may fail to be efficient under these conditions. For example, there is no apparent motivation for the "free rider" to pay for the information he enjoys. And even if he did willingly pay, efficiency would dictate individual specific prices in the general case where each individual values the information differently.[19] Hence, a more collective approach to production may be desirable. For example, an efficient solution can be achieved if some type of collective choice agency, such as the SEC or FASB, intervenes and appropriately determines both the information to be produced and the amount to be paid for its production by each individual. Observe that there is no reason to believe that it is desirable for firms to bear all the information production costs. Furthermore, it is not clear that the existing collective choice agencies have sufficient knowledge to identify the optimal level of information production. This

---

17. See Moonitz (1974) for a historical analysis of the various institutional arrangements that have been employed.

18. Appendix 8.1 illustrates the nature of public goods and the market failure that is associated with them.

19. With a normal type of commodity, individuals face the same price but adjust the quantity. With a public good, however, individuals face the same quantity and must, therefore, face individualistic prices or taxes for efficiency to obtain. (See Henderson and Quandt 1971 or Malinvaud 1972.)

latter point, plus the costs of intervention, should be considered in any decision to intervene in the market solution.[20]

The public good argument is not applicable, of course, if property rights and the market structure provide a mechanism for excluding nonpurchasers from either receiving or using the information.[21] However, in this context the existence of nontrivial information production (as opposed to transmittal) costs will lead to a single, monopolistic producer of particular types of information. Otherwise, resources would be needlessly consumed in the production of information by various individuals. This, in turn, brings us to another source of market failure: that of increasing returns to scale. The difficulty here arises because efficiency—in an otherwise classical economy—dictates pricing at marginal cost; but this implies a negative profit for such an information producer since the marginal cost of supplying another user only encompasses copying and transmittal costs, and not the costs of producing that information per se. Hence, the question of designing some intervention policy, such as a system of user taxes or reservation fees, arises (Henderson and Quandt 1971; Malinvaud 1972).

Another and potentially far deeper problem associated with information arises because an asymmetric distribution of information across competing decision makers may advantage or disadvantage various individuals. In this sense, it is not automatic in a multiperson setting that more (free) information is always as desirable as less information—as indicated in Proposition 2.1 for the single decision-maker setting. Rather, the distribution of information becomes critical, as illustrated by blackmail.[22] There appear to be two general concerns raised by this characteristic: inefficient resource allocations and undesirable resource allocations.

Anytime there are interdependencies between the production or consumption of a commodity by one person and the well-being of others, we have the potential for inefficient resource allocations.[23] This arises because the individual selects investment and consumption actions in accordance with his own preferences; and while market prices reflect his demand for commodities, they do not reflect other ways in which his actions may affect others. That is, he does not naturally internalize the effect of his actions on others. The classic (present-day) example of this type of impact is pollution; the polluters do not internalize their effect on others and this creates, other things equal, a tendency toward overproduction of pollution. In turn, we observe intervention by collective choice agencies. Polluters may be taxed, as in the Ruhr River Valley, or standards may be established as in the case of domestic automobile use.

---

20. See Gonedes et al. (1976) for further discussion of financial reporting and disclosure issues in terms of production of a public good.

21. For example, patent laws are designed to exclude nonpurchasers from using certain technological information. Gonedes (1975) formulates and analyzes an information production model under the assumption that nonpurchasers can be excluded. Also see Demsetz (1970).

22. Putting the two phenomena together, we might characterize information in terms of a community good that is subject to congestion, somewhat similar to national parks or fishing. (This particular insight is reported in the *Cowles Foundation Report of Research Activities: 1970–1973*, p. 19.) Also see Malinvaud (1972), Chapter 9, for discussion of congestion phenomena.

23. Appendix 8.1 illustrates the general nature and impact of interdependencies (externalities).

The view by collective choice agencies that some resource allocations are undesirable appears to be motivated by concerns other than restoration of efficiency. In particular, they often appear to be concerned with the accumulation of wealth by actions that, in the agency's view, constitute taking "unfair" advantage of others. Of course, different people may have different views as to what constitutes an "unfair" action. For example, members of the Mafia may disagree with the view that extortion is an "unfair" action.[24]

A simple poker game illustrates the distributive effects of information. Each players knows his own cards and any that are face up; and we might consider a player to have "unfair" information if he had marked the cards so that he knew at least some of his opponents' cards. This would give him an advantage in predicting the consequences of each player's actions (for example, bets) and thereby increase the likelihood that he would obtain the other players' stakes. Of course, the player will lose his advantage if his actions convey to the others that he has "unfair" information. Similarly, "bluffing" is unlikely to be productive if the private information is not concealed.[25]

In short, games exist in which information possessed and acted upon by one player affects the other players' outcomes.[26] Indeed, further analysis would demonstrate that the value of such information depends on the information available to the other players. Of course, rules are designed to limit the information-gathering opportunities. Dealing is supposed to provide a random distribution, the marking of cards is forbidden, communication patterns are strictly defined (as in bridge via the bidding convention), and so on.

Now consider activities that are more generally labeled as "economic." Concern over the distribution of information across economic actors is clearly present. Disclosure policies of the SEC and insider trading rules are paramount examples. Yet they are not unique. Agricultural crop production statistics are closely guarded during assembly and are publicly released when compiled. (The object is to prevent some actor from early acquisition of the statistics and use of them as a basis for speculation in the commodity markets.) Moreover, the mere fact that the government produces the agricultural data suggests that at least some view the problem as a public good issue, requiring collective choice among the production alternatives.[27]

---

24. Similarly, the individual who moves next door to a steel mill and then petitions for relief is different from the individual who petitions for relief when the steel mill moves next door.

25. The importance of not letting your actions reveal the information you have was dramatically illustrated during World War II. The British broke the German code early in the war and used the resulting information to advantage. But they did not take "full" advantage of this information since to do so would have revealed its availability. See Winterbotham (1974).

26. This does not hold for all games, however. For example, in a game of chess or checkers that is completely formulated and analyzed, both players know all there is to know about the game—such as current deployments, feasible alternatives, and opponent actions. This is, in fact, an illustration of decision making under subjective certainty; and information acquisition by one player is of no concern to the other.

27. See Hayami and Peterson (1972) for an analysis of the benefits from increasing the accuracy of these statistics.

   The impact of the distribution of information on economic activities and their resulting allocations can be illustrated by considering specific phenomena. "Moral hazard" is one such phenomenon. Consider two parties who engage in a fire insurance contract. The insured has superior information about his own behavior; and it is his behavior, in conjunction with that of nature, that determines the occurrence and outcome of fires. Hence, provision of insurance may alter the insured's decision-making incentives and in the process alter the lotteries faced by the insurer. (In turn, the insurer limits the amount of insurance he will provide.) The difficulty stems from the distribution of information. The objective is to insure against choices by nature; but nature is not completely observable. Rather, the observable events are more the joint product of nature and the insured. The insured, of course, observes his own behavior; but the insurer can only observe part of that behavior—as illustrated by fire inspections. The net result is that the inability to observe the behavior of the insured party creates a situation in which incentives are altered by the provision of insurance. Consequently, mutually acceptable insurance contracts are not consummated and risk sharing is not efficient.[28]

   A similar example is provided by the "adverse selection" phenomenon. This may occur when suppliers of commodities, such as labor services or used automobiles, have superior information about the commodity's "quality." This superior information provides an opportunity to misrepresent a low quality item in one manner or another. For example, without quality distinctions in the marketplace, the low quality supplier will have a strong incentive to enter the market. Put another way, the information discrepancy may affect the trades that are consummated; high quality suppliers may be unable to sell at other than a low quality price. Indeed, it is conceivable that no trades whatever will be consummated.[29] In turn, countervailing institutions may arise. Warranties may be issued; brand names may be fostered. Certification may be sought, as in the tendering of professional services (for example, auditors and lawyers) and the provision of certified annual reports. Yet there is no necessary guarantee that these information-providing activities are efficient.

   Other examples are provided by analyzing the impact of information distribution in a conventional market setting where state-dependent trades are consummated.[30] The basic theme, once again, is that the outcomes available to one individual may depend on the information possessed by others; and market failures may occur because existing markets do not separate these effects. For example, production of public information before an equilibrium allocation of goods and services has been achieved may be harmful because of the additional risk to which individuals are exposed. But with insurance for this risk (that is, creation of the

   28. See Spence and Zeckhauser (1971) for an analysis of the moral hazard issue and the effect of the insurer's inability to measure the insured's act. Also see Kihlstrom and Pauly (1971) and Ross (1973).

   29. See Akerlof (1970) for one such example. Additional discussion of adverse selection and its attendant inefficiencies is available in Arrow (1973) and Spence (1973, 1974). Further note that the FTC is presently considering disclosure regulations for used car dealers.

   30. Fama and Laffer (1971) and Hirshleifer (1971) initiated this type of analysis.

appropriate markets) the potential for harm is removed.[31] Similarly, a monopolistic producer of information may be able to make speculative investments prior to releasing his information to other investors.[32] In an exchange setting with homogeneous beliefs and costless information, the result is but a redistribution of wealth to the monopolistic producer.[33] But it is an inefficient solution if the producer uses resources to acquire the information.

The types of difficulties that are signaled by these findings are illustrated by the following proposition.

Proposition 8.4:[34]

Consider an economy with a set of individuals I and three alternative *costless* information systems: η^i, which provides private information to individual i; η^p, which provides public information to all $i \in I$; and η^0, which provides no information. We then have

(i) $\quad E(U_i \mid \alpha_i^*(\eta^i), \eta^i) \geq E(U_i \mid \alpha_i^*(\eta^0), \eta^0);$

(ii) $\quad E(U_i \mid \alpha_i^*(\eta^p), \eta^p) \gtreqless E(U_i \mid \alpha_i^*(\eta^0), \eta^0);$

and

(iii) $\quad E(U_i \mid \alpha_i^*(\eta^p), \eta^p) \geq E(U_i \mid \alpha_i^*(\eta^0), \eta^0)$

does not imply that

$$E(U_j \mid \alpha_j^*(\eta^p), \eta^p) \geq E(U_j \mid \alpha_j^*(\eta^0), \eta^0)$$

for $j \neq i$.

In short, in this type of market setting, unless the information is private, more information may not be regarded as better than less,[35] and individuals may not be unanimous in comparing information alternatives.

Moreover, some concerns over these distributive aspects center around concepts of "fairness" or "justness" as opposed to efficiency. One issue is whether allowing insiders to act on the basis of the inside information they acquire is efficient. At another level, however, there are questions of whether acting on such information provides gains that are "unfair" or "unjust." This, in turn, leads to questions of distribution, which appear to have public good, externality, and ethical overtones. (The distribution of wealth creates a social climate "enjoyed" by all, we may be affected by our neighbor's consumption, etc.)

---

31. See Marshall (1974), Ng (1975a), and Appendix 8.3 for examples.

32. As with the card marker in poker, the monopolist's ability to speculate is limited by the fact that his actions may convey his information to others. See Kihlstrom and Mirman (1975) for an exploration of the information conveyed by changes in equilibrium prices.

33. See Hirshleifer (1971), Demski (1974), Ng (1975a), and Appendix 8.3 for examples.

34. *Proof:*

(i) follows from Proposition 2.1; the necessary counterexamples for (ii) and (iii) are provided in Appendix 8.3. $E(U_i \mid \alpha_i^*(\eta), \eta)$ is defined in Equation [8.2] in the preceding section. Further note that η^i does not alter individual i's outcome structure in our setting. This may not be the case if others learn of i's use of η^i, as in Baiman (1975) and Kihlstrom and Mirman (1975).

35. The notion of more or less information can be given unambiguous meaning by using the finenss relation employed in Proposition 2.1.

The conclusion, then, is that in principle market failure possibilities in the information sphere are immense. Indeed, with distributive aspects involved, the concern is much deeper than the usual suspicion of less than complete private appropriability and economies of scale leading to underproduction of information. To our knowledge, however, the precise nature and extent of these failures are largely undocumented.[36]

2.3 INTERVENTION AND THE ROLE OF THE FASB

A final question concerns what form of intervention might be desirable. With market failure documented in principle but not in fact, discussion of this issue is somewhat conjectural. Moreover, market failure itself does not imply that intervention is desirable. Intervention is costly; and we must therefore concern ourselves with the allocations that will obtain with and without the proposed intervention.

For example, analysis of the existing regulatory mechanisms would recognize the use of standards to define the acceptable set of reporting policies and subsequent auditing to ensure the actual reporting is consistent with these standards. In turn, regulation of auditing firms would become an issue. Indeed, the SEC has recently called for an independent audit of the quality control of one of the large auditing firms.

In any event, the purpose of such intervention is to "improve" upon the laissez faire solution. Two subquestions emerge: What mapping from individual to social preference is to be followed and what institutional mechanism will be efficient in effecting this particular mapping? We consider these two issues in turn.

2.3.1 SOCIAL PREFERENCE

Suppose, now, that we compare alternative financial reporting systems for the various firms. We assume that the reports generated by any system will result in an equilibrium, that for at least some reports the equilibria under alternative systems are substantively different in terms of resource allocation, and that individual preferences with respect to the system alternatives may differ. The overall information content may be identical, with distribution of information costs being

---

36. Special cases do, of course, exist (see Demski 1973a; Marshall 1974; Ng 1975). Indeed, we have an emerging literature that addresses various aspects of the information production and allocation problem. Recent reviews are provided by Hirshleifer (1973), Rothschild (1973), and Radner (1974). In more specific terms, Kihlstrom (1974) studies the demand for information; Fama and Laffer (1971), Hirshleifer (1971), Demski (1974), Marshall (1974), Gonedes et al. (1976), and Ng (1975, 1975a) study inefficiency issues; Radner (1968), Wilson (1974), and Gonedes (1975) study equilibrium existence issues; and Radner (1972) and Kihlstrom and Mirman (1975) study incomplete markets, expectations, and learning from observed price behavior.

Specific numerical examples of some of these phenomena are presented in Appendices 8.2 and 8.3. Appendix 8.2 presents an example in a personal setting where two competing individuals are affected by the distribution of information. Appendix 8.3 presents a series of examples in an impersonal market setting, where the ultimate resource allocations are affected by the distribution of information.

the only question. Or the systems may offer substantively different information content.[37]

In pursuing the social preference question, it is convenient to summarize the individual preferences expressed by the utility measure in Equation [8.2] in terms of their associated binary relations. That is, if individual i regards system η^1 as at least as desirable as η^2 $(E(U_i \mid \alpha_i^*(\eta^1), \eta^1) \geq E(U_i \mid \alpha_i^*(\eta^2), \eta^2))$, we express that preference as $\eta^1 \succsim_i \eta^2$, for $\eta^1, \eta^2 \in H$. Our rationality assumptions (discussed in Chapter 2) ensure that the binary relation $\succsim_i$ for each individual is *complete* and *transitive* over the set of possible systems H.

Similarly, if η^1 is at least as desirable at the social level as η^2, we denote this $\eta^1 \succsim \eta^2$. The optimality question then takes the form of specifying the relationship between the social preference relation $\succsim$ and the individual preference relations $\succsim_i, i = 1, \ldots, I$. We seek, that is, a collective choice rule $f(\cdot)$:

$$\succsim = f(\succsim_1, \ldots, \succsim_i, \ldots, \succsim_I).$$

Note, in particular, that the domain of the choice rule extends to all individuals in the economy, not merely to those who "use" the resulting data. Nonusers may be affected by those who obtain the data and are, therefore, included in the basic statement.[38]

Countless collective choice rules exist. Arrow, however, discovered that the imposition of a set of seemingly desirable and innocuous requirements reduces the set of acceptable rules to the null set (that is, there is no such rule). This problem does not arise, of course, unless we have at least two people and three alternative financial reporting systems. We also limit our search for collective choice rules to those that provide complete and transitive social rankings. Within this setting, the four conditions Arrow imposed on $f(\cdot)$ are

(i) *Universal Domain:* All logically possible orders of H are admissible. The domain of $f(\cdot)$ must, that is, include all possible combinations of complete and transitive orders of H. "Weird" people are not disallowed —as long as they are completely and transitively "weird."

(ii) *Pareto Optimality:* If, for any pair $\eta^1, \eta^2 \in H$, all individuals strictly prefer η^1 to η^2, $f(\cdot)$ must guarantee social preference for η^1 over η^2. This is, of course, a close to unassailable requirement. Dropping it would amount to constructing a theory of choice among financial reporting policies based on systematically denying individuals what they want.

---

37. For expositional convenience we treat financial policy determination as exogenous. Endogenous determination could be introduced as in Radner (1968) and Gonedes (1975). But the policy-regulation issue that we are moving toward would still arise. Furthermore, treating information production as endogenous creates significant technical equilibrium existence difficulties. (See Wilson 1974.)

38. For example, construction of a setting where all direct users are indifferent between η^1 and η^2 but nonusers strictly prefer η^1 to η^2 is a straightforward task; and it appears capricious not to select η^1 in such a setting.

(iii) *Independence of Irrelevant Alternatives:* For any subset of H, any two sets of individual orderings that identically rank the reporting policies in the specified subset must have identical social choices of the policies in the subset. This condition rules out interpersonal utility comparisons. For example, it requires that choice between any pair $\eta^1, \eta^2 \in H$ be determined solely by the individual preferences for η^1 and η^2; other alternatives (such as might be used to "establish" or calibrate interpersonal comparisons) are not allowed to influence the social choice between η^1 and η^2.

(iv) *Nondictatorship:* There is no individual i such that $\succsim = \succsim_i$ regardless of other individuals' preferences.

We now have

Proposition 8.5 [39]

The set of collective choice rules $f(\cdot)$ that provides complete and transitive ranking of H and also satisfies the universal domain, Pareto optimality, independence of irrelevant alternatives, and nondictatorship conditions is null.

The four conditions are, that is, mutually inconsistent.

Two implications of this disturbing result should be noted. First, if we accept Arrow's formulation and conditions, this result precludes viewing the financial reporting problem in terms of the optimization of some aggregate level utility, social welfare, or cost-benefit function. Consequently, we cannot directly extend the single-person analysis in earlier chapters into this sphere. Rather, alternative formulations must be sought.

Second, since these choices must be made and since the conditions imposed by Arrow are inconsistent, we must violate at least one of them regardless of the manner in which financial reporting policies are to be determined. For example, we could relax the universal domain conditions and place restrictions on admissible individual preferences. If all preferences are single peaked, majority voting will work (Arrow 1963). Similarly, with exponential utility functions we can construct social utility and probability functions such that an aggregate form of the expected utility hypothesis is operative.[40]

In this regard, it is often thought that designing special purpose reports for disparate user groups will solve the problem of serving a heterogeneous group of financial statement users. This, however, is a form of liberalism in which certain issues are resolved solely by certain people; and no degree of liberalism will eliminate the Arrow paradox (Sen 1970, Ch. 6*).

An intriguing relaxation of Arrow's conditions is provided by dropping the requirement that a complete and transitive social ordering be provided. This

---

39. See Arrow (1963). Further discussion can be found in Luce and Raiffa (1957), Quirk and Saposnik (1968), and Sen (1970).

40. This result is due to Wilson (1968). Extension to information production and use is contained in Demski (1973a).

avenue has led to Bloomfield and Wilson's (1973) axiomatization of game theory. Moreover, it is closely related to the notion of a constitutional game. Here we focus on the conjunction of power and preference at the individual level and define social preference in terms of the wishes of those individuals who have the "power" to ensure their wishes in the social or political sphere. In particular, one reporting system is regarded as at least as desirable as a second if some set of individuals unanimously regards it as such *and* has sufficient power to enforce this choice in the social arena. Although exogenous specification of the critical power relationships is called for, a certain amount of structure is provided by this approach. Indeed, placing Pareto optimality, independence of irrelevant alternatives, and responsiveness conditions on the collective choice rule $f(\cdot)$ guarantees this formulation of the problem.[41] Addition of other conditions on $f(\cdot)$ will further limit the possibilities, such as guaranteeing existence of some "dictatorial" group.

In any event, we must remain partially agnostic in addressing this optimality question. There is no straightforward method of moving from individual to social preference. Rather, the concept of social preference is intertwined with the institutions we employ to sort out social choices. Optimality, in turn, is a reflection of what the political process defines it to be.

2.3.2 THE ROLE OF THE FASB

The FASB (along with the SEC) is clearly a social choice agency. In particular, it is the accounting profession's latest institutional arrangement for deciding which external reporting systems firms ought to use. In effect, it provides a mapping from individual preferences to a social preference function with respect to external reporting alternatives. Unfortunately, the mapping it provides is not well understood. The members of this agency have their own preferences, but its choices are obviously influenced by the information it receives as to the preferences of others (particularly those of the SEC and the accounting profession) and the predicted consequences of the alternatives available to it. The particular preferences and consequences it considers, as well as the relative weights given to them, are obviously important factors in defining the collective choice rule that is in operation here. But we have had little evidence or analysis of either.

The mapping this agency "should" provide has received some attention. For example, the AICPA Objectives Study Group apparently calls for maintenance of Pareto optimality along with deferral to "those users who have limited authority, ability, or resources to obtain information and who rely on financial statements

---

41. These results are provided by Bloomfield (1971) and Bloomfield and Wilson (1973). Application to financial reporting is discussed in Beaver and Demski (1974). Note that the Pareto optimality and independence of irrelevant alternative conditions employed here are slightly different from Arrow's. And the responsiveness condition noted requires that if society ranks η^1 as desirable as η^2, this ranking remains for any alteration of individual preferences for which the set of individuals with strictly opposed preferences does not grow.

as their principal source of information...."[42] Yet, whether this or any other balancing of preferences is desirable is an unsettled question. There simply has been very little systematic research into the issue.

On the other hand, the basic nature of the issues involved here should be apparent. We continue, that is, in the manner depicted in Chapter 2. Reporting alternatives are evaluated in terms of the consequences of the agent actions they induce. This applies to evaluation of alternative reporting standards by the FASB, to evaluation of disclosure requirements by the SEC, or to evaluation of the intervention question itself.[43]

3.0 COST-BASED PROCUREMENT METHODS AND THE CASB

In this section we extend our discussion of interorganization reporting to issues that arise in cost-based procurement contracts and the role of the Cost Accounting Standards Board (CASB). To appreciate the breadth of issues involved here, we need only consider some of the topics initially tackled by the CASB: capitalization policy, allocation of central expense, direct material costs, allocation of vacation pay, use of standard cost systems, and pension costs.

In principle, our analysis of these issues is identical to that in the financial reporting case. Intervention considerations arise in the light of possible market failures; and the optimality question remains intertwined with the institutions we devise to determine the preferred accounting methods.[44] In fact, the only departure from the previous analysis occurs in developing a model of consequences. Indeed, it is tempting to directly cast the problem in the full equilibrium framework employed in the above section. But the number of decision makers directly affected by the cost assessment alternatives is often small in this setting; and the nature of the difficulties that appear to have led to the CASB's creation are adequately examined by focusing on those directly involved. Hence, we pursue the topic using a partial equilibrium analysis.

The discussion is divided into two major parts. The first sketches a model of the consequences of relying on one as opposed to another method of cost assessment in this type of setting. The second then addresses the intervention question and the role of the CASB. For expositional purposes we concentrate on

---

42. AICPA Objectives Study Group (1973), p. 12. See Beaver and Demski (1974) and Cyert and Ijiri (1974) for further discussion of this mapping issue and the Objectives Report.

43. Benston (1973) has attempted to empirically assess the impact of the disclosure requirements contained in the legislation that created the SEC; and Hagerman (1975) has examined reporting regulation in the banking industry.

44. One might argue that, conceptually, the difficulties are an order of magnitude smaller in this case because whatever amount of national defense (a public good) is provided ought to be provided efficiently. Hence, the source should be paid its marginal (economic) cost. The price equals marginal cost dictum follows, however, from a classical economy. If nonclassical conditions are present (such as imperfect and incomplete markets) the marginal cost rule may not be desirable. This is the theory of the second best. See Lipsey and Lancaster (1956) and Due and Friedlaender (1973).

defense procurement, though the same issues (and applicability of CASB regulations) are found in nondefense procurement as well. In fact, the same issues are found in the private sector, when one firm agrees to supply another on some cost reimbursement basis.

3.1 A Bilateral Negotiation Model of Consequence

Defense procurement is a continuous process, encompassing basic and applied research, design, production, evaluation, and the like. Numerous projects are involved at all stages, and significant interdependencies among the various projects are usually present. Moreover, strict competitive bidding is rarely used in source selection, and the method of payment is often something other than a fixed price contract.

To develop a model of the consequences of relying on alternative cost assessments in the procurement process, we abstract from much of the potential complexity and concentrate on acquisition of a single project (for example, some type of aircraft) from a specified source. This setting is not far removed from many acquisitions, and it captures the essential characteristics of the defense procurement environment.

Following Berhold (1967), we concentrate on three distinct, sequential points in time. The first, denoted t_1, is the time at which the government selects the supply source and negotiates the essential contract provisions. The second, denoted t_2, is the time at which the source makes its production decisions. These decisions are likely to be adaptively selected over an interval of time; but, for convenience, we suppress the adaptive sequencing and concentrate on a specific, static decision point. The third, denoted t_3, is the time at which the source's remuneration is determined. Observe that $t_3 > t_2 > t_1$.

The nature of the decision process at each of these points is discussed below.

3.1.1 Contract specification at time t_1

Consider a setting in which a specific project and source have been selected. Numerous cost assessment issues undoubtedly arise in deciding whether to acquire or to supply this project. These do not differ from those discussed in prior chapters, however, and we therefore concentrate on the cost assessment issues that arise in the pricing practices typically employed.

To explore the price determination role of cost assessment in this context, we partition the source's outcome into benefit and cost components,[45] $x = p(s, a, \eta) = p^B(s, a, \eta) - p^C(s, a, \eta)$, such that $p^B(\cdot)$ is the price paid by the government to the

---

45. This partitioning follows from our discussion in Chapter 4. Observe, however, that for expositional convenience we assume that x^B and x^C are defined such that $x = x^B - x^C$, as opposed to $x = (x^B, x^C)$. This is appropriate in the present discussion because all three elements are assumed to be measured in monetary units.

source and $p^C(\cdot)$ is the cost, to the source, of carrying out the project. We assume that the source will fulfill all technical aspects of the contract.

Precisely which price schedule the source and government will agree upon is a little understood bargaining problem. However, Pareto optimality is a close to unassailable requirement to impose on that schedule. (Which point on the Pareto surface will be chosen is, recall, a much deeper question.) The set of Pareto optimal price schedules can be constructed by maximizing the government's position while holding the source's position constant (or vice versa). That is, for a given source expected utility level of θ, the Pareto optimal price schedule is located by

[8.3] $$\max_{p^B(\cdot)} \sum_{s \in S} U_g(p^B(s, \alpha^*(s, \eta), \eta) \phi_g(s)$$

subject to

$$\sum_{s \in S} U_f(p^B(s, \alpha^*(s, \eta), \eta) - p^C(s, \alpha^*(s, \eta), \eta)) \phi_f(s) = \theta$$

where $U_g(\cdot)$ and $\phi_g(\cdot)$ represent the government's preferences and beliefs, $U_f(\cdot)$ and $\phi_f(\cdot)$ the source's (firm f) preferences and beliefs, and $\alpha^*(s, \eta) = \alpha^*(\eta(s), \eta)$.[46]

Note that two extreme price schedules are possible: (i) a state-dependent and action-dependent price schedule

$$p^B(s, \alpha^*(s, \eta), \eta) = p^C(s, \alpha^*(s, \eta), \eta) + p^\pi(\theta)$$

where

$$U_f(p^\pi(\theta)) = \theta,$$

or (ii) a price invariant to the source's behavior and cost outcome

$$p^B(s, \alpha^*(s, \eta), \eta) = p^B(\theta)$$

where

$$\sum_{s \in S} U_f(p^B(\theta) - p^C(s, \alpha^*(s, \eta), \eta)) \phi_f(s) = \theta.$$

Under the first schedule the firm is guaranteed a profit of $p^\pi(\theta)$ and the government completely absorbs the state occurrence risk. The second schedule, on the other hand, provides the government with a fixed price of $p^B(\theta)$ and the source completely absorbs the risk.

---

46. In this model we assume, for expositional convenience, that the government's behavior can be represented with an expected utility measure. We further assume that the government knows both the source's information system and optimal decision rule. If the government does not know these, its expected utility should be modified to recognize the additional uncertainty about these elements. Further note that a private sector interpretation of this formulation obtains when the second firm is indexed by g.

To illustrate, let $U_f(x) = 1 - e^{-x/100}$ and consider a case where completion of the project will cost either \$100 or \$200. Both the source and government assess equally likely outcomes. Letting $\theta = 0.20$, we observe that the source is indifferent between the first price schedule with a guaranteed profit of $p^\pi(\theta) = \$22$ or the second price schedule with a fixed price of $p^B(\theta) = \$184$. If, however, the government is risk neutral (that is, $U_g(x^B) = -x^B$), it will strictly prefer the first schedule, since the expected cost of that schedule is \$172 as opposed to \$184 for the second. Alternatively, if the source is risk neutral and $U_g(x^B) = 1 - e^{x^B/100}$, a fixed price of \$150.2 will be employed.

The basic observation is that risk sharing is an important feature in this setting. Indeed, with the source risk averse and the government risk neutral, the government will absorb all the risk; and state-dependent price schedules will be the rule. Conversely, with the firm risk neutral and the government risk averse, the firm will absorb all the risk; and fixed prices will be the rule. But in the general case, with both parties risk averse, each will absorb part of the risk.[47]

Unfortunately, several difficulties emerge. Of particular importance is the fact that the government cannot directly observe the state; rather, it observes a cost outcome dependent on both state occurrence and choice by the source. Thus, if the source is relieved of a significant portion of the risks associated with its cost outcome, its incentive to minimize cost will likely be lowered. That is, risk sharing may dull the decision making (including cost control) incentives of the source.[48] This reduced incentive, in turn, leads to postoutcome audits and renegotiation to try to ensure that the source does not lose its cost minimization incentive.

We must also recognize that the formulation in [8.3] is somewhat ideal in that it ignores significant negotiation and information costs. For example, use of an event-contingent price schedule presupposes some postdecision information system that will reveal which event actually obtains. (See the examples in Appendix 8.3.) Construction and use of such a system is, however, simply too expensive to be practical, and use of simplified pricing arrangements is therefore encouraged.

Further reinforcement for a form of simplified, cost-based pricing is found in the fact that advanced (and highly uncertain) technologies are often involved. Thus it may not be very clear at the time of negotiation precisely what the source is to accomplish; and a simplified contracting arrangement allows the parties to

---

47. Of course, with perfect and complete markets, prices would exist for evaluation of state-contingent claims and $U_f(\cdot)$ would merely be the market evaluation. Incomplete markets, however, raise the possibility of risk averse behavior by the firm and attendant concern for efficient risk sharing. In any event, we have here a fairly straightforward application of agency theory. What incentives will properly motivate the source? See Wilson (1969a), Demski (1972b, 1976), Ross (1973), Groves (1973), Stiglitz (1974, 1975), and Williamson et al. (1975).

48. This is the moral hazard phenomenon discussed in the preceding section. See Kihlstrom and Pauly (1971) and Spence and Zeckhauser (1971). Additional discussion of the optimal level of risk sharing can be found in Berhold (1967).

avoid much of the cost of specifying performance contracts for each of the various possibilities.[49,50]

The net result is that numerous state distinctions are not made, and simplifications are tolerated. We find state occurrence replaced by one or a few outcome parameters. Cost is, of course, the dominant outcome parameter; others relating to product performance and time are also used but we shall concentrate on cost alone.[51]

The price schedules typically used can be viewed, therefore, as depending on the source's accounting cost. Let y_1^C denote the predicted cost that is negotiated at time t_1, y_3^C the agreed actual cost as determined at time t_3, π a target fee or profit, and β some scalar risk-sharing coefficient ($0 \leq \beta \leq 1$).[52] Then, in the typical case, we have

$$[8.4] \qquad\qquad p^B(\cdot) = y_1^C + \beta(y_3^C - y_1^C) + \pi.$$

Under a fixed price contract we have $\beta = 0$, the cost plus fixed fee contract has $\beta = 1$, and $0 < \beta < 1$ corresponds to the fixed price incentive and cost plus incentive fee contracts.

Although the predicted cost will be subject to negotiation, much of the information on which it is based comes from the source. Consequently, the prediction will depend on the cost assessment procedures used in making it. We denote that cost assessment procedure η_1 and let $y_1^C = \eta_1(s)$. The impact of the government on the prediction may be viewed as constraining the set of allowable assessment procedures to $\overline{H}_1$.

We leave the discussion of y_3^C until later and now consider the source behavior at time t_2. The price schedule is taken as given.[53]

3.1.2 SOURCE ACTION CHOICE AT TIME t_2

We view the source's choice problem at time t_2 in terms of selecting an optimal action, given the price schedule, technical possibilities, and other considerations. Two aspects of this characterization are particularly important.

---

49. Not surprisingly, we often find employment contracts vaguely defined, apparently in response to the cost of specifying specific performance contracts. These vague contracts allow the employer to select (from an admissible set) specific activities, as the need arises, for the employee to perform. See Williamson et al. (1975) and Stiglitz (1975).

50. Another difficulty here stems from the government's inability to precisely motivate the source under some conditions. That is, the government may not be able to devise a payment plan that will induce the source to select the precise action preferred by the government unless it observes the action actually taken. See Wilson (1969a), Ross (1973), and Demski (1976).

51. See Peck and Scherer (1962) and Scarborough (1968) for further discussion of noncost parameters in the price function.

52. Use of a scalar risk-sharing coefficient does not, however, imply that risk can in fact be completely collapsed into a single parameter. See the important paper by Borch (1962) for further discussion.

53. Precisely how such a schedule is or should be established is a deep and open question. Bargaining aspects are certainly involved. Scherer (1964) and Fox (1974) suggest a tendency for acquiescence to the source's technical expertise in agreeing upon the cost prediction; and existing evidence suggests a tendency by the source to provide downward biased cost predictions. The fee, in turn, ap-

First, significant production externalities may exist. The source's commercial activities and other defense activities, both current and future, may be affected by the manner in which the contract in question is performed. For example, the level of subcontracting may affect the level of technical knowledge that accrues to the source. To more precisely reflect these externalities, we partition the source's cost component outcome into an outlay cost, $p^{C1}(\cdot)$, and an externality cost, $p^{C2}(\cdot)$, as we did in Chapter 5 (section 2).[54]

Second, the actual cost reported on the contract in question is determined by the cost assessment method, η_2, employed by the source. Denoting this reported cost y_2^C we then have $y_2^C = \eta_2(s, a)$.[55] Observe that the assessment method used here is part of the information system η_f that is used by the source. Therefore, its cost and effect on future periods are recognized by the inclusion of η_f in $p^{C1}(\cdot)$ and $p^{C2}(\cdot)$.

The source, then, has two types of choices: production decisions and cost assessment method. Further suppose that the source and government agree upon a particular set of allowable assessment methods, which we denote $\bar{H}_2$. We may, for example, view $\bar{H}_2$ as restricting the assessment alternatives to being consistent with those used in η_1, pronouncements of the Cost Accounting Standards Board, Generally Accepted Accounting Principles, prior decisions by the Boards of Contract Appeals, Armed Services Procurement Regulations, and so on.

If we take the cost assessment procedures (η_1) and contract parameters (y_1^C, π, β) determined at time t_1 as given and assume that the source's cost assessment will be accepted by the government ($y_2^C = y_3^C$), then the source's time t_2 decision is given by[56]

$$E(U_f \mid (y_1^C, \pi, \beta), a^*, (\eta_1, \eta_2^*))$$

$$= \max_{\substack{a \in A \\ \eta_2 \in \bar{H}_2}} \left[\sum_{s \in S} U_f((y_1^C + \beta(\eta_2(s, a) - y_1^C) + \pi) - p^{C1}(s, a, \eta_f) - p^{C2}(s, a, \eta_f)) \right.$$

[8.5]
$$\left. \cdot \phi_f(s \mid y_1^C, \eta_1) \right]$$

where $\eta_f = (\eta_1, \eta_2)$.

---

pears to be related to the cost prediction. Scherer (1964), for example, uses the results of prior negotiations to establish a relationship among the (y_1^C, π, β) parameters and then presents a model (using these prior results to predict the negotiation outcome) to determine the optimal β. Also see Berhold (1967) and Cummins (1973).

54. Following Keynes, Scherer (1964) terms $p^{C2}(\cdot)$ the "user cost" and defines it as "the expected sacrifice of future profits or benefits, discounted to present value, caused by some present economic action." (P. 158.) Further note that a timing issue arises here in that the action choices are made at t_2 but the revenue is received at t_3. If the time span is significant, we may interpret $U_f(\cdot)$ as appropriately transforming $p(\cdot)$ to account for the timing difference. Progress payments may also be involved.

55. This cost assessment comes at the end of the project period, not at time t_2, and is therefore affected by both the state and the actions selected by the source.

56. This model differs from those of Scherer (1964) and Berhold (1967) only in its inclusion of accounting alternatives. Berhold, for example, assumes that "accounting cost is determined by an accounting system which is agreed upon between the contractor and the government." (P. 7.) Ours is a highly simplified view; but, as we shall see, it highlights the accounting issues that appear to have given rise to the CASB.

An interesting aspect of this formulation is that the typical accounting system focuses on the outlay cost and either ignores many elements of the externality cost or represents them in a very simplified manner. This applies to both interproject externalities within the current period and the future period effects of current projects. Consequently, the government's incentive system does not encompass these externalities when it relies on an incentive function, $p^B(\cdot)$, whose cost considerations are limited to the typical accounting system contract costs.[57] For example, performance on a given contract may significantly increase the source's technical capability. The effect of such an increase, depending on the state and action selected, is imbedded in the $p^{C2}(\cdot)$ term. But these effects are not directly reflected in the contract cost y_2^C and are, therefore, not encompassed by the typical incentives in $p^B(\cdot)$.

3.1.3 PRICE DETERMINATION AT TIME t_3

The actual price is determined following contract performance by the source. This may be based solely on the contract parameters, (y_1^C, π, β), and the actual cost reported by the source, y_2^C, as we assumed in [8.5]. But several factors suggest that provision of audit and renegotiation possibilities may be desirable. First, again recognizing negotiation costs, there is a tendency to leave $\bar{H}_2$ vaguely specified (or unspecified) and to therefore address the appropriateness question *ex post*. For example, questions about the method of allocating common costs to the contract may arise. Similarly, questions of allocating contract-related expenditures to recognize future source benefits, embodied in the $p^{C2}(\cdot)$ term, may also arise.

Second, audit and renegotiation may be pursued in light of information asymmetries. The initial bargaining, that is, may be significantly affected by the allocation of information between the parties; and there is a presumption that the source has superior information.[58] Similarly, moral hazard or incentive considerations may be present.

Finally, we also recognize that the parties' behavior may not be strictly cooperative. Prior agreements may not necessarily be honored.

Introduction of audit and renegotiation possibilities alters the analysis from both the government's and the source's perspective. To develop this theme, suppose that the contract has been completed and a cost of y_2^C reported by the source. Further suppose the government then engages in some audit activity, denoted $\eta_g \in H_g$. Although the cost to the government of this activity will likely depend on a number of factors, for simplicity, we confine its dependence to s, $y_f^C = (y_1^C, y_2^C)$, and $\bar{H} = (\bar{H}_1, \bar{H}_2)$ and denote it $\gamma(s, \eta_g, y_f^C, \bar{H})$. Then, if the audit re-

---

57. Recognizing these externalities also leads to a model quite consistent with the cost "overrun" phenomenon. See Cummins (1973) and Fox (1974).

58. An example, due to Ponssard and Zamir (1973), of the effect of superior information in a zero-sum sequential game is summarized in Appendix 8.2.

sults in a final contract cost of $y_3^C = \eta_g(s, y_f^C, \bar{H})$, the net cost to the government will be[59]

$$y_1^C + \beta(y_3^C - y_1^C) + \pi + \gamma(s, \eta_g, y_f^C, \bar{H}).$$

Hence, upon observing the reported cost, the government's optimal audit alternative is selected by

$$E(U_g \mid y_f^C, \pi, \beta, \bar{H}, \eta_g^*)$$

[8.6]
$$= \max_{\eta_g \in H_g} \left[\sum_{s \in S} U_g((y_1^C + \beta(\eta_g(\cdot) - y_1^C) + \pi) + \gamma(\cdot))\phi_g(s \mid y_f^C, \bar{H}) \right].$$

Recognition of this audit-renegotiation possibility also alters the original description of the source's choice problem at time t_2. Assessment method η_2 is no longer viewed in terms of producing a cost datum that is directly used in the price schedule. Rather, y_2^C is merely a preliminary measure that may subsequently be altered by the audit-renegotiation activities. This provides the following alteration of [8.5]:

$$E(U_f \mid (y_1^C, \pi, \beta), a^*, (\eta_1, \eta_2^*, \eta_g))$$

$$= \max_{\substack{a \in A \\ \eta_2 \in \bar{H}_2}} \left[\sum_{s \in S} U_f((y_1^C + \beta(\eta_g(\cdot) - y_1^C) + \pi) - p^{C1}(s, a, \eta_f) - p^{C2}(s, a, \eta_f)) \right.$$

[8.5a]
$$\left. \cdot \phi_f(s \mid y_1^C, \eta_1) \right]$$

where the anticipated government audit-renegotiation procedures, η_g, are exogenously specified.[60]

Finally, we must recognize that our descriptive model has been necessarily simplified. Most obviously, the choices at times t_1, t_2, and t_3 are dependent on information flow, an item we have not fully introduced. Moreover, both the government and sources operate in multicontract environments. We might view the basic models as reflecting appropriate modifications to focus on a single contract primary action space, but this remark is more gratuitous than informative. Interproject externalities appear to be quite significant. On the other hand, this formulation does capture enough of the procurement environment to discuss the regulation of cost assessment systems employed by the sources.

3.2 Intervention and the Role of the CASB

We now ask the same questions as in the financial reporting case: Is regulation of cost assessment practices in government procurement likely to be desirable

---

59. Quite clearly, the audit-renegotiation activity may also affect other contract parameters, but focusing on the reported cost datum is sufficient for our purpose.

60. In a more general formulation, we could treat η_g as uncertain as well as allow for the possibility that the source might choose a system not in $\bar{H}$. Moreover, a game formulation would provide a richer description, allowing for simultaneous determination of source and government policies, encompassing bargaining, contract design, performance, and the like.

and, if so, what type or form is likely to be desirable? And we arrive at essentially the same answers: in principle, inefficiencies may exist and intervention may, therefore, be desirable; but the entire area is so poorly understood at this stage that policy recommendations are largely conjectural.

Initially we note that cost assessment may be subject to intercontract externalities. Quite simply, assessing the actual cost of any project is so complex and approachable in so many different ways that merely comprehending the specific assessment employed in any particular case is likely to be a significant undertaking. Hence, provision of some set of guidelines may be efficient.[61] That is, when we recognize that the government engages in a large number of contracts, we observe that negotiation, audit, and renegotiation costs may be less in total if one set of assessment guidelines, $\overline{H}$, is specified for all such contracts. In this narrow sense, the CASB's role is to design a set of admissible assessment alternatives that, in recognition of the various costs, is efficient.

On a more subtle level, the source is, presumably, more informed than the government. In turn, it may be able to use this differential information to advantage and thereby gain abnormal returns. Use of disclosure guidelines, such as the CASB standard requiring consistency between assessment methods η_1 and η_2, may diminish the advantage conferred to the source by its superior information. This argument is not, however, entirely clear-cut. For example, other contract provisions may counteract the source's information advantage. Hence, unilateral changes in the reporting guidelines need not be "desirable," even though they remove information differences. The guidelines must, that is, be viewed in terms of the resource allocations they produce, and not merely in terms of the nature of the cost assessments they provide.[62]

Further note that influencing the cost assessment used by the source firms may, because of economies of scale in information production, also affect, say, their financial reporting practices. If so, we return to the discussion of the FASB's role. The question becomes, then, vastly deeper than one of designing efficient procurement procedures. Rather, far more basic resource allocation questions are involved; and in seeking a movement from individual to social preference we again arrive at a comingling of the nature of optimal cost assessments with the institutions we devise to determine them.

In this respect, two conclusions emerge. First, the question of determining the most preferred cost assessment methods in a cost-based procurement setting does not, in principle, differ from that of determining most preferred cost assessment methods in other settings. The analysis described in Chapter 2 remains applicable.

---

61. Anthony (1970) is particularly eloquent on this point. Another way of expressing this argument is that the government is uncertain as to the "quality" of the cost assessment methods employed by the source. Provision of guidelines may, therefore, reduce this uncertainty and result in efficiency gains. With extensive guidelines, for example, postperformance litigation may be reduced.

62. For example, questions of maintaining the firm's capability to perform government defense contracts often arise, and myopic focus on extant contract cost assessment procedures may be inconsistent with these more long-run maintenance objectives.

In particular, regulatory pronouncements should be selected in light of their anticipated consequences. The CASB's problem (like that of the FASB) is not one of definition; it is one of conscious choice.

Second, as in the FASB case, we adopt at least a partially agnostic position in detailing what criteria or goals should be pursued in selecting among alternative standards. We simply have not researched either side of the intervention question; and a very deep question of social optimality continues to underlie the problem.

4.0 SUMMARY

This chapter has provided a sketch, in conceptual terms, of the evaluation of cost assessment alternatives used in external reporting. In particular, we have focused on the regulation of financial reporting and reporting under cost-based procurement contracts. In the financial reporting discussion, we stressed that the assessment procedures selected may affect resource allocations among members of the economy because of the impact this information has on production, consumption, and investment decisions. In the cost-based procurement discussion, we stressed that the assessment procedures selected may affect resource allocations between the government and the producer because of its direct impact on the price paid and its indirect impact on the producer's production decisions. The models introduced in these discussions were not sufficiently rich to permit extensive analysis, but it is hoped we have provided an indication of the nature of the difficulties.

Analysis of cost assessment issues in the external reporting setting follows the basic theme of earlier chapters. That is, whether dealing with the alternatives themselves or regulatory mechanisms designed to control selection of the assessment methods, we evaluate the alternatives in terms of the consequences of the decision makers' actions they induce. More profoundly, however, Arrow's theorem precludes generally viewing evaluation of these consequences via some well-defined collective choice function. In particular, the expected utility hypothesis and its attendant structure extend only to special cases at this point. This makes the evaluation question more difficult; indeed, it points to a gaping hole in accounting theory.

In closing, we observe that many of the issues that arise in external reporting also arise in reporting among the subunits of a firm (for example, divisions and central management). Subunits often influence, and may even select, the cost assessment procedures used in their "external" reporting, but central management usually imposes severe constraints on the assessment procedures they may use. Selection of these constraints, in turn, would be predicated on the fact that these assessment procedures influence both the information available to the various decision makers within the firm and the prices paid to the subunits for the services they have provided.

In particular, design of interdepartmental cost allocation procedures raises the same issues as were discussed in this chapter. Resource allocations among the firm's members (including the owners) are influenced by the distribution of information among these members, as well as the cost allocation procedures that are used. Appropriately selected procedures may combat inefficiencies and undesirable resource allocations (where "undesirable" reflects, say, central management's view). Indeed, the design question takes on the flavor of specifying internal market prices (transfer prices) and restrictions, as opposed to imposing external market prices and restrictions.

APPENDIX 8.1
EXTERNALITIES, PUBLIC GOODS, AND MARKET FAILURE

In our society we usually view questions of resource allocation across individuals in terms of a market setting. Each individual pursues his private interest by selecting a most preferred consumption bundle subject to a budget constraint. (See Equation [2.6].) Prices adjust to equate supply and demand in the various markets; and, under appropriate conditions (see Propositions 8.1 and 8.2), the system operates efficiently. In turn, attempts to interfere—via "regulation"—with this essentially laissez faire determination are based on some form of dissatisfaction with the resource allocation it produces.

The purpose of this appendix is to review the nature and impact of these dissatisfactions, or market failures. To keep the discussion uncluttered, we formulate a highly idealized economy consisting of two goods and two types (of equally sized groups) of individuals. Subjective certainty is assumed, and both goods are traded in perfect markets.

The utility functions, endowments, and equilibrium consumption schedules are displayed in Table 8.1. Observe that, for a given price vector $P = (P^1, P^2)$, the choice problem for a type i individual is

$$E(U_i \mid a_i^*) = \max_{a_i' = (x_{i1}, x_{i2})} \ln(x_{i1} x_{i2})$$

subject to

$$x_{i1} P^1 + x_{i2} P^2 \leq W_i = \bar{x}_{i1} P^1 + \bar{x}_{i2} P^2.$$

And, with λ_i denoting a Lagrange multiplier associated with the budget constraint, differentiation readily establishes the following optimality conditions:

$$\frac{1}{x_{i1}^*} - \lambda_i P^1 = 0$$

$$\frac{1}{x_{i2}^*} - \lambda_i P^2 = 0$$

$$x_{i1}^* P^1 + x_{i2}^* P^2 = W_i.$$

It is apparent that (with $\lambda_i = 1/(x_{i1}^* P^1)$) the individual spends half of his wealth

TABLE 8.1   EXCHANGE ECONOMY EXAMPLE

	Individual Type	
	$i = 1$	$i = 2$
Preferences: $U_i(x_{i1}, x_{i2})$	$\ln(x_{11}x_{12})$	$\ln(x_{21}x_{22})$
Endowment:		
$\bar{x}_{i1}$	10	0
$\bar{x}_{i2}$	0	10
Equilibrium Consumption:		
x_{i1}^*	5	5
x_{i2}^*	5	5

on each commodity. Prices are only relative, so we normalize with $P^1 = 1$. Equating supply and demand (for a pair of representative individuals) for the first commodity, we then obtain

$$(1/2)(10) + (1/2)(10\, P^2) = 10$$

which implies $P^2 = 1$; and we therefore conclude that

$$x_{11}^* = x_{12}^* = x_{21}^* = x_{22}^* = 5.$$

Two observations are important at this point. First, note that the particular allocation is Pareto optimal. We cannot strictly improve one individual's well-being without harming another's. This is reflected by the fact that the marginal rate of substitution between the two goods is identical for all individuals.[63] Second, any dissatisfaction with this particular allocation can be viewed in terms of dissatisfaction with the initial endowments. This follows from the fact that in this

---

63. To see this we maximize the well-being of, say, $i = 1$ subject to a constraint of constant well-being for $i = 2$ (at level θ):

$$\max U_1(x_{11}, x_{12})$$

subject to

$$U_2(x_{21}, x_{22}) = \theta$$
$$x_{11} + x_{21} \leq \bar{x}_{11} + \bar{x}_{21}$$
$$x_{12} + x_{22} \leq \bar{x}_{12} + \bar{x}_{22}.$$

First order conditions then provide

$$\frac{\partial U_1(\cdot)/\partial x_{11}^*}{\partial U_1(\cdot)/\partial x_{12}^*} = \frac{\partial U_2(\cdot)/\partial x_{21}^*}{\partial U_2(\cdot)/\partial x_{22}^*}$$

TABLE 8.2 EXTERNALITY EXAMPLE

	Individual Type	
	$i = 1$	$i = 2$
Preferences: $U_i(x_{i1}, x_{i2})$	$\ln(x_{11}x_{12})$	$\ln(x_{21}x_{22} - x_{11})$
Endowment: $\bar{x}_{i1}$	10	0
$\bar{x}_{i2}$	0	10
Equilibrium Solution ($P^1 = P^2 = 1$):		
Consumption: x_{i1}^*	5	5
x_{i2}^*	5	5
Utility:	$\ln 25$	$\ln 20$
A Superior Pareto Optimal Solution: [1]		
Altered Endowment (with a tax of		
0.21 on x_{11} and $P^2 = 1.1$):		
$\bar{x}_{i1}$	10	0
$\bar{x}_{i2}$	1.41	8.59
Consumption:		
x_{i1}^*	4.77	5.23
x_{i2}^*	5.25	4.75
Utility:	$\ln 25.04$	$\ln 20.07$

1. With the indicated reallocation and tax, the first individual's decision problem becomes

$$\max \ln(x_{11}x_{12}) \quad \text{subject to} \quad (1 + 0.21)x_{11} + 1.1x_{12} \le 10 + (1.1)(1.41)$$

with $x_{11}^* \cong 4.77$ and $x_{12}^* \cong 5.25$. Similarly, the second individual's is

$$\max \ln(x_{21}x_{22} - x_{11}) \quad \text{subject to} \quad x_{21} + 1.1x_{22} - 0.21x_{11} \le (1.1)(8.59)$$

with $x_{21}^* \cong 5.23$ and $x_{22}^* \cong 4.75$.

setting all possible equilibrium allocations (subject to $x_{ij}^* > 0$) can be achieved by redistributing the initial endowments. For example, equilibrium allocation $x_{11}^* = x_{12}^* = 2$ and $x_{21}^* = x_{22}^* = 8$ can be achieved by redistributing the endowments to $\bar{x}_{11} = 4, \bar{x}_{12} = 0, \bar{x}_{21} = 6,$ and $\bar{x}_{22} = 10$. Thus, in this setting, any dislike of the resulting market allocations may be expressed as a dislike of the initial distribution of wealth.[64]

To this point, then, intervention in the operation of the market is a questionable exercise. But the situation changes if we admit to externalities—consumptive or productive interdependencies. Examples abound: a newly painted home

---

64. This is a fairly general result, due to Arrow, in welfare economics. The general conditions are summarized in Proposition 8.3. See Debreu (1959), Quirk and Saposnik (1968), and Arrow and Hahn (1971) for more complete discussion.

creates neighborhood benefits, productive processes may produce pollution, driving may cause congestion (as well as pollution), fishing may cause depletion, police protection acquired by one member of a community automatically provides some protection for others, etc.

To illustrate the difficulties created by externalities, return to our simple exchange economy in Table 8.1 and alter the second individual's preferences to depend on the consumption enjoyed by the first in the following specific manner:

$$U_2(\cdot) = \ln(x_{21}x_{22} - x_{11}).$$

With this single alteration, the equilibrium market solution is the same as in the preceding example (see Table 8.2). But this is no longer a Pareto optimal allocation.[65]

This difficulty arises because the first individual has not internalized the effect he has on the second individual. Put another way, the market arrangement has failed to provide a separation among the individuals such that private interest seeking is jointly efficient. (Indeed, when one individual imposes a cost on another, he tends to overproduce or consume the good that causes this external effect.)

Such inefficiencies lead us to consider corrective mechanisms. If the affected individuals are small in number and readily identified, direct negotiation among the parties may produce an efficient solution. With a large number of affected individuals, however, direct negotiation becomes infeasible and some form of intervention may be desirable.

Putting aside the mechanics of precisely how this would be accomplished, one possible approach is to impose a tax on the first individual's consumption of commodity one. Alternatively, if the necessary property rights and market can be established, we could achieve the same result by defining a third commodity representing the first individual's right to "pollute" the second. Of course, unless the first individual is in some way compensated, both of these approaches will make the first individual worse off. In Table 8.2 we present a Pareto optimal solution that is preferred by both individuals; it may be obtained by reallocating 1.41 units of the second commodity from the second to the first individual and then imposing a tax of 0.21 per unit of x_{11}.

Although intervention removes the inefficiency in this example, we cannot conclude that all externalities should be corrected by some form of intervention.

---

65. To see this, we maximize the well-being of $i = 1$ subject to $U_2(\cdot) = \theta$ as in footnote 63. With the specific data in Table 8.2, first order conditions produce

$$\frac{x_{12}^*}{x_{11}^*} = \frac{x_{22}^* + 1}{x_{21}^*}$$

while the market solution gives an allocation such that

$$\frac{x_{12}^*}{x_{11}^*} = \frac{x_{22}^*}{x_{21}^*}$$

Table 8.3   Public Good Example

	Individual Type	
	$i = 1$	$i = 2$
Preferences: $U_i(x_{i1}, x_2)$	$\ln(x_{11} x_2)$	$\ln(x_{21} x_2^2)$
Endowment: $\bar{x}_{i1}$	10	10
Public Good Production:[1]	$x_2 = \displaystyle\sum_{i=1}^{2} (\bar{x}_{i1} - x_{i1})$	
Equilibrium Solution ($P^1 = P^2 = 1$): Consumption: x_{i1}^*	8	4
x_2^*	8	8
Utility:	$\ln 64$	$\ln 256$
A Superior Pareto Optimal Solution: Altered Endowment: $\bar{x}_{i1}$	12.8	7.2
Consumption: x_{i1}^*	6.4	2.4
x_2^*	11.2	11.2
Utility:	$\ln 71.68$	$\ln 301.06$
Sustaining Public Good Price for Individual i ($P^1 = 1$):	4/7	3/7

1. We assume that the public good, x_2, may be produced by transforming either individual's endowment on a one-to-one basis.

Quite clearly, intervention is not required if the externality does not result in an inefficient allocation. For example, the symmetric utility functions

$$U_1(\cdot) = \ln(x_{11} x_{12} - x_{21}) \quad \text{and} \quad U_2(\cdot) = \ln(x_{21} x_{22} - x_{11})$$

obviously display consumptive interdependencies, but with the initial endowments in Table 8.1 the market solution is efficient. More important, even if inefficiencies occur, intervention may not be desirable when we recognize the cost of that intervention. For example, if one unit of each good is required to determine and administer the tax/subsidy scheme in Table 8.2, it is clearly not in the individuals' interests to intervene in the original, inefficient market solution.[66]

   An extreme form of the market failure phenomenon occurs when there is a *public good*—that is, when provision of a commodity by one individual makes that commodity equally, automatically, and costlessly available to all individuals. National defense is a familiar example. An important characteristic of a public good

66. See Buchanan and Stubblebine (1962) and Demsetz (1969) for further discussion of the point that observation of an externality creates a suspicion, but not a prima facie case, that some form of intervention is desirable.

is that while everyone receives the same quantity they value it differently. Consequently, efficiency requires that different individuals pay different prices for the public good. Thus the conventional price system fails entirely at this point.

Details of a specific numerical illustration are displayed in Table 8.3, where the second commodity is the public good. If the individuals do not cooperate and merely act in their own interests, they might arrive at the equilibrium solution in which the first individual provides two units of the public good and the second provides six units.[67] Neither individual acting alone is motivated to move from this solution, but it is not Pareto optimal. However, if they cooperate (and in this case both provide more of the public good) they can achieve a Pareto optimal solution that is better for both.[68]

For example, they might agree that the individuals would contribute, respectively, 3.6 and 7.6 units of endowment toward production of the public good —producing a total of 11.2 units. (See Table 8.3.) Alternatively, a properly informed collective choice agency could achieve the same result by redistributing the endowments and appropriately taxing the individuals. In particular, redistributing 2.8 units of endowment from the second to the first individual coupled with taxing them, respectively, at a rate of 4/7 and 3/7 per unit of the public good will result in a total supply of 11.2 units of the public good as well as each demanding precisely this amount.

Observe, however, that such an approach presumes that the collective choice agency knows the individuals' preferences. In turn, lack of such knowledge gives rise to a deep conundrum because of obvious incentives for individuals to misrepresent their preferences for public goods to that collective choice agency.[69]

In any event, intervention or regulation becomes a potentially interesting

---

67. This solution presumes that both are aware of the other's public good acquisitions even though they do not cooperate.

68. Maximizing $U_1(\cdot)$ subject to $U_2(\cdot) = \theta$ and $x_{11} + x_{21} + x_2 \leq 20$ results in the following conditions for Pareto optimality:

$$x_{21}^* = 20/3 - (2/3)x_{11}^*$$
$$x_2^* = 20 - x_{11}^* - x_{21}^*.$$

The marginal rates of substitution between the private and the public good are

$$\frac{\partial U_1(\cdot)/\partial x_2}{\partial U_1(\cdot)/\partial x_{11}} = \frac{x_{11}}{x_2} \quad \text{and} \quad \frac{\partial U_2(\cdot)/\partial x_2}{\partial U_2(\cdot)/\partial x_{21}} = \frac{2x_{21}}{x_2}.$$

Substituting the allocation in Table 8.3 we obtain

$$\frac{x_{11}}{x_2} = 4/7 \quad \text{and} \quad \frac{2x_{21}}{x_2} = 3/7.$$

That is, marginal valuations differ and individual relative prices must therefore differ if efficiency is to be achieved. (Indeed, efficiency requires that the sum of the individual's marginal rate of substitution equal the marginal rate of transformation—unity in this case—between the private and public goods.) See Malinvaud (1972) or Due and Friedlaender (1973) for further discussion.

69. See Due and Friedlaender (1973), Kurz (1974), and Groves and Loeb (1975) for discussions of the misrepresentation problem.

question when externalities are present in an otherwise classical perfect market setting.

APPENDIX 8.2
ILLUSTRATION OF THE IMPACT OF INFORMATION IN A TWO-PERSON COMPETITIVE SETTING

The purpose of this appendix is to present a simple example of the acquisition and use of information in a competitive setting. As we shall see, the desirability of information depends, in general, on what information others possess; and the affected decision makers will not generally agree on what information is most desirable. Indeed, some information may convey a strategic advantage (such as knowing the technological requirements or your competitors' precise capacities in a competitive bidding situation).

Numerous modes of behavior could be emphasized at this point. In part because the examples in Appendix 8.3 are essentially ones of cooperative behavior (all parties agree to a trade), we concentrate on a noncooperative setting. The following example is due to Ponssard and Zamir (1973).

Consider a strictly competitive, zero-sum game played by two decision makers ($i = 1, 2$). Each decision maker has two possible actions, and one of two states (denoted s^1 and s^2) may occur. The outcome, then, will depend on which action each takes as well as which state occurs. Denoting decision maker i's action a_i and outcome x_i, we then have $x_1 = p(s, a_1, a_2)$ and, with the zero-sum assumption, $x_2 = -x_1 = -p(s, a_1, a_2)$. Specific data are presented in Table 8.4.

We further assume that each decision maker is risk neutral (so that the expected outcome is sufficient for evaluation) and that both hold the same state probability assessments. Finally, the game is sequential in the sense that decision

TABLE 8.4 TWO-PERSON GAME: OUTCOME DATA FOR FIRST DECISION MAKER

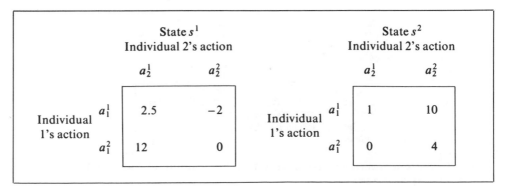

		State s^1 Individual 2's action				State s^2 Individual 2's action	
		a_2^1	a_2^2			a_2^1	a_2^2
Individual 1's action	a_1^1	2.5	−2	Individual 1's action	a_1^1	1	10
	a_1^2	12	0		a_1^2	0	4

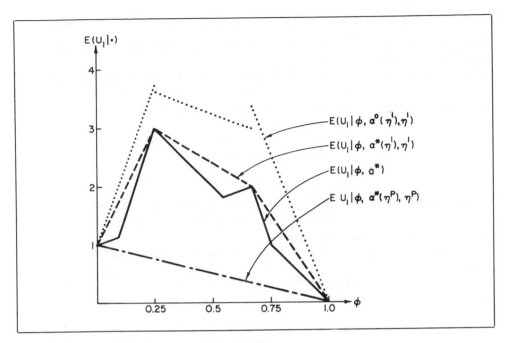

$E(U_1|\cdot)$

$E(U_1|\phi, a^0(\eta^1),\eta^1)$

$E(U_1|\phi, a^*(\eta^1),\eta^1)$

$E(U_1|\phi, a^*)$

$E\,U_1|\phi,\ a^*(\eta^P),\ \eta^P)$

ϕ

Fig. 8.1. Expected utility for two-person example.

maker 2 observes decision maker 1's action choice before selecting his own action choice.

Observe, now, that if s^1 will obtain with certainty, the (a_1^2, a_2^2) combination will be employed, resulting in a net outcome of precisely \$0. This follows from the fact that if the first decision maker selects a_1^1, the second has the option of paying \$2.5 or $-\$2.0$ and will surely opt for the latter (select a_2^2). Alternatively, if the first decision maker selects a_1^2, the second has the option of paying him \$12 or 0 and will surely opt for the latter (select a_2^2). And faced with the choice between losing \$2.0 or breaking even, the first will surely select a_1^2. Similarly, if s^2 will obtain with certainty, the solution will be (a_1^1, a_2^1) with an outcome of \$1 to the first decision maker.

Now suppose that s^1 will obtain with probability $\phi_1(s^1) = \phi_2(s^1) = \phi$. Then the expected outcomes are given by

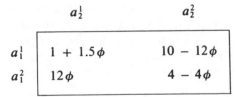

	a_2^1	a_2^2
a_1^1	$1 + 1.5\phi$	$10 - 12\phi$
a_1^2	12ϕ	$4 - 4\phi$

and the solution, from the first decision maker's point of view, is the following function of ϕ:

$$E(U_1 \mid \phi, a^*) = \max\{\min(1 + 1.5\phi, 10 - 12\phi), \ \min(12\phi, 4 - 4\phi)\}$$

where $a^* = (a_1^*, a_2^*)$ is the optimal action for both individuals. $E(U_1 \mid \phi, a^*)$ is plotted in Figure 8.1.

Now consider the acquisition and use of information by the two decision makers. To begin, suppose that both will receive costless state revelation from some source, denoted η^P. If both parties obtain the state revelation before selecting their optimal actions, the outcome will be 0 under s^1 and \$1 (to the first decision maker) under s^2. Hence, the expected value, from the first decision maker's perspective, under costless public revelation is

$$E(U_1 \mid \phi, \alpha^*(\eta^P), \eta^P) = \phi(0) + (1 - \phi)(1) = 1 - \phi.$$

And we see, in Figure 8.1, that public revelation may work to the disadvantage of the first decision maker. That is, the first would never pay to acquire and may pay to suppress public state revelation.

On the other hand, acquisition of *private*, costless state revelation by the first decision maker may work to the disadvantage of the second. For example, if the second does not know that the first has private information and merely selects actions in accordance with his prior beliefs, his strategy and the optimal strategy for the first will be

Second's Action Given First's Action			First's Optimal Action Given Revealed State			for
	a_1^1	a_1^2		s^1	s^2	
	a_2^1	a_2^1		a_1^2	a_1^1	$0 \le \phi \le 1/4$
$\alpha_2^0(a_1) =$	a_2^1	a_2^2	$\alpha_1^0(s) =$	a_1^1	a_1^2	$1/4 \le \phi \le 2/3$
	a_2^2	a_2^2		a_1^2	a_1^1	$2/3 \le \phi \le 1.$

Denoting this private information system η^1 and the somewhat naive strategies by the two decision makers as $\alpha^0(\eta^1)$, we have an expected utility for the first of [70]

$$E(U_1 \mid \phi, \alpha^0(\eta^1), \eta^1) = \begin{cases} 1 + 11\phi & 0 \le \phi \le 1/4 \\ 4 - 1.5\phi & 1/4 \le \phi \le 2/3 \\ 10 - 10\phi & 2/3 \le \phi \le 1. \end{cases}$$

We refer to the above strategies as naive in that they fail to recognize that the action selected by the first decision maker may convey his information to the second. In fact, if the second knows that the first has private state revelation, the above strategy will inform the second of the state and we have η^1 equivalent to η^P. In that case, the first would be better off to suppress the information. Al-

---

70. The expected utility at $\phi = 1/4$ and $\phi = 2/3$ is unclear since the second decision maker is indifferent between his two actions if the first selects a_1^2 and $\phi = 1/4$ or he selects a_1^1 and $\phi = 2/3$.

ternatively, he can develop a strategy that makes more effective use of the information.

Let $\alpha^*(\eta^1)$ denote the optimal strategies for the two decision makers and $E(U_1 \mid \phi, \alpha^*(\eta^1), \eta^1)$ the associated expected utility. The latter is plotted in Figure 8.1; and we observe that for $\phi = 1/8$, $E(U_1 \mid \phi, a^*) = 1.5$, $E(U_1 \mid \phi, \alpha^*(\eta^P), \eta^P) = 0.875$, and $E(U_1 \mid \phi, \alpha^*(\eta^1), \eta^1) = 2$. Furthermore, the latter is a simple combination of $E(U_1 \mid \phi = 0, a^*) = 1$ and $E(U_1 \mid \phi = 1/4, a^*) = 3$; in particular, since $\phi = 1/8 = (1/2)(0) + (1/2)(1/4)$, $E(U_1 \mid \phi = 1/8, \alpha^*(\eta^1), \eta^1) = (1/2)E(U_1 \mid \phi = 0, a^*) + (1/2)E(U_1 \mid \phi = 1/4, a^*)$. In fact, the first individual's optimal use of the revelation is to employ a strategy that results in a game that is equivalent to the $\phi = 0$ and $\phi = 1/4$ games with equal probability. The following strategy accomplishes this.

The first decision maker explicitly or implicitly informs the second that he is acquiring perfect state revelation and will employ an optimal strategy. If s^1 is revealed, he selects a_1^2; but if s^2 is revealed, he selects a_1^1 with conditional probability 4/7 (and a_1^2 with conditional probability 3/7). Starting with a prior assessment of $\phi = 1/8$, this implicit signaling strategy leads to the following beliefs being held by the second decision maker:

$$\phi_2(a_1^1) = (1/8)(0) + (7/8)(4/7) = 1/2,$$

$$\phi_2(s^1 \mid a_1^1) = 0,$$

and
$$\phi_2(s^1 \mid a_1^2) = \frac{1(1/8)}{1/2} = \frac{1}{4}.$$

The strategy, that is, induces the second decision maker to revise his assessment of ϕ to either 0 or 1/4 (with equal probability).

When faced with such a strategy, the second decision maker's best response is to select a_2^1 when he observes a_1^1, but upon observing a_1^2 select a_2^1 with conditional probability 3/4 (and a_2^2 with conditional probability 1/4). Any other strategy would allow the first decision maker to change his strategy and obtain a larger transfer. And these two strategies are equivalent to playing either the $\phi = 0$ or $\phi = 1/4$ games with equal probability.

In terms of optimal use we see that the first decision maker utilizes his information, but stops short of signaling its full content. With s^1 revealed, he selects his preferred action; but with s^2 revealed, he selects his preferred action part of the time and "bluffs" the remainder of the time. There is, therefore, an optimal amount of information to pass on to the opponent; and such judicious use of the information increases the possessor's advantage (for $\phi = 1/8$).[71]

---

71. As sketched in Figure 8.1, $E(U_1 \mid \phi, \alpha^*(\eta^1), \eta^1)$ is, in fact, the concavification of $E(U_1 \mid \phi, a^*)$, the least concave function that never falls below $E(U_1 \mid \phi, a^*)$. Clearly, $E(U_1 \mid \phi, \alpha^*(\eta^1), \eta^1)$ would never be less than $E(U_1 \mid \phi, a^*)$. But it is also concave with respect to ϕ and must, therefore, be *at least as large as* the concavification of $E(U_1 \mid \phi, a^*)$. On the other hand, the second decision maker can always revise his beliefs according to the first decision maker's strategy and choice, and then work with the corresponding outcomes. This, however, entails taking convex combinations of points along $E(U_1 \mid \phi, a^*)$. Thus $E(U_1 \mid \phi, \alpha^*(\eta^1), \eta^1)$ is the concavification of $E(U_1 \mid \phi, a^*)$. See Ponssard and Zamir (1973).

APPENDIX 8.3
ILLUSTRATIONS OF THE IMPACT OF INFORMATION
IN A CONVENTIONAL MARKET SETTING

In this appendix we present a series of examples of the use and effect of information in the type of conventional market setting originally sketched in Chapter 2, section 3. Specifically, we consider a classical competitive economy in which a single good is produced, traded, and consumed. Two distinct dates are recognized: present and future. In addition, the supply of the good available at the future time will depend upon production decisions and which state of nature obtains. For simplicity, we recognize only two states, s^1 and s^2.

We might interpret this setting as an agrarian society in which corn is produced, traded, and consumed. The future corn supply, in turn, will depend on planting decisions as well as whether the rainfall is heavy (s^1) or light (s^2).

Recognizing time- and event-contingent utility, this gives rise to three distinct types of corn: present, future if s^1 obtains, and future if s^2 obtains. We assume all three are traded in perfectly competitive markets and denote individual i's consumption of each by x_{i0} (current), x_{i1}^1 (future if s^1 obtains), and x_{i1}^2 (future if s^2 obtains).

For simplicity, each individual's preferences are represented by an additive logarithmic utility function. Individual i's utility evaluation of the consumption schedule $a_i' = (x_{i0}, x_{i1}^1, x_{i1}^2)$ is, therefore, given by

$$E(U_i \mid a_i) = \ln x_{i0} + \phi_i(s^1) \ln x_{i1}^1 + \phi_i(s^2) \ln x_{i1}^2$$

where $\phi_i(s)$ is the individual's subjective probability that state s will occur.

The set of consumption schedules available to individual i is delineated by assuming that he cannot spend more than his wealth. That wealth consists of $\bar{x}_{i0}$ units of current corn, $\bar{x}_{i1}^1$ units of future s^1 corn, and $\bar{x}_{i1}^2$ units of future s^2 corn, evaluated at respective market prices of $P_0 = 1$, P_1^1, and P_1^2; that is, his wealth is $W_i = \bar{x}_{i0} + P_1^1 \bar{x}_{i1}^1 + P_1^2 \bar{x}_{i1}^2$. (Note that prices are normalized so that the price of current corn is unity.) Similarly, the cost of consumption schedule $a_i' = (x_{i0}, x_{i1}^1, x_{i1}^2)$ is $P \cdot a_i = x_{i0} + P_1^1 x_{i1}^1 + P_1^2 x_{i1}^2$. Hence, as in relation [2.6], we model individual i's consumption choice problem as

$$E(U_i \mid a_i^*) = \max_{a_i} E(U_i \mid a_i)$$

subject to

$$P \cdot a_i \leq W_i.$$

Assuming positive wealth and applying the usual Lagrangian technique, we obtain the following optimal consumption schedule:

$$x_{i0}^* = W_i/2$$
$$x_{i1}^{1*} = W_i \phi_i(s^1)/2P_1^1$$
$$x_{i1}^{2*} = W_i \phi_i(s^2)/2P_1^2.$$

Table 8.5   Basic Data for Equilibrium Examples

	Current	Future	
		s^1 Obtains	s^2 Obtains
Endowment:			
Individual $i = 1$	50	10	10
$i = 2$	50	10	10
$i = 3$	20	0	0
Productive Alternatives:			
($i = 1, 2$ only):			
Null	0	0	0
s^1 only	-10	20	0
s^2 only	-10	0	20
Certain	-10	15	15
Expected Utility:			

$$E(U_1 \mid a_1) = \ln x_{10} + (1/4)\ln x_{11}^1 + (3/4)\ln x_{11}^2$$
$$E(U_2 \mid a_2) = \ln x_{20} + (3/4)\ln x_{21}^1 + (1/4)\ln x_{21}^2$$
$$E(U_3 \mid a_3) = \ln x_{30} + (1/5)\ln x_{31}^1 + (4/5)\ln x_{31}^2$$

To close the model and determine an equilibrium set of prices and consumption schedules, we add the belief, endowment, and production possibility assumptions listed in Table 8.5. We assume there are three equal-size classes of individuals and concentrate on one representative member of each class ($i = 1, 2, 3$). The first possesses an endowment of 50 units of current corn and 10 units of future corn and believes that state s^1 will obtain with probability $1/4$. He also has the option of transforming 10 units of current corn into (i) 20 units of future corn only if s^1 obtains, (ii) 20 units of future corn only if s^2 obtains, or (iii) 15 units of future corn regardless of which state obtains.

The second individual is identical in all respects to the first, except he believes that s^1 will occur with probability $3/4$. The third individual has an endowment of 20 units of current corn, believes that state s^1 will occur with probability $1/5$, and possesses no productive opportunities.

Equilibrium price and consumption schedules are determined by equating supply and demand for each type of corn. Observe that the optimal production for $i = 1, 2$ is the option that guarantees 15 units of future corn. Hence, the total supply of current corn will be $40 + 40 + 20 = 100$ units and the total supply of future corn in each state will be $25 + 25 + 0 = 50$ units. Using the solution to the individuals' consumption problem and equating supply and demand for current corn provides

$$100 = (1/2)[40 + 25(P_1^1 + P_1^2) + 40 + 25(P_1^1 + P_1^2) + 20].$$

Similarly equating supply and demand for future corn if s^1 obtains provides

TABLE 8.6   EQUILIBRIUM PRICE AND CONSUMPTION SCHEDULES

	Current	Future	
		s^1 obtains	s^2 obtains
Supply:			
Individual $i = 1$	40	25	25
$i = 2$	40	25	25
$i = 3$	20	0	0
	100	50	50
Demand:			
Individual $i = 1$	45	11.97	31.84
$i = 2$	45	35.90	10.61
$i = 3$	10	2.13	7.55
	100	50	50
Price:	$P_0 = 1$	$P_1^1 = 0.94$	$P_1^2 = 1.06$

Expected Utility:

$$E(U_1 \mid \alpha_1^*(\eta^0), \eta^0) = \ln 45 + (1/4)\ln 11.97 + (3/4)\ln 31.84 = 7.02$$

$$E(U_2 \mid \alpha_2^*(\eta^0), \eta^0) = \ln 45 + (3/4)\ln 35.90 + (1/4)\ln 10.61 = 7.08$$

$$E(U_3 \mid \alpha_3^*(\eta^0), \eta^0) = \ln 10 + (1/5)\ln 2.13 + (4/5)\ln 7.55 = 4.07$$

Note: Throughout Tables 8.6 to 8.10, we denote postdecision state revelation η^0, public predecision revelation η^1, unanticipated public revelation after trading occurs η^2, and no predicision or postdecision information η^3.

$$50 = \frac{1}{2P_1^1}\left[\frac{1}{4}(40 + 25(P_1^1 + P_1^2)) + \frac{3}{4}(40 + 25(P_1^1 + P_1^2)) + \frac{1}{5}(20)\right].$$

Hence, $P_1^1 = 0.94$ and $P_1^2 = 1.06$. The equilibrium consumption schedules are displayed in Table 8.6.

Now consider the provision and use of information in this simple economy. Two roles need to be distinguished. First, information may be provided *before* the various individuals select their optimal (equilibrium) actions. Here the information plays the usual prechoice probability revision role. Second, information may be provided *after* optimal actions are implemented and events obtain. Here the information supports a system of event-contingent trades.[72] For example, trading in future corn if state s^1 obtains requires knowledge of whether s^1 obtains. For this reason we observe life insurance contracts (death-contingent claims) but not

---

72. Observe that these two roles would also be present in a typical performance evaluation setting. Analysis of prior performance may improve future decisions. Similarly, a manager's rewards (psychic and otherwise) may be related to how well he actually performs. (See Demski 1972b.)

TABLE 8.7 PUBLIC PREDECISION STATE REVELATION

	s^1 will obtain		s^2 will obtain	
	Current	Future: s^1 obtains	Current	Future: s^2 obtains
Supply:				
$i = 1$	40	30	40	30
$i = 2$	40	30	40	30
$i = 3$	20	0	20	0
	100	60	100	60
Demand:				
$i = 1$	45	27	45	27
$i = 2$	45	27	45	27
$i = 3$	10	6	10	6
	100	60	100	60
Price:	1	5/3	1	5/3

Expected Utility:

$$E(U_1 \mid \alpha_1^*(\eta^1), \eta^1) = (1/4)(\ln 45 + \ln 27) + (3/4)(\ln 45 + \ln 27) = 7.10$$

$$E(U_2 \mid \alpha_2^*(\eta^1), \eta^1) = (3/4)(\ln 45 + \ln 27) + (1/4)(\ln 45 + \ln 27) = 7.10$$

$$E(U_3 \mid \alpha_3^*(\eta^1), \eta^1) = (1/5)(\ln 10 + \ln 6) + (4/5)(\ln 10 + \ln 6) = 4.09$$

salvation insurance (salvation-contingent trades)—Faust aside. These two roles are discussed in turn.

PREDECISION INFORMATION

To illustrate the predecision case, we consider a *costless* system η^1 that, prior to any trading or productive acts, publicly reveals the state that will obtain. If it is revealed that state s^1 will occur, individuals 1 and 2 will clearly adopt the productive alternative guaranteeing 20 units of corn if that state obtains. A guaranteed future supply of 60 (as opposed to 50) units will exist, P_1^1 will move from 0.94 to 5/3, and, of course, P_1^2 will drop to zero. Details are summarized in Table 8.7. Note, in particular, that all individuals strictly prefer such public revelation; all would contribute nontrivial resources toward development of the public information.

Such unanimity is not, however, guaranteed. Suppose we add one individual to our setting. (Recall that there are "many" of each type $i = 1, 2, 3$ and addition of a single individual will not significantly affect the prior equilibrium computations.) This single individual possesses only future s^1 corn but believes s^2 to be certain. If there is public state revelation before any trades are consummated, the

TABLE 8.8   UNANIMOUSLY OPPOSED PUBLIC REVELATION

Preferences: $E(U_i \mid a_i) = \ln x_{i0} + \phi_i(s^1) \ln x_{i1}^1 + \phi_i(s^2) \ln x_{i1}^2$

Beliefs:			$\phi_i(s^1)$	$\phi_i(s^2)$
$i = 1$			1/4	3/4
$i = 2$			3/4	1/4
$i = 3$			1/5	4/5

Fixed Supply:

		Current	Future	
			s^1 obtains	s^2 obtains
$i = 1$		40	25	25
$i = 2$		40	25	25
$i = 3$		20	0	0
		100	50	50

Equilibrium without information (η^0):

Demand:

	Current	s^1 obtains	s^2 obtains
$i = 1$	45	11.97	31.84
$i = 2$	45	35.90	10.61
$i = 3$	10	2.13	7.55
	100	50	50
Price:	1	0.94	1.06

Expected Utility:

$E(U_1 \mid \alpha_1^*(\eta^0), \eta^0) = \ln 45 + (1/4)\ln 11.97 + (3/4)\ln 31.84 = 7.02$

$E(U_2 \mid \alpha_2^*(\eta^0), \eta^0) = \ln 45 + (3/4)\ln 35.90 + (1/4)\ln 10.61 = 7.08$

$E(U_3 \mid \alpha_3^*(\eta^0), \eta^0) = \ln 10 + (1/5)\ln 2.13 + (4/5)\ln 7.55 = 4.07$

Costless Public Revelation Before Trading (η^1):

	s^1 Revealed		s^2 Revealed	
	Current	Future: s^1 obtains	Current	Future: s^2 obtains
Demand:				
$i = 1$	45	22.5	45	22.5
$i = 2$	45	22.5	45	22.5
$i = 3$	10	5.0	10	5.0
	100	50	100	50
Price:	1	2.0	1	2.0

Expected Utility:

$E(U_1 \mid \alpha_1^*(\eta^1), \eta^1) = \ln 45 + (1/4)\ln 22.5 + (3/4)\ln 22.5 = 6.92$

$E(U_2 \mid \alpha_2^*(\eta^1), \eta^1) = \ln 45 + (3/4)\ln 22.5 + (1/4)\ln 22.5 = 6.92$

$E(U_3 \mid \alpha_3^*(\eta^1), \eta^1) = \ln 10 + (1/5)\ln 5.0 + (4/5)\ln 5.0 = 3.91$

Continued on next page

TABLE 8.8 *(Continued)*

Costless Unanticipated Public Revelation after Trading
Coupled with a Second Trading Round (η^2):

		Future	
	Current	s^1 obtains	s^2 obtains
Supply:			
(from no information case)			
$i = 1$	45	11.97	31.84
$i = 2$	45	35.90	10.61
$i = 3$	10	2.13	7.55
	100	50	50

	s^1 Revealed		s^2 Revealed	
	Current	Future: s^1 obtains	Current	Future: s^2 obtains
Demand:				
$i = 1$	34.47	17.24	54.34	27.17
$i = 2$	58.40	29.20	33.11	16.55
$i = 3$	7.13	3.56	12.55	6.28
	100	50	100	50
Price:	1	2	1	2

Expected Utility:

$$E(U_1 \mid \alpha_1^*(\eta^2), \eta^2) = (1/4)(\ln 34.47 + \ln 17.24) + (3/4)(\ln 54.34 + \ln 27.17) = 7.07$$

$$E(U_2 \mid \alpha_2^*(\eta^2), \eta^2) = (3/4)(\ln 58.40 + \ln 29.20) + (1/4)(\ln 33.11 + \ln 16.55) = 7.16$$

$$E(U_3 \mid \alpha_3^*(\eta^2), \eta^2) = (1/5)(\ln 7.13 + \ln 3.56) + (4/5)(\ln 12.55 + \ln 6.28) = 4.14$$

only conceivable signal, from this individual's view, is s^2. Hence, *in his opinion,* the price of future s^1 corn will be zero, his wealth will be zero, and he will starve. He will, that is, pay to suppress the public information. We thus have a counter-example to Proposition 2.1 in a multiperson setting. Public state revelation prior to trading affects the individual's opportunity set. Without access to the same alternatives he may be and is, in this case, indeed harmed by public revelation. Of course, he would not pay to suppress costless private information.[73]

Another example of the distributive effects of information is provided in Table 8.8. Here, in a strict exchange setting, all individuals are unanimously op-

73. For example, if the private information can be conveyed to others and thereby induce a second round of trading, the individual might gain by investing his wealth in s^2 corn prior to revealing that information. That is, he might gain by speculating on the price change that will occur in the second round of trading and then using some proceeds from his investment to buy current corn. Indeed, it may even be optimal to produce s^1 corn to further increase these speculative gains.

TABLE 8.9 PRIVATE POSTDECISION REVELATION

| | | Future | |
	Current	s^1 obtains	s^2 obtains
Supply:			
$i = 1$	40	25	25
$i = 2$	40	25	25
$i = 3$	20	0	0
	100	50	50
Demand:			
$i = 1$	45	11.25	33.75
$i = 2$	45	33.75	11.25
$i = 3$	10	5.00	5.00
	100	50	50
Price:	1	1	1

Expected Utility:

$$E(U_1 \mid \alpha_1^*(\eta^3), \eta^3) = \ln 45 + (1/4)\ln 11.25 + (3/4)\ln 33.75 = 7.05$$
$$E(U_2 \mid \alpha_2^*(\eta^3), \eta^3) = \ln 45 + (3/4)\ln 33.75 + (1/4)\ln 11.25 = 7.05$$
$$E(U_3 \mid \alpha_3^*(\eta^3), \eta^3) = \ln 10 + \ln 5 \qquad\qquad\qquad = 3.91$$

posed to public revelation *before* any trades are consummated. The difficulty is that such revelation precludes mutually acceptable trades. Conversely, if they trade to an equilibrium before the information is received and then unexpectedly receive it, a second round of trading places them all in superior positions.

POSTDECISION INFORMATION

Alteration of postdecision information may also benefit some individuals and harm others. The nature of the effect is, however, somewhat different. In this case, altering the information system alters the trading opportunities that are available. That is, trading event-contingent corn requires an ability to distinguish among the various events. In our simple illustration, individuals 1 and 2 can, for example, distinguish between s^1 and s^2 as a mere by-product of their productive activities. Communication of this revelation to $i = 3$ is then sufficient to permit state-dependent trading in future corn among all individuals. But without such revelation, from some source, the uninformed individuals could not contract for event-contingent exchanges. For example, if individual 3 could not distinguish between s^1 and s^2, he could not make trades that depended on which of the two states did occur. Hence, he would require $x_{31}^1 = x_{31}^2$.

Thus, the trading of state-dependent commodities (such as corn if s^2 obtains)

TABLE 8.10 OPPOSED POSTDECISION REVELATION

Preferences: $E(U_i \mid a_i) = \ln x_{i0} + \phi_i(s^1)\ln x_{i1}^1 + \phi_i(s^2)\ln x_{i1}^2$

Beliefs:	$\phi_i(s^1)$	$\phi_i(s^2)$
$i = 1$	1	0
$i = 2$	1	0
$i = 3$	1/2	1/2

	Current	Future s^1 obtains	s^2 obtains
Fixed Supply:			
$i = 1$	40	25	1
$i = 2$	40	25	1
$i = 3$	20	0	0
Public Postdecision Revelation (η^0):			
Demand:			
$i = 1$	45	23.68	0
$i = 2$	45	23.68	0
$i = 3$	10	2.63	2
	100	50	2
Price:	1	1.9	2.5

Expected Utility:

$E(U_1 \mid \alpha_1^*(\eta^0), \eta^0) = \ln 45 + \ln 23.68 = 6.97$

$E(U_2 \mid \alpha_2^*(\eta^0), \eta^0) = \ln 45 + \ln 23.68 = 6.97$

$E(U_3 \mid \alpha_3^*(\eta^0), \eta^0) = \ln 10 + (1/2)\ln 2.63 + (1/2)\ln 2 = 3.13$

Private Postdecision Revelation (η^3):			
Demand:			
$i = 1$	45	24	0
$i = 2$	45	24	0
$i = 3$	10	2	2
	100	50	2
Price:	1	1.875	3.125

Expected Utility:

$E(U_1 \mid \alpha_1^*(\eta^3), \eta^3) = \ln 45 + \ln 24 = 6.98$

$E(U_2 \mid \alpha_2^*(\eta^3), \eta^3) = \ln 45 + \ln 24 = 6.98$

$E(U_3 \mid \alpha_3^*(\eta^3), \eta^3) = \ln 10 + \ln 2 = 3.00$

requires that each party possess an information system that will reveal which state does in fact obtain. If these systems do not reveal unique states, they effectively limit the number of trades that may be desirable. That is, less than unique state revelation produces an incomplete set of commodity markets.

However, systems that provide unique state revelation are not necessarily desirable. Such a set of systems and markets has a cost; moreover, an increase in the number of state distinctions may benefit some individuals while harming others.

To illustrate, suppose individuals 1 and 2 will naturally observe state occurrence as a by-product of their productive activities, but individual 3 will not be able to distinguish between s^1 and s^2. Adding the $x^1_{31} = x^2_{31}$ constraint to the choice model for $i = 3$ results in the equilibrium price and consumption schedules displayed in Table 8.9. On the other hand, costlessly informing $i = 3$ of which state obtains returns us to the original example in Table 8.6; and in this case we note that $i = 2$ strictly prefers informing $i = 3$. In a similar example presented in Table 8.10 we observe that neither $i = 1$ nor $i = 2$ prefers to inform $i = 3$.[74]

---

74. Alternatively, the reader can readily verify that with homogeneous beliefs and $\phi_i(s^1) = 0.9$ all individuals would be indifferent toward receiving or providing costless postdecision revelation.

EPILOGUE

In any context involving cost determination, there are typically alternative cost assessments that may be used. The purpose of this study has been to identify the nature of those alternatives and to present an explicit model of rational choice for selecting from among them. The accounting literature has presented and discussed many alternatives, and some consideration has been given to the "cost-benefit" trade-offs involved. However, this literature has often failed to explicitly consider many of the choice theoretic aspects of selecting a particular alternative.

In this final chapter we briefly review our analysis and suggest some possible directions for future research.

1.0 WHAT HAVE WE DONE?[1]

We can gain some overall perspective of this study by recognizing that it consists of three major types of analyses: (i) exploration of models of rational or consistent choice under uncertainty; (ii) exploration of the nature of cost assessment and its role in facilitating and influencing decisions; and (iii) exploration of the evaluation of cost assessment alternatives in specific decision contexts.

Our discussion of models of rational choice appears in Chapters 2, 3, and 8. Chapters 2 and 3 focus on decisions made within the firm (with primary emphasis

---

1. Assuming, of course, that the reader accepts that we have done something.

on a single user of cost assessment data). Chapter 8 focuses on decisions made by those external to the firm (with primary emphasis on multiple users of cost assessment data). And, as we briefly consider the multidivisional firm, the two explorations merge together.

Our discussion of internal decisions focuses on the rational choice of information systems and decision models. Evaluation of these alternatives is assumed to be a costless activity, but recognition is given to the costs of providing and processing information and of constructing and using decision models to select actions. Much of the discussion assumes that the evaluation is made by a rational evaluator who selects alternatives in accordance with his preferences.[2] Some consideration is given, however, to the case where the evaluator's preferences are assumed to be congruent with the unanimous preferences of the firm's owners.

The discussion in Chapters 2 and 3 also stresses the fact that selection of information systems and decision models must be made *ex ante,* under conditions of uncertainty. Explicit recognition of uncertainty is an important characteristic of the analyses in this study.

Much of the discussion in Chapters 2 and 3 assumes that the decision model used to select actions fully reflects the beliefs and preferences of the evaluator. Chapter 3 first explores the fact that this model has many equivalent forms, and then goes on to recognize that the cost of constructing and using such models makes model simplification desirable, despite the possible selection of nonoptimal actions.

The general analysis in Chapters 2 and 3 provides a basis from which to explore the nature of cost assessment and its role in facilitating and influencing decisions within the firm. This exploration is found in Chapters 4 and 5. Chapter 4 focuses on action costs while Chapter 5 extends the discussion to input and output costs. Both chapters stress that cost is an inherently arbitrary concept and that the cost of a particular object can be any of a number of amounts depending on how a decision maker chooses to approach his decision problem. Furthermore, the process of providing and using cost assessments requires the use of scarce resources and, consequently, rational choice of a particular cost assessment must be based on the evaluator's preferences with respect to the predicted (net) consequences of each of the available alternatives. These alternatives may take the form of alternative cost functions, cost parameter prediction methods, or cost information.

The discussion of input and output costs in Chapter 5 assumes that the cost functions used in a decision model will fully reflect the decision maker's beliefs and preferences. This assumption is obviously unrealistic, but it allows us to explore the complexity and requirements of any cost function that is to fulfill this idealistic role. Of particular importance is the requirement that the input and output de-

---

2. Of course, these preferences are influenced by incentives and deterrents provided by the evaluator's superiors. (See Ijiri 1975 for a particularly eloquent discussion of motivating or controlling the evaluator.)

scriptions reflect all aspects of the action alternatives that affect the cost component outcome (that is, they must constitute a sufficient cost statistic).

Chapters 6 and 7 explicitly recognize the desirability of simplified cost functions and explore their general nature and the evaluation of alternatives in specific
decision contexts. Chapter 6 focuses on decisions that have a relatively short-run
impact on outcomes, while Chapter 7 focuses on investment decisions that have a
relatively long-run impact. The analysis in both chapters is limited both in terms
of the variety of cost assessment alternatives considered and in the extent of the
analysis for those that are considered. Our objective has been to illustrate the diverse nature of cost assessment alternatives and to point out the basic "cost-
benefit" issues to be considered in evaluating those alternatives.

We emphasize that we make no attempt to provide policy recommendations.
Whether one cost assessment alternative is preferred to another is an inherently
contextual question. We may pose a situation and then proceed to analyze the
question of preference (as we have done in Chapters 6 and 7), but the situation
must be specified. More general prescriptions are the product of repeated analyses.

Chapter 8 focuses on the evaluation of cost assessment alternatives that arise
in preparing reports for investors and in determining costs in cost-plus contracting.
Both situations are characterized by the fact that the selected alternatives affect
the actions of more than one decision maker, at least one of which is external to
the firm. And in each case, boards have been established to specify "standards"
that restrict the cost assessment alternatives available to management. Our discussion stresses that the preferences of those affected by these standards are likely
to differ, thus raising problems of social choice. Such choices require ethical
judgments. Consequently, even determination of preferences among standards in
specific contexts is beyond the scope of this study. Our analysis merely provides
a choice theoretic framework that could be used in conjunction with ethical judgments.

2.0 WHAT "SHOULD" WE DO?[3]

The analyses presented in this study have clearly not exhausted the subject.
Further research is likely to prove fruitful. But what form of research is likely to
be desirable? We conclude this final chapter with some suggestions. These suggestions fall into two broad categories: research into the consequences of various cost
assessment alternatives and research into the usefulness of various surrogate evaluation procedures.

In this study we have avoided making prescriptive statements about the de-

---

3. If the reader is tempted to provide an answer to this question, please recognize that "we"
is meant to encompass both the readers and the authors. Moreover, we now step into the realm of
personal opinion, as opposed to applying the analysis in Chapter 8 to the selection of research
projects.

sirability of particular cost assessment alternatives. Such desirability depends on the specific context. However, determination of the consequences of particular alternatives in a variety of specific contexts is likely to provide useful information to those who must make selections in other contexts. This will be particularly likely if we can identify some general characteristics of situations in which particular alternatives tend to dominate. It might also be useful to determine the sensitivity of the consequences to the selection of nonoptimal alternatives.

This research may be either analytical or empirical.[4] Analytical research, such as that illustrated in Chapters 6 and 7, is useful in identifying extreme cases, for example those under which a particular alternative is guaranteed to dominate or under which two or more alternatives are guaranteed to be equivalent. Analytical research may also be able to isolate the impact of varying particular characteristics of a situation.

More specifically, analytical research can be used to more extensively explore each of the areas discussed in Chapters 6 and 7. For example, it seems likely that more extensive recognition of uncertainty and the information alternatives involved in those areas would produce useful information.[5] More extensive analysis of the impact of cost assessment alternatives on influencing decisions may also provide useful results. This latter research will require more extensive recognition of the multiperson facets of firm decisions, including such factors as risk sharing[6] and the coordination of multiperson decisions. Finally, we also conjecture that more extensive recognition of the problems of facilitating and influencing decisions in contexts that are dynamically changing over time will prove a useful exercise. Simulation, as illustrated in Appendix 7.1, may be a particularly productive analytical device for exploring the more complex situations that are created by recognizing multiperson and multiperiod issues.

Evaluation of cost assessment alternatives requires explicit predictions about how decision makers will react to alternative cost information and about how their actions will affect outcomes.[7] Empirical evidence about the nature of these relationships is likely to be useful. Most of our models of these relationships are currently based on *a priori* reasoning and general "wisdom" derived from anecdotal evidence. Extensive systematic evidence is generally not available.

Of course, some of the behavioral research conducted by accountants attempts to provide evidence as to how decision-maker choices differ under alternative cost assessments. However, this research has been somewhat fragmented; and

---

4. This is a logical "or"; we do not view research as being necessarily exclusively analytical or empirical.

5. For example, see Feltham (1975) for this type of analysis of the aggregation issue discussed in Chapter 6.

6. For example, see Demski (1976).

7. These predictions are required both in specific evaluation in specific contexts and in the analytical research mentioned above. If we have little information about these relationships our uncertainty can be appropriately reflected in the evaluation model we construct. See Smallwood (1968).

systematic development and testing of hypotheses in both decision-facilitating and decision-influencing contexts appear to be a fruitful area for future research.[8]

More analytical and empirical research is also a useful prospect in the social choice areas discussed in Chapter 8. This research must necessarily focus on the prediction of consequences leaving evaluation of those consequences to policy-makers.[9] These consequences may, observe, be associated with particular assessment alternatives or with institutional mechanisms. We may, for example, address the question of consequence predictions for use of LIFO versus FIFO inventory methods in a financial reporting setting. Alternatively, we may address the question of what consequences are likely to result from some specific alteration of the existing institutional arrangements. For example, what consequences might follow from abandoning the current FASB arrangement in favor of some type of voting structure?[10]

Finally, recall that rationality and costless analysis on the part of the evaluator are central assumptions throughout the study. Analysis is clearly not costless; and many would argue that no one is completely rational. Since we are conducting research to assist the evaluator, we choose to assume that he at least desires to be rational. The form of rational evaluation changes, however, if we admit to costly analysis.

Admission of costly analysis moves us from the construction of models that completely reflect the evaluator's preferences and beliefs to the construction of simplified evaluation models. Consequently, it now becomes potentially worthwhile to study the ability of various simplified evaluation procedures to produce acceptable cost assessment decisions. For example, does selection from among alternative overhead allocation models on the basis of historical correlation produce acceptable results? Systematic evidence on how well such a heuristic evaluation procedure works would, no doubt, be interesting as well as useful.

"Standards" represent another example of surrogate evaluation. We know from Proposition 2.1 that no set of conventional standards (such as objectivity, reliability, fairness, etc.) can completely and correctly rank information alternatives—if we place no restrictions on the evaluator other than his preferences admit to characterization by the expected utility hypothesis. With costly analysis, however, the use of standards as a basis for simplified analysis becomes interesting. Yet, at present, we know very little about how well they work.

Again, the research here may be either analytical or empirical. Analytical

---

8. Examples of prior research in decision-facilitating contexts are provided by Dyckman (1964), Bruns (1965), and Barefield (1972). Examples of research in decision-influencing contexts are provided by Cook (1967) and Hopwood (1972, 1974).

9. We can, of course, impose a criterion such as Pareto optimality and use analytical research to identify alternatives that satisfy that criterion. However, except in some highly constrained circumstances, many alternatives will not be comparable in terms of that criterion.

10. Examples of institutional research are provided by Sen (1970), Fishburn (1973), and Benston (1973).

research may be used, for example, to identify conditions under which a particular simplified procedure will yield decisions equivalent to a complete analysis.[11] Analysis may also be used to identify how sensitive the consequences are to choice errors in particular postulated situations. Again, simulation is likely to be particularly useful if the situation is at all complex.[12]

An obvious drawback of analytical research is that the postulated situations must have a relatively simple and well-specified structure in order to be tractable. This, coupled with less than perfect understanding of the "real world," brings us to empirical research. Such research might, for example, attempt to determine the actual consequences of using alternative evaluation procedures. A major problem, however, is that it is often difficult to determine what would have happened after the fact. Furthermore, each case is but a single observation of a state realization. The latter problem can be attenuated if a sufficient number of observations can be obtained under appropriately similar conditions; but that is often difficult when we are dealing with internal decisions. Of course, even a small sample provides some information.

In any event, whether the evaluator operates in the complete or simplified domain, and whether he faces choice among cost assessment alternatives at the individual, firm, or social levels, the *conceptual nature* of his analysis remains. He selects among the alternatives by focusing on the evaluation of the consequences of the decision behavior they induce. The challenge is the identification of efficient, reliable methods of making these analyses.

---

11. See, for example, Itami (1975a) for an analysis of the "amount" of information as an evaluation criterion.

12. See Demski and Feltham (1972) for an illustration of this. Further note that in pursuing this type of research we continually encounter the conundrum of being forced into a complete analysis to unequivocally answer the question of how well a particular simplification works. A parallel situation arises, for example, in transfer pricing where, in many cases, the information necessary to set an optimal price structure is sufficient to determine the optimal actions.

BIBLIOGRAPHY

Abdel-khalik, A. R., "User Preference Ordering Value: A Model," *Accounting Review* (July 1971).

Abernathy, W. J., and Demski, J. S., "Simplification Activities in a Network Scheduling Context," *Management Science* (May 1973).

AICPA, Report of the Study Group on *Objectives of Financial Statements* (AICPA, 1973).

————, Report of the Study Group on *Objectives of Financial Statements,* Volume 2: Selected Papers (AICPA, 1974).

Akerlof, G., "The Market for 'Lemons': Quality Uncertainty and the Market Mechanism," *Quarterly Journal of Economics* (Aug. 1970).

American Accounting Association, "Statement of Accounting Principles Affecting Corporate Reports," *Accounting Review* (June 1936).

————, Committee on Cost Concepts and Standards, "Tentative Statement of Cost Concepts Underlying Reports for Management Purposes," *Accounting Review* (Apr. 1956).

————, Committee on External Reporting, "An Evaluation of External Reporting Practices," *Accounting Review Supplement* (1969).

————, "Report of the Committee on Accounting and Information Systems," *Accounting Review Supplement* (1971).

Amey, L. R., "On Opportunity Costs and Decision Making," *Accountancy* (July 1968).

Anthony, R. N., "What Should 'Cost' Mean?" *Harvard Business Review* (May-June 1970).

Anton, H. R., "Some Aspects of Measurement and Accounting," *Journal of Accounting Research* (Spring 1964).

Arrow, K. J., "Economic Welfare and the Allocation of Resources for Invention," in *The Rate and Direction of Economic Activity: Economic and Social Factors,* National Bureau of Economic Research (Princeton University Press, 1962).

———, *Social Choice and Individual Values,* Cowles Foundation Monograph 12 (Wiley, 1963).

———, "Control in Large Organizations," *Management Science* (Apr. 1964).

———, "The Role of Securities in the Optimal Allocation of Risk Bearing," *Review of Economic Studies* (1964a).

———, "Political and Economic Evaluation of Social Effects and Externalities," in M. Intriligator (ed.), *Frontiers of Quantitative Economics* (North-Holland, 1971).

———, "Higher Education as a Filter," *Journal of Public Economics* (July 1973).

Arrow, K. J., and Hahn, F. H., *General Competitive Analysis* (Holden-Day, 1971).

Arrow, K. J., and Lind, R. C., "Uncertainty and the Evaluation of Public Investment Decisions," *American Economic Review* (June 1970).

Avriel, M., and Williams, A. C., "The Value of Information and Stochastic Programming," *Operations Research* (Sept.-Oct. 1970).

Baiman, S., *Optimal Forecasting in Selected Organizational Models,* unpublished Ph.D. dissertation (Stanford University, 1974).

———, "The Evaluation and Choice of Internal Information Systems within a Multiperson World," *Journal of Accounting Research* (Spring 1975).

Baloff, N., "Startups in Machine-Intensive Production Systems," *Journal of Industrial Engineering* (Jan. 1966).

Baloff, N., and Kennelly, J., "Accounting Implications of Product and Process Start-ups," *Journal of Accounting Research* (Autumn 1967).

Barefield, R. M., "The Effect of Aggregation on Decision Making Success: A Laboratory Study," *Journal of Accounting Research* (Autumn 1972).

Baumol, W. J., *Economic Theory and Operations Analysis* (Prentice-Hall, 1972).

Baumol, W. J., and Bushnell, R. C., "Error Produced by Linearization in Mathematical Programming," *Econometrica* (July-Oct. 1967).

Beaver, W. H., "The Information Content of Annual Earnings Announcements," *Journal of Accounting Research Supplement* (1968).

———, "The Behavior of Security Prices and Its Implications for Accounting Research (Methods)," *Accounting Review Supplement* (1972).

Beaver, W. H., and Demski, J. S., "The Nature of Financial Accounting Objectives: A Summary and Synthesis," *Studies on Financial Accounting Objectives: 1974, Journal of Accounting Research Supplement* (1974).

Benston, G. J., "Multiple Regression Analysis of Cost Behavior," *Accounting Review* (Oct. 1966).

———, "Required Disclosure and the Stock Market: An Evaluation of the Securities Exchange Act of 1934," *American Economic Review* (Mar. 1973).

Berhold, M. H., *An Analysis of Contractual Incentives,* unpublished Ph.D. dissertation, Working Paper No. 129 (Western Management Science Institute, University of California, Los Angeles, 1967).

Bernhard, R. H., "Mathematical Programming Models for Capital Budgeting—A Survey, Generalization, and Critique," *Journal of Financial and Quantitative Analysis* (June 1969).

Bierman, H., and Dyckman, T. R., *Managerial Cost Accounting* (Macmillan, 1971).

Blackwell, D., and Girshick, M. A., *Theory of Games and Statistical Decisions* (Wiley, 1954).

Bloomfield, S., "An Axiomatic Formulation of Constitutional Games," Technical Report No. 71-18 (Operations Research House, Stanford University, 1971).

Bloomfield, S., and Wilson, R., "The Postulates of Game Theory," *Journal of Mathematical Sociology* (July 1973).

Borch, K., "Equilibrium in a Reinsurance Market," *Econometrica* (July 1962).

Brenner, V. C., "Financial Statement User's Views of the Desirability of Reporting Current Cost Information," *Journal of Accounting Research* (Autumn 1970).

Browne, D. E., "The Risk/Return Relationship in Military Procurement," *Management Accounting* (Mar. 1971).

Bruns, W. J., "Inventory Valuation and Management Decisions," *Accounting Review* (Apr. 1965).

Buchanan, J. M., *The Demand and Supply of Public Goods* (Rand-McNally, 1968).

———, *Cost and Choice: An Inquiry in Economic Theory* (Markham, 1969).

Buchanan, J. M., and Stubblebine, W. C., "Externality," *Economica* (1962).

Buchanan, J. M., and Thirlby, G. F., *L.S.E. Essays on Cost* (London School of Economics and Political Science, 1973).

Buffa, E. S., *Reading in Production and Operations Management* (Wiley, 1966).

———, *Production-Inventory Systems: Planning and Control* (Irwin, 1968).

Burns, A. E., "Profit Limitation: Regulated Industries and the Defense Space Industries," *Bell Journal of Economics and Management Science* (Spring 1972).

Butterworth, J., "The Accounting System as an Information Function," *Journal of Accounting Research* (Spring 1972).

———, "The Evaluation of Information Alternatives for Uncertain Decision Problems," Working Paper 73-47 (European Institute for Advanced Studies in Management, Brussels, 1973).

Caplan, E. H., *Management Accounting and Behavioral Science* (Addison-Wesley, 1971).

Chambers, R. J., *Accounting, Evaluation, and Economic Behavior* (Prentice-Hall, 1966).

Clark, J. M., *Studies in the Economics of Overhead Costs* (University of Chicago Press, 1923).

Coase, R. H., "The Nature of Costs," in Solomons (1968a).

———, "The Theory of Public Utility Pricing and Its Application," *Bell Journal of Economics* (Spring 1970).

Cohen, K., and Elton, E., "Inter-temporal Portfolio Analysis Based on Simulation of Joint Returns," *Management Science* (Aug. 1967).

Comptroller General of the United States, *Report on the Feasibility of Applying Uniform Cost-Accounting Standards to Negotiated Defense Contracts* (U.S. Government Printing Office, 1970).

———, *Defense Industry Profit Study* (U.S. Government Printing Office, 1971).

Cook, D. M., "The Effect of Frequency of Feedback on Attitudes and Performance," *Journal of Accounting Research Supplement* (1967).

Cummins, J. M., "Contractual Incentives and Efficient Performance: The Case of Cost Overruns in Defense Procurement," unpublished working paper (Graduate School of Business, Stanford University, 1973).

Cyert, R. M., and Ijiri, Y., "Problems of Implementing the Trueblood Objectives Report," *Studies on Financial Accounting Objectives: 1974, Journal of Accounting Research Supplement* (1974).

Dano, S., *Industrial Production Models: A Theoretical Study* (Springer-Verlag, 1966).

Debreu, G., *Theory of Value,* Cowles Foundation Monograph 17 (Wiley, 1959).

Debreu, G., and Scarf, H., "A Limit Theorem on the Core of an Economy," *International Economic Review* (1963).

DeGroot, M. H., *Optimal Statistical Decisions* (McGraw-Hill, 1970).

Demsetz, H., "Information and Efficiency: Another Viewpoint," *Journal of Law and Economics* (Apr. 1969).

———, "The Private Production of Public Goods," *Journal of Law and Economics* (Oct. 1970).

Demski, J. S., "Some Considerations in Sensitizing an Optimization Model," *Journal of Industrial Engineering* (Sept. 1968).

———, "Some Decomposition Results for Information Evaluation," *Journal of Accounting Research* (Autumn 1970).

———, *Information Analysis* (Addison-Wesley, 1972).

———, "Information Improvement Bounds," *Journal of Accounting Research* (Spring 1972a).

———, "Optimal Performance Measurement," *Journal of Accounting Research* (Autumn 1972b).

———, "The General Impossibility of Normative Accounting Standards," *Accounting Review* (Oct. 1973).

———, "Rational Choice of Accounting Method for a Class of Partnerships," *Journal of Accounting Research* (Autumn 1973a).

———, "Choice among Financial Reporting Alternatives," *Accounting Review* (Apr. 1974).

———, "Uncertainty and Evaluation Based on Controllable Performance," *Journal of Accounting Research* (Autumn 1976).

Demski, J. S., and Feltham, G. A., "Forecast Evaluation," *Accounting Review* (July 1972).

Demski, J. S., and Swieringa, R. J., "A Cooperative Formulation of the Audit Choice Problem," *Accounting Review* (July 1974).

Demski, J. S.; Feltham, G. A.; Horngren, C.; Jaedicke, R.; and Sprouse, R., *Cost Concepts and Implementation Criteria: An Interim Report* (American Institute of Certified Public Accountants, 1969).

Devine, C., "Cost Accounting and Price Policies," *Accounting Review* (Oct. 1950).

Diamond, P. A., "The Role of a Stock Market in a General Equilibrium Model with Technological Uncertainty," *American Economic Review* (Sept. 1967).

Dopuch, N.; Birnberg, J. G.; and Demski, J. S., *Cost Accounting: Accounting Data for Management's Decisions* (Harcourt, Brace and World, 1974).

Dorfman, R. (ed.), *Measuring Benefits of Government Investments* (The Brookings Institution, 1965).

Dorfman, R.; Samuelson, P. A.; and Solow, R. M., *Linear Programming and Economic Analysis* (McGraw-Hill, 1958).

Drake, H. B., "Major DOD Procurements at War with Reality," *Harvard Business Review* (Jan.–Feb. 1970).

Due, J. F., and Friedlaender, A. F., *Government Finance: Economics of the Public Sector* (Irwin, 1973).

Dyckman, T. R., "The Effects of Alternative Accounting Techniques on Certain Management Decisions," *Journal of Accounting Research* (Spring 1964).

———, "The Investigation of Cost Variances," *Journal of Accounting Research* (Autumn 1969).

Eckstein, O., *Water Resource Development* (Harvard University Press, 1965).

Ekern, S., "On the Theory of the Firm in an Economy with Incomplete Markets: An Addendum," *Bell Journal of Economics* (Spring 1975).

Ekern, S., and Wilson, R., "On the Theory of the Firm in an Economy with Incomplete Markets," *Bell Journal of Economics and Management Science* (Spring 1974).

Fair, W. R., "The Next Step in Management Controls," in D. G. Malcom and A. J. Rowe (eds.), *Management Control Systems* (Wiley, 1960).

Fama, E. F., "Multiperiod Consumption-Investment Decisions," *American Economic Review* (Mar. 1970).

Fama, E. F., and Laffer, A. B., "Information and Capital Markets," *Journal of Business* (July 1971).

Fama, E. F., and MacBeth, J., "Tests of the Multiperiod Two-Parameter Model," *Journal of Financial Economics* (1974).

Fama, E. F., and Miller, M., *The Theory of Finance* (Holden-Day, 1972).

Farquharson, R., *Theory of Voting* (Yale University Press, 1969).

Feltham, G. A., "The Value of Information," *Accounting Review* (Oct. 1968).

———, *Information Evaluation,* Studies in Accounting Research #5 (American Accounting Association, 1972).

———, "Cost Aggregation: An Information Economic Analysis," unpublished working paper (University of British Columbia, 1975).

Feltham, G. A., and Demski, J. S., "The Use of Models in Information Evaluation," *Accounting Review* (Oct. 1970).

Fishburn, P. C., *Decision and Value Theory* (Wiley, 1964).

———, *Utility Theory for Decision Making* (Wiley, 1970).

_____, *The Theory of Social Choice* (Princeton University Press, 1973).

Fox, J. R., *Arming America: How the U.S. Buys Weapons* (Harvard Graduate School of Business, Division of Research, 1974).

Garman, M. B., and Kamien, M. I., "The Paradox of Voting: Probability Calculations," *Behavioral Science* (July 1968).

Godfrey, J. T., "Resource Allocation in the Long Run—A Recursive Linear Programming Approach," in J. Blood (ed.), *Management Science in Planning and Control* (Technical Association of the Pulp and Paper Industry, 1969).

Gonedes, N. J., "Information Production and Capital Market Equilibrium," *Journal of Finance* (June 1975).

Gonedes, N. J., and Dopuch, N., "Capital Market Equilibrium, Information Production, and Selecting Accounting Techniques: Theoretical Framework and Review of Empirical Work," *Studies on Financial Accounting Objectives: 1974, Journal of Accounting Research Supplement* (1974).

Gonedes, N. J.; Dopuch, N.; and Penman, S., "Disclosure Rules, Information-Production and Capital Market Equilibrium: The Case of Forecast Disclosure Rules," *Journal of Accounting Research* (Spring 1976).

Gordon, M. J., "The Payoff Period and the Rate of Profit," *Journal of Business* (Oct. 1955).

Graaff, J. deV., *Theoretical Welfare Economics* (Cambridge University Press, 1967).

Greer, H. C., "Restoration of Fixed Asset Values to the Balance Sheet, Second Negative," *Accounting Review* (Apr. 1947).

Groves, T., "Incentives in Teams," *Econometrica* (July 1973).

Groves, T., and Loeb, M., "Incentives and Public Inputs," *Journal of Public Economics* (Aug. 1975).

Hadley, G., *Linear Programming* (Addison-Wesley, 1962).

Hadley, G., and Whitin, T. M., *Analysis of Inventory Systems* (Prentice-Hall, 1963).

Hagerman, R. L., "A Test of Government Regulation of Accounting Principles," *Accounting Review* (Oct. 1975).

Hamada, R. S., "Portfolio Analysis, Market Equilibrium and Corporation Finance," *Journal of Finance* (Mar. 1969).

Hanssman, F., and Hess, S. W., "A Linear-Programming Approach to Production and Employment Scheduling," *Management Technology* (Jan. 1960).

Harsanyi, J. C., "Games with Incomplete Information Played by 'Bayesian' Players, I–III," *Management Science* (Nov. 1967; Jan. 1968; Mar. 1968).

Hayami, Y., and Peterson, W., "Social Returns to Public Information Services: Statistical Reporting of U.S. Farm Commodities," *American Economic Review* (Mar. 1972).

Helpman, E., and Laffont, J., "On Moral Hazard in General Equilibrium Theory," *Journal of Economic Theory* (Feb. 1975).

Henderson, J. M., and Quandt, R. E., *Microeconomic Theory: A Mathematical Approach* (McGraw-Hill, 1971).

Hertz, D. B., "Risk Analysis in Capital Investment," *Harvard Business Review* (Jan.–Feb. 1964).

Hillier, F. S., "The Derivation of Probabilistic Information for the Evaluation of Risky Investments," *Management Science* (Apr. 1963).

———, "Supplement to 'The Derivation of Probabilistic Information for the Evaluation of Risky Investments,'" *Management Science* (Jan. 1965).

———, *The Evaluation of Risky Interrelated Investments* (North-Holland, 1969).

Hirshleifer, J., "On the Economics of Transfer Pricing," *Journal of Business* (July 1956).

———, "Investment Decision under Uncertainty: Applications of the State-Preference Approach," *Quarterly Journal of Economics* (May 1966).

———, *Investment, Interest, and Capital* (Prentice-Hall, 1970).

———, "The Private and Social Value of Information and the Reward to Inventive Activity," *American Economic Review* (Sept. 1971).

———, "Where Are We in the Theory of Information?" *American Economic Review* (May 1973).

Hitch, C. J., and McKean, R. N., *The Economics of Defense in the Nuclear Age* (Harvard University Press, 1963).

Ho, Y. C., and Chu, K. C., "Information Structure in Dynamic Multi-Person Control Problems," *Automatica* (1974).

Holt, C. C.; Modigliani, F.; Muth, J. F.; and Simon, H. A., *Planning Production, Inventories, and Work Force* (Prentice-Hall, 1960).

Hopwood, A. G., "An Empirical Study of the Role of Accounting Data in Performance Evaluation," *Journal of Accounting Research Supplement* (1972).

———, "Accounting Data and Performance Evaluation," *Accounting Review* (July 1974).

Horngren, C. T., *Cost Accounting: A Managerial Emphasis* (Prentice-Hall, 1972).

———, "Accounting Principles: Private or Public Sector?" *Journal of Accountancy* (May 1972a).

Howard, R. A., "The Foundations of Decision Analysis," *IEEE Transactions on Systems Science and Cybernetics* (Sept. 1968).

———, "Proximal Decision Analysis," *Management Science* (May 1971).

Ijiri, Y., *Management Goals and Accounting for Control* (Rand-McNally, 1965).

———, *The Foundations of Accounting Measurement: A Mathematical, Economic, and Behavioral Inquiry* (Prentice-Hall, 1967).

———, *Theory of Accounting Measurement,* Studies in Accounting Research #10 (American Accounting Association, 1975).

Intriligator, M. D., *Mathematical Optimization and Economic Theory* (Prentice-Hall, 1971).

Itami, H., "Evaluation Measures and Goal Congruence under Uncertainty," *Journal of Accounting Research* (Spring 1975).

———, "On the Relationships between the Value and the Amount of Information," unpublished working paper (Graduate School of Business, Stanford University, 1975a).

Jaedicke, R. K.; Demski, J.; Feltham, G.; Horngren, C.; and Sprouse, R., "Research Proposal for Cost Measurement Criteria," *Journal of Accountancy* (Feb. 1969).

Jennergren, L. P., *Studies in the Mathematical Theory of Decentralized Resource-Allocation,* unpublished Ph.D. dissertation (Stanford University, 1971).

———, "Decentralization on the Basis of Price Schedules in Linear Decomposable Resource-Allocation Problems," *Journal of Financial and Quantitative Analysis* (Jan. 1972).

Jensen, D. L., "Cost in Pricing Joint Products," *Accounting Review* (July 1974).

Jensen, M. C., "Risk, the Pricing of Capital Assets, and the Evaluation of Investment Portfolios," *Journal of Business* (Apr. 1969).

——— (ed.), *Studies in the Theory of Capital Markets* (Praeger, 1972).

Jensen, M. C., and Long, J. B., Jr., "Corporate Investment under Uncertainty and Pareto Optimality in the Capital Markets," *Bell Journal of Economics and Management Science* (Spring 1972).

Johnston, J., *Econometric Methods* (McGraw-Hill, 1972).

Jorgenson, D. W.; McCall, J. J.; and Radner, R., *Optimal Replacement Policy* (Rand-McNally, 1967).

Kaplan, R., "Optimal Investigation Strategies with Imperfect Information," *Journal of Accounting Research* (Spring 1969).

———, "The Significance and Investigation of Cost Variances: Survey and Extensions," *Journal of Accounting Research* (Autumn 1975).

Kaplan, R., and Thompson, G., "Overhead Allocation via Mathematical Programming Models," *Accounting Review* (Apr. 1971).

Kaplan, R., and Welam, U., "Overhead Allocation with Imperfect Markets and Nonlinear Technology," *Accounting Review* (July 1974).

Kassouf, S., *Normative Decision Making* (Prentice-Hall, 1970).

Kihlstrom, R., "A General Theory of Demand for Information about Product Quality," *Journal of Economic Theory* (Aug. 1974).

Kihlstrom, R., and Mirman, L. J., "Information and Market Equilibrium," *Bell Journal of Economics* (Spring 1975).

Kihlstrom, R., and Pauly, M., "The Role of Insurance in the Allocation of Risk," *American Economic Review* (May 1971).

Kohler, E. L.. "Why Not Retain Historical Cost?" *Journal of Accountancy* (Oct. 1963).

———, *A Dictionary for Accountants* (Prentice-Hall, 1970).

Koopmans, T. C., "Representation of Preference Orderings with Independent Components of Consumption," in McGuire and Radner (1972).

Krantz, D. H.; Luce, R. D.; Suppes, P.; and Tversky, A., *Foundations of Measurement* (Academic Press, 1971).

Kurz, M., "Experimental Approaches to the Determination of the Demand for Public Goods," *Journal of Public Economics* (Nov. 1974).

Lancaster, K., *Mathematical Economics* (Macmillan, 1968).

Lasden, L. S., *Optimization Theory for Large Systems* (Macmillan, 1970)

LaValle, I. H., "On Cash Equivalents and Information Evaluation in Decisions under Uncertainty, Parts, I, II, and III," *Journal of the American Statistical Association* (Mar. 1968).

Lea, R. B., "Comments on Mock's Concepts of Information Value," *Accounting Review* (Apr. 1973).

Lintner, J., "The Valuation of Risk Assets and the Selection of Risky Investments in Stock Portfolios and Capital Budgets," *The Review of Economics and Statistics* (Feb. 1965).

Lipsey, R. G., and Lancaster, K., "The General Theory of the Second Best," *Review of Economic Studies* (1956).

Littleton, A. C., "Concepts of Income Underlying Accounting," *Accounting Review* (Mar. 1937).

Long, J. B., "Consumption-Investment Decisions and Equilibrium in the Securities Market," in Jensen (1972).

Luce, R. D., and Raiffa, H., *Games and Decisions* (Wiley, 1957).

Luenberger, D. G., *Optimization by Vector Space Methods* (Wiley, 1969).

———, *Introduction to Linear and Nonlinear Programming* (Addison-Wesley, 1973).

Magee, R. R., "Cost-Volume-Profit Analysis, Uncertainty and Capital Market Equilibrium," *Journal of Accounting Research* (Autumn 1975).

Malinvaud, E., *Lectures on Microeconomic Theory* (North-Holland, 1972).

Mao, J. C. T., *Quantitative Analysis of Financial Decisions* (Macmillan, 1969).

March, J. G., and Simon, H. A., *Organizations* (Wiley, 1958).

Marschak, J., "The Payoff-Relevant Description of States and Acts," *Econometrica* (Oct. 1963).

———, "Economics of Information Systems," *Journal of the American Statistical Association* (Mar. 1971).

———, "Optimal Symbol Processing: A Problem in Individual and Social Economics," *Behavioral Science* (May 1971a).

Marschak, J., and Radner, R., *Economic Theory of Teams,* Cowles Monograph 22 (Yale University Press, 1972).

Marschak, T., "Centralization and Decentralization in Economic Organizations," *Econometrica* (1959).

Marshall, J., "Private Incentives and Public Information," *American Economic Review* (June 1974).

Marshall, R., "Determining an Optimal Accounting Information System for an Unidentified User," *Journal of Accounting Research* (Autumn 1972).

May, K. O., "A Set of Independent, Necessary and Sufficient Conditions for Simple Majority Decisions," *Econometrica* (1952).

McCall, J. J., "The Simple Economics of Incentive Contracting," *American Economic Review* (Dec. 1970).

———, "Probabilistic Microeconomics," *Bell Journal of Economics and Management Science* (Autumn 1971).

McGuire, C. B., "Comparisons of Information Structures," in McGuire and Radner (1972).

McGuire, C. B., and Radner, R. (eds.), *Decision and Organization* (American Elsevier, 1972).

McKinsey, J. O., *Budgetary Control* (Ronald Press, 1922).

Mesarovic, M. D.; Macko, D.; and Takahara, Y., *Theory of Hierarchical, Multilevel Systems* (Academic Press, 1970).

Moonitz, M., *Obtaining Agreement on Standards in the Accounting Profession,* Studies in Accounting Research #8 (American Accounting Association, 1974).

Moonitz, M., and Nelson, C. L., "Recent Developments in Accounting Theory," *Accounting Review* (Apr. 1960).

Morris, W. T., "On the Art of Modeling," *Management Science* (Aug. 1967).

———, *Decentralization in Management Systems* (Ohio State University Press, 1968).

Myers, S. C., "A Time-State Preference Model of Security Valuation," *Journal of Financial and Quantitative Analysis* (Mar. 1968).

National Association of Accountants, Committee on Management Accounting Practices, "Concepts for Contract Costing," *Management Accounting* (Mar. 1972).

National Association of Cost Accountants, "Direct Costing" (Research Series No. 23), *NACA Bulletin* (Apr. 1953, Section 3).

Nemhauser, G. L., *Introduction to Dynamic Programming* (Wiley, 1966).

Ng, D., "Information Accuracy and Social Welfare under Homogeneous Beliefs," *Journal of Financial Economics* (Mar. 1975).

———, *Essays on the Effects of Information in Financial Markets,* unpublished Ph.D. dissertation (University of California, Berkeley, 1975a).

Nikaido, H., *Convex Structures and Economic Theory* (Academic Press, 1968).

North, D. W., "A Tutorial Introduction to Decision Theory," *IEEE Transactions on Systems Science and Cybernetics* (Sept. 1968).

Owen, G., *Game Theory* (W. B. Saunders, 1968).

Peck, M. J., and Scherer, F. M., *The Weapons Acquisition Process: An Economic Analysis* (Harvard Graduate School of Business, Division of Research, 1962).

Ponssard, J., *Information Usage in Non-Cooperative Game Theory,* unpublished Ph.D. dissertation (Stanford University, Sept. 1971).

Ponssard, J., and Zamir, S., "Zero-Sum Sequential Games with Incomplete Information," *The International Journal of Game Theory* (1973).

Porteus, E., "An Informal Look at the Principle of Optimality," *Management Science* (July 1975).

Prest, A. R., and Turvey, R., "Cost-Benefit Analysis: A Survey," *Economic Journal* (Dec. 1965).

Quirk, J., and Saposnik, R., *Introduction to General Equilibrium Theory and Welfare Economics* (McGraw-Hill, 1968).

Radner, R., "Competitive Equilibrium under Uncertainty," *Econometrica* (Jan. 1968).

———, "Existence of Equilibrium of Plans, Prices, and Price Expectations in a Sequence of Markets," *Econometrica* (Mar. 1972).

———, "Market Equilibrium and Uncertainty: Concepts and Problems," in M. D. Intriligator and D. A. Kendrick (eds.), *Frontiers of Quantitative Economics, Volume 2* (North-Holland, 1974).

———, "A Note on Unanimity of Stockholders' Preferences among Alternative Production Plans: A Reformulation of the Ekern-Wilson Model," *Bell Journal of Economics and Management Science* (Spring 1974a).

Raiffa, H., *Decision Analysis* (Addison-Wesley, 1968).

Raiffa, H., and Schlaifer, R., *Applied Statistical Decision Theory* (MIT Press, 1961).

Rappaport, A., "Sensitivity Analysis in Decision Making," *Accounting Review* (July 1967).

Reiter, S., "Surrogates for Uncertain Decision Problems: Minimal Information for Decision Making," *Econometrica* (1957).

Rosing, J., *The Formation of Groups for Cooperative Decision Making under Uncertainty,* unpublished Ph.D. dissertation (Stanford University, 1968).

Ross, S., "The Economic Theory of Agency: The Principal's Problem," *American Economic Review* (May 1973).

Rothschild, M., "Models of Market Organization with Imperfect Information: A Survey," *Journal of Political Economy* (Nov.–Dec. 1973).

Rubinstein, M., "An Aggregation Theorem for Securities Markets," *Journal of Financial Economics* (Sept. 1974).

Rudin, W., *Principles of Mathematical Analysis* (McGraw-Hill, 1964).

Samuelson, P. A., *Foundations of Economic Analysis* (Atheneum, 1965); originally published by Harvard University Press as Harvard Economic Studies, Volume 80.

Savage, L. J., *The Foundations of Statistics* (Wiley, 1954).

Scarborough, C. W., "The Structure of Incentive Contracts," in T. A. Goldman (ed.), *Cost-Effectiveness Analysis* (Praeger, 1968).

Scherer, F. M., *The Weapons Acquisition Process: Economic Incentives* (Harvard Graduate School of Business, Division of Research, 1964).

Schlaifer, R., *Analysis of Decisions under Uncertainty* (McGraw-Hill, 1969).

Schoenfeld, H. W., *Cost Terminology and Cost Theory: A Study of Its Development and Present State in Central Europe* (Center for International Education and Research in Accounting, University of Illinois, 1974).

Scitovsky, T., *Welfare and Competition* (Irwin, 1971).

Sen, A. K., *Collective Choice and Social Welfare* (Holden-Day, 1970).

Sharpe, W. F., *Portfolio Theory and Capital Markets* (McGraw-Hill, 1970).

Shepard, R. W., *Theory of Cost and Production Functions* (Princeton University Press, 1970).

Shillinglaw, G., *Cost Accounting: Analysis and Control* (Irwin, 1972).

Shubik, M., "Incentives, Decentralized Control, the Assignment of Joint Costs and Internal Pricing," *Management Science* (Apr. 1962).

Simon, H. A., "Theories of Decision-Making in Economics and Behavioral Science," *American Economic Review* (June 1959).

———, "Theories of Bounded Rationality," in McGuire and Radner (1972).

Smallwood, R. D., "A Decision Analysis of Model Selection," *IEEE Transactions on Systems Science and Cybernetics* (Sept. 1968).

Solomons, D., *Divisional Performance: Measurement and Control* (Irwin, 1968).

——— (ed.), *Studies in Cost Analysis* (Irwin, 1968a).

Sorter, G. H., "An 'Events' Approach to Basic Accounting Theory," *Accounting Review* (Jan. 1969).

Spence, M., "Job Market Signaling," *Quarterly Journal of Economics* (Aug. 1973).

———, "Competitive and Optimal Responses to Signals: An Analysis of Efficiency and Distribution," *Journal of Economic Theory* (Mar. 1974).

Spence, M., and Zeckhauser, R., "Insurance, Information, and Individual Action," *American Economic Review* (May 1971).

Starrett, D., "Fundamental Nonconvexities in the Theory of Externalities," *Journal of Economic Theory* (Aug. 1972).

———, "On the Nature of Externalities," Report No. 129 (Institute for Mathematical Studies in the Social Sciences, Stanford University, 1974).

Staubus, G. J., *Activity Costing and Input-Output Accounting* (Irwin, 1971).

Sterling, R. R., *Theory of the Measurement of Enterprise Income* (University Press of Kansas, 1970).

Stigler, G. J., *The Theory of Price* (Macmillan, 1966).

Stiglitz, J. E., "On the Optimality of the Stock Market Allocation of Investment," *Quarterly Journal of Economics* (Feb. 1972).

———, "Risk Sharing and Incentives in Sharecropping," *Review of Economic Studies* (Apr. 1974).

———, "Incentives, Risk, and Information: Notes Toward a Theory of Hierarchy," *Bell Journal of Economics* (Autumn 1975).

Sundem, G. L., *Selecting the Optimal Capital Budgeting Decision Model,* unpublished Ph.D. dissertation (Stanford University, 1971).

———, "Evaluating Simplified Capital Budgeting Models Using a Time-State Preference Metric," *Accounting Review* (Apr. 1974).

Taussig, R., "Information Requirements of Replacement Models," *Journal of Accounting Research* (Spring 1964).

Thomas, A. L., *The Allocation Problem: Part Two,* Studies in Accounting Research #9 (American Accounting Association, 1974).

Trippi, R. R., and Khumawala, B. M., "Solution of the Multi-Asset Finite Horizon Investment Renewal Problem," *Management Science* (June 1975).

Tullock, G., *Toward a Mathematics of Politics* (University of Michigan Press, 1967).

Van Horne, J. C., "A Note on Biases in Capital Budgeting Introduced by Inflation," *Journal of Financial and Quantitative Analysis* (Jan. 1971).

———, *Financial Management and Policy* (Prentice-Hall, 1974).

Vatter, W. J., "Does Rate of Return Measure Business Efficiency?" *NAA Bulletin* (Jan. 1959).

———, "Standards for Cost Analysis" (Aug. 1969); contained in the Comptroller General's Feasibility Study (1970).

von Neumann, J., and Morgenstern, O., *Theory of Games and Economic Behavior* (Princeton University Press, 1947).

Wagner, H. M., *Principles of Operations Research: With Applications to Managerial Decisions* (Prentice-Hall, 1969).

Weingartner, H. M., *Mathematical Programming and the Analysis of Capital Budgeting Problems* (Markham, 1967).

———, "Some New Views on the Payback Period and Capital Budgeting," *Management Science* (Aug. 1969).

Williamson, O. E.; Wachter, M. L.; and Harris, J. E., "Understanding the Employment Relation: The Analysis of Idiosyncratic Exchange," *Bell Journal of Economics* (Spring 1975).

Wilson, R., "On the Theory of Syndicates," *Econometrica* (Jan. 1968).

_____, "Decision Analysis in a Corporation," *IEEE Transactions on Systems Science and Cybernetics* (Sept. 1968a).

_____, "An Axiomatic Model of Logrolling," *American Economic Review* (June 1969).

_____, "The Structure of Incentives for Decentralization under Uncertainty," in M. Guilbaud (ed.), *La Decision* (Centre National de la Recherche Scientifique, 1969a).

_____, "Information in an Equilibrium Model," Working Paper No. 42 (Institute for Mathematical Studies in the Social Sciences, Stanford University, 1974).

_____, "Vertical Integration and Communication," *Bell Journal of Economics* (Spring 1975).

Winterbotham, F. W., *The Ultra Secret* (Harper and Row, 1974).

Wright, H. W., "Uniform Cost Accounting Standards: Past, Present, and Future," *Financial Executive* (May 1971).

Zangwill, W. I., *Nonlinear Programming: A Unified Approach* (Prentice-Hall, 1969).

Zellner, A., *An Introduction to Bayesian Inference in Econometrics* (Wiley, 1971).

AUTHOR INDEX

SUBJECT INDEX